Mergers and Productivity

A National Bureau
of Economic Research
Conference Report

Mergers and Productivity

Edited by **Steven N. Kaplan**

The University of Chicago Press

Chicago and London

STEVEN N. KAPLAN is the Neubauer Family Professor of
Entrepreneurship and Finance at the Graduate School of Business of
the University of Chicago and a research associate of the National
Bureau of Economic Research.

The University of Chicago Press, Chicago 60637
The University of Chicago Press, Ltd., London
© 2000 by the National Bureau of Economic Research
All rights reserved. Published 2000
Printed in the United States of America
09 08 07 06 05 04 03 02 01 00   1 2 3 4 5
ISBN: 0-226-42431-6 (cloth)

Chapter 3 by Charles W. Calomiris and Jason Karceski was
previously published as a pamphlet by the AEI Press, © 1998
American Enterprise Institute for Public Policy Research,
Washington, D.C. It is reprinted here with permission.

Library of Congress Cataloging-in-Publication Data

Mergers and productivity / edited by Steven N. Kaplan.
    p.   cm. — (A National Bureau of Economic Research
    conference report)
    Includes bibliographical references and index.
    ISBN 0-226-42431-6 (alk. paper)
    1. Consolidation and merger of corporations—United
    States.   I. Kaplan, Steven N.
HD2746.55.U5 M475 2000
338.8'3'0973 21—dc21
                                                    99-045131

♾ The paper used in this publication meets the minimum
requirements of the American National Standard for Information
Sciences—Permanence of Paper for Printed Library Materials,
ANSI Z39.48-1992.

Since this volume is a record of conference proceedings, it has been exempted from the rules governing critical review of manuscripts by the Board of Directors of the National Bureau (resolution adopted 8 June 1948, as revised 21 November 1949 and 20 April 1968).

Contents

Acknowledgments

This volume is a collection of six papers that provide in-depth case studies of a small number of mergers. The papers were presented and discussed at a conference in January 1997 in Islamorada, Florida.

The studies were motivated by the reality that existing academic work on merger activity—mostly based on large sample studies—has yielded mixed results. In particular, the academic literature is mixed on the effects of mergers on operating performance, productivity, and efficiency. The case studies and this volume were undertaken with the goal of augmenting the existing literature and informing future large sample and field-based studies. The National Bureau of Economic Research (NBER), through Martin Feldstein and the Sloan Foundation, was the major force in encouraging this approach. With the completion of this volume, it is clear that the studies and the conference proved extremely successful in achieving their goals. This is particularly timely as the 1990s end in the midst of a new merger wave.

I am indebted to all the authors for agreeing to take part in this project. For many of the authors, this was their first attempt at undertaking field-based research. I also am grateful to the discussants, who provided thoughtful and insightful comments on the papers. The combination of the papers and the discussants made the conference one of the most interesting I have attended.

I want to thank the Sloan Foundation for their crucial role in sponsoring this research effort. This volume is part of a broader effort by the Sloan Foundation to encourage economic research at the firm level.

Finally, I want to thank those at the NBER for their central roles in this project. Martin Feldstein was the driving force behind this volume. He encouraged me to organize it, coordinated the participation of the Sloan Foundation and the NBER, and participated in the conference. Kirsten Foss Davis, Lauren Lariviere, and the NBER's conference department managed the logistics of the conference flawlessly. And Helena Fitz-Patrick has firmly shepherded the papers and discussions into book form.

Steve Kaplan

Introduction

Steven N. Kaplan

This volume is a collection of six papers that provide in-depth case studies of a small number of mergers. These studies were motivated by two primary factors. First, the existing academic work on merger activity—mainly based on large sample studies—has provided mixed results. Some findings are clear while others are inconclusive. In particular, the academic literature is quite mixed on the effects of mergers on operating performance, productivity, and efficiency. The National Bureau of Economic Research and the Sloan Foundation sponsored the case studies in this volume with the intent of augmenting the existing literature and informing future large sample and field-based studies.

Second, these studies were undertaken in the midst of substantial merger activity in the latter half of the 1990s. The dollar volume of merger and acquisition (M&A) activity has set new records each year since 1995 (see fig. 1). More significantly, M&A activity in those years has exceeded 6 percent of total stock market value, approaching the levels of the 1980s (see fig. 2). Given the mixed results from previous studies, an additional goal of this volume is to increase our understanding of the current merger activity.

In this introduction, I briefly discuss the existing evidence on mergers and acquisitions; summarize the studies in this volume; and, finally, discuss the general lessons of these studies.

Steven N. Kaplan is the Neubauer Family Professor of Entrepreneurship and Finance at the Graduate School of Business of the University of Chicago and a research associate of the National Bureau of Economic Research.

Comments from Jeremy Stein, Luigi Zingales, and conference participants were very helpful. This research has been supported by the Sloan Foundation through a grant to the National Bureau of Economic Research.

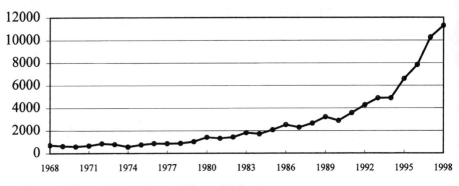

Fig. 1   All acquisition volume (billions of dollars)
Source: Mergerstat.

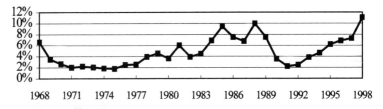

Fig. 2   All acquisition volume as a percentage of average total stock market capitalization
Source: Mergerstat; author's calculations.

Existing Evidence on Mergers and Acquisitions

The existing evidence on the effects of mergers and acquisitions on productivity or value comes from two basic types of large sample studies: event studies and performance studies.[1]

Event studies consider the returns to the shareholders of targets and acquirers in the days before and after an acquisition announcement. These studies consistently find that the combined returns to acquirer and target stockholders are unequivocally positive. These positive returns imply that the market anticipates that acquisitions on average will create value. These studies (and reactions) do not, however, provide insight into the sources of the value changes in mergers or whether the expectations of value changes are ultimately realized. Furthermore, the combined returns cover a broad range of responses from very positive to very negative.

Cross-sectional analyses of event-period returns provide some evidence that the broad range of combined announcement-period returns reflects the market's ability to forecast an acquisition's success. For example, both

1. See Kaplan, Mitchell, and Wruck (chap. 4 in this volume) for a more detailed version of this section.

Mitchell and Lehn (1990) and Kaplan and Weisbach (1992) find that there is a relation between (1) acquirer and combined returns and (2) the ultimate outcome of the acquisition. Other studies examine a number of different determinants of the cross-sectional variation in returns associated with acquisitions. (See, e.g., Lang, Stulz, and Walkling 1991. Maloney, McCormick, and Mitchell 1993; Morck, Shleifer, and Vishny 1990; and Servaes 1991.) These cross-sectional analyses of event-period returns provide some understanding of the nature of the market reaction to acquisition announcements. They do not, however, examine whether the anticipated value creation or improved productivity materializes. Nor do they have a great deal to say about the organizational mechanisms and management practices that drive acquisition success or failure.

Studies of postmerger performance attempt to measure the longer-term implications of mergers and acquisitions using both accounting and stock return data. Studies of accounting data fail to find consistent evidence of improved performance or productivity gains. (See, e.g., Healy, Palepu, and Ruback 1992, and Ravenscraft and Scherer 1987.) Similarly, studies that focus on acquirers' long-term stock performance find mixed results: abnormally negative stock returns after the acquisition (Agrawal, Jaffe, and Mandelker 1992), no abnormal returns (Franks, Harris, and Titman 1991), and negative abnormal returns only for stock mergers (Mitchell and Stafford 1996). Like the announcement-period event studies, longer-term performance and event studies document substantial cross-sectional variation in performance, but do not study the sources of value changes in mergers and acquisitions.

In sum, there are a number of questions that the existing economics and finance literature on mergers and acquisitions leaves unanswered. Existing work provides mixed results on the average impact of mergers and acquisitions. More importantly, existing work offers little insight into the determinants of an acquisition's success or failure.

The Studies in This Volume

The six papers in this volume are in-depth studies of a small number of mergers. Most of the papers study a particular industry. Unlike large sample studies, they cannot and do not consider the average effect of a large sample of acquisitions. Instead, they do an excellent job of analyzing the factors that lead to acquisitions and determining which factors account for the ultimate success or failure of the acquisition.

The first two studies focus more on the factors that lead to acquisition. In "Consolidation in the Medical Care Marketplace," Barro and Cutler study the hospital consolidation in the Massachusetts hospital market. They find that the consolidation is driven by a large decline in the demand for hospital beds over the last several years. That decline, in turn, has been driven by the proliferation of managed care and by technological change. Barro and Cutler find three manifestations of consolidation: (1) merger for closure of excess capacity; (2) merger for economies of scale on administrative, laboratory and other costs; and (3) merger for network creation and greater bargaining power. This paper, then, finds an economic rationale for consolidation and suggests that the effects of those consolidations have been to increase efficiency.

In "The Eclipse of the U.S. Tire Industry," Rajan, Volpin, and Zingales study the consolidation in the U.S. tire industry in the 1980s. This consolidation primarily consisted of foreign tire manufacturers acquiring U.S. tire manufacturers. The authors consider possible explanations for this activity. They argue that the acquisitions were not driven by efficiency gains through acquisition by more efficient producers. The authors also reject the argument that the acquisitions forced downsizing on U.S. manufacturers that had overinvested. Instead, the authors argue that the acquisitions were motivated by global economies of scale in production, product development, and marketing.

While the remaining four papers discuss the factors that lead to acquisitions, they focus more on the outcomes of those acquisitions and the determinants of those outcomes.

In "Is the Bank Merger Wave of the 1990s Efficient?" Calomiris and Karceski study nine bank mergers. They collect detailed data to determine if those nine mergers were successful ex post. The authors conclude that the bank mergers they study do create value, for the most part in the ways expected by the acquirers ex ante. The stock price reactions to the mergers and the value creation are, however, very noisy. Calomiris and Karceski also find that it is possible to obtain revenue gains or synergies via cross-selling in addition to those from cost cutting.

In "A Clinical Exploration of Value Creation and Destruction in Acquisitions," Kaplan, Mitchell, and Wruck study two mergers with extreme stock price reactions. They conclude that merger success or failure is a function of initial due diligence or information gathering, postmerger incentives, and organizational design. They also find that traditional measures of postmerger operating performance are very noisy measures of the actual performance of the merger.

In "Workforce Integration and the Dissipation of Value in Mergers," Kole and Lehn study USAir's acquisition of Piedmont Aviation. The acquisition turned out to be very unsuccessful. Kole and Lehn find that the key stumbling block came in integrating the workforces of the two companies. After the acquisition, USAir made the disastrous decision to increase the wages at Piedmont (the lower wage firm) rather than do nothing or reduce wages at USAir (the high wage firm). Kole and Lehn also argue that part of the reason for the acquisition and its lack of success was that the top executives involved cared more about survival than about shareholder value. Finally, Kole and Lehn report that the stock market reacted very positively to the acquisition when it was announced. As in several of the other studies in this volume, that reaction turned out to be wrong.

In "Paths to Creating Value in Pharmaceutical Mergers," Ravenscraft and Long study mergers in the pharmaceutical industry. They argue that large deals involving similar companies—horizontal deals—create the most value. This value is created from reducing costs in manufacturing, marketing and sales, headquarters, and research and development after the merger.

Conclusions and Generalizations

The question remains, what can be learned in this volume from the in-depth analyses of a small number of mergers that cannot be learned from large sample studies. The answer is a great deal.[2]

The studies do an excellent job of discussing the forces that lead to mergers and acquisitions. The success here is partially due to the fact that most of the studies consider industries. In particular, Barro and Cutler do an excellent job of discussing the reasons for hospital consolidation in Massachusetts as do Rajan, Volpin, and Zingales for the acquisitions in the U.S. tire industry.

The success in identifying these forces is noteworthy because a general pattern emerges from these studies. It is striking that most of the mergers and acquisitions were associated with technological or regulatory shocks. This is true in every industry studied in this volume—the airline, banking, hospital, pharmaceutical, and tire industries. This pattern supports the large sample results of Mitchell and Mulherin (1996) that merger activity is related to industry shocks.

At the same time that these studies shed light on the forces that lead to mergers, they also provide useful information—to both academics and practitioners—concerning what factors influence a merger's success or failure. Perhaps the most interesting factor, found in several of the studies, is the extent to which the acquirer understood the target before the acquisition. While this finding seems obvious and commonsensical, the fact that acquisitions fail because acquirers do not gain sufficient information on the target is important. For practitioners, it provides a strong incentive to get information before completing an acquisition. For academics, it provides some possible topics for further study. Why do executives undertake acquisitions without sufficient information gathering? What is the optimal amount of information to gather?

2. I particularly thank Jeremy Stein for helpful comments here.

The studies also suggest some issues that should be of interest to finance and organizational theorists. In particular, several of the papers yield interesting results concerning the boundaries of the firm. For example, the Kole and Lehn analysis of the USAir-Piedmont merger suggests that workers respond in substantially different ways to having low wages relative to similar workers in the same industry versus having low wages relative to similar workers in the same firm. The analysis of the Cooper-Cameron acquisition in Kaplan, Mitchell, and Wruck suggests that different organizational structures lead to important differences in productivity.

Finally, the studies should be of methodological interest for those who perform large sample studies. These papers indicate that large sample studies—whether accounting-based or stock-based—cannot possibly capture the richness of the economic effects of mergers. And, with some frequency, those large sample measures will not even capture the direction of the economic effect.

In summary, then, the studies in this volume do exactly what they are supposed to do. They augment and inform the existing literature on mergers and acquisitions. They also suggest areas for future work—both large sample and small.

References

Agrawal, A., J. Jaffe, and G. Mandelker. 1992. The post-merger performance of acquiring firms: A re-examination of an anomaly. *Journal of Finance* 47: 1605–21.

Comment, R., and G. Jarrell. 1995. Corporate focus, stock returns and the market for corporate control. *Journal of Financial Economics* 37:67–88.

Franks, J. R., R. Harris, and S. Titman. 1991. The post-merger share price performance of acquiring firms. *Journal of Financial Economics* 29:81–96.

Healy, P., K. Palepu, and R. Ruback. 1992. Do mergers improve corporate performance? *Journal of Financial Economics* 31:135–76.

Kaplan, S. 1989. The effects of management buyouts on operations and value. *Journal of Financial Economics* 24:217–54.

Kaplan, S., and M. Weisbach. 1992. The success of acquisitions: Evidence from divestitures. *Journal of Finance* 47:107–38.

Lang, L., R. Stulz, and R. Walkling. 1991. A test of the free cash flow hypothesis: The case of bidder returns. *Journal of Financial Economics* 29:315–35.

Lichtenberg, F. 1992. *Corporate takeovers and productivity.* Cambridge, Mass.: MIT Press.

Maloney, M., R. McCormick, and M. Mitchell. 1993. Managerial decision making and capital structure. *Journal of Business* 66:189–217.

Mitchell, M., and K. Lehn. 1990. Do bad bidders become good targets? *Journal of Political Economy* 98:372–98.

Mitchell, M., and H. Mulherin. 1996. The impact of industry shocks on takeover and restructuring activity. *Journal of Financial Economics* 41:193–229.

Mitchell, M., and E. Stafford. 1996. Managerial decisions and long-term stock price performance. Working paper. University of Chicago, November.

Morck, R., A. Shleifer, and R. Vishny. 1990. Do managerial motives drive bad acquisitions? *Journal of Finance* 45:31–48.

Ravenscraft, D., and F. M. Scherer. 1987. *Mergers, selloffs and economic efficiency.* Washington, D.C.: The Brookings Institution.

Servaes, H. 1991. Tobin's Q and the gains from takeovers. *Journal of Finance* 46: 409–19.

Consolidation in the Medical Care Marketplace
A Case Study from Massachusetts

Jason R. Barro and David M. Cutler

1.1 Introduction

"Merger mania" is sweeping the health care industry. Hospitals are merging with other hospitals. Hospitals are purchasing or merging with physician practices. Insurers are merging with other insurers. Why are these consolidations occurring? What are their implications for consumers, employers, and the government? In this paper we start to address these questions. Because so little is known about health care consolidation, we focus on consolidation in a particular state—Massachusetts—and largely on the hospital sector. Hospital consolidation in Massachusetts has been as rapid as anywhere in the country. Between 1980 and 1996, two-thirds of the state's 108 acute care hospitals were involved in some type of merger or contractual affiliation, as were many physicians and a number of insurers. We analyze the Massachusetts experience using standard economic tools as well as a set of interviews of virtually all of the major hospitals in the Boston area. Our results cannot be generalized to the nation as a whole, but they do tell us about consolidation in a situation where it has been pervasive.

The fundamental factor driving health care consolidation, we argue, is managed care. Traditional health insurance was very generous. It paid

Jason R. Barro is assistant professor at Harvard Business School. David M. Cutler is professor of economics at Harvard University and a research associate of the National Bureau of Economic Research.

The authors are grateful to Richard Gaintner, Lawrence Kaplan, Anthony Komaroff, Francis Lynch, Robert Norton, Mitchell Rabkin, Andrew Riddell, Howard Rotmer, and Thomas Trailor for speaking with them; to Matthew Barmack, Paul Healy, Steve Kaplan, and Frank Lichtenberg for comments; and to the National Institute on Aging and the Olin Foundation for research support.

providers on a fee-for-service basis; it did little to control utilization; and it allowed patients unlimited access to the providers of their choice. Managed care changes all that. Managed care policies typically pay primary care physicians a fixed amount per enrollee ("capitation"), making the provider bear all of the marginal cost of services. They require patients to see a primary care physician ("gatekeeper") before getting a referral to a specialist. And they set up a network of "preferred" providers (physicians, hospitals, and pharmaceutical companies) who accept much lower fees from insurers in exchange for having access to the insurance pool. More generally, this phenomenon of an exogenous shock by health maintenance organizations (HMOs) causing a consolidation wave is not necessarily unique to the hospital industry. The defense industry in recent years probably fits this model as well.

Managed care has spurred provider consolidation in three primary ways. The first effect we term *consolidation for closure*. Managed care— along with technological innovation in medicine more generally—has reduced the demand for inpatient hospitals substantially. Between 1980 and 1994, admissions to Massachusetts hospitals fell by 0.8 percent annually and inpatient days fell by 3.5 percent annually. By any assessment, hospital capacity in Massachusetts (and the nation as a whole) was substantially above demand. Some hospitals have closed outright, while others have merged to facilitate, or substitute for, closure.

The second effect we term *consolidation for economies of scale*. Access to managed care networks is guaranteed largely on the basis of cost. Low cost providers will be better positioned to join networks than high cost providers. In many cases, overall costs can be lowered through hospital mergers. Fixed costs of administrative services, laboratories, or specialized clinical facilities, for example, require a minimum scale to be efficient. Particularly as hospital admissions fall, mergers to achieve these economies of scale have become more common.

The third effect we term *consolidation for network creation*. The cottage industry of local hospitals and physicians in each town is giving way to the regionalization of medical care. To improve their bargaining position with insurers, hospitals want to be part of bigger networks. To ensure access to patients, hospitals want to affiliate with primary care physicians and hospitals in outlying areas. The medical market is moving toward a position of large provider networks, potentially three to five in major cities, that consist of hospitals, primary care physicians, and specialist groups.

In the remainder of the paper, we document the role of health care consolidation in closures, economies of scale, and network creation and consider the implications of mergers for health care costs and patient outcomes. We begin in section 1.2 with a discussion of the terminology of consolidation. In section 1.3 we discuss the growth of managed care and show trends in patient care. Section 1.4 discusses the rationales for consolidation. Section 1.5 shows aggregate trends in consolidation in Massachusetts, and section 1.6 presents a series of case studies. Section 1.7 looks at some of the implications of mergers for medical care costs. Section 1.8 concludes.

1.2   Definition of Terms

Hospital consolidations encompasses a range of different factors. Because health care is so local—a laboratory three blocks away is practically useless for an emergency patient—not all consolidations can involve the same changes. We differentiate consolidations along three lines.

The first type of consolidation is an agreement to coordinate on medical treatments. For example, two hospitals can set up a joint seminar to learn about patient care or can agree to transfer patients back and forth in a specified way. This type of consolidation is not our primary concern.

The second type of consolidation is an agreement to negotiate jointly with third parties. For example, hospitals might agree to purchase inputs together or to negotiate together with insurers. This type of consolidation was contemplated in Boston before mergers became widespread.

Neither of these first two types of consolidation involves the combination of production activities. Perhaps the most extreme form of consolidation is the complete closure of a medical facility, with all of its services being consolidated into other hospitals. We define a *closure* as an acute care facility's closing or converting such that it is no longer an acute care facility. "Acute care" means a general medical and surgical hospital as defined by the American Hospital Association. A conversion would be if an acute care facility became a rehabilitation center or an elderly care facility, and conversions as well as situations where the building is no longer used in the medical care industry are all considered to be closures.

There are many situations where there is a partial combination of services between facilities with all involved facilities remaining open. We define a *merger* as a consolidation of at least some aspects of hospital production. Mergers can occur at several different levels. The easiest type of merger is an *administrative merger.* This involves combining the nonpatient aspects of the hospitals—billing, information services, purchasing, facilities and maintenance, and so forth.

Administrative mergers are relatively easy because there is no need for the hospitals to be physically close to one another. If the hospitals are close in proximity, they can merge along several other dimensions: *ancillary services* such as laboratories, x-ray machines, magnetic resonance imaging (MRI), and so forth; *nursing staff;* and *clinical services* such as medical/surgical units, emergency rooms, and obstetrics units.

The degree to which these services can be merged depends on the exact physical structure of the hospitals. Services such as organ transplantation or obstetrics can be combined at one institution even if the hospitals are several miles apart, since there is typically sufficient time to move patients back and forth between institutions. Core services such as laboratories or radiology cannot be far apart from general medical and surgical units, however.

Very few mergers involve full integration of two hospitals into one facility, although many merged institutions claim they intend to move toward this type of integration. Determining the implications of steps short of full integration is extremely important and is a subject we pay close attention to.

To get a sense for what economies of scale are possible, table 1.1 shows a breakdown of hospital employees by type in 1988. The average hospital had roughly one thousand employees, of which close to one-half were not involved with patient care (laundry, cafeteria, custodial staffs, etc.), another third were nurses, and the residual were administrators, technical workers and physicians. Economies of scale seem quite possible. An average hospital had a total budget of $100 million in 1994, of which approximately 50 percent came from labor expenses. If a hospital could cut 10 percent of its labor force, it would save approximately 5 percent of total spending.

1.3   Trends in the Medical Care Industry

Before considering health care consolidation, we begin with a discussion of the changes that are taking place in the delivery of medical services and health insurance. Traditional insurance was very generous for providers. Reimbursement was on a fee-for-service basis, so that every additional test or procedure brought in additional income. Providers had complete say about what treatments they thought were appropriate, with few controls on utilization. And patients paid very little at the time they used services, giving them little incentive to monitor the care they received.

The result was an industry that expanded far beyond the level of truly necessary services. The expansion was in two directions. First, specialist care became dominant over primary care. Why see an internist for chest pains when a cardiologist is around and can be seen at little additional cost? Since specialists tend to perform procedures related to their specialty more frequently than do generalists seeing similar patients (Greenfield et al. 1992), the result was high levels and rapid growth of medical services. In addition, hospitalizations became frequent and lengthy. Marginal cases were generally hospitalized, and people admitted to hospitals tended to stay there for long periods of time to make sure everything was OK.

Further, because health care is primarily a local good, the industry developed a local orientation. Practically every community had local

Table 1.1   **Distribution of Hospital Employment, 1988**

| | | | FTEs/Bed | | |
Area of Hospital	FTEs	FTEs/Bed	Less Than 100 Beds	100–300 Beds	More Than 300 Beds
Doctors	56	.25	.06	.04	.47
Nurses	305	1.38	1.30	1.19	1.55
Administrators	23	.1	.12	.10	.10
Technical workers	88	.4	.39	.38	.41
Dietitians	8	.04	.08	.03	.04
Social workers	7	.03	.02	.02	.04
Psychologists	2	.01	.003	.005	.01
Other	501	2.26	1.56	1.71	2.85
Total	988	4.59	3.66	3.61	5.58

Source: American Medical Association 1988 Annual Survey of Hospitals.

physicians and hospitals, which were the entry points to the medical system along with specialized, high-tech hospitals in big cities. Figure 1.1 shows the distribution of acute care hospitals in Massachusetts in 1980—a year roughly at the high-water mark for the hospital industry. Each dot in the figure is an acute care hospital.[1] There were 108 acute care hospitals in 1980. Many towns had one or two community hospitals or were near a town that had one. The map also indicates which of the 1980 acute care hospitals are no longer acute care hospitals today. The smaller symbols indicate that the hospital closed before 1996.

We divide the hospitals in the state into five groups (differentiated on the map): 24 hospitals were located in major cities;[2] 53 hospitals in suburban areas immediately surrounding these major cities;[3] 12 hospitals in smaller cities;[4] 12 hospitals in suburbs of these smaller cities; and 7 hospitals in rural areas.

Because towns took great pride in their hospitals, and hospitals were such an important local institution, medical cultures developed quite locally. Patients and physicians in neighboring towns or across the street might each see their hospital as the better institution. The most difficult aspect of hospital mergers, in many cases, are these cultural issues.

The past few years have seen a dramatic reversal of these trends (see Zelman 1996 for an overview). Most prominent in the reversal is the rise of managed care insurance.[5] One fundamental difference between managed care and traditional insurance is that managed care insurers generally do not pay providers on a fee-for-service basis. Primary care physicians, for example, are typically capitated—they receive a fixed amount per patient per month, independent of actual services provided. Hospitals and specialists are generally paid on a fee-for-service basis, but there are often financial incentives facing the specialist and the primary care physician to encourage lower utilization. For example, primary care physicians might get additional income if hospital utilization rates remain low, or hospital payments could depend on utilization rates. As a result, there are substantial incentives toward reduced utilization of medical care, particularly hospital and specialist care (Cutler 1995).

1. Acute care means that the hospital is a general medical or surgical hospital, as defined by the American Hospital Association. The primary medical institutions excluded by this definition are psychiatric and rehabilitation hospitals.

2. Major cities are Boston, Springfield, and Worcester.

3. We define a suburb loosely as a town near a city. Large towns near larger cities are considered suburbs rather than their own city. For example, Cambridge is considered a suburb of Boston.

4. The smaller cities are Lawrence, Lowell, New Bedford, Fall River, Fitchburg/Leominster, and Pittsfield.

5. The lexicon of managed care has traditionally been divided into such terms as health maintenance organizations (HMOs), preferred provider organizations (PPOs), and independent practice associations (IPAs), but for our purposes the terminology is less important than the economic effects.

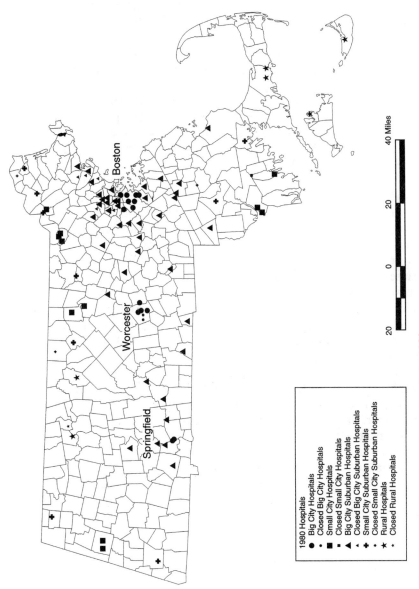

Fig. 1.1   Massachusetts acute care hospitals, 1980

1980 Hospitals

- ● Big City Hospitals
- ■ Closed Big City Hospitals
- ■ Small City Hospitals
- ◄ Closed Small City Hospitals
- ◄ Big City Suburban Hospitals
- ◄ Closed Big City Suburban Hospitals
- + Small City Suburban Hospitals
- + Closed Small City Suburban Hospitals
- ★ Rural Hospitals
- · Closed Rural Hospitals

Boston

Worcester

Springfield

20   0   20   40 Miles

Financial pressures are not limited to private insurance but have become most extensive there. Beginning in fiscal year 1984, for example, Medicare moved to paying hospitals on a per-case basis, much the way managed care does now. Medicaid followed as well, and managed care is an increasing part of both of these programs. But the dominant effect for providers has been managed care in the private sector.

In addition to its financial restrictions, managed care removes equal choice of providers. Managed care insurers set up a "network" of providers who agree to lower fees in exchange for access to the network. Patients are steered toward the network providers by increasing the cost sharing required for out-of-network usage. A typical plan, for example, might charge a ten dollar copayment if the person uses a network provider but require a five hundred dollar deductible and 20 percent coinsurance for care received outside of the network.

Even within the network, moreover, patients do not have free choice of providers. Most managed care insurers use the primary care physician as a "gatekeeper"—care from specialists will only be available if the primary care physician has authorized it. Limiting access to medical specialists limits the use of expensive, high-tech medical care.

Finally, managed care insurers bargain strenuously with providers. Because access to the network is so important and managed care limits the network substantially, managed care insurers receive rates far below what non-managed care insurers are paying. No systematic evidence on payment rates across insurers is available, but our informal conversations suggest that a large managed care insurer can pay up to 30 percent below insurers without a tight network.

Managed care is a large and growing part of the health insurance marketplace (Cutler, McClellan, and Newhouse 1996). Figure 1.2 shows the expansion of managed care into Massachusetts and the nation as a whole between 1984 and 1994. The figure shows just one part of managed care—closed panel HMO enrollment. Other types of insurance such as preferred provider organizations (PPOs) and looser forms of HMOs do not have data that extend back as far. Even with this restriction, more than a third (34.5 percent) of the Massachusetts population was enrolled in an HMO in 1994. This is triple the rate a decade earlier and over twice the national average. Massachusetts thus seems to be a natural case study for examining the impact of managed care on the medical marketplace.

1.4 Trends in the Hospital Marketplace

Managed care is not the only factor affecting the hospital marketplace, although it is a dominant one. The movement of Medicare and Medicaid to a per-admission payment basis reduced the intensity of medical treatment substantially (Feder, Hadley, and Zuckerman 1987). And technologi-

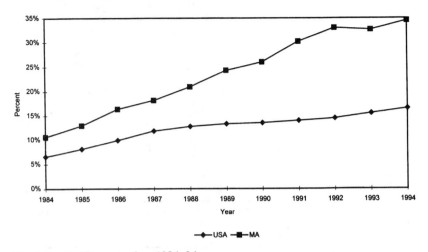

Fig. 1.2   HMO penetration, 1984–94

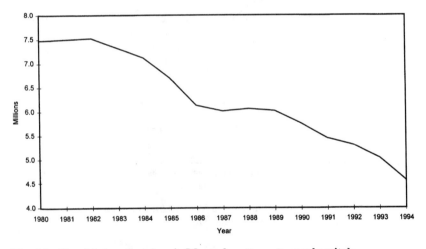

Fig. 1.3   Trend in inpatient days in Massachusetts acute care hospitals

cal change has also reduced the demand for inpatient care. In the early 1980s, for example, the typical cataract surgery operation involved several days in the hospital. By the late 1980s, essentially all cataract surgeries were done on an outpatient basis. Treatment of ulcers used to require surgery, but better knowledge of gastrointestinal processes has led to the development of pharmaceutical methods of treatment. The net effect of all of these factors has been a substantial reduction in the demand for inpatient hospitals.

The demand reduction has been dramatic. Figure 1.3 shows the trend in inpatient days in Massachusetts hospitals. Between 1980 and 1994, in-

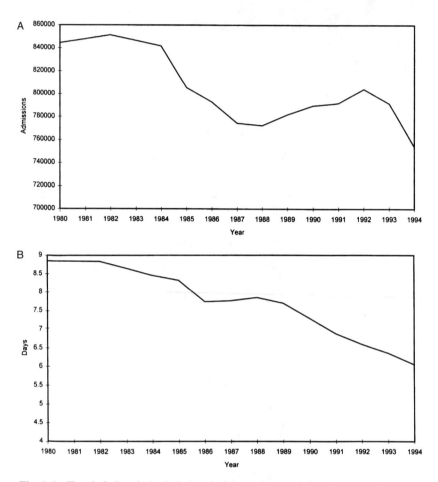

Fig. 1.4   Trends in hospital admissions in Massachusetts (*A*) and average length of stay in Massachusetts acute care hospitals (*B*)

patient days have declined by 3.5 percent annually, even with a growing and aging population. This decline is so dramatic that by the turn of the century, inpatient hospital utilization will be roughly 50 percent of its level in 1980. Indeed, a common estimate among market participants is that long-run demand will be 50 percent or less of its peak level.

Figure 1.4 decomposes the change in inpatient days into changes in the number of admissions and changes in the length of stay per admission. Both have fallen over time. Admissions fell by 1.1 percent annually between 1980 and 1994, and length of stay fell by 2.2 percent annually. The reduction in average length of stay is particularly notable since most research suggests that the pool of patients being admitted to hospitals is sicker now than it used to be (Cutler and Staiger 1996).

The reduction in inpatient demand has had three implications for the organization of the medical system.

1.4.1 Consolidation for Closure

Clearly, demand reductions of this magnitude cannot be met without substantial hospital closures and downsizing of surviving hospitals. The first implication of managed care has therefore been to force a contraction of inpatient beds. We term this implication *consolidation for closure.*

Some hospitals have closed outright. Smaller hospitals without strong ties to particular local communities, for example, are generally the first to close. Figure 1.5 shows the drop in the number of acute care hospitals in Massachusetts.

But it is often difficult for hospitals to close. The community and cultural factors noted above make people want to preserve their access to nearby, neighborhood health care and make providers eager to ensure continuity of this access. In such circumstances, hospital mergers are often a way to facilitate, or substitute for, closure. For instance, for a community that has had two hospitals but now only needs one, merging may make it easier for the combined institution to shut down one of the physical buildings and move operations to the other. The building may move out of the medical sector entirely (as happened in Lynn, where the old hospital was razed and converted into a supermarket). Or the facility may be converted into a psychiatric hospital, rehabilitation hospital, nursing home, outpatient center, or similar service (as happened in Winthrop where Boston University Medical Center purchased Winthrop Community Hospital and converted it into an outpatient facility).

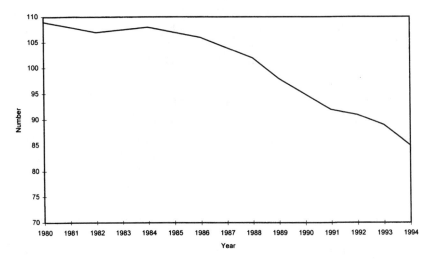

Fig. 1.5 Number of acute care hospitals in Massachusetts

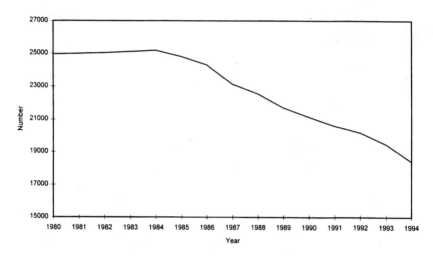

Fig. 1.6   Number of beds in acute care hospitals in Massachusetts

Alternatively, merging hospitals can reduce the inpatient supply of each hospital but maintain both physical institutions as acute care facilities. This is what occurred in Framingham and Natick, where both local hospitals remain open but at substantially lower capacity than before.

A reduction in hospital beds has indeed occurred. Figure 1.6 shows the number of acute care hospital beds from 1980 to 1994. Inpatient capacity has fallen by 30 percent. This is near the reduction in hospital days, although a bit smaller. It seems that further facility closure will be needed.

Managed care penetration varies considerably across different states, and one may therefore expect consolidation for closure to differ across states as well. Indeed, California, which along with Massachusetts has high managed care penetration, has also seen a large number of hospital closings and consolidations. In future research, we intend to examine how much of hospital closings nationwide results from managed care.

1.4.2   Consolidation for Economies of Scale

The second implication of managed care is to increase the emphasis on cost savings. In addition to closing or curtailing services, hospitals have incentives to provide care more efficiently. Mergers can help hospitals realize efficiency savings. This is particularly true as demand is falling. A hospital that was producing at minimum cost with four hundred beds may be above minimum cost if it falls to two hundred beds. In order to reduce average costs, the hospital may need to merge. We term this rationale *consolidation for economies of scale.*

As noted above, hospitals can merge at several levels. Hospitals can combine their administrations, their ancillary services (laboratories, x-rays, etc.), nursing services, and their entire medical services. The ease with which hospitals can combine each of these levels decreases after administrative and ancillary, and increases as the distance between the hospitals becomes smaller. Hospitals that are not located next to each other cannot share certain facilities such as laboratories or cafeterias. Recent mergers have run the gamut of these possibilities.

1.4.3   Consolidation for Network Creation

The third implication of managed care is somewhat more subtle. As managed care has increased in importance, the value of being part of a larger network has increased as well.

Networking regionally meets two needs. First, it is a way to secure access to patients in a market with falling demand. Patients are generally not loyal to insurance companies (other than the government), but they are very loyal to their doctor (witness the advertising on television and radio). Given that hospitals need patients, that patients value stable provider contacts, and that patients are increasingly affiliating themselves with primary care physicians, the key to ensuring a continuous stream of patients is to affiliate with primary care physicians. Hospitals' buying or affiliating with primary care practices or community hospitals to meet this demand has become a substantial market.

Specialists are less well positioned than are primary care physicians in this market, in part because specialists have much higher costs than primary care physicians, and in part because the relative supply of specialists is so much greater than the relative supply of primary care physicians. Thus, affiliations between hospitals and specialists are a much smaller part of the managed care revolution.

Networks also increase the bargaining power of providers relative to insurers. For small hospitals, the reality is that managed care insurers will not even bother to contract with a small hospital that does not offer the full range of services. As a merged institution, two small hospitals can offer a complete medical package to insurers that the two separately might not be able to support.

Large hospitals can also gain by merging. Even large hospitals face price pressure from insurers. If hospitals can affiliate with enough other hospitals so that an insurance company could not conceivably offer a plan to its customers without access to those hospitals, then the balance of power shifts toward the hospitals and the contracts become more favorable.

1.5   The Massachusetts Experience

To examine how these various trends have played out, we look in detail at the recent history of consolidation in Massachusetts. Our data on consolidation and its outcomes are from the Massachusetts Hospital Association and the American Hospital Association.

Table 1.2 shows the number of hospitals involved in at least one

Table 1.2 Hospital Consolidation in Massachusetts

Years	Number of Hospitals Beginning	Closed, No Merger	Consolidations			Hospitals without Consolidation
				Merged		
			Immediate Closure	Future Closure	Still Acute Care	
1980–85	108	3	1	2	8	94
1985–90	104	5	4	1	11	73
1990–92	93	0	1	0	8	64
1992–94	91	0	4	0	18	42
1994–96	87	0	0	0	11	31
Total	108	8	10	3	56	31

Source: Massachusetts Hospital Association.

consolidation over time. We divide consolidations into two broad types: closures without any prior affiliation with another hospital and mergers.[6] A merger need not be the end of the story. We subdivide mergers by what happened to the original hospital building: immediate closure, closure in the future, or survival as an acute care institution.

Closure has been an important part of hospital consolidation. Of the 108 acute care facilities in Massachusetts in 1980, 8 closed without any prior consolidation activity, and 13 closed subsequent to a merger. Thus, there has been a net reduction of 20 percent (21/108) in the number of acute care hospitals. Three-quarters of the hospitals that have closed either closed or first merged with another hospital in the 1980s. This fact suggests that there were stronger and weaker hospitals in 1980, and that the first effect of falling demand is to force the weaker institutions to leave the market.

In addition to the hospitals that closed, another 56 hospitals merged with another institution and remain open as inpatient facilities. This type of consolidation has increased over time, from roughly 2 per year in the 1980s to 6 per year in the 1990s. Nearly all of the mergers of large hospitals are later in the period (Partners, CareGroup, Columbia/HCA).

All told, 69 percent of the hospitals in Massachusetts have closed or been involved in some kind of consolidation since 1980; only 31 institutions have neither closed nor merged with another hospital (and many of these are the subject of consolidation rumors).

The extent of consolidation, and the form that consolidation takes, differs along two dimensions. The first is the hospital's location within the state. The upper panel of table 1.3 shows the rate of consolidation by hospital location. Consolidation is more common in cities than in suburbs or rural areas. Seventy-five percent of big city hospitals and 83 percent of small city hospitals have engaged in some consolidation, compared to 60 or 70 percent of other hospitals.

The form of consolidation differs as well. Closure—whether coupled with a merger or not—is more common in big cities or their suburbs than in other areas of the state. In big cities and their suburbs, 21 percent of the hospitals in 1980 ultimately closed, compared to 16 percent of hospitals in other areas. Merger without closure, in contrast, is about equally likely in all of the areas.

The second dimension is the size of the institution. The lower panel of table 1.3 shows the rate of consolidation by the number of beds in the hospital in 1980. Smaller facilities are much more likely to consolidate than are larger facilities. Eighty percent of hospitals with less than one hundred beds underwent some form of consolidation, compared with 67 percent of large hospitals. The biggest difference is in the likelihood that

---

6. Mergers are sometimes differentiated into holding company mergers, acquisitions, and contractual arrangements, but we do not view this distinction as particularly relevant.

Table 1.3   Consolidation by Hospital Location and Number of Beds

Characteristic	Number of Hospitals, 1980	Percent Consolidating	Percent Closing	Percent Merging without Closure
Total	108	71	19	52
Location				
Big city	24	75	21	54
Suburb of big city	53	68	21	47
Small city	12	83	8	75
Suburb of small city	12	67	25	42
Rural	7	71	14	57
Number of beds, 1980				
Less than 100 beds	25	80	52	28
100–300 beds	56	70	10	59
More than 300 beds	27	67	7	59

Note: Big cities are Boston, Springfield, and Worcester. Small cities are Lawrence, Lowell, New Bedford, Fall River, Fitchburg/Leominster, and Pittsfield. Suburbs are generally defined as towns in close proximity to large cities. Small cities very close to large cities are considered suburbs, rather than their own city (e.g., Cambridge is a suburb of Boston). Fig. 1.1 shows the distribution of hospitals by location.

a hospital will close. Over half of the small hospitals in Massachusetts in 1980 were no longer acute care facilities by 1996. Hospitals with less than one hundred beds in 1980 accounted for approximately one-fourth of the acute care hospitals, and yet 62 percent of the closures came from that group.

But the downsizing of the industry is more than just hospitals closing. As table 1.4 shows, even those hospitals that are still acute care institutions have seen reductions in the number of inpatient beds. Both those that consolidated and those that did not consolidate have reduced their inpatient beds by roughly 20 percent. As the last row of the table shows, only one-third of the reduction in inpatient beds has been a result of hospital closures; the remaining two-thirds represents downsizing among existing institutions.

A hospital involves a certain amount of physical space, and one might wonder what hospitals do with the space when it is no longer in use serving acute care patients. Table 1.5 presents data on this question. Generally, areas of the hospital that are no longer in use for acute patients are converted to subacute use—rehabilitation facilities, nursing home services, and psychiatric services. Between 1980 and 1994 the share of beds in acute care facilities that were rehabilitation beds rose from 0.3 percent to 1.1 percent, while nursing home beds and psychiatric beds rose even more substantially, from 0.2 to 4.3 percent and 0.3 to 7.2 percent, respectively. The shift of acute care institutions to subacute care services is one of the hallmarks of hospital consolidation.

Table 1.4   **Change in Average Number of Beds by Hospital Location and Consolidation**

Location	Year	Closed	Still Acute Care	No Consolidation	Average
			Consolidation		
Big city	1980	132	502	307	376
	1994	—	413	258	364
Suburb of big city	1980	122	202	219	191
	1994	—	164	175	166
Small city	1980	116	277	327	272
	1994	—	205	226	208
Suburb of small city	1980	51	142	167	128
	1994	—	124	138	130
Rural	1980	82	153	67	118
	1994	—	135	65	111
Average change (%)		—	−21	−22	−10
% of total change		35	44	21	100

Note: Location definitions are given in table 1.3.

Have these mergers been largely for closure, economies of scale, or network creation? It is difficult to say *ex ante,* and more than one may be at work in any particular case. We can give some sense of this by looking at the extremes. Given the reduction in the number of hospitals, consolidation for closure seems quite important. So does consolidation for economics of scale. In several mergers, the two hospitals were physically joined.

But these are only crude estimates. We try to get a better sense of why some hospitals are merging in the next section by analyzing a series of case studies.

1.6   Case Studies

In this section, we consider how some of the mergers that have occurred in Massachusetts fit into our typology above. We focus on five mergers in particular, which are detailed in table 1.6: (1) the merger of Brigham and Women's Hospital and Massachusetts General Hospital to form Partners Health Care (1993); (2) the merger of Beth Israel Hospital, the Pathways Group (build around the Deaconess), and Mount Auburn Hospital to form CareGroup (1994 and 1996); (3) the merger of Boston City Hospital and the Boston University Hospital to form Boston Medical Center (1996); (4) the merger of Framingham Union Hospital and Leonard Morse Hospital to form MetroWest (1991), and its subsequent acquisition by the for-profit Columbia/HCA chain (1996); and (5) the merger of Union Hospital and Lynn Hospital to form AtlantiCare (1985).

We chose these mergers because we felt they represent a good cross

Table 1.5   **Distribution of Hospital Beds by Type of Bed and Institution**

Location	Year	Total	Rehabilitation	Non–Acute Care Services		
				Nursing Home	Psychiatric	Other Subacute
Acute care institutions	1980	25,005	65	50	64	77
	1994	19,914	215	813	1,364	296
Percent of acute care	1980	—	0.3	0.2	0.3	0.3
beds	1994	—	1.1	4.3	7.2	1.5

Note: Acute care institutions are defined as general medical and surgical facilities by the American Hospital Association.

Table 1.6   Summary of Consolidation Case Studies

Consolidation	Year	Number of Beds		Type	Rationale
		1980	1994		
Partners (Boston)	1993			Single parent	Network formation
Massachusetts General Hospital		1,092	899		Economies of scale (administration)
Brigham and Women's		655	712		
Total beds		1,747	1,611		
CareGroup (Boston)	1993–96			Full integration (BI/Deaconess)	Economies of scale
Beth Israel		452	447		Network formation
N.E. Deaconess		489	314		Closure
Mount Auburn		300	279		
N.E. Baptist		245	173	Single parent (Others)	
Waltham		311	206		
Nashoba		102	59		
Glover		101	58		
Total beds		2,000	1,536		
Boston Medical Center (Boston)	1996			Full integration	Economies of scale
Boston City Hospital		454	282		Closure
Boston University Hospital		379	311		Network formation
Total beds		833	593		
MetroWest (Framingham)	1991, 1996			Full integration (MetroWest)	Economies of scale
Framingham Union		311	469		Closure
Leonard Morse		259		Takeover (Columbia)	Access to capital
Total beds		570	469		Debt relief
AtlantiCare (Lynn)	1985			Full integration	Closure
Union Hospital		210	318		Economies of scale
Lynn Hospital		305			Debt relief
Total beds		515	318		

Note: Rationale for merger drawn from hospital interviews.

section of the different types of consolidations occurring in the Boston area. Partners and CareGroup are large health care networks. Boston Medical Center brings a concern about public hospitals and the implications for the poor. AtlantiCare and MetroWest are smaller suburban hospitals, where survival is more of a concern.

Our analysis is based on both economic evidence and detailed interviews with hospital executives from all of these consolidations. In each case, our interviews lasted about one and one-half hours and covered the history of mergers at that institution and in the state as a whole. All of the institutions that we approached agreed to speak with us.

Table 1.6 gives a brief summary of each consolidation. The table shows the number of beds in each of the hospitals in 1980 and 1994 and provides an overview of the rationale for the merger. The mergers that we examine represent a large share of the Massachusetts hospital industry. In 1980, for example, these institutions accounted for 23 percent of the state's 25,005 hospital beds in acute care facilities.

1.6.1   Partners Health Care

The Partners merger, agreed to in 1993, was the most important hospital consolidation in Massachusetts, if not the country, at the time. The merger brought together Massachusetts General Hospital and Brigham and Women's Hospital, two of the five leading downtown teaching hospitals (the others were Beth Israel, New England Medical Center, and Boston University Medical Center). The merger sent shock waves throughout the rest of the market. Indeed, a fair part of the subsequent merger activity in the Boston area was a response to the Partners merger.

The first thing to note about this merger, as shown in figure 1.7, is that Massachusetts General Hospital and Brigham and Women's Hospital are not near each other. Massachusetts General Hospital is close to downtown Boston, while Brigham and Women's Hospital is located in the Longwood Medical Area, a dense concentration of hospitals near the Boston-Brookline border. The two hospitals are located three miles apart, a drive of perhaps twenty minutes. Thus, complete integration is not the goal of the merger. The only way that would be feasible would be to move the operations from one facility over to the other.

The Partners merger is primarily a merger for network creation. At one level, the new institution is so prestigious that most insurers virtually cannot afford not to contract with it. This improves substantially Partners' bargaining position with insurers. At another level, Partners has a strategy of affiliating with many physician groups in the periphery as well as setting up local ambulatory clinics in suburban areas, to extend the hospitals' patient base.

Having a combined institution makes it easier to engage in this practice, in part because the financial resources of the combined institution are

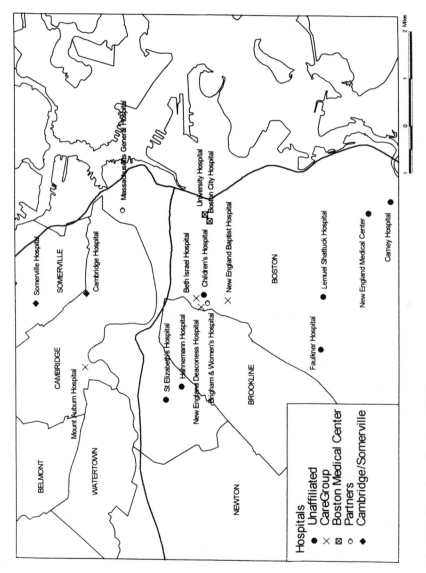

Fig. 1.7 Downtown Boston affiliations

much greater. Indeed, this strategy was aided by the fact that, prior to the merger, the two hospitals had primarily drawn patients from different parts of the city (Brigham and Women's to the north; Massachusetts General to the south), so that market share among the two hospitals was complementary.

Part of the Partners merger is also for economies of scale, but these are largely administrative savings. For example, there are goals of consolidating the information services departments, as well as human services and building and construction. The lack of full clinical integration is not particularly surprising given the physical distance between the two institutions. But even the services that might be consolidated are not being consolidated. For example, Massachusetts General Hospital went ahead with its plans to build a new obstetrics unit after the merger, even though Brigham and Women's has perhaps the preeminent obstetrics unit in the country. This was seen as some evidence that the merger between these institutions is more difficult than had been thought originally.

Finally, as is relatively obvious, the Partners merger was not a merger for closure. The current combined institution is financially strong, even stronger than the hospitals themselves expected. Part of the reason for that may be that the new network has been successful in increasing their customer base even in an overall declining market. The continued financial strength has put little pressure on Partners to close or consolidate any services. This does not mean that the hospitals have not reduced their scale. Table 1.6 shows that between 1980 and 1994, the two hospitals combined reduced their bed capacity by 8 percent. This is not nearly as large as many other reductions, but it illustrates that even the most powerful hospitals in the market realized the need to downsize.

1.6.2   CareGroup

CareGroup is the result of a three-way merger between Pathways—which was Deaconess Hospital's fledgling network—Beth Israel Hospital and Mount Auburn Hospital. Beth Israel and the Deaconess were perhaps hospitals number three and four in the Boston market prior to the consolidations. Geographically, Beth Israel and the Deaconess are right next to each other in the Longwood area (in fig. 1.7, they are the two X's directly north of Brigham and Women's Hospital). Mount Auburn (also indicated with an X) is in Cambridge, to the northwest and across the Charles River from the two central hospitals.

Beth Israel and the Deaconess had each held out hope of affiliating in some way with either Massachusetts General Hospital or Brigham and Women's Hospital prior to the Partners merger, and the hospitals spent the three years after that shock trying to solidify their positions as powerful Boston area teaching hospitals.

There are two fundamentally different events taking place in Care-

Group. The first is the integration of Deaconess and Beth Israel. Beth Israel and the Deaconess are going to become one institution. The name has been changed to the Beth Israel Deaconess Hospital; they are appointing only one service chief for each department; and they are going to physically relocate parts of the two institutions to combine activities such as emergency rooms, obstetrics, and so forth. Indeed, the hospitals have gone so far as to plan a bridge to connect the two facilities. Full consolidation may take several years, but the hospitals envision a single, unified institution. This part of the merger appears to be for economies of scale: the hospitals envision large cost savings from eliminating duplicative services.

The second factor involved is the network that the combined institution is forming. This is the primary rationale for keeping the other (smaller) hospitals with Beth Israel Deaconess. Mount Auburn and New England Baptist (one of the former Pathways members) are the more substantial of these other hospitals, but as table 1.6 shows Deaconess and Beth Israel as a combined institution dwarf the other members of the network. Several of the other hospitals (they are outside the map boundaries of fig. 1.7) will, in all likelihood, survive as acute care facilities; it is generally less expensive to provide routine care outside of the major downtown center. The future of the smaller suburban hospitals in areas where demand has fallen substantially, however, is more perilous.

Table 1.6 shows the extent to which CareGroup has already reduced its size. In 1980, the hospitals making up CareGroup actually would have been larger than Partners. By 1994, however, the combined institution is smaller, having cut a quarter of their inpatient beds.

CareGroup's strategy of maintaining suburban hospitals contrasts with the Partners strategy of affiliating with doctors but not hospitals. Of course, if there is only one local hospital, having affiliated with either the doctors or the hospital is equivalent to having affiliated with both. But more generally, there is a debate about the right strategy for interaction of the powerful, downtown hospitals and the weaker, suburban communities that these two strategies reflect.

1.6.3   Boston Medical Center

Boston Medical Center is the result of a merger between Boston City Hospital and Boston University Hospital. As with the Deaconess–Beth Israel merger, University Hospital and Boston City Hospital are physically adjacent to each other, making it feasible for the two institutions to combine. Figure 1.7 shows the two hospitals isolated in east-central Boston.

The primary reason for the merger appears to be economies of scale. It was clear to everyone involved that with the reduction in inpatient demand, there was no need for two large hospitals located in that part of town. Because the projected size of two scaled-down hospitals would be too small to operate efficiently, merging was the only real option. Table

1.6 shows the extent to which the two hospitals had already reduced their capacity prior to the merger. By 1994, the institutions had cut 34 percent of their inpatient beds. The new hospital expects to shrink even more. The likely outcome is that the new, combined institution will have half as many beds as the two hospitals together had just fifteen years ago.

Boston City Hospital and Boston University Hospital were synergistic in some ways, helping to ease the merger. Boston City Hospital had relationships with community health centers, which meant access to patients. University Hospital never had much affiliation with primary care practices. Surprisingly for a public hospital, Boston City Hospital was in good financial shape, due in large part to generous payments by the state for Medicaid and care for the uninsured. University Hospital, on the other hand, was a private institution, which provided Boston City Hospital a way to remove itself from the controls of city government.

Boston City Hospital and University Hospital had been de facto integrated for several years before the merger. They shared medical staff for at least three years prior to the merger, and the administrative positions had been merged through attrition for several years as well, in anticipation of the consolidation.

The only real problem with the merger was the cultural issues over access for the poor and treatment of the public workers. The workers were largely ignored and the merger was approved despite their objections. The access issue was really a nonissue, as for now the new hospital intends to continue the policy of the old City Hospital, particularly if the city money continues to flow in.

The two hospitals are currently in the process of merging all services into one institution. They are actually planning to close down some of the buildings (the hospitals are a mix of excellent new facilities and decaying older ones) as the institution shrinks.

1.6.4   MetroWest—Columbia/HCA

MetroWest is a story of two mergers. First there was a merger between two small, financially troubled hospitals, Framingham Union and Leonard Morse (Natick), that went very wrong. Second there is the purchase of the resulting hospital by Columbia/HCA, the largest for-profit hospital chain in the country.

MetroWest was created in 1991 by a merger of Leonard Morse Hospital in Natick and Framingham Union Hospital in Framingham (the two towns are adjacent, west of Boston). This merger was largely a form of closure. It was clear to everyone associated with the hospitals that the Framingham-Natick market was not big enough to support two hospitals. The strategy employed by Framingham was to wait for Natick to close, and to actually facilitate that closure by writing contracts with insurance companies to exclude Leonard Morse. Leonard Morse's strategy was to beg for a merger, which ultimately took place.

The merger was unsuccessful. Part of the difficulty was cultural. Framingham Union was the teaching hospital with the star doctors, while Leonard Morse was the friendly community hospital where the doctors paid attention to their patients. Framingham ignored Leonard Morse after the merger. The physical facility fell into disrepair and the services disappeared. The Natick community was upset, and the local outcry to save Leonard Morse hospital helped to bring about a change of management.

Beyond the cultural issues, the financial health of the new hospital deteriorated. The hospitals continued to lose patients and were in need of capital to improve the physical structure of the two institutions. The decision of the management was that the two hospitals would not be able to survive alone. An outside partner would be needed to provide capital and access to favorable insurance contracts.

As a result, MetroWest was sold to Columbia/HCA. Before that, MetroWest was offered to the other major players in the Boston market, but Columbia was the only hospital that would guarantee to keep both facilities open. The deal allowed each of the institutions, and the hospital as a whole, to survive. Columbia benefited by getting a foothold in the Boston area.

Since the takeover, MetroWest has done better financially. The turnaround in performance under Columbia/HCA is in part a result of cost cutting and in part a result of converting inpatient facilities into more profitable services. The Leonard Morse building, for example, has transitional care units (TCUs), rehabilitation units, and a child psychology facility. TCUs are a way for hospitals to increase Medicare reimbursement.[7] The result of all of this is that the Leonard Morse facility has almost no unused space in the hospital even though it has seen its patient base decline substantially.

1.6.5 AtlantiCare

AtlantiCare is the story of a town struggling to preserve local, acute-care hospital services. The city of Lynn, a poor, working class community in the North Shore section of the Boston area, once had two hospitals: Union Hospital, which is where the current AtlantiCare hospital is, and Lynn Hospital. Like MetroWest, the two hospitals were more related by geography than culture. Union was more suburban while Lynn was an inner-city hospital, even though the two are within three miles of each other.

---

7. A patient admitted to the hospital with a hip fracture, for example, will be treated in the hospital unit and the hospital will receive a diagnosis-related group (DRG) payment. Afterward, the patient may be transferred to the rehabilitation unit, and the hospital is paid a per-diem rate for care.

In the mid-1980s, it became clear that two institutions could not survive in the city. The obvious solution was to consolidate hospital services into the nicer facility (Union Hospital); the Lynn Hospital structure was old and substantially depreciated. The merger was predominately one for closure.

The merger was not handled well politically, however, and the town essentially forced the hospitals to consolidate in the poor facility. The result was an exodus of patients and doctors to nearby Salem Hospital. The hospitals learned the hard way that patients are attached to their doctors more than their hospital, and that small community hospitals cannot force doctors or their patients to stay.

Eventually, the hospital relocated to the good facility at Union, but by then a great deal of damage had been done. For example, obstetrics and pediatrics, which had fled for Salem Hospital from the old facility, never returned to the new facility.

It is now clear that even the combined institution cannot survive in the new marketplace. The hospital has cut its costs, but that will not be enough. The key to survival in the long run is access to patients. The North Shore as a whole has a substantial oversupply of beds, and Atlanti-Care cannot offer insurers the full-service hospital they desire. Without an additional merger, AtlantiCare is almost certain to close. Indeed, AtlantiCare has tried to merge with each of the networks of the North Shore: the Salem group (which is affiliated with Partners), Beverly, and Lahey (a doctor's hospital in Burlington). None of these have worked out.

1.6.6   Summary

Our case studies document all three roles for mergers. In many cases, mergers are a way of facilitating or substituting for closure. MetroWest and AtlantiCare are prime examples of this. In one case, the merger facilitated closure (AtlantiCare); in the other case, the merger substituted for closure (MetroWest). Fundamentally, however, the two examples are more similar than they are different. The stereotype of this type of consolidation is a smaller hospital in a metropolitan area or the suburban area just surrounding a metropolitan area where demand is falling. In these markets, there is generally an oversupply of hospital beds and patients have the ability to move across institutions. Some form of closure is often the result.

Our case studies also show the potential role of economies of scale, particularly when neighboring hospitals merge. Hospitals can combine two service staffs into one at the administrative level or all the way down to moving departments across facilities. Economies of scale are most important for Boston Medical Center and Beth Israel Deaconess, both of which are consolidating to operate more efficiently. Unfortunately, both mergers are too new to know much about how successful they will be in reducing costs.

But perhaps most strongly, the mergers show the growing regionalization of medical care delivery. The Boston area is building up several large provider networks: Partners, CareGroup, Boston Medical Center, Lahey, and Columbia/HCA (if it enters the city). Each network will be affiliated with suburban physicians and potentially hospitals.

Columbia was recently dealt a blow in its attempts to enter the Boston hospital market when New England Medical Center, the last remaining unaffiliated, major teaching hospital downtown decided to merge with Lifespan, a Rhode Island not-for-profit hospital group associated with the Brown University Medical School. Columbia's potential entry into the Boston market was a source of concern for all of the hospitals with whom we spoke, and all had assumed that New England Medical Center was the most likely target. With New England Medical Center having merged, it is less likely that Columbia will be able to establish a dominant position among the downtown teaching hospitals in Boston. Columbia will no doubt continue to be a major source of concern to the other Boston hospitals as it decides how or whether it will enter the market.

Most of the consolidations we examine have network creation as one of the goals, if not the central goal. Network creation is valuable to the hospitals both because it ensures access to primary care physicians and their patients and because it gives them more leverage in bargaining with insurers.

The five potential networks in the Boston area is likely too many, however. The networks that are already established employ predatory strategy toward the other networks, and some are in financial trouble. If inpatient demand continues to fall, financial difficulties will increase and further consolidation is likely. This has been the experience in markets where consolidation is more advanced than it is in Boston, such as California and Minneapolis. A common conjecture is that there will eventually emerge roughly three networks in Boston, each with its own group of primary care physicians, specialists, and insurance contracts.

In principle, the provider networks that are being formed could turn into insurance companies, since they will have the inpatient facilities and physician base to do so. It is generally believed, however, that this is unlikely to occur, since hospital administrators do not know the insurance business and may fare poorly in it, and they would risk antagonizing insurers who they otherwise need to negotiate with.

The future of medical care in the area thus appears to be a few large insurers negotiating with a few large provider groups. This is quite a big difference from the older organization of medical care. There may also be a growing role of for-profit hospitals in the Massachusetts market, if Columbia/HCA becomes a major player in the Boston area. Columbia is thought to be advantaged because of its easier access to capital, because of economies of scale in purchasing and negotiating, and because it has less need to worry about care for the uninsured than do not-for-profit hospitals. If the criterion for survival in the Boston health care market is the ability to survive for-profit entry, then fewer networks than five at the end is probably the right number.

1.7   Are the Mergers Successful?

For many hospitals, particularly the smaller ones, the question of whether the mergers are successful is answered simply by noting whether the hospital has managed to remain open. For the big hospitals, such as those in Pathways or Partners, the question is harder. There are three indicators one can examine to measure the success of consolidations. First, the mergers have implications on the revenue side. The mergers for network creation are intended, partially, to increase revenues from insurance companies through increased bargaining power. The data necessary for this sort of analysis are unavailable, although the anecdotal evidence from our interviews suggests that Partners and Pathways have been somewhat successful in improving their contracts. Examining this in more detail is a key issue for future research.

The second indicator is reductions in costs. If these mergers move hospitals to their efficient scale, then one should expect a fall in average cost following the consolidations. That is perhaps the most direct implication of mergers for economies of scale; medical care should now be provided more efficiently. There is some evidence that the mergers are having a positive effect on costs. Figure 1.8 shows the trend in real costs per adjusted admission in Massachusetts and in the United States as a whole since 1980, and table 1.7 shows summary statistics. Massachusetts has been

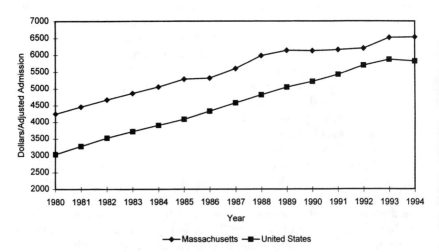

Fig. 1.8   Trend in real costs per adjusted admission

Table 1.7   Annual Growth Rate of Real Costs/Admission (%)

Years	Massachusetts	United States
1970–80	4.0	4.8
1980–85	4.4	5.9
1985–90	3.0	4.9
1990–95	1.6	2.8

Source: American Hospital Association data.

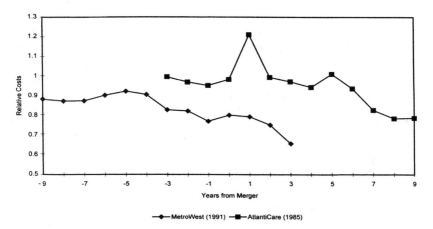

Fig. 1.9   AtlantiCare and MetroWest—costs per adjusted admission relative to the rest of Massachusetts in years around their mergers

affected more by managed care than have most areas, and if managed care is one of the primary driving forces behind mergers for economies of scale, we should expect greater cost reductions there. This is indeed the case. Massachusetts has long had higher medical costs than the nation as a whole, but over the last fifteen years costs have been falling relative to the rest of the country. This is particularly true in the last decade. In the 1980s, cost growth in Massachusetts was below growth in the nation as a whole by 0.8 percentage points. Between 1985 and 1995, the differential has been about 1.5 percentage points.

Of course, what we would like to look at are the cost changes before and after particular mergers we can identify. We are hampered in this effort by the fact that several of the mergers are very recent and thus the potential cost reductions would not have taken place. Two of our mergers are more complete than the others: MetroWest and AtlantiCare. Figure 1.9 shows the hospitals' combined real costs per adjusted admission in the years leading up to and after their respective mergers. Year zero is normalized as the year in which the merger took place: 1985 for AtlantiCare and 1991 for MetroWest. In each case, we scale costs by the average costs in the state as a whole.

There is some evidence that the mergers did lead to cost savings. In the AtlantiCare merger, the time of the merger is likely not the time when cost reduction began, since there were several years of difficulty over the ultimate location of the combined institution. Indeed, the cost reductions appear to come several years later. MetroWest experienced a drop in costs after their merger as well. It will be important to follow the effects of the more recent mergers over the next several years to estimate the degree of cost savings.

The third indicator of merger success is the allocation of customers. One characteristic of the recent consolidations has been the outreach of the big city hospitals into the suburbs, through either the integration of neighborhood clinics or the purchase of neighborhood hospitals. A downtown hospital that purchases a hospital in a suburb should expect to see an increase in its share of patients from that suburb who go downtown for hospital care.

The most natural test of this hypothesis is the Pathways network. Deaconess purchased three suburban hospitals while creating Pathways: Ayer's Nashoba Community Hospital in 1993, Needham's Glover Memorial Hospital in 1994, and Waltham/Weston Hospital in 1995. Table 1.8 shows the Deaconess's share of hospital admissions from the towns of Ayer, Needham, and Waltham/Weston. If network creation is successful, then Deaconess should attract a higher percentage of the hospital admissions in the peripheral towns, particularly those patients that go downtown for care.

The Waltham/Weston acquisition probably occurred too late to have an impact on the admission rates in 1995, and it is therefore not surprising that there is very little movement of patients toward Deaconess relative to its principal downtown competitors. It is perhaps also the case in Needham that the acquisition has not had enough time to adjust admission patterns. If behavior has adjusted as much as it ultimately will, then the story is not very good for network creation; Deaconess's share of patients has actually fallen. The Nashoba acquisition looks to be more successful. Deaconess has gone from a nonentity in the Ayer hospital market to the leading downtown hospital presence, even if it is only 2.6 percent of the market.

Even if the downtown hospital does not succeed in attracting more patients, the alliance can be successful from the local perspective if it strengthens the local hospital. Tables 1.9 and 1.10 show where patients from Ayer and Needham respectively are admitted to the hospital. In both cases, the hospitals that merged with Deaconess have seen their market power improve. In the case of Ayer, Nashoba's gain seems to have come from taking patients from the other large regional hospitals rather than from large, downtown hospitals.

Table 1.8   Changes in Market Share (1988–95) in Pathways Suburbs

Market	Deaconess Market Share (%)			Massachusetts General Hospital Market Share (%)			Brigham and Women's Market Share (%)			Beth Israel Market Share (%)		
	1988	1995	Change	1988	1995	Change	1988	1995	Change	1988	1995	Change
Ayer[a]												
Ayer	0.29	2.63	2.34	0.49	0.95	0.46	1.85	2.11	0.26	0.88	0.53	−0.35
Needham[b]												
Needham	2.41	1.99	−0.42	3.00	2.89	−0.11	11.38	10.34	−1.04	5.44	5.75	0.32
Waltham/Weston[c]												
Waltham	0.77	1.33	0.56	2.51	3.02	0.51	5.36	5.12	−0.25	1.74	2.57	0.83
Weston	2.26	2.58	0.32	10.57	10.91	0.34	12.38	13.41	1.03	7.14	7.66	0.52

Source: Massachusetts Rate Setting Commission.

[a]Nashoba Community Hospital purchased in 1993.

[b]Glover Hospital purchased in 1994.

[c]Waltham-Weston Hospital purchased in 1994.

Table 1.9   Hospital Admissions from Ayer, 1988, 1995

Hospital	Market Share (%)			Number of Admissions	
	1988	1995	Change	1988	1995
Nashoba Community[a]	41.93	43.31	1.38	431	411
Emerson Hospital	26.85	20.76	−6.09	276	197
Leominster Hospital	9.53	6.11	−3.42	98	58
Burbank Hospital	5.84	4.00	−1.83	60	38
Deaconess Hospital[a]	0.29	2.63	2.34	3	25
Brigham and Women's	1.85	2.11	0.26	19	20
Waltham-Weston[a]	0.00	1.16	1.16	0	11
Massachusetts General Hospital	0.49	0.95	0.46	5	9
N.E. Baptist Hospital[a]	0.49	0.74	0.25	5	7
Beth Israel Hospital	0.88	0.53	−0.35	9	5

Source: Massachusetts Rate Setting Commission.
[a]This hospital is a member of Pathways.

Table 1.10   Hospital Admissions from Needham, 1988, 1995

Hospital	Market Share (%)			Number of Admissions	
	1988	1995	Change	1988	1995
Glover Hospital[a]	38.83	42.27	3.44	1,371	1,594
Newton-Wellesley	18.38	20.90	2.52	649	788
Brigham and Women's	11.38	10.34	−1.04	402	390
Beth Israel Hospital	5.44	5.75	0.32	192	217
Massachusetts General Hopsital	3.00	2.89	−0.11	106	109
St. Elizabeth's	2.92	2.23	−0.69	103	84
Deaconess[a]	2.41	1.99	−0.42	58	75
N.E. Baptist Hospital[a]	2.07	1.54	−0.53	73	58

Source: Massachusetts Rate Setting Commission.
[a]This hospital is a member of Pathways.

1.8   Conclusions

Hospital consolidations in Massachusetts have resulted primarily from the pressure imposed on the hospital market by the rise of managed care and changes in technology that reduced the demand for inpatient care. The reduction in demand is manifest in three ways: the need to close, the desire for economies of scale, and the value of health care networks.

Consolidation in the medical care marketplace is likely to fundamentally change the relations between insurers and providers. The old medical system was one where insurers had little power and providers operated at a local level. The new system will have several large insurers bargaining hard with large networks of providers. A widely expressed view is that by the end of the decade, the Boston area will have been transformed from a market with near fifty hospitals to a market with essentially three to four regional networks of doctors, downtown, and local hospitals.

There are three issues that the consolidation of medical care raises that will ultimately determine the success of this transformation. The first is the effect of these consolidations on the level and growth rate of medical costs. Consolidation seems destined to reduce the level of medical spending. Much of medical costs are the return on past investment (for example, specialist physicians), and the new medical system seems likely to eliminate these rents. The long-run driver of medical costs is new technology, however (Aaron 1991; Newhouse 1992; Cutler and McClellan 1996), and it is less certain what effect consolidation will have on the nature of technological change.

The second issue is the effect of the increased market power of hospitals on the costs ultimately faced by patients. The increased bargaining position of hospitals should shift some rents from their contracts with doctors and insurance companies toward the hospitals. This may raise the premiums individuals pay for insurance, depending on how competitive the insurance industry is. The antitrust implications of mergers are not entirely clear, but essentially all proposed mergers have been approved by state and federal regulators.

The third issue is how the new system will deal with the uninsured and underinsured. A hallmark of the noncompetitive medical care system was the extraordinary amount of "uncompensated care" it provided to the poor. Of course, the care was ultimately paid for in the form of higher prices to governments and the privately insured. As public and private payers become increasingly reluctant to subsidize these activities, the care for those unable to afford insurance may suffer. Medical care consolidation may bring issues of equity and social values to the front even as they push worries over medical costs to the rear.

References

Aaron, H. 1991. *Serious and unstable condition: Financing America's health care.* Washington, D.C.: The Brookings Institution.

Cutler, David M. 1995. The incidence of adverse medical outcomes under prospective payment. *Econometrica* 1 (January): 29–50.

Cutler, David M., and M. McClellan. 1996. The determinants of technological change in heart attack treatments. NBER Working Paper no. 5751. Cambridge, Mass.: National Bureau of Economic Research, September.

Cutler, David M., M. McClellan, and J. Newhouse. 1996. How does managed care do it? Unpublished paper, Harvard University, Department of Economics.

Cutler, David M., and Douglas Staiger. 1996. Measuring the benefits of medical progress. Mimeo, Harvard University, Department of Economics, September.

Dranove, D., and M. Shanley. 1995. Cost reductions or reputation enhancement as motives for mergers: The logic of multihospital systems. *Strategic Management Journal* 16:55–74.

Feder, Judith, Jack Hadley, and Stephen Zuckerman. 1987. How Medicare's prospective payment system affected hospitals. *New England Journal of Medicine* 317 (14): 867–73.

Ginsburg, Paul. 1996. RWJF Community Snapshots Study: Introduction and overview. *Health Affairs* 15, no. 2 (summer): 7–20.

Greenfield, S., et al. 1992. Variations in resource utilization among medical specialties and systems of care: Results from the Medical Outcomes Study. *Journal of the American Medical Association* 267:1624–31.

Newhouse, J. P. 1992. Medical care costs: How much welfare loss? *Journal of Economic Perspectives* 6, no. 3 (summer): 3–21.

Zelman, Walter. 1996. *The changing health care marketplace: Private ventures, public interest.* San Francisco: Jossey-Bass.

Comment   Paul M. Healy

Overview of Study

This study examines factors underlying the high frequency of mergers and acquisitions in the hospital industry during the late 1980s and 1990s. Based on their analysis of consolidations in the state of Massachusetts, the authors conclude that mergers were a response to the dramatic decline in demand for hospital beds after 1980. By 1994 demand for beds in the state had fallen to 67 percent of 1980 demand. This trend is expected to continue, with demand forecasted to decline to 50 percent of the 1980 level by 2000.

The authors trace the decline in demand for hospital beds to changes in health insurance and to improved medical technology. In the early 1980s, private managed care insurers as well as public insurers (Medicare and Medicaid) began paying providers on a per-patient basis, rather than on a fee-for-service basis. These fee changes gave health providers greater incentive to economize on health costs and hospital stays. In addition, new medical technologies enabled procedures that would formerly have required a hospital stay to be performed on an outpatient basis.

The authors hypothesize that the sharp decline in hospital demand provided three motivations for mergers: to facilitate hospital closures or bed reductions, to enable small hospitals to survive by consolidating to take advantage of economies of scale, and to help providers create networks to

Paul M. Healy is the MBA Class of 1949 Professor of Business Administration at Harvard University.

improve their bargaining power with insurers. The evidence provided in the paper, which is derived from aggregate hospital data and individual firm case studies, is consistent with all three explanations. For example, the field studies suggest that the consolidation of Union and Lynn Hospitals occurred to reduce bed capacity in Lynn, whereas the merger of Massachusetts General and Brigham and Women's Hospitals was aimed at increasing efficiency through economies of scale and creating a powerful network of providers in the Boston area.

The paper has several very positive features. First, by providing evidence on the economic forces underlying hospital mergers, closures, and network creation, it can inform the public policy debate on the merits of hospital mergers, both in Massachusetts and elsewhere in the United States. Second, by using both aggregate data and individual firm case studies, the authors are able to provide stronger evidence on hospital consolidations than would be possible using each of these sources alone. The aggregate data provide evidence on the broad changes taking place in the industry, whereas the field studies provide evidence on management motivations for hospital mergers.

I anticipate that this paper will stimulate additional research on health care provider consolidation, particularly in light of the ongoing public policy debate on the economic implications of provider mergers. I therefore focus my comments on areas where such research could be directed: further examination of reasons for mergers and additional empirical tests.

Further Examination of Reasons for Hospital Mergers

The paper provides a useful overview of the major motives for hospital merger. However, each of the three explanations presented in the paper merits additional consideration.

Mergers to Close Hospitals

Although the authors argue that mergers facilitate hospital closures or capacity declines, they provide relatively little explanation of the forces that make mergers necessary to induce hospitals managers to downsize their facilities. Several explanations are plausible. First, target managers may be reluctant to voluntarily reduce hospital capacity either because of concern about their own job security or because of public pressure to keep community hospitals open. Alternatively, hospital managers may be reluctant to downsize if they believe that their competitors may downsize first, leaving their own firm as the industry survivor. For example, consider two competing hospitals of comparable size and operating efficiency that face a 50 percent decline in demand. Each has an incentive to wait for the other to close, so that it can become the sole provider for the region. The optimal strategy for each provider may therefore be to avoid reducing capacity, even though demand is shrinking. By agreeing to merge, the two eliminate this destructive private incentive and permit an orderly reduction in capacity to take place within the region.

The above explanations of merging as a form of facilitating closure have different empirical predictions. If mergers occur so that efficiently run hospitals can close or consolidate weaker operations, acquirers are likely to be hospitals that have already reduced their own bed capacity, whereas targets would not. Alternatively, if mergers arise to eliminate private incentives by hospitals in the same region to avoid downsizing, neither partner in the combination will have had to reduce its capacity prior to the merger. In addition, both merger partners would compete in the same geographic region.

Mergers for Economies of Scale

Hospitals may also merge to generate economies of scale. These arise if merging hospitals can reduce the cost of expensive equipment that is currently not fully utilized or can reduce administrative personnel and nursing and medical staff. As the authors note in the paper, "an average hospital had a total budget of $100 million in 1994, of which approximately 50 percent came from labor expenses. If a hospital could cut 10 percent of its labor force, it would save approximately 5 percent of total spending."

However, the evidence in table 1.1 suggests that economies in personnel may not be easy to achieve. Indeed, full-time hospital employment per bed is higher for larger hospitals than for smaller. Hospitals with fewer than one hundred beds have an average of 3.66 full-time employees per bed, compared to 5.58 for hospitals with more than three hundred beds. These data suggest that there may actually be diseconomies of scale for physicians, nurses, and other hospital employees, raising questions about the sources of economies of scale in hospital mergers.

Mergers for Network Creation

The third explanation for mergers provided in the paper—the creation of area networks to increase bargaining power with insurers—raises several questions. For example, what are the implications of the combinations for patients? At one level increased provider power is likely to increase the costs of health care for users. However, this need not be the case. For example, if it is difficult for users to evaluate the quality of their health care, powerful providers may counteract insurers' incentives to increase profits by lowering health care quality. Many communities are increasingly wary of managed care insurers' incentives to reduce the quality of care and have passed or proposed legislation to regulate insurers.[1] It would be

1. Regulations have been passed in at least twenty states to protect the rights of managed care patients. These regulations cover such issues as assuring managed care patients of continuity of care and access to emergency services, specialists, and experimental procedures, as well as limiting travel and waiting times and providing grievance procedures.

interesting to examine whether these regulations are effective in maintaining health care quality, or whether the creation of powerful provider networks are more effective regulators of insurer incentives.

Management's justification of many of the largest recent hospital mergers on network grounds, rather than consolidation grounds, has an alternative explanation to that provided in the paper. The authors note that by 2000 the demand for hospital beds in Massachusetts is expected to fall by 50 percent relative to its 1980 level, although the number of hospital beds has declined by only 25 percent. Considerable additional capacity reduction is therefore likely to occur. Yet target and acquirer management apparently prefer to focus on creating provider networks rather than on making painful cuts in their own bed capacity. Is management simply avoiding making these difficult downsizing decisions? Certainly, there is casual evidence consistent with this hypothesis. For example, in January 1997, New England Medical Center (NEMC), a struggling nonprofit hospital in Boston, was acquired by Lifespan (a Providence not-for-profit group affiliated with Brown University Medical School). Other bidders for the hospital included Columbia/HCA, the nation's largest for-profit hospital company. Lifespan argued that the acquisition would help it create a strong regional network. The failure of Columbia to acquire NEMC was greeted with relief by all the major area groups, perhaps because Columbia would be more likely to reduce capacity at NEMC and to provide more cost competition in the Boston hospital market. It remains to be seen whether these types of acquisitions provide the intended benefits or whether they have simply delayed inevitable capacity reductions.

Additional Empirical Evidence on Mergers

Because the data used in the study are relatively coarse, there remain opportunities to undertake additional empirical research on hospital consolidations. For example, the evidence on reductions in hospital bed capacity is based on the number of beds available in only two years (1980 and 1994) for both the aggregate tests and the case studies. These data are difficult to interpret since they do not provide evidence on changes in capacity before and after the merger. As a result it is not possible to assess whether mergers actually led to reductions in capacity, as hypothesized, or whether the observed reductions had already taken place prior to the mergers. To distinguish between these competing explanations, additional time-series data must be collected so that beds available at each hospital can be aligned in event time.

Time-series data on hospital capacity will also provide insights into the characteristics of target and acquirer firms, and hence the forces that lead to consolidating acquisitions. For example, are acquisitions to reduce capacity made by acquirers that have successfully downsized their own facilities? Have these acquirers taken over and downsized other providers' facilities? Are targets in these acquisitions firms that have been slow to reduce capacity? Alternatively, have both partners been unable to make reductions (perhaps because they want to be the survivor in their region)?

Other ways to improve our understanding of the forces underlying acquisitions include examining the premerger characteristics of targets and acquirers. For example, if acquirers merge with providers that have been slow to reduce capacity, there are likely to be differences in operating efficiency for the two firms prior to acquisition. Data on operating costs per patient, operating costs per bed, and occupancy rates can show whether acquirers have lower costs per patient and costs per bed and higher occupancy rates than target hospitals. Also, in areas where there is a mix of not-for-profit and for-profit hospitals, are acquirers more likely to be for-profits, where operating efficiency is viewed as more salient?

It will also be interesting to examine data on postmerger performance for the combined firm. If mergers are justified as a means of developing economies of scale, are they followed by reductions in employees per patient or employees per bed? Are there declines in capital, administrative, and operating costs per bed and/or per patient? Do mergers for the creation of regional networks enable the merged firm to negotiate better deals with insurers, and thereby have higher revenue growth, higher operating margins, and/or higher market share than they would otherwise have had? Do they lead to increased patient occupancy rates? The authors provide some data on these effects, but they are relatively limited. There is scope for additional work on these areas, particularly given questions about the benefits of network mergers noted earlier.

Finally, it would be interesting to examine whether the high frequency of hospital mergers in Massachusetts and the factors underlying these consolidations are also evident in other parts of the country. Are mergers also popular in regions where hospital demand has not declined as rapidly as Massachusetts, perhaps because of offsetting population or demographic changes? Are there nonmerger responses to the decline in hospital demand in other regions?

Summary

In conclusion, this paper provides a fascinating first look at the responses by the hospital industry in Massachusetts to a dramatic decline in demand. The paper is innovative in its use of both aggregate industry and field study data to examine this topic. The observed consolidation of the industry through mergers and acquisitions raises a number of interesting follow-up questions. For example, do the mergers really cause reductions in hospital beds? If so, what forces make mergers the most effective way for providers to reduce capacity? Do firms realize anticipated economies of scale from mergers? How effective are network mergers in improving providers' bargaining power with insurers? Do these mergers permit providers to avoid costly downsizing? Answers to these questions are particularly relevant given the public debate on the changing health industry landscape.

Comment   Frank R. Lichtenberg

Jason Barro and David Cutler have written a very insightful case study of a market undergoing enormous transitions. They document that in 1980, there were 108 acute care hospitals in Massachusetts. By 1994, 21 had closed (or ceased to operate as acute care hospitals) and another 56 had engaged in some kind of affiliation; only 31 "remained the same." As they observe, the rapid structural change in the Massachusetts medical care marketplace is largely attributable to two major types—*organizational* and *technological*—of exogenous innovation in the delivery of health care.

The major organizational innovation was (and continues to be) the replacement of traditional fee-for-service health care by "managed care." Between 1976 and 1995, the fraction of the U.S. population enrolled in health maintenance organizations (HMOs) increased more than sixfold, from 2.8 percent to 17.7 percent (*Health, United States, 1995* [1996], table 136). There was also a shift in the character of managed care: in 1976, staff, group, and network model HMOs accounted for almost all HMO enrollments, whereas by 1995, they accounted for only about one-fourth of enrollments.[1]

It is widely believed that people enrolled in HMOs are less likely to be admitted to hospitals than traditionally insured people who are similar in other (observable) respects.[2] Data from the 1992 National Hospital Ambulatory Medical Care Survey—which provides data on a large random sample of hospital outpatient department visits—are consistent with this view. Overall, the patient is admitted (as an inpatient) to the hospital in about 1.2 percent of hospital outpatient visits. The probability that an HMO patient will be admitted to the hospital is about 0.6 percent lower than the probability that a fee-for-service patient will be admitted, controlling for single year of age, sex, race, ethnicity, (ICD-9 two-digit) diagnosis,

Frank R. Lichtenberg is the Courtney C. Brown Professor of Business at the Graduate School of Business of Columbia University and a research associate of the National Bureau of Economic Research.

1. By 1995, "individual practice associations" (IPAs), in which the HMO contracts with an association of physicians from various settings (solo and group practices), and "mixed" (IPA/group) models accounted for the majority of enrollments.

2. The admission rate may be lower, in part, because HMOs may place greater emphasis on preventive health care.

geographic region, "fixed hospital effects," and a few other variables. In other words, *the HMO patient is about 30 to 50 percent less likely to be admitted to the hospital,* and this difference is highly statistically significant.[3] This, of course, implies that the adoption and diffusion of the innovation known as managed care resulted in a sharp decline in the number of hospital admissions, which the authors document.[4]

The time-series evidence—the fact that the number of hospitals was declining when managed care penetration was increasing—is certainly consistent with the hypothesis that the managed care revolution precipitated consolidation in the medical care marketplace. It would be nice to test this hypothesis econometrically using longitudinal data on various health care markets. Although managed care penetration has increased in all regions of the country, it has increased more rapidly in some regions than in others. In the west, for example, the fraction of the population enrolled in HMOs increased from 9.7 percent in 1976 to 29.0 percent in 1995, whereas in the south it increased from 0.4 percent to 11.2 percent (*Health, United States, 1995* [1996], table 136). Was the rate of hospital consolidation in the south during this period significantly lower than what it was in the west?

Technological innovation was the second major cause of the decline in hospital utilization. One aspect of this alluded to by the authors was the substitution of outpatient surgery for inpatient surgery: the fraction of total surgeries performed on an outpatient basis increased from 16.4 percent in 1980 to 54.9 percent in 1993.[5] Another was the substitution of drugs for surgical treatment. In a recent paper (Lichtenberg 1996), I performed an econometric analysis of the effect of changes in the quantity and type of pharmaceuticals prescribed by physicians in outpatient visits on rates of hospitalization, surgical procedure, mortality, and related variables. I examined the statistical relationship across diseases between changes in outpatient pharmaceutical utilization and changes in inpatient

3. In the 1991 National Ambulatory Medical Care Survey—a random sample of outpatient visits to doctor offices—the HMO hospitalization rate is also lower than the fee-for-service hospitalization rate (controlling for similar covariates), but the difference is statistically insignificant. Patients visiting hospital outpatient departments tend to have lower incomes than those visiting doctors' offices, so this may indicate that managed care may limit hospitalization of low income individuals to a greater extent.
4. The difference between HMO and fee-for-service hospital admission rates may reflect a variety of factors, and may either overstate or understate the true "effect" of HMOs on hospitalization. One reason for overstatement is that exogenously healthier individuals may self-select for HMO coverage when they have a choice. On the other hand, as Laurence Baker and Martin Brown (1997) have hypothesized, there may be "spillovers" (e.g., "demonstration" or "threat" effects) from HMO practices to fee-for-service practices; this would cause the difference in probabilities to understate the effect of HMOs.
5. Health, United States, 1995 (1996), table 90. The outpatient share of total surgeries increased most rapidly in small hospitals: 62.5 percent of surgeries performed in 1993 in hospitals with fewer than one hundred beds were outpatient surgeries, compared to 47.0 percent in hospitals with five hundred beds or more.

care utilization and mortality during the period 1980–92. I found that the number of hospital stays, bed days, and surgical procedures declined most rapidly for those diagnoses with the greatest increase in the total number of drugs prescribed and the greatest change in the distribution of drugs, by molecule. The estimates implied that an increase of one hundred prescriptions is associated with 1.48 fewer hospital admissions, 16.3 fewer hospital days, and 3.36 fewer inpatient surgical procedures. Greater quantity and novelty of pharmaceuticals had a negative impact on average length of stay in hospitals, as well as on the number of hospital stays. The average number of inpatient procedures performed per stay increased more slowly for diagnoses with higher growth in drug quantity and novelty.

Barro and Cutler attempt to assess the *consequences* as well as the *causes* of hospital consolidation, but their ability to do so is limited by the recentness of most of the mergers and alliances and by incomplete data on hospital inputs, outputs, and prices. In principle, hospital mergers may be profitable because they enable the hospitals to reduce costs (increase productivity), raise prices, or both. As the authors note, cost savings are most likely to be realized in administrative departments (e.g., information services, human resources, and building and construction). My research (1992) on mergers and acquisitions in the manufacturing sector of the economy is consistent with this view. I found that mergers had a much greater impact on the employment of administrators than they did on production workers, and that reductions in administrative costs accounted for almost half of the productivity gains associated with mergers.

Unfortunately, measuring the productivity of hospitals is much more difficult than measuring the productivity of manufacturing plants (and even that is subject to pitfalls!). Costs per admission and similar resource-intensity measures may be misleading because of substantial heterogeneity in case mix and severity of illness. The authors note that "most research suggests that the pool of patients being admitted to hospitals is sicker now than it used to be," so that the increase in deflated costs per admission overstates the true rate of cost increase. The data on AtlantiCare's and MetroWest's relative costs per adjusted admission presented in figure 1.9 suggest that these costs tend to decline following the merger, but there is also evidence of a downward trend premerger, which may simply continue (not accelerate) after consolidation.

The authors argue that an important reason for a hospital to join a network of health care providers is to increase its bargaining power vis-à-vis large-scale purchasers of health services (managed care organizations and insurance companies). Consolidation may enable hospitals to charge higher prices and enhance their "market power" in the face of the increased monopsony power that large-scale purchasers have acquired. Presumably due to lack of data, Barro and Cutler do not examine the behavior of prices of hospital services in relation to supplier consolidation;

hopefully they or others will do so in future research. According to Martin Gaynor (1997), the Federal Trade Commission has challenged several proposed hospital mergers on antitrust grounds, but it has not won any of these cases; the courts ruled that these mergers did not pose a threat to consumer welfare.

Standard models of perfectly or monopolistically competitive industries imply that a contraction in demand will result in industry restructuring and a reduction in the equilibrium number of "firms." Barro and Cutler have done an excellent job of vividly describing both the main features and the nuances of that adjustment process in an actual, and very interesting, market.

References

Baker, Laurence, and Martin Brown. 1997. Effect of managed care on health care providers: Evidence from mammography. Paper read at NBER Health Care Program meeting, 15 May, in Cambridge, Mass.

Gaynor, Martin. 1997. Presentation at NBER Not-For-Profit Hospitals Program meeting, 16 May, Cambridge, Mass.

Health, United States, 1995. 1996. National Center for Health Statistics. Hyattsville, Md.: Public Health Services.

Lichtenberg, Frank. 1992. *Corporate takeovers and productivity.* Cambridge, Mass.: MIT Press.

———. 1996. Do (more and better) drugs keep people out of hospitals? *American Economic Review* 86 (May): 384–88.

2

The Eclipse of the U.S. Tire Industry

Raghuram Rajan, Paolo Volpin, and Luigi Zingales

It is difficult to think of an industry that was affected more by the wave of mergers and acquisitions (M&A) in the 1980s than the U.S. tire industry. Seventy-five percent of the companies in the industry (accounting for 90 percent of the value) experienced a takeover bid or were forced to restructure during the period 1982–89 (Mitchell and Mulherin 1996). As a result of this activity, control changed hands in over half the companies in this industry. Even more remarkable, in the majority of cases, control was transferred to foreign owners. By the end of the decade, traditional American firms like Firestone, Uniroyal, Goodrich, Armstrong, and General Tire belonged to foreign companies. As a consequence, large U.S.-owned tire manufacturers, who in 1971 represented 59 percent of the world production and included four out of the top five producers, in 1991 represented only 17 percent of world production with only one of the top five producers (see table 2.1 below). These changes are even more dramatic

Raghuram Rajan is the Joseph L. Gidwitz Professor of Finance at the Graduate School of Business of the University of Chicago and a research associate of the National Bureau of Economic Research. Paolo Volpin is a Ph.D. student in economics at Harvard University. Luigi Zingales is professor of finance at the Graduate School of Business of the University of Chicago and a research associate of the National Bureau of Economic Research.

Rajan and Zingales acknowledge financial support from NSF grant no. SBR-9423645, and Volpin from an NSF graduate fellowship. The authors are grateful for the insights provided by tire industry executives, especially Mr. Maki, Mr. Mihelick, and Mr. Tee. The authors benefited from the comments of Mike Jensen, Robert Porter, and participants at the conference and at a seminar at the University of Chicago. The authors also thank the Bureau of the Census and the NBER for making available the Longitudinal Research Database (LRD). In particular, they acknowledge the help of Joyce Cooper, Wayne Gray, and Arnold Resznek. The opinions expressed in the paper do not necessarily represent the views of the Bureau of the Census or the NBER. The LRD matched sample has been screened to ensure that no confidential data have been revealed. Whenever a single company's name is mentioned, there is no intention to suggest that such a company is in the LRD sample.

when compared with the stability of the relative market shares of U.S. tire manufacturers for the previous fifty years.

The U.S. tire industry therefore presents an intriguing example of the changes wrought by the M&A wave that swept through the United States in the 1980s, and of its effect on the position of U.S. manufacturers in a global market. Anyone interested in the effects of M&A on the productivity and the long-term competitiveness of the U.S. economy cannot ignore what has happened in this industry. The purpose of this paper, then, is to undertake an in-depth industry analysis of the events that led to the demise of U.S. ownership in the tire industry, and of the effects of mergers on industry restructuring and productivity. To do so we call upon a variety of different sources, ranging from plant-level data to industry analyses (including contemporary reports in trade publications), interviews with executives, and accounting data. The goal is to attempt to explain why the merger wave occurred, why it was led by foreign producers, and what its effects have been.

We are able to test (and reject) two main interpretations of these events. The first (neoclassical) hypothesis is that foreign manufacturers were more efficient in producing tires, and that this advantage (be it superior know-how or better management) could not be transferred to U.S. manufacturers without acquiring their plants. According to this view, the takeovers in the 1980s in the tire industry were simply a reflection of the fundamental tendency for assets to move to the most efficient producers. Contrary to this view, we find that plants are not acquired by the most efficient producers (at least as far as plant-level productivity is concerned) and we do not find any evidence of an increase in plant-level productivity after an acquisition.

A second explanation of the phenomena is advanced by Jensen (1993). He suggests that the evolution of the U.S. tire industry during the 1980s is a textbook example of the effects of what he calls "the third industrial revolution." According to Jensen, rapid technological change generates overcapacity in certain industries, requiring some firms to downsize or exit. But "managers fail to recognize that they themselves must downsize; instead they leave the exit to others while they continue to invest. When all managers behave this way, exit is significantly delayed at substantial cost of real resources to society. The tire industry is an example. Widespread consumer acceptance of radial tires meant that worldwide tire capacity had to shrink by two-thirds (because radials last three to five times longer than bias ply tires). Nonetheless, the response by the managers of individual companies was often equivalent to: 'This business is going through some rough times. We have to make major investments so that we will have a chair when the music stops'" (Jensen 1993, 847). Since internal control systems do not force managers to shrink, only the intervention of outside raiders can force these companies to downsize or exit.

That the acquirers were foreign rather than domestic is not relevant for this interpretation, all that matters is that they were outsiders to the industry.

We do not find much support for this interpretation either. While, as suggested by Jensen (1993), there were some delays in closing bias ply capacity (also see Sull 1996), the industry had made most of the necessary closures by the early 1980s—before the takeovers started! More specifically, we find no evidence that acquisitions hastened the closure of plants in general and more inefficient plants in particular. We also find that capital expenditures increase after an acquisition, which is inconsistent with the overinvestment hypothesis.

We then try to explore the reasons for the demise of the U.S. ownership in the tire industry by looking at the historical evolution of the tire industry in the United States and the rest of the world, with particular emphasis on the relationship between the car and the tire industries. The car industry plays an important role for two reasons. First, original equipment sales represent about one-quarter of all sales. Moreover, they have an important effect on the replacement sales given the tendency of consumers to buy the same type of tires. Second, major changes in type of tires used, like the introduction of radials, require some modifications in the design of cars. This raises an important coordination problem.

The most striking aspect of the U.S. tire industry is its delay in the introduction of radials. Michelin first commercially produced radials in France in 1948, and by 1970, 98 percent of tires sold in France were radials. The rest of Europe and Japan followed a similar path. Yet, in 1970 radials represented only 2 percent of the tires sold in the United States. The technology was well known to U.S. manufacturers, who were using it in their European subsidiaries. An attempt by Goodrich to launch radial production in the United States in 1965 failed because of the strong opposition of U.S. car manufacturers, who did not like the fact that radial tires required a new suspension system in the cars. Only in the beginning of the 1970s did the car producers announce that they wanted to switch to radials. Therefore, U.S. tire manufacturers delayed the transition to radials until the 1970s, a period characterized by the oil crisis and a severe recession in the car industry.

The switch to the radial technology required major capital investments because it was not economically feasible to convert the existing bias-ply capacity to producing radials; Firestone's attempt to do so ended in fiasco. As a result, tire producers faced the prospect of making major capital investment in a low margin sector at the same time as the growth prospects for the entire sector looked grim. The major diversified tire companies (Goodrich in particular) made the conscious decision to reduce their capital and development expenditure in the tire business, sell their foreign operations, and look for a buyer for domestic operations. Others, like Uniroyal, were less clear-cut about their prospects. However, barring Goodyear, all the tire manufacturers reduced their focus on tires. It is entirely possible that this was indeed the optimal strategy, since foreign producers had already sunk their investment in radials, while U.S. producers had to sink at a time when the long-term growth prospect of the car industry (and thus indirectly of the tire industry) had worsened.

One possible solution at this stage was a consolidation of the U.S. tire industry. There were two reasons, however, why that could not occur without the cooperation of outsiders. First, it was unclear whether such a move would be accepted by the Federal Trade Commission. Second, and most important, automobile manufacturers strongly opposed any consolidation among their suppliers. They liked having a number of independent tire suppliers to ensure competition. As a result, a merger between two tire suppliers would inevitably result in a redistribution of some of their share of the original equipment business to other tire manufacturers. The importance to tire manufacturers of having original equipment sales to the automobile manufacturers therefore precluded a large domestic tire manufacturer from merging with another large domestic manufacturer (unless, of course, one of the manufacturers had no original equipment sales as was the case with Goodrich, which merged with Uniroyal).

In the meantime, the economics of the industry were changing in other ways. Most important, automobile sales and manufacture were becoming increasingly international and there was a growing need for tire manufacturers to follow their customers across countries. If Honda cars are equipped with Bridgestone tires, then Honda's exports in the United States automatically generate demand for Bridgestone tires in the U.S. replacement market. It is only natural for Bridgestone, thus, to take advantage of this demand by starting to sell in the United States. Given the high transportation costs, this will generate also the need for producing in the United States.

The globalization of the car industry also produced the need for a higher level of research and development (R&D), which could be borne only if spread over a higher volume of sales. For example, Goodyear's R&D and advertising expenses as a fraction of sales rose 27 percent between 1970–75 and 1980–90. As a result, only large multinational companies could survive.

If only multinationals could survive and there was not much room to build new capacity in any of the major industrialized countries, then only two possibilities were left: either the foreign producers acquired U.S. firms or U.S. firms acquired foreign producers. The latter alternative, however, was not feasible since most of the foreign companies could not be acquired. Michelin, for example, which is the major French tire producer, is fully controlled by a limited partnership, whose unlimited partner is Francois Michelin. He, rather than a majority of Michelin shareholders, determines the future of Michelin. Similarly, the major German producer, Continental, is controlled by a complicated web of shareholdings that prevented Pirelli from taking it over in 1990. The Japanese firms are even harder to acquire. By contrast, acquisitions, even acquisitions by foreign firms, were extremely easy in the United States during the 1980s. Although it is hard to establish how much of a role this asymmetry played, it is an important (and often ignored) factor that should be taken into consideration.

We therefore conclude that the roots of the dramatic change in the world and U.S. tire markets between 1970 and 1990 lie largely in the failure of U.S. tire manufacturers to adopt the radial technology when the rest of the world did so. Of course, hindsight is always 20/20. But even manufacturers such as Goodrich who realized the potential of the technology back in 1965 could not force its widespread acceptance. The structure of the domestic market, and specifically the relationship between the automobile manufacturers and the tire producers, was probably instrumental in retarding adoption of the technology. In other words, even though they acted rationally and in their own self-interest, the structure of the domestic market led U.S. tire manufacturers—like characters in a Greek tragedy—inexorably toward their doom. By contrast, the domestic market structure in countries like France probably spurred innovation. Thus the paper highlights a possible link between domestic market structure, innovation, and the ability to compete internationally.

The rest of the paper is organized as follows. In section 2.1, we discuss the structure of the tire industry; in section 2.2, we discuss the reasons for the delay in the introduction of radials into the United States. Section 2.3 tests the "neoclassical" and "overinvestment" hypotheses, while section 2.4 examines the hypotheses that the U.S. manufacturers willingly quit a business they were too weak to compete in. Section 2.5 concludes with policy conjectures.

2.1   The Structure of the Tire Industry

2.1.1   History

The tire industry had its beginnings in tires made for bicycles.[1] At first, bicycles used solid rubber tires, but the invention of the pneumatic tire by John Dunlop in 1888 soon made it the dominant product. The industry took off on the back of an explosion in the demand for bicycles in the 1890s. By the time the craze for bicycles waned in the beginning of the twentieth century, automobiles started driving the demand for tires, and they account for the majority of tires manufactured today.

---

1. This section draws heavily from French (1991) and Tedlow (1991).

The early focus in product innovation was on making the tire fit the wheel without slipping, while at the same time making it easily removable. But the demand for product innovation did not cease once this was achieved. Automobiles became heavier and faster, which triggered major innovations in tire manufacture including the introduction of patterned treads. French (1991) argues that these innovations enabled smaller firms such as Goodyear and Firestone to compete with the large bicycle tire manufacturers.

Even though the basic form of the automobile tire was set by 1910, there have since been tremendous advances in the product. The introduction of balloon tires in the 1920s and, as we will detail shortly, radials in the 1970s were fundamental changes. Tires became flatter and wider, and tire life improved rapidly, especially in the 1920s and 1970s. Changes in manufacturing technology accompanied the changes in product technology. The industry had moved to mass production using tire-building machines by the 1920s. French (1991, xv) suggests that "technical changes increasingly disadvantaged smaller producers and consolidated the position of larger firms, leading to a decline in the number of firms after 1920." Interestingly, innovation seems to have enabled small manufacturers to establish themselves when the industry was in its infancy, but as the industry matured, it seemed to become a barrier to entry. This relationship between innovation and number of firms has been formalized and applied to the tire industry by Jovanovic and MacDonald (1994).[2]

This is reflected in the market shares of the various manufacturers. Four of the five biggest producers of tires in 1970 (Goodyear, Firestone, U.S. Rubber [later Uniroyal], and Goodrich) were also among the five biggest in 1910. This is not to say that there was no entry or exit early on. For instance, sixty firms entered the industry in 1919–20 alone. But the turnover was largely confined to the small firms and new entrants. The large firms and their market shares remained surprisingly stable. Moreover, entry eventually dropped off with virtually no entry between 1929 and 1970.

The major tire manufacturers in 1970—the starting point for much of our analysis—had somewhat different origins. BFGoodrich and U.S. Rubber (Uniroyal) were primarily rubber goods manufacturers before they began producing tires. The tire business was a form of diversification for them. By contrast, Goodyear and Firestone started out in the tire business. The differences in their origins seemed to reflect the extent to which they diversified outside the tire industry. Goodrich and Uniroyal had approximately 60 percent of their sales in the tire industry in 1970, while the figure was over 80 percent for both Firestone and Goodyear. The exception to this pattern is General Tire which started in 1915 by supplying repair ma-

---

2. Interestingly, they end their analysis in 1973 on the basis that the introduction of radials did not increase the optimal scale of production of tires.

terial but soon began tire production in 1916. It had only 40 percent of its sales in tires by 1970. As we will see, the extent to which the firm was diversified appeared to influence top management's commitment to stay in the business.

2.1.2   Structure of the Industry circa 1970

Table 2.1 shows the share of the world market for tires held by the major producers. Michelin was the only non-U.S. manufacturer in the top five in 1971. The top four producers controlled 60 percent of the world market. According to Dick (1980), the tire industry has been heavily concentrated in this way since the thirties: in the U.S. market in 1935, the four largest producers accounted for 80 percent of the total sales; in 1958 their share was 74 percent, and at the end of the 1960s, 72 percent.

Economies of scale in production do not seem to explain such a level of concentration. Plants in 1976 had capacity varying from 300 tires per day to 30,000 tires per day, with a mean capacity of 14,500 tires. *Modern Tire Dealer* reports there were fifty-five plants of significant size in 1976. That the minimum economic scale is not very large seems to be obliquely confirmed by John Ong, Chairman of the Board of BFGoodrich, "Today, under normal competitive conditions, it's not economically feasible to operate a tire plant with capacity lower than 9,000 to 12,000 tires a day. Mixing, calendering, and other equipment investments mandate a mini-

Table 2.1   **World Market Share of the Largest Tire Producers**

Company	Home Country	1971	1979	1986	1993
Goodyear	U.S.	24	23	19	17
Michelin	France	11	16	18	19
Firestone	U.S.	17	14	7	
Dunlop	U.K.	4	4		
Pirelli	Italy	6	6	6	5
Bridgestone	Japan	3	7	9	18
Uniroyal	U.S.	8	5	6	
Goodrich	U.S.	6	4		
General Tire	U.S.	4	4		
Continental	Germany	2	3	8	7
Sumitomo	Japan			6	6
Yokohama	Japan			4	5
Toyo	Japan			2	3
Concentration indexes					
C4		60	60	54	61
Herfindahl		12	11	10	11

Sources: West (1984) and *Financial Times,* 1988 and 1995.

Note: This table presents each manufacturer's tire sales as a percentage of world sales. C4 is the sum of market shares of the four largest producers. The Herfindahl index is the sum of the squared market shares of each producer.

mum size." This estimate would allow for about one hundred plants in the United States.

2.1.3 Channels of Distribution

The tire industry essentially serves two markets: the original equipment (OE) market and the replacement market. OE manufacturers are the automobile producers who, historically, have had tremendous bargaining power. In the words of William O'Neil Sr., founder of General Tire, "Detroit wants tires that are round, black, and cheap—and it don't care whether they are round and black" (Tedlow 1991, 15). The automobile manufacturers have been content to play tire manufacturers against each other without actually building their own tire factories (though Ford briefly did so in 1938). But despite its low profitability, the OE market has historically been important because it provides large orders (and hence the scale) as well as the prospect of future replacement sales (car owners typically replace tires with the same original equipment brand).

A possible explanation for the concentration of tire sales is that sales to the OE market are critical. The primary requirement of an OE supplier according to *Rubber World* (January 1966) is that the supplier must be a technological innovator. As a tire veteran put it "You just can't stand still with those boys [the automobile manufacturers]. . . . Your tires have to carry heavier loads, last longer and go faster. The smaller firms cannot afford the kind of R&D operation this entails." Another requirement is that the tire manufacturer must be able to deliver the product. In other words, it must have "a distribution set-up capable of giving Detroit what it wants, where it's wanted—and on time. . . . It must have acceptance as [a] national supplier . . . it must be able to warehouse Detroit's requirements well ahead of the call, stockpiling them, in order to avoid the risk of strikes." Finally, a sales network that is capable of servicing the OE tires is an added advantage in obtaining OE orders. Thus the economies of scale in research and distribution appear to be an important element of this industry.

Table 2.2 shows the share of the domestic OE market held by U.S. manufacturers. Smaller manufacturers had a presence only in the replacement market, but even there, the majors controlled a significant fraction of the overall sales.[3] The automobile manufacturers did not buy from one tire supplier. Instead, they spread their orders among the tire manufacturers, though they had their favorites. For instance, Goodyear and Chrysler, Uniroyal and General Motors, and Firestone and Ford were thought to enjoy

---

3. Most major manufacturers also produced for private labels. As a result, it is not easy to obtain an exact figure for the share of the replacement market controlled by each manufacturer. If we restrict our attention to the share of the market controlled by the majors under their original names, Goodyear controlled 13 percent of the replacement market in 1974 and Firestone 10 percent.

Table 2.2   **Tire Manufacturer Shares of Original Equipment Market in the United States**

Company	1968	1975	1980	1985	1990
Goodyear	31.0	35.0	28.0	32.0	36.5
Firestone	24.0	24.0	21.5	21.5	17.0
Uniroyal	25.0	20.0	24.4	22.0	17.0
Goodrich	15.0	8.0	10.3	0.0	
General Tire	5.0	11.5	10.8	13.0	12.0
Michelin		1.5	5.0	11.0	15.7
Continental				0.4	
Pirelli				0.1	
Dunlop					1.5
Bridgestone					0.3

Source: Modern Tire Dealer (1991).

Note: This table presents each tire manufacturer's share of sales to the OE market. All the figures are percentages of total sales of tires to automobile manufacturers in the United States.

special relationships. Since no foreign tire manufacturer produced locally, this explains why virtually the entire OE market was held by the five major U.S. manufacturers in 1970.

The OE sales of 37.5 million tires in 1970 accounted for 22 percent of the market. The rest is accounted for by replacement sales that were a further 130 million tires and accounted for 77 percent of the market, while exports represented less than 1 percent. Buyers in the replacement market range from mail order and retail chains like Sears and Montgomery Ward, which became significant buyers in the 1920s, to oil companies that entered tire retailing in the 1930s, tire company stores, and independent merchants. In 1970, replacement sales were composed of sales to the service stations of large oil companies (15 percent), large department stores (15.5 percent), tire company stores (11 percent), and independent tire dealers (56 percent). Profits in the replacement market have historically been higher than in the OE market. Rosenbloom and Benioff (1990) report that in 1966 the profit margins were between 3 percent and 5 percent in the OE market and between 5 percent and 8 percent in the replacement market.

In the replacement market, not all tires are sold under the producer's own name. Part of the output sold to large oil companies and to department and chain stores were distributed under private names specific to the outlet. This market was especially important for smaller companies such as Armstrong and Mohawk, since they did not need to advertise in order to sell. The tire producers distributed the rest under their own names (the national brands), or under less well-known names called "associate brands." As a result, even though the tires were produced by only a small number of companies, they were sold under more than 170 brand names.

The market was effectively segmented; national brands that were highly advertised across the United States and were used as original equipment could command a higher price, while the other brands were sold in a very price-competitive market.

2.1.4 Technology

In the 1960s, there were fundamentally two different types of tire construction: bias ply and radial ply. Technically, the two tires differ in the way the body cords are layered in the body of the tire. In bias ply tires, the cords are at an angle to the direction of rotation, while in radials they are perpendicular. In practice, the two tires differ substantially in performance. On well-maintained roads, bias tires ensure a smoother ride, but they are inferior to radials on bumpy roads and they do not hold the road as well when it is wet. The radial tire offers more safety with better braking and cornering power. Radial tires also give better gas mileage. The major difference, though, is in life expectancy: a bias ply tire lasts about twelve thousand miles while the radial lasts forty thousand miles.

For reasons we shall discuss shortly, the tire manufacturers by and large continued to produce bias ply tires, though Goodrich made a failed attempt to introduce radials in 1965. From 1967 onward, however, they quickly switched to an intermediate product, the belted bias ply tire. This tire had much of the ride characteristics of the bias ply tire but lasted about twenty-four thousand miles. The belted bias tire had one advantage over radials: it was much cheaper to convert existing production lines to produce belted bias tires. In 1970, approximately 85 percent of tires manufactured were belted bias ply tires.

2.1.5 Investment and Financial State

The majors invested substantial amounts in the 1960s as they expanded production and switched production to belted bias ply (while conversion was cheaper than converting to radials, it was not costless). Goodyear opened four new plants over this decade while Firestone opened three. Both Goodyear and Firestone were largely in tire production, so Compustat firm-level data can be used as an approximate measure of their investment in tires (domestic and foreign). Both firms invested 6 percent of sales, on average, in the first half of the 1960s, and 8 percent on average in the second half.

Despite the substantial investment (the majors did not invest such large amounts relative to sales again), the majors entered the 1970s in reasonably good financial condition. Interest coverage (earnings before interest, taxes, depreciation, and amortization (EBITDA)/interest expense) ranged from a low of 3 for Goodrich to a high of 7 for Firestone. Netting out cash from both debt and assets, the debt-to-assets ratio ranged from a high of 0.38 for Goodrich to a low of 0.23 for Firestone. Interestingly, Goodyear, which was the only major to survive, entered the 1970s right in the middle of the pack in terms of leverage.

2.1.6   Industrial Relations

The last important aspect of the tire industry to be considered is industrial relations. Workers in the tire industry were organized by the United Rubber Workers (URW) during the 1930s and early 1940s. Historically, wages in tire plants have moved in tandem with increases in the Big Three auto contracts. This principle has underlined URW bargaining since the forties. Competition from imports, however, placed greater pressure on tire companies to reduce costs over the 1970s and 1980s. In response, management attempted less expensive settlements. Also, they shifted production by opening new plants in the southern part of the United States, where unions were less strong. As a result, of the nine plants constructed since 1970, only one has been organized, while all twenty-one plants built during the 1960s were organized.

2.2   Radial Technology and Its Delayed Entry in the U.S. Market

In 1970, U.S. manufacturers were the largest in the world with extensive international operations. Looming ahead, however, was the specter of wrenching change for the tire manufacturers. Even though they had just converted to the intermediate technology of belted bias ply tires, the single most important issue faced by the tire industry in the beginning of the 1970s was the impending arrival of radial tires. Contrary to popular belief, neither were radials a new technology nor did the oil crisis in late 1973 precipitate their introduction. This raises the question why the U.S. manufacturers sunk so much in the intermediate belted bias technology rather than moving directly to radials, and why they then took so long to introduce radials. We argue that both the U.S. automobile and tire industries were in a low technology equilibrium that was disrupted only by the entry of foreign manufacturers.

2.2.1   Brief History of the Radial Tire

The radial tire was invented in 1913 by Gray and Sloper of the Palmer Tyre Company (United Kingdom). In 1948, Michelin first introduced the tire into commercial production (the Incredible X) and patented a radial with a steel belt. In 1951, Pirelli patented its own radial tire, with rayon belts (named Cinturato), and in the late fifties, Continental, Dunlop, and the European subsidiaries of Goodyear, Firestone, and Uniroyal started the production of radial tires. In 1970, when over 98 percent of tires manufactured in the United States were bias ply or belted bias ply, 97 percent of tires in France and 80 percent of tires in Italy were radials. Thus, radial technology was not commercially new, nor was it unknown to U.S. manufacturers. It simply was not used in the United States.

2.2.2   Production Technology

In 1970, radial production required 20 to 35 percent more labor than bias tires. Furthermore, it required substantial investment and changes in the method of production. "One of the certainties about radial-ply manufacture is that, new production equipment will be a necessity . . . new tire building machines, fabric and wire bias-cutters, new or modified curing, special stacking and handling systems, and (perhaps) new feeding equipment. This is due to the radial's unique construction" (*Rubber World,* November 1965). Moreover, radials necessitated closer tolerances, stricter quality control, and frequent inspections, and the percentage of scrap and defective radial tires was twice as high as with conventional tires. Another reason for their increased cost was that the raw materials needed to produce a radial tire cost 35 percent more than for a bias tire.

2.2.3   The Attitude of the Automobile Manufacturers

Automobile manufacturers in the United States had grown complacent over the 1960s. Tedlow (1991, 24) points out that the 1967 Cadillac Eldorado was "priced at $6,277" and, weighing in at three thousand pounds, "plowed through tight corners in ungainly fashion and got only ten miles to the gallon." The Mercedes Benz 250 of that year weighed half a ton less, cost two thousand dollars less, was more than a foot and a half shorter, and ran twice as long on a gallon of gas. American cars were built to be land cruisers, floating on large highways and fueled by cheap gas. The smooth, mushy ride that manufacturers thought consumers required could only be provided by the bias ply tires. The emphasis in automobile design was not so much on the handling or product quality but on looks. "There was only one kind of car headquarters wanted to hear about: A Car Just Like Last Years" (Easterbrook 1992, 317). The problem, however, was that customer preferences had changed considerably: they now wanted better handling, quality, and—after the oil crisis—mileage. This was reflected in the rising tide of automobile imports as Detroit failed to meet the needs of its customers.[4]

2.2.4   The Diffusion of the Radial Tire in the United States

Seeing the changing preferences of consumers, Ford in 1970 and General Motors in 1972 announced plans to introduce models with steel belted

---

4. It is also possible that the driving experience with car imports led customers to acquire a taste for radials.

radials. "Suddenly [the tire manufacturer's] expectations were confounded by dramatic external changes, and the switch to radials had to be undertaken swiftly. . . ." (French 1991, 101). What were the changed expectations? In 1972, *Rubber Age* projected the growth of the radial market in the United States based on the diffusion of the tire in the German and U.K. markets. It estimated that the radial ply would grow from 3 percent of the OEM market in 1972 to 65 percent in 1976. It was somewhat more conservative in its estimate of penetration in the replacement market, given the popularity of belted bias ply tires. *Rubber Age* felt radials would have 30 percent of the replacement market by 1976. Sull (1996) also argues that two tire manufacturers in 1973 made similar projections for 1976.

These estimates are important because they preceded the oil crisis (recall that the trebling of oil prices was unimaginable until it actually occurred in late 1973). It is amazing that the actual penetration of radials in the OE market in 1976 was 64 percent, while in the replacement market it was 29 percent (table 2.3). This suggests that at least some industry sources could see the writing on the wall, and the forces precipitating the change to radials were in place even prior to the oil crisis. This view is confirmed by our conversations with industry sources.

What is puzzling about the switch to radials is not that it occurred so fast. In fact, the switch from bias ply to belted bias ply toward the end of the 1960s occurred even faster. The puzzle is why radials were not introduced while belted bias ply tires were—the latter almost as soon as they could be produced commercially. As we will argue, this delay in adopting an innovation that the rest of the world had already implemented put U.S. industry at a disadvantage. We will also attempt to explain why the introduction took place when it did. These are critical to understanding the takeovers in the 1980s.

2.2.5 Causes for the Delayed Introduction of the Radial Tire

Three special characteristics of radials explain why U.S. manufacturers settled into a low technology equilibrium. First, car suspensions have to be built differently to accommodate radials. This involves substantial redesign and investment. Thus, unlike the change from bias to belted bias, the change to radials required the support of the automobile manufacturers. As we have already pointed out, the car manufacturers were reluctant to abandon the cushy ride offered by the bias ply tires even though consumer preferences may have been changing. Thus the reluctance to innovate upstream hampered innovation downstream. To complicate matters, radials were a radically different technology, unlike the belted bias ply tires. While U.S. manufacturers had some experience in manufacturing radials in their European subsidiaries, they were certainly not the leaders (see *Rubber World,* April 1976). Adapting radials to U.S. cars and U.S. production

Table 2.3   **Relative Importance of Original Equipment and Replacement Tire Markets**

Year	Original Equipment Market		Replacement Market		Car Production
	Total Shipments	% Radials	Total Shipments	% Radials	
1965	51,413	0.0	94,893	0.0	9,329
1966	47,362	0.0	101,812	0.0	8,599
1967	40,827	0.0	108,499	0.0	7,405
1968	49,873	0.0	121,088	0.0	9,843
1969	46,172	0.4	129,112	1.5	8,219
1970	37,535	0.3	129,608	2.1	6,545
1971	48,609	0.1	135,009	3.6	8,578
1972	51,292	4.6	141,295	6.2	8,821
1973	55,960	17.6	142,002	12.1	9,661
1974	43,307	43.1	123,460	22.4	7,290
1975	39,281	63.9	122,469	27.0	6,706
1976	49,905	64.3	122,690	29.1	8,492
1977	55,689	66.3	129,270	32.7	9,211
1978	54,963	67.2	135,151	37.5	9,173
1979	48,188	76.6	121,922	42.4	8,423
1980	34,932	80.0	106,912	50.0	6,373
1981	35,979	83.3	125,263	60.9	6,251
1982	33,981	83.6	130,539	65.9	5,074
1983	43,845	83.5	133,964	70.1	6,782
1984	50,993	83.8	144,580	75.7	7,774
1985	54,839	83.5	141,455	81.6	8,185
1986	54,392	84.2	144,267	86.7	7,829
1987	52,913	85.0	151,892	90.2	7,098
1988	54,131	85.5	155,294	93.7	7,136
1989	51,170	87.3	151,156	95.3	6,825
1990	47,199	87.6	152,251	96.7	6,076
1991	41,859	88.4	155,400	97.9	5,439
1992	46,307	89.1	165,794	98.9	5,667
1993	52,335	88.7	165,146	99.2	5,982
1994	58,448	90.0	169,983	99.4	6,601

Note: Passenger tire shipments in the OE market and the replacement market are in thousands of units and are taken from the Rubber Manufacturers Association (1994). The number of cars produced (also in thousands of units) is from *Ward's Automotive Year Book, Shipments.*

methods still required considerable innovation. Thus U.S. automobile manufacturers did not have an assured supply of high quality radials if, in fact, they decided to switch.

Second, unlike with belted bias tires, radials could not be manufactured on the same machinery as bias ply tires. Enormous investment in new machinery was required to change to radial manufacture. But the third factor comes in here. In the OE market, much of the rents from the improved technology would be extracted by the automobile manufacturers. And the technology had the potential to shrink the replacement market even more than belted bias ply tires. Thus rents from the new technology would accrue largely to the automobile manufacturers, and indirectly to consumers, while the investments costs would be wholly borne by the tire manufacturer.[5] To summarize, there were two barriers to switching to the radial technology: a coordination problem and a rent sharing problem. The coordination problem was that car manufacturers were afraid to change their designs absent a serious commitment to radials by tire manufacturers. Tire manufacturers, on the other hand, were unwilling to make the massive investments in moving to radials without the assurance of rents from a large market.[6] Yet, in all likelihood, it appeared that their most profitable market (the replacement market) would shrink as a result of the longer life of the new product. This appears to be a textbook example of the hold-up problem as modeled by Grossman and Hart (1986).

What was different in the other countries? Consider France, which was the first to switch to radials. When Michelin introduced the radial tire, it controlled Citroen, having acquired it in the 1930s when Citroen was unable to repay the debts owed to the tire company. Thus the coordination and rent sharing problem in upstream and downstream innovation was solved by the simple expedient of vertical integration. Moreover, the tire market in France was dominated by Michelin (it had 63 percent of domestic market share in 1975 with the second producer having only 12 percent; see West 1984, 44). So not only could it keep some of the rents from innovation while dealing with other car manufacturers, it could also capture rents in the replacement market from the improved product. As in Grossman and Hart (1986), the hold-up problem is resolved by integration.

Even though tire manufacturers in Italy, Germany, and the United Kingdom did not own automobile manufacturers, they adopted quickly. This was because once Michelin had shown the success of the radial, it could offer it in neighboring countries where it had a foothold.[7] This forced tire manufacturers in the other countries to offer radials.

---

5. Implicit in this argument is that the OE market and the replacement market are only loosely connected so that the automobile manufacturer does not extract all the rents from replacement sales also. If consumers always replaced tires on their car with the same brand, then presumably the automobile manufacturer could extract not only the profits on the OE tire but also the profits on the replacement.

6. West (1984) focuses on this last issue: "the way in which the US transnationals delayed launching the radial tire in their home market is a classic example of the use of market power by large firms to slow down the pace of innovation in an industry." We, however, believe that automobile manufacturers also played an important part in the delay.

7. West (1984) reports that Michelin had 30 percent of the Italian market in 1973, 23 percent of the U.K. market in 1972, and 21 percent of the German market in 1975. It should also be noted that Pirelli independently made substantial innovations in radial manufacture. Furthermore, unlike Michelin, it appropriated the rents not by manufacturing elsewhere but by licensing the technology out.

What changed in the United States in the early 1970s to propel adoption? Ford and GM expressed the intent to start manufacturing cars with radials. An important factor in this decision was Michelin's decision in 1970 to reenter the U.S. market (which it had abandoned in 1930) and produce radials from a plant in Nova Scotia. Not coincidentally, it obtained a contract to produce radials for the 1970 Ford Continental at the same time (see Tedlow 1991). In mid-1973 Michelin also announced plans to build two tire plants in the United States (*Wall Street Journal,* 28 August 1973).

Another factor was the growing volume of automobile imports from Europe and Japan that convinced manufacturers of changing consumer preferences, even before the oil crisis. Once the automobile manufacturers signed on to the new tire technology, and there was a credible high-quality producer (Michelin) to supply it, the low technology equilibrium was broken. Now the competitive nature of the industry forced all the manufacturers to either adopt the technology or exit. The oil crisis in 1973 did not initiate the move to radials. It simply reinforced and perhaps accelerated it.

2.2.6   The Structure of the Tire Industry and Innovation

A number of issues have been highlighted about the industry that will help us in our later discussion of the causes of the takeovers. First, rents in this business exist only in markets where firms interact with individuals; the intermediate goods market is very competitive. Second, the tire industry is mature enough that it is hard for manufacturers to get a sustainable advantage through innovation. Finally, there is a coordination problem especially when both the upstream tire manufacturers and downstream automobile manufacturers have to innovate.

These features of the market explain why the returns to innovation accrue, if at all, to the largest tire manufacturers who have a substantial presence in the replacement market, while the costs of innovation are borne by all. Goodrich failed in its early attempt to introduce radials in the United States in 1965 because it could not convince the automobile manufacturers to switch. Goodyear, on the other hand, was not the first out with the belted bias ply tire. But once it saw customer acceptance of the belted bias, it accelerated development and retained its share of both the OE market and the replacement market. Of course, once Goodyear switched to producing belted bias, the automobile manufacturers demanded it of the other manufacturers.

Similarly, when radials were introduced, Goodyear was not in the vanguard of innovators. It misjudged the acceptability of the tire and lost a few points in OE market share between 1972 and 1974. But once it was convinced the radial was there to stay, it switched its substantial resources to developing and producing them. Its large (and somewhat inertia bound) position in the replacement market gave it an advantage in recovering market share in the OE market. The nod of approval from Goodyear then made radials the de facto industry standard. The other manufacturers had to scramble to adapt.

With this understanding of the industry and the dramatic impact of the introduction of radials, we will return to the question of why the major U.S. producers were acquired by foreign firms. Before doing so, however, we next review the major events in the merger and acquisition wave.

2.2.7   The Corporate Control Events

The tire industry has a long M&A history. In 1968, shortly after the failed attempt to introduce radials, Goodrich was the target of one of the first hostile takeover attempts in U.S. history. Goodrich, however, succeeded in fending off that attempt and there is no record of any major corporate control transaction until 1985.

As table 2.4 indicates, in 1985 Uniroyal had to undertake a defensive leverage buyout in response to a hostile bid by Carl Icahn. At the same time, Sumitomo (a Japanese company) emerged as a white knight to rescue Dunlop (a British company) from a hostile bid. In the next five years, every major U.S. tire producer had to face a hostile bid and all but one, Goodyear, ended up being acquired by foreign manufacturers. Table 2.4 also shows the relationship between acquisitions and plant closure. Clearly, most plant closures took place between 1978 and 1981, well before the beginning of the intense takeover activity.

2.3   An Empirical Analysis of the Possible Causes of the Acquisitions by Foreign Firms

We now test the "neoclassical" and "overinvestment" hypotheses set forth earlier in the introduction.

2.3.1   Higher Productivity of Foreign Producers?

The first hypothesis is that the acquisition of existing plants by foreign producers was the best way to transfer plants into the hands of more efficient producers. To address this question, we analyze plant-level productivity following an acquisition. In particular, we test two direct implications of the hypothesis that foreign manufacturers acquired U.S. plants because they were more efficient. First, we should observe higher productivity in plants owned by foreign manufacturers. Second, we should observe an increase in the productivity following an acquisition, especially an acquisition by foreigners.

Table 2.4 Chronology of Events in the U.S. Tire Industry

Year	Corporate Control Events	New Plants	Closed Plants
1966		Firestone (Bloomington, Ill.)	
1967		Goodyear (Danville, Va.)	
1968		General (Charlotte, N.C.)	
		Goodyear (Union City, Tenn.)	
		Mohawk (Salem, Va.)	
		Mohawk (Salem, Va.)	
1969	Hostile takeover attempt against Goodrich by Northwest Ind.	Dunlop (Huntsville, Ala.)	
		Firestone (Oklahoma City, Okla.)	
		Goodyear (Fayetteville, N.C.)	
		Uniroyal (Ardmore, Okla.)	
1970			
1971			
1972		Firestone (Lavergne, Tenn.)	
1973	Armstrong buys Nashville (Tenn.) plant from Gates	Firestone (Wilson, N.C.)	
1974			
1975		General (Mt. Vernon, Ill.)	
1976		Michelin (Greenville, S.C.)	
1977			
1978		Goodyear (Lawton, Okla.)	
1979		Michelin (Dothan, Ala.)	Goodrich (Akron, Ohio)
			Goodyear (Akron, Ohio)
			Mansfield (Mansfield, Ohio)
			Mohawk (Akron, Ohio)
			Uniroyal (Los Angeles, Cal.)
1980			Iri (Louisville, Ky.)
			Mohawk (West Helena, Ark.)
			Firestone (Barbeton, Ohio)
			Firestone (Dayton, Ohio)
			Firestone (Los Angeles, Cal.)
			Firestone (Salinas, Cal.)
			Goodyear (Los Angeles, Cal.)

Year	Event	Michelin	Other locations	Cooper
1981		Michelin (Lexington, S.C.)	Uniroyal (Chicopee Falls, Mass.) Uniroyal (Detroit, Mich.) Armstrong (West Haven, Conn.) Firestone (Akron, Ohio)	
1982	Firestone and Bridgestone agreement for Lavergne (Tenn.) plant ($52 million)			
1983	Cooper buys Tupelo (Miss.) plant from Mansfield		Firestone (Memphis, Tenn.)	
1984			Goodyear (Conshocken, Pa.) Goodyear (Jackson, Mich.)	
1985	Hostile takeover (BTR) attempt against Dunlop, bailed out by Sumitomo Hostile takeover attempt (C. Icahn) against Uniroyal			
1986	Uniroyal and Goodrich merge in Uni-Goodrich Hostile takeover attempt (Goldsmith) against Goodyear		Goodrich (Miami, Okla.) Goodrich (Oaks, Pa.) Firestone (Albany, Ga.) General (Waco, Tex.) Goodyear (Cumberland, Md.)	
1987	Continental buys General ($650 million) Goodrich adopts antitakeover plan			
1988	Pirelli's bid for Firestone Bridgestone buys Firestone ($2.6 billion) Pirelli buys Armstrong ($197 million)			
1989	Yokohama buys Mohawk ($150 million)			
1990	Cooper buys Firestone's Albany (Ga.) plant Michelin buys Uni-Goodrich			Cooper (Albany, Ga.)
1991				
1992				
1993				

Sources: *Modern Tire Dealer* and *Wall Street Journal Index.*

Data

The plant-level data we use come from the Longitudinal Research Database (LRD) maintained at the Center for Economic Studies (CES) at the Bureau of the Census. The LRD file is a time series of economic variables collected from manufacturing establishments in the Census of Manufactures (CM) and Annual Survey of Manufactures (ASM) programs.

The census universe covers approximately 350,000 establishments. The CM reports data on all these establishments every five years (in years ending in "2" and "7"), while the ASM covers a subset of the universe in each of the four years between censuses. The ASM, though, contains a complete time series for establishments with 250 or more employees.

The LRD file contains identifying information at the establishment level, basic information on the factors of production (inputs such as levels of capital, labor, energy, and materials) and the products produced (outputs), and other basic economic information used to define the operations of a manufacturing plant. In addition to these items, since 1972, establishments in the ASM sample panel have been asked to supply detailed information on assets, rental payments, supplemental labor costs, consumption of specific types of fuels, and other selected items. Unlike the census, the ASM does not request data on individual materials consumed and products shipped, although product class information is collected. These data, thus, are available only in census years.

Because we are interested in U.S. tire plants, we extracted from the LRD all the data on manufacturing establishments with SIC code 3011 (tire and inner tubes). We identified 3,061 plant-year observations from 493 plants and 402 firms. The first year for which we have comprehensive data is 1967. The next year of data is 1972, after which we have data for all the years until 1993.

To maximize the homogeneity of the group we analyze, we restrict our analysis to passenger tire plants (primary product code 1), ignoring truck tires and other special tires. This reduces our sample to 71 plants and 741 plant-years. Twenty-one observations and four plants lack some or all of the data required by our specification. This leaves us with 67 plants corresponding to 720 plant-years.

Table 2.5 contains the summary statistics for this data set. Note that the census data are confidential and this prevents us reporting data when it would reveal the identity of a single company in the sample. All the reported analysis based on LRD data will, by necessity, be aggregated.

To check how exhaustive the ASM is, to obtain data on plant ownership from an independent source, and to produce a series of dummy variables (foreign, acquisition, and nonunionization), we collected a data set on passenger tire plants from the trade magazine *Modern Tire Dealer.* Starting in 1976, the January issue of the journal lists all U.S. tire plants, their

Table 2.5   **Summary Statistics**

A. Continuous Variables

	Means	Stand. Dev.	N. Obs.
Value added	11.08	0.99	720
Capital	4.92	0.95	720
Labor	7.90	0.68	720
Capital expenditures	0.05	0.17	720
Employment	7.20	0.68	720

B. Discrete Variables

	Frequency	Percent	N. Obs.
Closure	13	1.82	712
Foreign	107	14.86	720
Acquisition	110	15.28	720
Nonunion	96	13.33	720

Note: Value added is the logarithm of a plant's value added measured in thousands of U.S. dollars. Capital is the logarithm of the net amount of property, plant, and equipment. Labor is the logarithm of production-worker-equivalent man-hours, as defined in Lichtenberg (1992). The foreign ownership indicator is one if the plant is owned by a foreign company in that particular year. The acquisition indicator is one in all plant-years following a change in control taking place in the period 1970–93. The nonunion indicator is one for those plants that were not unionized. All the data are from the LRD, except for foreign ownership and unionization indicators, which are constructed from data in *Modern Tire Dealer.*

production capacity, their location, the company they belong to, and (starting in 1984) whether the plant is unionized or not. We identified a sample of 66 plants. Overall our impression is that the LRD data set is representative of passenger tire plants operating in the United States.[8]

Methodology

We want to compare productivity across different plants and over time. It is standard in this literature (see Lichtenberg 1992) to use the notion of total factor productivity, defined as output per unit of total input:

(1) $$\pi = \frac{VA}{F(L, K)},$$

where *VA* is output net of purchased intermediate goods and *F(L, K)* is a production function, with *L* denoting labor input and *K* capital input.

If we assume that the production function is Cobb-Douglas so that $F(L, K) = L^\alpha K^\beta$ and we take logarithms, we obtain

(2) $$\log VA = \alpha \log L + \beta \log K + \log \pi.$$

8. For disclosure-related reasons we cannot give further detail about the nature of and exact differences between the two samples.

If we assume the technical parameters α and β are invariant across plants, we can test our hypotheses using the following specification:

(3) $\log VA_{it} = f(X_i) + \alpha \log L_{it} + \beta \log K_{it} + \delta \text{Year}_t + \varepsilon_{it},$

Where $f(X_i)$ are plant-specific characteristics (like ownership, unionization, etc.), Year_t is a calendar year dummy, and ε_{it} is an error, which we assume orthogonal to the input quantities.

Results

Panel A of table 2.6 reports the results obtained by estimating equation (3). Columns (1) to (3) estimate equation (3) with ordinary least squares (OLS) on the entire sample of plants. The plant-specific characteristics we test are an acquisition indicator (equal to one in the years subsequent to an acquisition), a foreign ownership indicator (equal to one if the plant belongs to a subsidiary of a foreign manufacturer), an indicator if the plant is not unionized, and the age of the plant measured as years since the plant was built.[9]

Column (1) tests whether foreign-owned plants are more or less productive in general. The estimates indicate that the total factor productivity of foreign-owned plants is 20 percent less than that of U.S.-owned plants. This effect is highly statistically significant. There is no evidence that non-unionized plants are more productive. Column (2) adds the acquisition indicator to the basic specification. Plants that have been acquired are 9 percent less productive after an acquisition, but this effect is not statistically significant even at the 10 percent level. The results are substantially unchanged if we insert a measure of a plant's age (col. [3]).

It is possible that the estimated adverse effects of foreign ownership are the result of some misspecification. We might miss some plant-specific characteristics that reduce productivity and happen to be correlated with the foreign ownership indicator. For example, since foreigners bought, rather than started, most of their U.S. plants, it is possible that the observed effect captures adverse selection rather than inefficiency: foreigners buy less-productive plants. For this reason we reestimate equation (3) (estimates not reported) restricting the sample to new plants. Productivity of foreign-owned plants is again significantly less than U.S.-owned plants.

Is it that foreign acquirers pick poor plants, or are they poor managers? We try to control better for plant-specific characteristics by reestimating equation (3) with plant fixed effects. Since our measure of capital is a noisy proxy for the real level of capital, it is not surprising that the coefficient on capital drops by 50 percent and becomes insignificant. However, the indicators are the variables of interest. Controlling for the plant-specific

9. Since we do not have data on construction years before 1960, for any plant built before 1960 we set the year of construction to 1959.

Table 2.6   **Effects of Ownership on Productivity**

A. Whole Sample

	OLS			Fixed Effects		
	(1)	(2)	(3)	(4)	(5)	(6)
Capital	0.091	0.091	0.088	0.061	0.056	0.056
	(0.033)	(0.032)	(0.033)	(0.039)	(0.038)	(0.041)
Labor	1.022	1.015	1.018	1.102	1.111	1.111
	(0.038)	(0.038)	(0.038)	(0.051)	(0.051)	(0.055)
Foreign dummy	−0.196	−0.163	−0.145		0.184	0.184
	(0.056)	(0.071)	(0.076)		(0.094)	(0.101)
Acquisition dummy		−0.086	−0.085	−0.249	−0.354	−0.354
		(0.080)	(0.082)	(0.061)	(0.093)	(0.100)
Nonunion dummy	0.041	0.039	0.013			
	(0.047)	(0.048)	(0.051)			
Age			−0.002			0.061
			(0.001)			0.004
Adjusted R^2	0.846	0.846	0.852	0.908	0.908	0.920
N. obs.	720	720	720	720	720	720

B. Radial Sample

	(1)	(2)	(3)	(4)	(5)	(6)
Capital	0.115	0.139	0.159	−0.033	−0.051	−0.051
	(0.069)	(0.073)	(0.072)	(0.085)	(0.079)	(0.041)
Labor	0.952	0.961	0.941	0.838	0.853	0.853
	(0.077)	(0.076)	(0.074)	(0.097)	(0.097)	(0.097)
Foreign dummy	−0.487	−0.546	−0.543		0.226	0.226
	(0.056)	(0.079)	(0.079)		(0.147)	(0.147)
Acquisition dummy		0.124	0.095	−0.136	−0.307	−0.307
		(0.088)	(0.090)	(0.078)	(0.149)	(0.149)
Nonunion dummy	0.051	0.069	0.115			
	(0.049)	(0.049)	(0.055)			
Age			0.006			0.054
			(0.002)			0.007
Adjusted R^2	0.776	0.779	0.782	0.888	0.891	0.891
N. obs.	265	265	265	265	265	265

C. Whole Sample, Proxy for Capital

	(1)	(2)	(3)	(4)	(5)	(6)
Capital (energy)	0.280	0.284	0.281	0.207	0.209	0.209
	(0.054)	(0.052)	(0.052)	(0.079)	(0.078)	(0.078)
Labor	0.870	0.860	0.862	0.997	1.003	1.003
	(0.046)	(0.046)	(0.046)	(0.096)	(0.095)	(0.095)
Foreign dummy	−0.135	−0.094	−0.084		0.199	0.199
	(0.052)	(0.064)	(0.066)		(0.102)	(0.102)
Acquisition dummy		−0.102	−0.101	−0.227	−0.340	−0.340
		(0.078)	(0.077)	(0.063)	(0.099)	(0.099)
Nonunion dummy	0.052	0.049	0.033			
	(0.045)	(0.045)	(0.047)			

(*continued*)

Table 2.6   (continued)

	C. Whole Sample, Proxy for Capital					
	OLS			Fixed Effects		
	(1)	(2)	(3)	(4)	(5)	(6)
Age			−0.001			0.056
			(0.001)			0.004
Adjusted R^2	0.867	0.868	0.868	0.912	0.912	0.912
N. obs.	729	729	729	729	729	729

Note: The dependent variable is the logarithm of a plant's value added in a given year. Capital is the logarithm of the net amount of property, plant, and equipment. In panel C the logarithm of constant price energy consumption has been used as a proxy for capital. Labor is the logarithm of production-worker-equivalent man-hours, as defined in Lichtenberg (1992). The foreign ownership indicator is one if the plant is owned by a foreign company in that particular year. The acquisition indicator is one in all plant-years following a change in control taking place in the period 1970–93. The nonunion indicator is one for those plants that were not unionized. Age is the number of years since the plant was originally built. For plants built before 1960, we set the year of construction to 1959. All the data are from the LRD, except for foreign ownership, unionization indicators (which are constructed from data in *Modern Tire Dealer*), and age of the plant (which is from *Tire Business*). All the specifications contain calendar year indicators (coefficient estimates not reported). Heteroskedasticity robust standard errors are reported in parentheses.

characteristics, an acquisition reduces a plant's total factor productivity by a statistically significant 25 percent. This phenomenon is not just temporary. In an unreported regression we allowed for the impact of an acquisition to be different in the two years following an acquisition and in the long run. The effect is entirely concentrated in the long run. The effects are robust to the inclusion of a measure of the age of the plant. Older plants are less productive, 0.2 percent per year of age.

When we include plant-specific effects, the acquisition indicator is almost collinear with the foreign indicator (there are only few acquisitions that are not made by foreign firms). Nevertheless, we try including both variables in the regression. The effect of acquisition is still negative and bigger in absolute sign, while the incremental effect of foreign ownership (separate from that of acquisition) is positive and statistically significant. The combined effect of a foreign acquisition, though, remains negative: it reflects a 17 percent drop in total factor productivity. Interestingly, the coefficient of age becomes positive and highly statistically significant. This suggests that while newer plants are more productive, a plant itself becomes more productive with age. Hence the difference in coefficient between the OLS and the fixed effects estimates.

Although we could not reject the hypothesis that the production function for plants was the same independent of the quantity of radials produced, in panel B of table 2.6 we test the robustness of our result to restricting the estimates to plants producing at least 80 percent radials. The main thrust of the results is unchanged. If anything the results are more striking: foreign-owned plants are 50 percent (rather than 20 percent) less productive than U.S.-owned plants.

Since our measure of the capital stock is likely to be very noisy, in panel C of table 2.6 we report the basic regressions when the amount of energy consumed is used as a proxy for capital. The coefficient for capital and labor now appears more sensible, but all the other results remain substantially unchanged. In an unreported regression we also estimated the same specifications using the quantity of energy consumed as an instrumental variable. The results are substantially unchanged.

In sum, little support emerges for this narrow version of the neoclassical hypothesis, which focuses on plant-level productivity. Plants do not seem to be acquired by more efficient producers. Even more surprisingly, plants do not experience an increase in productivity following a change of ownership. This implies that if we want to explain the M&A activity of the late 1980s, we have to look elsewhere.

2.3.2   Failure of Internal Control Systems?

The second hypothesis we want to test is that acquisitions forced the closure of inefficient plants that were kept open long after they became unprofitable because of a failure of internal control systems. The argument is that internal systems do not force managers to downsize when needed (Jensen 1993), and market forces take a long time to act because internal resources take a long time to be fully dissipated.

This hypothesis has already been challenged by Sull (1996), who documents that 69 percent of the plant closures took place before 1981, the year of the first hostile takeover threat in the tire industry. He also shows that the adoption of antitakeover devices is not significantly related with the plant closure.

Here we extend Sull's analysis in three ways. First, we consider the effect of acquisitions themselves on the probability of plant closure. Second, we control for the total factor productivity of the plant. Third, we fully use the data on the time dimension by estimating the probability of closing a plant between time t and time $t + 1$, conditional on it not having been closed till time t. This captures the essence of Jensen's hypothesis that a failure of the internal control system delayed the closing of inefficient plants.

Results

The results obtained estimating a proportional hazard ratio model of the probability of closing a plant are shown in table 2.7. Column (1) reports the estimates obtained when the only determinants of plant closure are the logarithm of total factor productivity, as defined in equation (2), and calendar year dummies. Not surprisingly, more efficient plants are less

Table 2.7   Determinants of Plant Closures

	(1)	(2)	(3)	(4)
Total factor productivity	−1.73	−1.82	−1.85	−1.86
	(0.61)	(0.63)	(0.63)	(0.63)
Acquisition dummy		−0.78	−0.80	−0.94
		(1.26)	(1.36)	(1.56)
Acquisition × total			0.61	0.35
factor productivity			(1.92)	(1.69)
Foreign dummy				0.43
				(2.19)
Pseudo R^2	0.11	0.11	0.12	0.12
N. obs.	549	549	549	549

Note: We estimate a proportional hazard ratio model, where the dependent variable is the probability of closure between year t and year $t+1$ conditional on surviving up to time t. The explanatory variables are the total factor productivity as estimated with specification (3) in the text, a foreign ownership indicator, and an acquisition indicator. The foreign ownership indicator is one if the plant is owned by a foreign company in that particular year. The acquisition indicator is one in all plant-years following a change in control taking place in the period 1970–93. The nonunion indicator is one for those plants that were not unionized. All the data are from the LRD, except for foreign ownership and unionization indicators, which are constructed from data in *Modern Tire Dealer.* All the specifications contain calendar year indicators (coefficient estimates not reported). The standard errors are reported in parentheses.

likely to be closed, and this effect is statistically significant at the 5 percent level. More interesting for our purposes is column (2). It shows that acquisition of a company has no impact on the probability of closing a plant (after the efficiency of the plant is accounted for). If anything, the impact is negative (albeit not statistically significant). A more direct test of whether acquisitions improved the ability of managers to close inefficient plants is to examine the differential effect of productivity on plant closure when a firm is acquired. As column (3) shows, less productive plants were no more likely to be closed by acquirers. Similar results obtain when a plant is owned (or acquired) by a foreign firm. So there is no evidence that different corporate governance systems or external threats had any impact on the decision to close a plant.[10] Nor is there evidence that acquisitions changed the speed of plant closing.

A different approach to the same question is to analyze the behavior of capital expenditures following an acquisition. If acquisitions were aimed at disciplining managers who were overinvesting in their plants, we should observe a reduction in investment following an acquisition. In fact, as table 2.8 shows, the opposite is true. The level of capital expenditure (over sales) of a plant goes up by four percentage points after an acquisition

10. The raw data confirm this. No plant was closed by a foreign manufacturer and, as pointed out earlier, most of the closures took place prior to acquisition.

Table 2.8   Effects of Acquisitions on Capital Expenditure and Employment

| | Capital Expenditures | | | | Employment | | | |
| | OLS | | Fixed Effects | | OLS | | Fixed Effects | |
	(1)	(2)	(3)	(4)	(5)	(6)	(7)	(8)
Acquisition dummy	0.02	0.01	0.04	0.00	−0.43	0.15	−0.02	−0.19
	(0.01)	(0.01)	(0.02)	(0.02)	(0.11)	(0.09)	(0.08)	(0.10)
Foreign dummy		0.01		0.04		−0.50		0.09
		(0.01)		(0.01)		(0.10)		(0.05)
Nonunion dummy					0.15	0.13		
					0.07	0.07		
Adjusted R^2	0.01	0.01	0.61	0.61	0.02	0.02	0.81	0.79
N. obs.	731	731	731	731	731	731	731	731

Note: The dependent variables are either the level of capital expenditure over sales or the logarithm of the number of plant employees in the year. The foreign ownership indicator is one if the plant is owned by a foreign company in that particular year. The acquisition indicator is one in all plant-years following a change in control taking place in the period 1970–93. The nonunion indicator is one for those plants that were not unionized. All the data are from the LRD, except for foreign ownership and unionization indicators, which are constructed from data in *Modern Tire Dealer*. All the specifications contain calendar year indicators (coefficient estimates not reported). The heteroskedasticity robust standard errors are reported in parentheses.

and this effect is statistically significant at the 5 percent level. Interestingly, this effect is due entirely to foreign acquisitions.

The results are less clear for employment. If we control for plant-specific factors, acquisitions do not seem to have any effect on employment. However, decomposing acquisitions further, acquisitions increase employment, albeit not statistically significantly, while if the acquirer is foreign, employment falls.

Comments

In sum, we find no evidence supporting the idea that acquisitions were aimed at disciplining managers who were delaying the closure of inefficient plants or were overinvesting in existing plants. Assuming foreign acquirers made sensible investment decisions, we find quite the opposite; there was some underinvestment before the plants were acquired.[11]

This is not to say that internal control systems worked perfectly, only that much of the needed restructuring had taken place before the acquisitions. We will argue that the advent of radials and the inability of the conglomerate tire manufacturers (General, Goodrich, and Uniroyal) to improve their position even with such dramatic change simply confirmed for them the need to get out of the tire industry. Thus they were unlikely to overinvest in tires. Goodyear was fortunate in 1972 to get a CEO who was an outsider, understood the potential of radials, and quickly implemented the needed restructuring. Firestone best exemplifies a firm's failure to rationalize its operations (see Sull 1996), but even it got an outside CEO in 1979 who quickly closed down plants. Thus it was not the inability of internal systems to respond quickly to the radials that led to takeovers by the foreign firms.

Rather, we will argue that the conglomerate tire manufacturers did not have a secure enough position in profitable markets to justify the demand for continuous innovation. They were ready to sell out, though during the 1970s and early 1980s, there was no obvious domestic buyer. But during this time, car exports and cross-border car production by domestic car manufacturers increased. Large manufacturers with secure domestic markets—Michelin, Pirelli, Bridgestone, and Continental—were eager to move into the United States and realize the economies of scale in product development and marketing. Even if they wanted to, Goodrich and Uniroyal, who had neglected R&D and investment in the tire business and had withdrawn from international tire production in the 1970s, were poorly positioned to capture these economies. General Tire was too small and, furthermore, had little international experience to speak of. Firestone had

---

11. For instance, Bridgestone announced capital expenditures of $1.5 billion after it took over Firestone, and industry sources suggest that some of this was to compensate for past underinvestment by Firestone.

a severe liquidity problem in the late 1970s as a result of its problems in switching to radials. This forced it to withdraw from international operations, and it also became a willing candidate for acquisition. Only Goodyear maintained its international operations even as it switched to radials. It had the scale both domestically and internationally to justify the expenditures on R&D and advertising to keep it competitive with the large foreign manufacturers. As a result, only Goodyear survived the "internationalization" of the industry.

2.4   What Led to the Eclipse of the U.S. (Owned) Tire Industry?

We now elaborate on our explanation. Table 2.9 shows the fraction of total sales accounted for by tires for each of the five major manufacturers between 1970 and 1985. While Firestone and Goodyear tire sales were steady at approximately 80 percent of total sales, Goodrich tire sales dropped from 58 percent in 1970 to 44 percent in 1985 and Uniroyal sales dropped from 56 percent to 49 percent. This suggests that both Goodrich and Uniroyal were attempting to reduce their stake in the tire business. The exception among the diversified conglomerates is General Tire, which maintained a steady share at 39 percent, though as we shall see it decided to reduce its commitment to the tire business from the early 1980s onward.

Some of the tire manufacturers report data segment by segment. These data are available from Compustat from 1978 onward. While Goodyear and Firestone each invested an average of 5 percent of annual tire sales in their tire business in the period 1978–86, General Tire invested only 3.7 percent while Goodrich invested 3 percent. When we look at the ratio of investment in tires to total investment, the ratio fell from an average of 46 percent for General Tire in 1978–80 to 25 percent in 1984–86. Goodrich was already investing very little in the tire business, but this fell slightly further from 24 to 23 percent over this period.

Thus it appears that the diversified tire firms were investing more of their cash flows outside the tire business. They appeared eager to get out, a fact confirmed by published and industry sources.

Table 2.9   **Extent of Diversification away from the Tire Business by Major U.S. Producers**

	1970	1975	1980	1985
Goodyear	83	83	83	80
Firestone	83	83	79	89
Uniroyal	56	57	49	49
Goodrich	58	53	42	43
General Tire	39	36	44	41

Note: Percentage of total sales in tires (from company annual reports and from West 1984).

Consider Goodrich. It was the first to introduce radials in the United States (in 1965), and this turned out to be a miserable marketing failure as neither the automobile industry nor the other tire manufacturers responded. Tedlow (1991, 67) analyzes Goodrich's situation thus: "The failure to leapfrog the competition in radials was the beginning of the end of Goodrich's tire business. If they could not dramatically alter their position in the industry by pioneering a breakthrough of this magnitude, Goodrich management apparently realized they never would. . . . [P]laying second fiddle to Firestone and Goodyear was untenable on a long term basis . . . and it was [Firestone and Goodyear] . . . who would determine product policy in this industry. . . . In the mid-1970s, Goodrich realized that it had to get out of the tire business. . . . The strategy . . . was simplicity itself. The tire business was always to generate more cash than it used. . . . [The first step] was abandoning the Original Equipment market altogether [in the early 1970s]." By abandoning the OE market (table 2.2 shows that by 1985 Goodrich was out), it could focus on replacement sales which were highly profitable. Of course, the OE market was a way for a firm to invest in future replacement sales, so this move was again a form of cutting investment.

Uniroyal, by contrast, had historically been focused on OE sales, specifically sales to General Motors. It hoped to make a breakthrough in radials in the early 1970s with its Zeta 40M tire. But in order to make it profitable, and perhaps even to sell more in the OE market, Uniroyal had to establish a credible presence in the replacement market by expanding its retail stores (recall that automobile manufacturers like a supplier to have these stores because they can service tires sold as original equipment). But Uniroyal's internal cash flow was low because of the low profitability of the segments it served and it had an enormous debt burden, especially in the late 1970s (average interest coverage in the period 1976–80 was 2.4, the lowest in the industry). Moreover, it had an unfunded pension liability that, in 1979, amounted to 79 percent of its net worth. So Uniroyal faced a cash crunch just when it needed to expand its network of stores, and they dwindled from 535 in 1972 to none in 1981 (see Tedlow 1991, 59). Thus Uniroyal did not have the option of harvesting its OE sales, and limped along investing minimal amounts in maintaining its plants.

Finally, General Tire, which was run by the O'Neil family, was the only true conglomerate. Tedlow reports that "back in 1980, Jerry O'Neil was . . . determined about tires. He has no intention of getting out, he thinks Uniroyal probably will, and in the end, Goodrich. In the shrunken field, he sees General surviving and prospering." But by 1984, when our data show the fall in General Tire's investment in the tire business, "O'Neil was more willing to consider exiting the industry. The possibility of spinning the tire business off into a merger with another firm was on his mind" (Tedlow 1991, 84).

This suggests that the diversified majors initially perceived the advent of radials as a market opportunity where they could challenge the dominance of Goodyear and Firestone. Even though Firestone made a major misstep (see below) that General Tire and Michelin cashed in on, the industry was mature and innovation did not result in dramatic sustainable advantage. The market segment that was most ready to switch to the innovation (the automobile manufacturers) was unprofitable. There was substantial inertia in the profitable replacement segment, and by the time an innovator made some headway, the leaders would have their own products. At the same time, the smaller manufacturers had to constantly match the successful innovations or else lose market share. Therefore, even though we have argued that economies of scale in production were not significant for the major manufacturers, significant fixed investments had to be made in R&D, advertising, and the distribution network in order to keep up.

Table 2.10 shows the average investment in R&D and advertising over the 1970s and 1980s. The figures for the diversified tire firms should be interpreted with caution since they are not by segment but are for the overall firm. Nevertheless, the pattern of investment by both Goodyear and Firestone suggests that the requirement for R&D and advertising increased dramatically over the two decades, from 3.1 percent in 1971–75 for Firestone to 4.2 percent in 1986–87, and from 4.1 percent in 1971–75 for Goodyear to 5.2 percent in 1986–87. By contrast, the level of invest-

Table 2.10   **Investment in R&D and Advertising by Major U.S. Tire Producers**

	1970–75	1975–80	1980–85	1985–90
Goodyear				
R&D	2.40	2.00	2.70	2.90
Advertising	1.80	1.80	1.90	2.30
Sum	4.10	3.80	4.60	5.20
Firestone				
R&D	1.50	1.40	2.00	2.30
Advertising	1.70	1.60	2.00	1.90
Sum	3.20	3.10	4.00	4.20
Uniroyal				
R&D	2.70	2.00	1.90	
Advertising	2.00	1.80	1.50	
Sum	4.70	3.80	3.40	
Goodrich				
R&D	2.20	1.70	1.90	2.20
Advertising	1.50	0.90	1.10	0.90
Sum	3.70	2.70	3.00	3.10
General Tire				
R&D	1.90	1.40	2.70	2.20
Advertising	1.00	1.00	1.20	1.60
Sum	2.80	2.40	3.90	3.80

Source: Compustat.

Note: Average R&D and advertising expenses as a percentage of total sales in different periods.

ment by the diversified majors was smaller, and perhaps would look smaller still if we had tire segment data. Furthermore, it declined steadily for Uniroyal and Goodrich. Again, General is the exception, but recall that in the early 1980s it was doing all that was necessary to stay in the industry. In fact, General's investment in R&D seems to mirror its changing commitment to the industry. It peaked at 3.1 percent of sales in 1983 and then fell steadily every year to 1.7 percent of sales in 1988 when the tire division was sold.

To summarize, then, the diversified majors did not have the scale to compete on R&D and advertising, or in sustaining the distribution network. Their decision to sell out, though made at different times, was understandable. We still have to ask why Firestone was taken over, why Goodyear survived, and why the acquirers were foreign.

2.4.1   Goodyear and Firestone

In hindsight, Firestone's problems can be traced to its large investment in the late 1960s in the intermediate technology of belted bias ply tires. In order to avoid scrapping its existing investment, Firestone manufactured radials through a process that required relatively minor modification of the machinery. The resulting product, the Firestone 500 Steel-Belted radial, was initially successful but had tread separation problems. Even though top management knew about the problem, it was only in 1978 (six years after production began) that production was stopped and the tire recalled at enormous cost. The popular press was very critical. Tedlow (1991, 60) cites *Time* magazine as reporting, "The company just kept churning out the 500 tires; they just kept failing; customers kept returning them. And company lawyers just kept defending lawsuits brought by accident victims—and their heirs." The damage to the company's reputation was enormous. Firestone's OE sales fell from 24 percent of the OE market to 21.5 percent between 1975 and 1980 (see table 2.2), while its replacement sales under its own brand name fell from 11.8 percent of the market in 1977 to 9 percent in 1981.

Table 2.10 shows that Firestone's annual investment in R&D in 1971–75 was only 1.5 percent of sales while, by comparison, Goodyear's was 2.4 percent of sales (and Goodyear's sales were considerably more). Therefore, even though Firestone matched Goodyear in capital expenditure and advertising, it lagged behind in expenditure on R&D, which may partly explain its quality problems.

Soon after the recall, John Nevin, who had been CEO of Zenith, became Firestone's CEO. The firm had now become, he declared, "a company of limited resources. The day has passed when Firestone can say: We are a tire company and we will participate actively in every element of the tire business, throughout America and throughout the world" (Tedlow 1991, 42). The strategy now was to eliminate the least profitable aspects of the tire business and diversify. As we will argue, the economics of the business had changed to make this strategy infeasible.

Goodyear, by contrast, made all the right decisions early on. Even though it was not the first out with radials, it neither attempted to skimp on the investment necessary to convert to radial production nor did it compromise on the quality of radials produced. A key factor in this was Charles Pelliod, CEO from 1972 to 1982, who came with substantial experience of radials from Goodyear's European subsidiary. According to industry sources, he saw the writing on the wall and forced Goodyear to make the difficult decisions to close down old plants and invest heavily in new ones. As can be seen, Goodyear's spending on R&D and advertising also went up at this time. But Pelliod also wanted to diversify out of tires. This did not happen until he was succeeded by Robert Mercer as CEO, after which Goodyear bought the Celeron Corporation (an energy company) in 1983 and started investing in the All-American Pipeline. Despite the sudden attempt at diversification (which proved disastrous), Goodyear did not reduce its investments in the tire business. In fact, both R&D and advertising increased, even as the firm was diversifying outside the tire business.[12]

2.4.2 The Eclipse of the U.S. (Owned) Tire Industry

Even while the U.S. manufacturers were struggling to adapt to radials and shut down excess capacity, another dramatic change was taking place around the world. The automobile industry was becoming more global and its methods of design and production were changing. There was increasing talk of producing the same car for different markets at different locations. The Japanese were the first to do this with cars like the Honda Accord, which was produced in both Japan and the United States. Similarly, as U.S. and European tastes converged, the U.S. automobile manufacturers started planning for production in both the United States and Europe. It made sense to have close cooperation between the tire supplier and the car manufacturer at both the design and manufacturing stages. Just-in-time manufacturing made it almost imperative that tires be produced close to the locale for automobile assembly. The greater the number of markets in which a tire manufacturer produced, the shorter the supply cycle and the more valuable the supplier would be to the car manufacturer. A related reason for a global presence is that car exports increased tremendously. A tire manufacturer who had a presence both at the point of production and in the country to which the car was exported would be able to take advantage of replacement sales. Furthermore, the car manufacturer

---

12. It is unlikely that pipelines need much R&D and advertising. So even though we only have data on firm-level R&D and advertising to sales, the firm-level ratio is likely to underestimate the ratio devoted to tires.

would be able to get some of the benefits of the advertising done by the tire manufacturer in the export market. In sum, the increasing cross-border production and trade of cars increased the need for multinational tire producers.

But barring Goodyear, the U.S. tire manufacturers had spent the 1970s concentrating their resources on domestic radial production and withdrawing from foreign markets. West (1984) reports that Firestone exited, among others, the United Kingdom, Switzerland, Australia, Sweden, and Chile. Uniroyal sold its entire European tire operations to Continental in 1979 and also quit Australia. Goodrich exited Australia, Holland, West Germany, and Brazil, and General Tire quit Spain and Venezuela (it did not have much of an international presence anyway). Interestingly, many of the plants were sold to the big foreign producers such as Continental, Bridgestone, and Pirelli. In fact, Continental became a multinational producer largely as a result of its purchase of Uniroyal's European operations.

Thus the conglomerate tire manufacturers, in pursuit of their objective of reducing their exposure to the tire business, sold their foreign plants. As the car manufacturers geared up to produce transnationally, the conglomerates had the choice of either returning anew to foreign markets or exiting the tire business entirely by selling their U.S. holdings. By contrast, the foreign multinational tire producers such as Bridgestone, Continental, Michelin, and Pirelli only needed a U.S. base to round out their portfolio. Given that new capacity was not needed by the late 1980s even in radials, and that the multinationals' position in their domestic markets was much stronger than the U.S. conglomerates' position in the United States, a transfer of ownership of the tire business from the U.S. conglomerates to the multinationals made eminent sense.

One could ask why Goodyear or Firestone did not buy out the tire operations of the conglomerate manufacturers earlier. Apart from a lack of funds on the part of these two firms, the foreign manufacturers probably valued the conglomerates more: in order for the foreign manufacturers like Bridgestone, Pirelli, or Continental to be credible partners for the automobile firms, they needed a U.S. production base. By contrast, neither Goodyear nor Firestone needed additional U.S. capacity. Rather, in all likelihood, they would probably lose some of the OE sales of the acquired firm as automobile manufacturers rebalanced their portfolio of suppliers to avoid too much dependence on one vendor. Thus the nature of the industry made it hard for mergers between U.S. firms to take place. Not coincidentally, the only merger that was consummated, albeit temporarily, was between Goodrich and Uniroyal. This was clearly helped by the fact that Goodrich had no OE sales.

Firestone was not interested in exiting the tire business. But it was extremely difficult to be a major niche player—after exiting from various lines and countries—in what had become a full service, global business. Tedlow (1991, 44) cites the vice president of international sales thus: "When we withdrew from radial truck tires in the United States, our overseas customers whose business with us is 25 percent for trucks, saw it as a lack of commitment to tires. . . ." Firestone simply did not have the resources to compete. If one had to point to a single factor leading directly to its demise, it would have to be its lack of attention to R&D and quality control that, in turn, led to the Firestone 500 disaster.

2.5 Conclusions

Our analysis of the forces that led to the demise of the U.S. tire industry points to two major factors. First, the U.S. tire companies were the last to switch to radials. They faced this choice when the prospects of the entire tire industry were most grim. While their competitors had already paid the sunk costs, U.S. firms had not and, as a result, were more resistant to invest. If any major player had to leave, the U.S. firms were the most likely candidate. As a result, in this period they did not invest sufficiently in their plants, which may partly explain the large capital expenditure made by foreign acquirers after the takeover as well the lower productivity of these plants.

Second, the internationalization of the market for cars triggered the need for tire producers to follow their customers. Since the flow of cars was toward the United States, it was natural that foreign tire firms wanted to penetrate the U.S. market and not the other way around. In the absence of major growth in the market, the way to acquire a presence in the United States was to integrate with existing producers.

Of course, a number of factors may explain why U.S. manufacturers were taken over by foreign manufacturers rather than the other way around. Of these, the most interesting possibility is that takeover legislation is much more friendly to targets in other countries, making it easier for ownership to change in one direction than the other. Understanding the influence that these barriers have in shaping international competition is an important topic for future research.

From a policy perspective, it is not clear that any changes are warranted. While there may have been insufficient incentives to innovate in the competitive U.S. domestic market, the internationalization and consolidation of the market ensured each of the large manufacturers has the scale as well as enough pockets of market power to reward innovation. Also, an international manufacturer can ignore the U.S. market only at the risk of losing credibility elsewhere. Therefore, despite the eclipse of the U.S.-owned tire industry, the U.S. consumer has no cause for complaint.

References

Dick, John S. 1980. How technological innovations have affected the tire industry's structure. *Elastomerics* (September): 43–48.

Easterbrook, Gregg. 1992. Driving quality at Ford. In *The challenge of organizational change,* ed. R. Kanter, B. Stein, and T. Jack. New York: Free Press.

French, Michael J. 1991. *The US tire industry.* Boston: Twayne Publishers.

Grossman, S., and O. Hart. 1986. The costs and the benefits of ownership: A theory of vertical and lateral integration. *Journal of Political Economy* 94:691–719.

Jensen, M. 1993. The modern industrial revolution, exit and the failure of internal control systems. *Journal of Finance* 48:831–80.

Jovanovic, B., and G. M. MacDonald. 1994. The life cycle of a competitive industry. *Journal of Political Economy* 102:322–47.

Lichtenberg, F. R. 1992. *Corporate takeovers and productivity.* Cambridge, Mass.: MIT Press.

McGuckin, R., and S. Nguyen. 1995. On productivity and plant ownership change: New evidence from the Longitudinal Research Database. *RAND Journal of Economics* 26:257–76.

Mitchell, M., and H. Mulherin. 1996. The impact of industry shocks on takeover and restructuring activity. *Journal of Financial Economics* 41:193–230.

Modern Tire Dealer. 1991. *Facts edition.* Akron, OH: Bill Communications.

Olley, G. S., and A. Pakes. 1996. The dynamic of productivity in the telecommunications equipment industry. *Econometrica* 64:1263–99.

Rosenbloom, R. S., and S. Benioff. 1990. Tire industry 1973. Harvard Business School Case Study, Harvard University, Cambridge, Mass.

Rubber Manufacturers Association. 1994. *Tire industry facts.* Washington, D.C.

Sull, Donald. 1996. The ties that bind: Overcapacity, implicit contracts, and divestments from a declining industry. Unpublished manuscript, Harvard Business School.

Tedlow, Richard. 1991. Hitting the skids: Tires and time horizons. Unpublished manuscript, Harvard Business School.

West, Peter J. 1984. Foreign investment and technology transfer: The tire industry in Latin America. Contemporary studies in economic and financial analysis, vol. 31. Greenwich, Conn.: JAI Press.

Comment   Robert H. Porter

Rajan, Volpin, and Zingales are to be congratulated for carefully assembling evidence from a broad variety of sources and for providing an interesting interpretation of this evidence. Their story is well told and provocative. My role as a discussant, however, is to question whether their story stands up to scrutiny and to describe some issues that might warrant further research.

Robert H. Porter is the William R. Kenan, Jr., Professor of Economics at Northwestern University and a research associate of the National Bureau of Economic Research.

I cannot claim any expertise on the tire industry. I am not an avid, or even occasional, reader of *Rubber World*. Moreover, this industry has not been the subject of much previous research in industrial organization. For example, I could find no reference to the tire industry in the textbooks by Carlton and Perloff (1994) and by Scherer and Ross (1990). Hence my comments are those of an outsider.

Rajan, Volpin, and Zingales seek to discriminate among three explanations of why the U.S. tire industry experienced a series of hostile takeover bids in the 1980s, and why most of the acquired companies ended up under the control of foreign tire manufacturers. The authors call the first explanation "neoclassical." Essentially, according to this explanation the mergers were necessary to realize efficiency gains in production or distribution. Foreign firms were more experienced with radial production, which came relatively late to North America, and the takeovers may have been the only mechanism to achieve cost savings quickly.

The second explanation credits managerial factors associated with overinvestment. In particular, the existing management may have been intransigent or unwilling to make necessary changes. Changes may have been necessary because the increases in tire durability associated with the introduction of radials led to excess productive capacity.

The third explanation is an industrial organization story. According to this story, automobile production and marketing were becoming increasingly global, and as a consequence global production of tires became efficient. Foreign firms had greater relative expertise with radials. De novo entry by foreign companies in the United States would have led to excess capacity, and so takeovers were the least cost method of globalizing the U.S. industry. Why was there new entry rather than the necessary investments in R&D by the incumbent manufacturers once radials were introduced? Because the new entrants did not internalize the effect of new radial investments on the value of sunk investments in belted bias ply manufacturing, the old technology. It was not easy to convert existing belted bias ply plants to radial production. Why were the entrants foreign, not domestic? Because only they had sufficient expertise with radial technology. Why were there takeovers? Better that than going through a war of attrition to knock out inefficient or outmoded capacity (i.e., the inferior technology).

The authors prefer the third explanation. They rebut the second, managerial, explanation with two key facts. First, the transition of U.S. manufacturing capacity to radials was largely complete prior to the takeover wave. Second, radials were not that much more durable than belted bias ply tires, and replacement sales of tires actually increased in the relevant period, perhaps because of increasing awareness of and demand for safety, which might have induced more frequent tire replacement. Michael Jensen was one of the first proponents of the managerial explanation of takeovers in the tire industry, and considerations of comparative (and perhaps absolute) advantage dictate that I defer to him to defend this story.

In the case of the neoclassical explanation, the fact that radial conversion preceded the takeover wave does not preclude the possibility that there were unrealized efficiency gains that could be achieved only with a change in management. The centerpiece of their rebuttal of the neoclassical explanation is the total factor productivity computations summarized in table 2.6, which are based on a regression analysis of census of manufacturing plant-level data.

The regression analysis considers a panel of sixty-seven plants in the years 1967 and 1972–93, inclusive. There are 720 plant-years of data, so the average plant has a sample life of eleven years. The main regression equation employs ordinary least squares, and the logarithm of value added is regressed on the logarithm of labor (production worker equivalent man-hours), the logarithm of a capital stock measure (net property, plant, and equipment), and a variety of dummy variables, in many instances including plant fixed effects. The use of plant fixed effects is a major improvement on comparable studies, especially since the set of acquired plants does not seem to be similar to plants that were not acquired. I return to this point below.

The coefficients of most interest to Rajan, Volpin, and Zingales are associated with the dummies for plants that were owned by foreign manufacturers and those that were acquired after acquisition. The sum of these two coefficients is a measure of the average productivity change in plants that were acquired by foreign companies, in years after the acquisition. The sum of these coefficients is negative in all the regressions considered, although apparently not always significantly different from zero. I say "apparently" because standard errors are not reported for the sum of the two coefficients. Nevertheless, the coefficient sum indicates that there was not a productivity gain at the plant level associated with foreign takeovers, contrary to the neoclassical explanation.

I have some concerns with the reported regressions, however, and with the interpretation of the regression results. Because of these concerns, I believe that it may be premature to dismiss the neoclassical explanation.

First, the coefficient on the labor variable is greater than one in many of the reported regressions, and greater than 0.83 in all. These values are implausible, and probably inconsistent with the interpretation of the estimated equation as a production function. Measurement error of both the capital stock and labor input is a potential concern, as is potential endogeneity of the labor variable. Similar coefficients were found by Burnside, Eichenbaum, and Rebelo (1995, 67–110), for example, in their study of two- and three-digit manufacturing industry data. (One of their three-digit industries is tires.) Burnside et al. argue that their capital stock measure is suspect, and in particular that capital utilization is poorly proxied. Rajan, Volpin, and Zingales follow their lead in table 2.6C, which describes regressions that employ energy consumption as a proxy for capital utilization. The results are similar to the regression equations in table 2.6A that employ capital. However, Burnside et al. also correct for endogeneity of their labor and capital utilization regressors, and they then obtain more sensible production function parameters. Rajan, Volpin, and Zingales make no attempt to correct for simultaneity bias. The issue here is not that getting more reliable estimates of the capital and labor coefficients is of intrinsic interest, but rather that the foreign ownership and acquisition dummy variable coefficients may be biased because of biases elsewhere in the estimated equation.

Second, one wonders about potential sample selection bias associated with comparing plants that were closed during the sample period to those that remained open. In this sample, 20 percent of the plants were closed during the period considered. The positive coefficient on the age variable is symptomatic of a potential problem, if some older plants survive because they are relatively productive. Olley and Pakes (1996), who study productivity in telecommunications equipment plants using similar data from the Census Bureau, describe the potential biases and methods of correcting them in detail. If there is sample selection bias, then the equations reported in tables 2.6 and 2.7 should be estimated jointly. Note that the coefficient on the age variable is implausibly large in the fixed effects regressions. A coefficient of 0.05 implies that productivity grew 5 percent per year, for a productivity gain of more than 70 percent over the eleven-year sample life of an average plant. Again, the problem is that the coefficient seems inconsistent with a production function interpretation of the estimates.

Third, as the authors acknowledge, the capital stock is probably measured with error. I shall focus on one aspect. Many plants seem to have converted from belted bias ply to radial during the sample period. Surely some of the existing capital was rendered obsolete by the transition, yet no account is made of this. In short, it is not innocuous to use a standard capital stock construction with fixed and constant depreciation in a transitional environment. The regressions reported in table 2.6B employ a sample of plants with at least 80 percent radial production and therefore address concerns about whether one can pool observations from belted bias ply and radial plants. But splitting the sample will not necessarily solve the problem with capital measurement, for the capital stock of plants that were converted to radial may be measured with error in the years immediately following conversion.

Finally, there is a general issue of how to interpret plant-level productivity regressions in this instance. The firms under consideration are multiplant firms with global operations. It is possible that plant-level total factor productivity did not change, consistent with the reported regressions, and yet the takeovers led to firm-level efficiency gains due to the consolidation of nonproduction segments of the business, such as marketing, R&D, product design, advertising, or bargaining with the automobile manufacturers.

On the basis of the evidence presented in the paper, I would argue that the industrial organization explanation may be true, but also that the evidence is not sufficient to discredit the neoclassical, or efficiency-based, explanation.

The paper also raises a number of questions that may be worth pursuing in subsequent research. I shall describe a few.

First, the employment regressions reported in table 2.8 indicate that the plants that were acquired by foreign firms were much smaller than average, with about half the employment of the typical plant. (The coefficient on foreign ownership is -0.50 in the regression in column [6] explaining the logarithm of labor, and that on acquisition in column [5] is -0.43.) Again, one wonders whether it is appropriate to pool these smaller plants in the productivity regressions. But the coefficients also indicate that the acquired plants were atypically small. The fact that capital expenditures increased after acquisitions, as indicated by the capital expenditure fixed effects regressions in table 2.8, might be explained by underinvestment by domestic owners, as the authors claim. There may also have been an inefficient scale of operations in acquired plants prior to acquisition.

If the account in the paper is accurate, why was there a complete shift from belted bias ply to radial tires? Rajan, Volpin, and Zingales indicate that there are some advantages to belted bias ply in terms of their ride. Now that gas mileage is not as great a concern for consumers (as real gas prices have returned to pre-OPEC levels), why can't the two types of tires co-exist in the market to satisfy the various consumer preferences?

Another (small) puzzle is why, according to table 2.3, the replacement market went 100 percent radial before the original equipment (OE) market. In 1992, for example, 89 percent of original equipment sales were radials, yet radials accounted for 99 percent of replacement sales. Either the numbers are incorrect, or belted bias ply original equipment sales are for export, or belted bias ply replacement demand is being met by imports or retreads. Note that the car production numbers omit small trucks and minivans, which account for an increasing share of original equipment sales over the sample period.

A striking feature of table 2.1 is how stable global concentration measures have been over the period considered, especially given the pronounced cycles in the demand for tires (mirroring fluctuations in automobile sales), technological changes in the production of tires, and significant changes in the structure of the global automobile industry. Perhaps the global concentration of tire production is optimal, given the procurement requirements of the automobile industry. That is, it may be optimal for the car companies to have about nine effective competitors among tire suppliers. Nine is the approximate inverse of the Herfindahl index. This inverse is sometimes referred to as the number of effective competitors, for it is the number of symmetric firms consistent with the calculated Herfindahl index.

The data set used in the productivity and plant closure regressions of tables 2.6 and 2.7 does not seem to be as extensive as one might wish, especially in the case of the plant closure regressions. A total of thirteen plants closed in the sample studied in table 2.5, yet table 2.4 identifies twenty-four plant closures in the industry between 1976 and 1986. Virtually all of these closures preceded the takeovers, consistent with the story favored by the authors. But a full story of plant closure decisions might focus on the broader sample.

An important issue that is not considered in the paper is why mergers were necessary to realize efficiency, managerial, or strategic gains. Why were joint ventures or other contractual arrangements not employed?

It would also be interesting to learn more about what happened in this industry after the takeover wave. Are the mergers considered successful? For example, Milgrom and Roberts (1992, 510) cite the Bridgestone takeover of Firestone as an example of an extreme takeover premium. According to Milgrom and Roberts, the prebidding value of Firestone shares was on the order of $1 billion, and the final price paid by Bridgestone approximately $2.6 billion, amounting to a premium of 160 percent. Is this large takeover premium thought to be warranted? Michelin is described in a recent issue of the *Economist* ("Michelin Gets a Grip," 1 March 1997) as emerging from troubles associated with the debt it incurred in its acquisition of Goodrich. Is this merger a success? And how has Goodyear, the one U.S. company that survived without being acquired, fared in comparison to its rivals? The sample for the total factor productivity regressions does not cover many years after the takeovers, so that it is conceivable that a longer-run analysis may yield different conclusions. A return to the numbers a few years hence may provide a more definitive answer. It is also conceivable that the mergers occurred because of hubris or false expectations of synergies on the part of the acquiring firms' managers, consistent with the experience in several takeovers studied by other papers in this volume. The "eclipse" of the U.S. tire industry may have occurred because the acquired firms were offered a price far in excess of the value of the company, even under optimal management.

Finally, Rajan, Volpin, and Zingales argue in section 2.2.5 that the domestic tire industry faced a hold-up problem in converting to radials. They describe the necessity of coordinating conversion with the automobile manufacturers, as well as the automobile companies' ability to extract most rents from the original equipment market. The consequence, they claim, was inefficient delay in the introduction of radials. But the numbers of players involved is not large, and the tire and automobile companies were partners in longstanding relationships. One might expect that contractual remedies could have been found for any hold-up problem, and therefore that the delay in introducing radials may be due to other factors. As the authors argue elsewhere, the automobile industry was not a leader in the introduction of many other design innovations in the period around 1980.

None of the preceding skepticism should detract from the contributions of the paper. The authors have carefully combined data from a variety of sources, they employ appropriate techniques to analyze their data, and their economic analysis is novel and plausible. In short, this paper represents best practice methodology. But like most good research, it whets one's appetite for more, to corroborate results or to investigate alternative explanations.

References

Burnside, C., M. Eichenbaum, and S. Rebelo. 1995. Capital utilization and returns to scale. In *NBER macroeconomics annual 1995*, ed. B. Bernanke and J. Rotemberg. Cambridge, Mass.: MIT Press.

Carlton, D., and J. Perloff. 1994. *Modern industrial organization.* 2d ed. New York: HarperCollins.

Milgrom, P., and J. Roberts. 1992. *Economics, organization and management.* Englewood Cliffs, N.J.: Prentice Hall.

Olley, S., and A. Pakes. 1996. The dynamics of productivity in the telecommunications industry. *Econometrica* 64:1263–97.

Scherer, F. M., and D. Ross. 1990. *Industrial market structure and economic performance.* 3d ed. Boston: Houghton Mifflin.

Is the Bank Merger Wave of the 1990s Efficient?
Lessons from Nine Case Studies

Charles W. Calomiris and Jason Karceski

1 Bank Industry Trends

The U.S. banking system is undergoing dramatic consolidation. America's historical predilection for requiring the chartering of local banks and limiting the powers of commercial banks has given way to a new era of deregulation: nationwide banks with broad powers have taken over the industry after building themselves up largely through acquisitions. Is the current merger wave in American banking helping to promote efficiency by increasing the size and scope of banks, or is the bank merger wave driven by darker aspirations: the search for monopoly rents or the job security and personal perquisites of bank managers?

Researchers and industry analysts have approached this question in various ways: (1) cross-regime comparisons of historical bank performance, (2) identification of the influences that encourage bank concentration, and (3) econometric studies of the consequences of consolidation. Interestingly, these various perspectives on bank consolidation have not agreed in their assessment of the potential or actual efficiency gains from mergers and acquisitions. Econometric studies have tended not to identify large potential efficiency gains, on average, from bank mergers. Those results have sometimes been interpreted as evidence that bank mergers typically

Charles W. Calomiris is the Paul M. Montrone Professor of Finance and Economics at the Columbia University Graduate School of Business, a research associate of the National Bureau of Economic Research, and the director of the American Enterprise Institute's Project on Financial Deregulation. Jason Karceski is assistant professor of finance at the University of Florida.

This chapter was previously published as a pamphlet by the AEI Press, © 1998 American Enterprise Institute for Public Policy Research, Washington, D.C. It is reprinted here with permission.

are attempts to reap monopoly rents or attempts by managers to improve their positions at the expense of stockholders. In contrast, cross-regime comparisons of the performance of banking systems and analyses of the forces underlying bank mergers suggest large potential and actual gains over the past five years. We argue that detailed case studies of some recent merger transactions—provided in section 2—help to resolve some of these apparent inconsistencies and are particularly useful in an industry such as banking, in which rapid changes make even the recent past a poor guide to the future.

Cross-Regime Comparisons

Historical cross-country and cross-state comparisons suggest large potential gains from current bank consolidation. Studies comparing the banking system of the United States (where regulation has been hostile to bank branching and consolidation) with the banking systems of countries whose regulatory regimes allowed bank consolidation (especially Germany and Canada) have found significant deficiencies in U.S. banks. Those deficiencies included limits on bank diversification, operating efficiency, the capacity to lend or take deposits per unit of capital, and the banking system's ability to finance large-scale industrialization during the Second Industrial Revolution of 1870–1914 (Calomiris 1993, 1995; Calomiris and Ramirez 1996). These historical shortcomings of American banking are traceable in large part to branching limitations and to other regulations that constrained American banks by keeping them small, undiversified, and narrowly focused on lending and deposit taking.

Furthermore, U.S. states that were most liberal in their regulation of bank concentration (notably California, Ohio, and North Carolina) have historically enjoyed superior banking performance (Calomiris 1993). Banks originating from those states (including Bank of America, Banc-One, NationsBank, and First Union) have become industry leaders not only in size but also in profitability, innovativeness, and growth.

Consider differences in bank performance between the states of North Carolina (long a branching state) and Illinois (long a state that restricted bank branching). Illinois, by virtue of its commercial importance, might have produced nationwide leaders in banking, and yet North Carolina's banks have survived and prospered while Illinois' most prominent banks have all but disappeared. Chicago, in particular, has seen its most important local banking institutions acquired by international giants such as ABN Amro, Bank of America, Bank of Montreal, BancOne, and Citibank. With the exception of Northern Trust (and arguably First Chicago, which has merged with National Bank of Detroit), Chicago no longer has any major banking institution headquartered in Illinois. Table 1-1 reproduces a performance comparison of the rates of return on bank assets and bank equity for Illinois and North Carolina from 1984 to 1992 (a period

Table 1-1   **Bank Structure and Performance in Illinois and North Carolina,
1984–1992**

Year	Number of Banks		Return on Assets (%)		Return on Equity (%)	
	Illinois	North Carolina	Illinois	North Carolina	Illinois	North Carolina
1984	1,240	63	−0.11	0.97	−1.76	16.47
1985	1,233	63	0.63	0.98	9.55	16.82
1986	1,218	65	0.71	1.07	10.70	18.22
1987	1,209	68	−0.23	0.92	−3.88	15.38
1988	1,149	71	0.99	1.06	15.66	16.86
1989	1,119	78	0.88	0.97	13.53	15.62
1990	1,087	78	0.68	0.85	10.05	13.77
1991	1,061	81	0.67	0.74	9.40	10.99
1992	1,006	78	0.72	1.03	9.32	15.24

Source: Division of Research and Statistics, Federal Deposit Insurance Corporation, cited in McCoy, Frieder, and Hedges (1994).

coincident with the most important external acquisitions of Chicago banks). North Carolina-based institutions not only enjoyed much higher average return on equity (ROE) and return on assets (ROA) but saw much smaller fluctuations than did Illinois banks.

Superior historic performance in concentrated banking systems seems to reflect greater efficiency rather than higher rent extraction or inefficient managerial preferences for large size. Bank customers have shared in the efficiency gains from bank consolidation. Before World War I, narrowly focused unit banks in the United States offered an inferior menu of financial services to industrial firms than their German counterparts did and charged higher costs for lending and underwriting (which reflected both technological inferiority of American banks and greater rent extraction in less competitive local unit banking markets) (Calomiris 1995).

U.S. banks in rural areas were protected from competition by unit banking laws. Large fixed costs of setting up a bank—as opposed to a branch office—often ensured a local monopoly. Rural unit banks charged higher rates of interest on loans and paid less on deposits than urban banks. Branch banking regimes in other countries saw greater competition in rural areas and did not witness regional differences in loan-deposit spreads (Calomiris 1993). U.S. banks in unit banking states provided access to banking services inferior to that of rural offices in branch banking states, as measured by the number of bank offices per acre or per capita (Evanoff 1988). Shaffer's (1993) study of Canadian banking giants measured the extent to which they enjoyed market power. He concluded that the highly concentrated Canadian system (with six large banks) had been greatly competitive.

These cross-regime comparisons are telling. Since the nineteenth cen-

Table 1-2   U.S. Bank Mergers and Acquisitions, 1979–1994 (billions of 1994 $)

Year	Assets of All U.S. Banks	Assets of Banks Consolidating[a]
1979	3,257	174
1980	3,267	209
1981	3,250	180
1982	3,310	239
1983	3,398	287
1984	3,482	317
1985	3,658	368
1986	3,838	396
1987	3,823	510
1988	3,833	442
1989	3,866	327
1990	3,801	390
1991	3,707	388
1992	3,681	434
1993	3,803	329
1994	4,024	627

Source: Data for consolidating banks are derived from Berger, Saunders, Scalise, and Udell (1997), table 1A.

Note: A *family merger* is defined as a merger between banks that are owned by the same parent institution. A *merger* is defined as the consolidation of two banks within the same charter, while an *acquisition* is defined as the purchase of a bank that retained its charter.

[a]The sum of all nonfamily mergers and all acquisitions.

tury, banking systems both within and outside the United States uniformly have taken the form of large-scale, multiproduct, branch banking systems when that option was not precluded by restrictive regulations. There is strong evidence that regimes that are friendly to both consolidation and competition produce lower bank risk and higher bank productivity. Evidence from the current deregulation of U.S. banking, which we discuss below, provides a similar perspective: both banks and their customers have gained from deregulation, increased competition, and improvements in bank structure and services that have followed.

Competition and the New Face of Banking

One approach to evaluating the likely efficiency gains from the current merger wave (table 1-2) is to examine industry trends related to consolidation: to identify the origins of the merger wave and ask whether it has coincided with efficiency gains for the banking industry as a whole. The argument that increased competition motivates the recent bank merger wave and that industry performance has improved with consolidation provides some support for the view that consolidation has promoted efficiency. That is, if mergers result from competitive pressure, they are more likely value maximizing because in a highly competitive environment there is less opportunity for rent extraction by banks and less tolerance for inefficient managerial preferences for consolidation.

Competition and Deregulation in Financial Services

Increasing competition has been an important trend in the financial services industry over the past twenty years. Initially, competition was spurred by a combination of financial innovation and deregulation in the market for deposits, both reflecting the effect of inflation on real rates of return to bank depositors. The removal of interest rate ceilings, the relaxation of reserve requirements, the entry of money market mutual funds, and the growth in the commercial paper market, however, were just the beginning. Beginning in the early1980s, state laws and federal laws consistently favored increased entry into the previously protected banking industry.

Foreign bank entry was facilitated by the single-country approach adopted by the United States (codified in 1978), which treated the operating branches of foreign banks or chartered banks in the United States the same as domestic banks. The banking distress of the early 1980s was an important source of regulatory change allowing greater domestic bank entry, through holding company purchases of banks or bank branching. Weak and failing banks motivated regulators to relax entry restrictions within and across states so that troubled banks could be acquired by banks within their state through branching or by out-of-state holding companies.

Thirty-nine states relaxed their branching laws between 1979 and 1990 (Mengle 1990). In some states, bank branching was the result of a 1988 ruling by the Comptroller of the Currency requiring that banks be granted the same branching rights as thrifts. Regional pacts among states permitted interstate branching on a limited basis through most of the country by 1990. Finally, the Riegle-Neal Interstate Banking and Branching Efficiency Act of 1994 effectively repealed all limits on branching across states by January 1, 1997 (many states opted to comply with the act earlier).

Berger, Kashyap, and Scalise (1995, 166–67) traced the progress of interstate bank entry, state by state, over the period 1979–1994 and documented the sudden bursts of interstate entry that followed the removal of branching restrictions in each state. For the United States as a whole, the percentage of bank assets controlled by out-of-state banks rose from 2 percent in 1979 to 10 percent in 1986 and then rocketed to 28 percent by 1994. The consolidation in the banking industry over this period is remarkable. The total number of banking organizations fell from 12,463 in 1979 to 7,926 in 1994, while the percentage of assets controlled by banks with over $100 billion in assets (in 1994 dollars) rose from 9.4 percent to 18.8 percent (Berger, Kashyap, and Scalise 1995, 67).

While deregulation (especially the removal of branching restrictions) has been a key and necessary condition for the bank merger wave in the

United States, competition has been a key exogenous factor as well. Increased global competition among banks and competition from nonbank providers have spurred a reorganization of financial services worldwide. Technological changes that favor the repackaging of bank loans as securities (securitization) and computerization changes that allow greater access to consumers have been important in spurring the new global competition. As late as 1980, America's securities transactions with foreigners (gross sales and purchases of stocks and bonds) amounted to only 9 percent of the gross domestic product. By 1990, these transactions totaled 93 percent of GDP. International bank lending worldwide rose from $324 billion in 1980 to $7.5 trillion in 1991 (Crook 1992).

The importance of global competition in the new structure of the financial services industry is reflected in the international aspect of bank consolidation, affecting banks in many countries that have not shared the historic limitations on consolidation of the United States. Notable examples include Germany and Switzerland, where recent consolidations also reflect competitive pressure. Furthermore, the deregulation that has allowed bank restructuring in countries such as the United States itself largely reflects the effect of competitive pressure on regulators. In the new global environment, domestic bank regulators have been forced to choose between continuing heavy regulation of a shrinking system of banks or a healthy and deregulated domestic banking system.

Although banking distress can be credited with the relaxation of state branching laws, more fundamental long-run concerns shaped the policy of the Federal Reserve both on bank consolidation and on bank powers. The Fed's support for expanding the scale and scope of banks explicitly reflected concerns that nonbank intermediaries and foreign banks were outcompeting American commercial banks and that relaxation of regulation was necessary to give U.S. banks a fighting chance to survive. Alan Greenspan (1988, 1990, 1992), Fed chairman, has repeatedly argued that increased scale and scope in banking is essential to maintaining an internationally competitive U.S. banking sector. In a call for expanding bank powers, Greenspan (1988, 3–4) argued: "The ability of banks to continue to hold their position by operating on the margins of customer services is limited. Existing constraints, in conjunction with the continued undermining of the bank franchise by the new technology, are likely to limit the future profitability of banking. . . . If the aforementioned trends continue banking will contract either relatively or absolutely." Similarly, the Fed chairman (1990, 5) argued, "in an environment of global competition, rapid financial innovation, and technological change, bankers understandably feel that the old portfolio and affiliate rules and the constraints on permissible activities of affiliates are no longer meaningful and likely to result in a shrinking banking system."

Some of the Fed's concern about the competitiveness of American banks reflected the boom in foreign bank entry into the United States in the late 1980s. Foreign banks received a golden opportunity for entry into American banking markets during the capital crunch of 1985–1990. Calomiris and Carey (1994) report that foreign banks' share of nonmortgage commercial and industrial (C&I) lending in the United States rose from 7 percent in 1983 to 14 percent in 1991, while the share of U.S. banks fell from 30 to 16 percent.

Nonbank competition in C&I lending has also been important. Finance companies maintained a nearly constant share of 10–12 percent from 1983 to 1993. But the share of market debt (bonds, commercial paper, and asset-backed securities) rose during the 1980s and early 1990s, from 40–41 percent in 1983–1985 to 49–52 percent during 1991–1993. Loans to small businesses—traditionally reserved almost exclusively to banks—have become a hotly contested market. Merrill Lynch, with offices throughout the United States, now boasts its status as the seventh largest lender to small businesses in the United States. In consumer banking, the credit card market has long been a highly competitive national market. But potential new providers of other retail consumer banking services now threaten to enter the national electronic market, and some of these (notably those with easy access to large customer bases, such as Microsoft) could threaten the traditional consumer niches occupied by banks.

Competition should reduce monopoly rents, enhance efficiency, and weaken the power of inefficient bank managers to determine the goals and structure of their institutions. Empirical evidence is consistent with these predictions. Keeley (1990) and Berger and Humphrey (1992) found that local bank monopolies were undermined in the 1980s by relaxation of entry restrictions. Jayaratne and Strahan (1997) determined that the relaxation of branching restrictions in the United States produced competitive pressures that cut bank operating costs and loan losses and that these advantages were largely passed on to customers in the form of lower loan interest rates. Akhavein, Berger, and Humphrey's (1997) analysis of mergers uncovered no evidence of increased market power in deposit or lending markets as a result of consolidation during the 1980s.

The link between consolidation and competition is also visible in the growth accompanying consolidation. The new competition has resulted in an increase in the number of bank offices even as it has promoted a decline in the number of banks. From 1980 to 1989, the number of banks declined by 12 percent, but the number of banking offices increased from 38,350 to 51,300. By 1994, the number of bank offices had reached 65,610. Adding automated teller machines (ATMs) to the number of bank offices significantly adds to the measured growth in points of sale of bank services. ATMs increased in number from 13,800 in 1979 to 109,080 in 1994 (Berger, Kashyap, and Scalise 1995, 79).

As Boyd and Gertler (1994) and James and Houston (1996) emphasize, the decline in banks' share of financial assets should not be viewed as a decline in the importance of banks but rather as evidence of technological advances that have allowed banks to do more things. Despite the rapid growth in nonbank financial institutions (notably pensions and mutuals), banks' share of total financial institutions' income is roughly the same as it was in the 1960s (about 40 percent), which largely reflects the growth in fee income.

That the banking industry is not shrinking deserves emphasis. The movement to consolidation in banking is about competition and the enhancement of efficiency, not about the elimination of excess capacity. Unit banking (with its high overhead costs of setting up points of service) had restricted efficient growth. With a break from the legacy of unit banking, the costs of entry and of establishing new banking locations fell dramatically, and the capacity of the industry increased.

Retail banking and banking in less populated areas are not the only markets that have seen increased competition. Entry into cities in states with historic limits on banking has been particularly pronounced. Chicago is the prime example (Calomiris and Karceski 1994). According to the *New York Times* (February 21, 1995, C1, C9), competition in corporate lending has become so intense that some regulators are concerned that banks are no longer earning a sufficient return on large corporate lending within the United States. The *Times* reports:

> The average interest rate on a loan to a big company with a comparatively weak BB credit rating has fallen from 1.30 percentage points above Libor [London Interbank Offered Rate] in 1992 to 0.79 point above Libor at the end of last year, according to statistics compiled by the Loan Pricing Corporation. . . . Spreads for companies rated A fell from 0.40 to 0.25 point. And while statistics are not available, bankers say that rates for small businesses are declining at least that much.

The new competition is not limited to traditional banking products and services. Encroachment by new entrants into the traditional activities of U.S. banks has been a spur to deregulation of bank activities (particularly through the efforts of the Fed) and has helped to promote competition in financial services previously not provided by banks. The more competition banks received, the more they were able to convince their regulators (Congress, the Fed, and the Comptroller) to allow them to enter new areas. U.S. commercial banks have become significant players in underwriting, derivatives intermediation, venture capital finance, and mutual fund management and have begun to provide life insurance and annuities. Brewer (1989) found that bank holding companies that have taken advantage of the new permissible activities significantly have improved their risk-adjusted returns as a consequence. This consolidation wave reflects not only the demise of branching and other scale restrictions in banking but also the desire on the part of banks to take advantage rapidly of the broadening of their new powers.

The New Era of Client-Based Universal Banking

The era of dividing the financial sector into fragmented niches, protected by regulatory entry barriers, has ended. But if the financial services industry is becoming more competitive, why are banks so keen to enter into new product lines? The answer is that commercial banking strategies are driven by a belief in the value of *relationships,* which translates into economics as *quasi rents.* Bankers have come to believe that there are strong economies of scope in combining products within a single intermediary. These economies of scope take the form not of physical production economies but rather of economies that arise in the context of relationship management. There are, for example, marketing and sales cost economies from cross-selling—a lending relationship provides an opportunity to discuss additional products with a client. There are also information and monitoring cost economies of scope in relationships. A bank providing a loan or credit enhancement already tracks a firm's performance and perhaps is enforcing a set of covenants or holding a collateral interest in the firm. Consequently, it is easier to evaluate and bear the counterparty risk of a swap with that customer or to evaluate the customer's potential for a private or public equity offering.

Because these client economies of scope provide a competitive advantage on any single transactional dimension to intermediaries that already provide other transactional or advisory services to clients and because such economies also imply costs of searching and switching on the part of clients, client economies of scope offer banks the opportunity to reap quasi rents from their relationships. As Rajan (1992) points out, however, such an ex post relationship advantage need not translate into ex ante economic profit. The competition for new relationships may imply that much of these rents will be dissipated by front-loaded concessions to customers (so-called loss leaders). Indeed, underpricing loans as a means to attract customers into a relationship (sometimes referred to as tying) has become a common practice. Bankers are trained to judge profitability not on the basis of individual transactions but rather by evaluating the total resources the bank devotes to a client (consisting predominantly of man-hours and funds) and the total fees and interest paid by the client.

This approach to commercial banking accounted for the rebirth of Continental Bank in the late 1980s and for the attractive acquisition offer it received from Bank of America in 1994. After its demise and rescue by the government in 1984, Continental shed its retail operations and outsourced its noncore functions to focus on its core operations in corporate banking. The bank's niche was defined not as a set of products per se but rather as a set of employees (and hence a base of knowledge about certain customers) and as a type of client it wanted to have. Continental's internal training program emphasized total client profitability, the sharing of information within and across client teams and deal teams within the bank, and the development of special internal accounting to allocate overhead costs and measure client profitability. Continental's strategy was to use new products as a way to lock in a "share of mind"—to move from simple to complex transactional services and to provide financial and business advisory services so that clients would rely more on the bank. By acquiring Continental and moving its headquarters of corporate banking to Chicago, Bank of America expressed its confidence in that approach.

The new emphasis on the economics of relationships, as opposed to productivity or profitability measured at the level of the product or service, is not unique to Continental. Chase's motto, "The right relationship is everything," bespeaks the same approach. Harris Bank's "Vision 2002" is also based on a relationship-focused strategy, in determining both the combination of services and the location of its branches (Calomiris and Karceski 1994, 55–59; 1995, 14–26). Similarly, BancOne's profitability accounting emphasizes tracking overhead expenditure and evaluating the value of product lines in light of general client relationships (McCoy, Frieder, and Hedges 1994). McCoy and his coauthors devote an entire chapter of their book to relationship banking ("The New Search for Growth: Relationship Banking"). In explaining the value of relationships, they explicitly point to the importance of quasi rents resulting from search and switch costs, though they use a different language (p. 18): "Capturing a greater share of existing customers' wallets through relationships has the potential of raising profitability significantly and locking in a bank's customer base. That is, if customers maintain several products and significant balances with a given bank, they will be less likely to switch to a competitor."

Bankers clearly agree with this assessment and have been aggressive advocates of the deregulation of bank powers. Banks were successful in 1996 and 1997 in pushing for substantial relaxation of firewalls that had separated the activities of underwriting (section 20) affiliates and banks and in broadening the range of permissable transactions in nonbank affiliates. Recently, one of the most prominent bank industry representatives (the Bankers' Roundtable) has advocated the rolling back of deposit insurance protection for banks to make it possible for Congress to grant even greater powers to bank holding companies (Bankers' Roundtable 1997).

New banking powers not only permit banks to provide new services to customers, they also give banks greater flexibility in meeting customers' financing needs. During the 1980s and early 1990s, for example, some of the largest bank holding companies (including Citicorp, Chase, Chemical, First Chicago, Continental, Norwest, J. P. Morgan, and Bank of America) earned a substantial fraction of their earnings from private equity investments.

It is hard to find bankers opposed to relationship-based strategy. The most prominent contrarian had been Bankers Trust, which had long espoused a transactional vision of banking and had argued that profitable relationship banking had been undermined by competition. The view that competition had undermined the profitability of relationship banking— held by some academics and journalists as well as Bankers Trust executives—failed to distinguish between the old (disappearing) monopoly rents of noncompetitive banking and the new quasi rents of universal banking. That confusion led Bankers Trust to discount the value of a client-based strategy and to see its business as a sequence of independent transactions. In the wake of large losses in trading and derivatives deals in Latin America and the United States, Bankers Trust has changed management and strategy. In 1995–1997, management focused on reducing the importance of trading activities and increasing the emphasis on relationship banking.

That lesson holds for emerging market risk exposure of banks, as well as domestic strategy. The losses that Bankers Trust suffered in 1994 and 1995 from its Latin American portfolio contrast with the experiences of Bank Santander, Bank of Boston, and Citibank in Latin America. Those banks have seen significant growth with far less exposure to country risk because they have established large branching networks, which they use to pursue profitable consumer and small business relationships in Mexico, Argentina, and elsewhere.

The importance of customer lending relationships and the quasi rents they create for banks through the valuable information and control technology banks enjoy (compared with arm's-length debtholders) has been widely documented in recent academic work. Over the past decade, an outpouring of empirical research has documented the special role of banks as information collectors and enforcers of contracts under asymmetric information (James 1987; James and Wier 1988; Hoshi, Kashyap, and Scharfstein, 1990a, 1990b, 1991; Booth 1991; Slovin, Sushka, and Polonchek 1993; Best and Zhang 1993; Petersen and Rajan 1994; Billett, Flannery, and Garfinkel 1995; Kashyap and Stein 1995; and Calomiris and Wilson 1997).

Focusing on customer relationships also proves important in understanding the way new entry occurs in lending markets and differences in the profitability of new and existing lenders. Calomiris and Carey (1994) argue that foreign bank entry into the U.S. corporate lending market during the 1980s reflected a cost of funds advantage on the part of foreign banks during the U.S. bank capital crunch. But foreign bank entrants suffered an information cost disadvantage, which is visible in the form and pricing of foreign bank entry. Foreign banks were able to underprice U.S. banks significantly only in the high-quality segment of the market. For high-risk customers (where information costs are more important), foreign bank pricing was similar to that of domestic banks. Moreover, compared with domestic banks, foreign banks were much more likely to lend in the low-risk segment of the market and were much more likely to lend as passive members of syndicates or through the purchase of loans originated by domestic banks. The relationship cost advantage of domestic banks is also visible in loan performance differences. Nolle (1994) found that foreign-owned banks in the United States had much lower returns on assets in the 1990s and that this difference reflected both higher overhead costs and higher loan-loss rates for foreign banks.

Our case analyses provide evidence that this new approach to client-based universal banking is central to understanding the merger wave of the 1990s in U.S. banking and its potential efficiency gains. A bank's mixture of products and services and its locational strategy are primarily set in reference to the client base that the bank is targeting rather than according to the technological costs or synergies associated with particular sets of products or services. Thus, mergers and acquisitions should be seen in the context of client-based universal banking strategies.

Client-based strategies underlie many choices of acquisition targets in the nine case studies that we discuss. In searching for merger targets, acquiring banks may be attempting to achieve operating cost economies of scale (a primary stated goal in the cases of Firstar's acquisition of First Colonial, Roosevelt's acquisition of Farm and Home, the merger of equals between Comerica and Manufacturers and, to a lesser extent, in the cases of Firstar's acquisition of Investors, Mercentile's acquisition of United Postal, and First Chicago's acquisition of Lake Shore). But often targets were at least as important because they provided missing links in a client-based strategy. They did so sometimes by providing a branching network to a targeted group of people whom the bank felt were its natural client base (as in the cases of Harris Bank's acquisition of Suburban, First Chicago's acquisition of Lake Shore, First Bank's acquisition of Boulevard, and NationsBank's acquisition of MNC). In other cases, targets provided a quick and inexpensive means of acquiring expertise in a set of services that fit the needs of the acquiring bank's strategy (as in Mercentile's takeover of United Postal, Firstar's acquisition of Investors, and the Comerica-Manufacturers merger).

Competition, Consolidation, and Efficiency Gains in the 1990s

Given the deregulation of entry and the new client-based universal banking strategy made possible by the expansion of bank powers, competition should encourage efficient consolidation. Thus, one would expect the mergers that coincide with the heightened competition of the 1990s to be associated with greater efficiency gains. Competition should promote efficient consolidation in two ways.

First, competition magnifies the rewards for efficiency and the penalties for incompetence. If there are economies of scale, economies of scope (for example, due to the opportunities to cross-sell products within any given bank-customer relationship), or x-efficiencies associated with managerial skill, a competitive environment will encourage those potential efficiency gains to be realized by allowing efficient strategies to produce larger relative earnings differences among competitors.

Second, because competition widens the distribution of earnings, it changes the incentives of inefficient, entrenched bank managers and makes them more willing to step aside. In a noncompetitive environment, weak managers may be insulated from stockholder discipline. If stockholders rebel against managers only when earnings are low, then even inefficient managers may do well enough in a noncompetitive environment to avoid discipline. In the face of increasing competition, poor managers who see their time running out will have an incentive to hasten their exit before the stockholders rebel and before all the franchise value of their local monopoly is eroded by competing entrants.

Thus, an emphasis on the new client-based approach to banking, along with the acceleration in competition as the result of the repeal of branching restrictions during the early to mid-1990s, suggests that motivations for mergers and the consequences of mergers during the 1990s could differ greatly from those of the preceding years. In fact, there is some evidence that the early 1990s have been a watershed not only for mergers but for bank efficiency. Despite the increased competition in lending markets, a combination of cost savings and the introduction of new fee-generating products and services seems to have produced a significant improvement in bank industry performance.

No available measure of performance for banks is ideal as a measure of long-run efficiency. Ideally, bank earnings must be adjusted for the riskiness of bank activities, and some measures of short-term trends in bank performance can reflect exogenous cyclical influences on bank loan quality or interest rates more than technological improvements. Furthermore, efficiency gains associated with increased competition may accrue to customers, not to banks, and may coincide with reductions in performance attributable to reduced monopoly rents. Thus, bank performance improvements during deregulation will understate productivity gains.

Despite these caveats, it is hard not to be impressed by the past five years' improvement in bank performance, which bankers and bank analysts interpret as a long-run improvement in productivity. Average market-to-book values for banks rose from an average of roughly unity for the period 1980–1991 to an average of 1.4 for the period 1992–1995 (James and Houston 1996). Bank earnings have also shown permanent improvement. Perhaps the most popular measure of operating performance is the return on equity. As table 1-3 shows, commercial bank return on equity since 1992 has been high and stable compared even with the return in the early 1980s (before the deterioration in bank loan quality that lowered ROE in the late 1980s).

Higher bank profitability today is not driven by higher loan ratios (which are roughly constant over time). Part of the improvement in bank performance is due to a widening of net interest margin (net interest income relative to interest-earning assets). This has grown over time despite the reductions in lending spreads for corporate loans. As bankers emphasize, the key to the growth in net interest margin has been new retail lending products (such as home equity loans) that have permitted banks to move into relatively high margin consumer lending. The other primary contributor to improved bank performance has been noninterest income. Relative to assets, noninterest income has doubled over the past twelve years. While noninterest expenses (essentially salaries and wages) have risen relative to assets (because of the growth of off–balance sheet activities), the growth in noninterest expense has more than paid for itself in generating new sources of income and higher interest margins. That trade-off is captured (albeit imperfectly) in a measure known in the banking industry as the efficiency ratio: the ratio of noninterest expense (not including chargeoffs) relative to net interest and noninterest income. In table 1-3, we report that measure, which shows virtual constancy during the period 1981–1991 but falls dramatically afterward.

One of the clearest indicators of the effects of the new competition on bank performance is the changing composition of earnings and expenses for Midwestern banks. These banks have seen a decline in net interest margin alongside growth in noninterest income and a decline in noninterest expense. That region more than any other had been characterized by branching restrictions that limited competition in local lending markets and kept banks from realizing cost savings and relationship synergies. As shown in table 1-3, banks in the Midwest saw a decline in their net interest margin from 4.57 percent in 1993 to 2.89 percent in 1997, while noninterest expenses fell from 4.18 percent of assets to 3.43 percent and noninterest income rose from 2.15 percent to 2.63 percent. The simultaneity of these changes provides evidence of improved productivity. Midwest banks found ways to improve their noninterest earnings per asset dollar while cutting their noninterest costs per asset dollar. Thus, despite declining interest margins, Midwest banks have maintained their ROE.

Of course, the cost reductions in American banking are not entirely attributable to consolidation. Changes in technology (notably the replacement of teller-originated transactions with ATMs) would have produced cost savings even without any consolidation. Nevertheless, the improvement in bank efficiency reflects favorably on the case for bank mergers in

Table 1-3 Commercial Bank Performance, 1981–1997 (percent)

Year	Asset Growth	Ratio of Loans to Assets	Net Interest Margin[a]	Ratio of Noninterest Income to Assets	Ratio of Noninterest Expense to Assets	Efficiency Ratio[b]	Return on Equity
All U.S. Insured Domestic Commercial Banks							
1981	6.30	55.91	3.75	0.90	2.77	68.23	13.09
1982	8.30	56.82	3.82	0.96	2.93	68.94	12.10
1983	7.52	56.46	3.78	1.03	2.96	69.16	11.24
1984	7.04	57.67	3.80	1.19	3.05	68.54	10.60
1985	5.96	58.38	3.93	1.32	3.19	67.87	11.32
1986	8.47	57.86	3.81	1.40	3.22	68.80	10.23
1987	5.15	59.12	3.91	1.43	3.35	69.07	1.29
1988	4.31	59.80	4.02	1.50	3.38	67.06	11.61
1989	4.56	60.64	3.99	1.62	3.42	66.67	7.33
1990	4.74	60.53	3.94	1.67	3.49	68.16	7.29
1991	1.23	59.55	4.10	1.79	3.73	69.07	7.71
1992	1.86	57.30	4.42	1.95	3.87	66.15	12.66
1993	3.60	56.25	4.42	2.13	3.94	65.23	15.34
1994	8.33	56.06	4.38	2.00	3.76	64.94	14.64
1995	7.40	58.39	4.31	2.02	3.65	63.48	14.71
1996	5.54	59.91	4.33	2.19	3.73	62.69	14.60
Midwestern Banks							
1993	14.86	61.49	4.57	2.15	4.18	66.37	14.70
1994	42.92	60.66	4.19	2.05	3.79	64.67	15.10
1995	11.20	61.87	3.96	2.12	3.61	63.19	14.60
1996	5.18	64.08	3.78	2.42	3.84	65.53	15.90
1997	14.28	59.85	2.89	2.63	3.43	65.28	16.00

Source: Federal Reserve Bulletin (July 1987, 538–42; June 1997, 479–81) for all U.S. banks; Value Line Investment Survey (July 4, 1997) for 1993–1996 Midwest data; 1997 data are estimates.

[a](Interest income − interest expense)/earning assets.

[b]Noninterest expense/(interest income + noninterest − interest expense).

two ways. First, it provides prima facie evidence that the cost savings programs that coincide with many bank consolidation transactions may actually be having some effect. In that regard, it is noteworthy that the Midwest region (where the regime change has been most dramatic) is also the region that has seen some of the greatest efficiency gains. Second, the evidence of dramatic improvements in bank efficiency supports the view that competitive pressures have been particularly pronounced during the merger wave, which reflects favorably on the likely motives for mergers.

Microeconometric Analyses of Bank Consolidation

From the standpoint of the preceding arguments about the likely efficiency gains from the merger wave currently transforming U.S. banking, econometric evidence of efficiency gains at the level of individual banks has been surprisingly weak. Three decades of microeconomic empirical research in banking have failed to produce clear evidence of large gains from consolidation. That fact has not done much for the reputation of academic analysis within the banking industry, where the gains from consolidation are generally regarded as beyond reasonable doubt. How have the academics arrived at their conclusions, and how might one reconcile the econometric results of these studies with other evidence (and bankers' beliefs) that consolidation is the child of competition and the mother of efficiency?

Studies that have failed to find economies of scale in banking and thus question the potential gains from consolidation are relatively easy to discount. First, under a regulatory regime that limited bank branching (the regime under which scale economies were estimated), it is not surprising that economies of scale were hard to find. If the advantages of large size include operating economies of scale (back office consolidation across bank offices), portfolio diversification, and economies associated with widespread marketing and client-access, then they depend on the ability to branch. But the branching networks that would have allowed such economies of scale to be realized were absent. Thus, past measures of realized scale economies are likely to be a poor guide to potential scale economies. Berger and Mester (1997) provide evidence consistent with that view. Using a database taken from the 1990s, they found potential scale economies significantly larger than those of previous studies.

Second, measures of inputs and outputs are controversial in banking, and incomparability across banks of different sizes in inputs and outputs makes it particularly hard to render convincing scale comparisons. Banking consultants, with access to better data, argue that economies of scale are important but are hard to identify with publicly available data. Toevs (1992) provides evidence from line-of-business data that show large economies of scale and great potential for cost savings from within-market consolidation.

Empirical studies of merger and acquisition transactions bear more directly on the question of the gains from consolidation. The results of these studies divide into two broad categories: (1) analyses of the effects of transaction announcements on stock prices of targets and acquirers and (2) analyses of postmerger bank performance through bank income and balance sheet data. Both sets of findings have tended to produce evidence of meager expected or actual postconsolidation improvement, on average. But interpreting the evidence from these studies is difficult because of a variety of problems. The pitfalls that we outline in our criticism of the extant empirical work on mergers help to motivate our use of the case-study approach.

Average Stock Price Reactions

Studies of stock price reactions to consolidation announcements (for various dates covering the period before 1992) have reported negative average returns for acquirers, positive average returns for acquirees, and a zero average change in the value of the combined institutions (Beatty, Santomero, and Smirlock 1987; James and Wier 1987; Wall and Gup 1988; Dubofsky and Fraser 1988; Kaen and Tehranian 1988; Sushka and Bendeck 1988; Cornett and Tehranian 1992; Houston and Ryngaert 1994). Should one conclude that mergers account for little of the gains in the 1990s (or before) or that measures of gains based on stock price reactions are flawed?

Studies that focus on stock price reactions and measure performance by announcement effects face several difficulties. First, stock issues (including stock swaps associated with acquisitions) tend to be associated with negative price reactions for issuers and acquirers, which is generally explained as a result of adverse-selection (pooling) problems (Myers and Majluf 1984). That interpretation suggests that it is inappropriate to view negative average price reactions to acquirers' announced acquisition plans as evidence that consolidation is value reducing.

Second, the efficiency gains from consolidation may be reaped largely by bank customers in a competitive market (as suggested by the evidence in Jayaratne and Strahan 1997). In that case, stock prices of banks might capture little of the efficiency gains of consolidation. Measures of consumer surplus (convenience, transaction cost, interest rate spreads) might be more useful measures of efficiency gains than bank stock prices or bank earnings.

Third, if acquisitions are anticipated, their positive effects on bank value may not show themselves at the announcement date. Many banks have clearly expressed their acquisition strategies (NationsBank, Banc-One, and Harris Bank, for example). Acquisition announcements may provide details about timing and specific targets but less information about the future shape of the bank, which may have been known to the market before the announcement.

Fourth, a negative market reaction could itself reflect market disappointment with the announced transaction because of anticipated gains for consolidation transactions if some such transactions become less likely as the result of the announced consolidation. As we argue in our analysis of Firstar's acquisitions, a possible interpretation of the market's negative reaction to Firstar's acquisition announcements is that the market believed Firstar's value-maximizing strategy was to become acquired by a larger superregional bank. Despite Firstar's impressive record before these acquisitions and despite its reasonable expectation of achieving gains through consolidation, the market may have been disappointed by the implication of these announcements for the long-run strategy of the bank.

Fifth, market reactions may reflect an incomplete understanding of the transactions. McCoy, Frieder, and Hedges (1994) contend that the nature of the gains from consolidation has changed over short periods during the past twenty years. Given the limited information from experience available in the market to judge the likely success of consolidations, market expectations may be formed largely from the record of a few transactions, which may provide an inaccurate picture of anticipated gains when the motivations for mergers are changing.

Average Postmerger Performance

Studies of postconsolidation performance often provide mixed evidence on typical cost savings and revenue gains from mergers and acquisitions. The various studies all report that acquisition targets tend to be relatively inefficient banks. They disagree, however, about the extent to which acquisitions help to realize potential efficiency gains. Results are sensitive to the type of bank being analyzed and the benchmark used for comparison. Some studies report little average performance improvement from consolidation. Berger and Humphrey (1992), for example, examined a sample of bank consolidations from 1981 to 1989 and found little realized gains from mergers. Srinivasan and Wall (1992) and Rhoades (1993a) discovered no cost savings from mergers.

More recent work suggests that mergers may produce significant revenue gains, despite scant cost savings. Akhavein, Berger, and Humphrey (1997); Berger (1997); and Peristiani (1997) found no significant cost savings from consolidations but did find increases in profits after consolidation, which largely reflected portfolio reallocations—the switch from government securities holdings to loans—or improvements in asset quality. The first and last of these studies examine data from the 1980s, while the second uses data only for the period 1991–1994. Together, those findings suggest that some combination of greater loan diversification opportunities or perhaps the profitability of lending as part of a multiproduct delivery strategy (quasi rent creation) accompanies consolidation—that is, bank management is either more willing or more able to take on lending risk than before.

Other studies of this same period do detect significant cost savings from consolidation. Spindt and Tarhan (1992a, 1992b) used a matched-sample approach to construct their performance benchmark. They concluded that large gains were realized by acquirers and that the prices paid for targets were fair measures of expected discounted future gains from the acquisition. Toevs (1992) provides a similarly optimistic perspective on cost savings, using data on lines of business rather than total banking costs. Cornett and Tehranian (1992), who confined their analysis to large bank holding companies, found large increases in postmerger performance; also, cross-sectional differences in ex post performance and cost savings were reflected in cross-sectional differences in stock market reactions to announcements.

Some differences across studies—especially the differences regarding cost savings—reflect different definitions of costs and profits. Cornett and Tehranian (1992) focused on measures that excluded interest costs but have been criticized for doing so since banks with high operating costs may be spending more on operations to avoid higher interest costs (Berger 1997). Differences in the samples of banks studied may also produce different measures of cost savings. Spindt and Tarhan's findings may reflect a high proportion of small banks in their sample.

In general, the conclusions from the performance-based studies of mergers are mixed. Still, they provide a more optimistic picture than the evidence on average stock price reactions. They also tend to emphasize potential gains from revenue increases rather than cost savings and show that those gains in revenue are not traceable to increases in market power.

The scant evidence of postmerger improvement from some performance studies may be attributable to methodological pitfalls. Some problems are similar to those encountered in the literature about reactions of stock prices—for example, the possibility that efficiency gains will not show up as net earnings improvements because of competition. Other pitfalls in measurement are peculiar to performance comparisons. First, there is a selectivity bias. Nonmerging banks (which serve as the benchmark for comparison) may be avoiding consolidation for good reason. Perhaps they are pursuing de novo branching as a method for expansion, or perhaps they are in a different service niche, where consolidation is not as useful. This selectivity bias implies that measured improvements from consolidation relative to some benchmark will understate actual improvements.

Second, lags in performance improvement may be extensive. Transactions motivated by pure cost cutting show benefits fastest, but even in these cases most industry estimates claim that cost savings take roughly three years to become fully realized. In the first year after a merger, costs often rise because of special costs from the merger itself (including special accounting charges and severance pay). Transactions motivated by strategic factors (marketing synergies or diversification) may take much longer to show themselves. Diversification advantages may take years to appear. Revenue gains from combining services to foster more profitable client contacts may not be realized for several years. Furthermore, some acquirers deliberately pursue a slow path when integrating targets into the parent institution because they believe that doing so enhances the long-run profitability of the acquisition (through its effects on customer relationships and employee morale).

Third, during a merger wave, it is hard to construct a believable benchmark of performance to gauge the gains from consolidation, and this problem is exacerbated by the lags in realizing the gains of mergers. Panel data analysis of mergers seeks to take advantage of within-firm and across-firm differences in consolidation status to identify gains from consolidation. But, in the midst of a merger wave, banks that did not acquire an institution in a given year are still likely to have been involved in a previous consolidation or are likely to be involved in one in the near future. The econometrician faces the difficult task of identifying firm-years that should reflect the influence of consolidation as opposed to firm-years that should not. Recall that the gains of consolidation (according to bankers) show themselves in bank performance with a lag and the first year of consolidation often sees large expenses associated with the transaction itself. Thus, constructing a meaningful comparison of merging and non-merging institutions to evaluate performance consequences may be difficult. (We return to the problem of constructing counterfactual benchmarks in our case discussions.)

Fourth, because one story does not fit all bank mergers, the econometrician has difficulties in identifying the benefits of mergers. Suppose that there are many different ways in which mergers might improve efficiency (including operating cost savings, x-efficiency gains, and product sales synergies) but that any one merger typically is motivated primarily by only one of the many possible sources of gain (a supposition that we argue below is quite realistic). In that case, econometric modeling that treats all mergers as the same may lead to false conclusions. Suppose that only one in three mergers is motivated by operating cost savings. Then the measured cost savings implied by simple regression analysis of the entire sample of mergers understates by a factor of three the benefits (and overstates coefficient standard errors) from cost reduction for the subset of mergers that are motivated by cost reduction.

From the perspective of this last critique of econometric studies of cost reduction, case studies may be helpful. One benefit from an analysis of cases is the information provided about bank characteristics associated with particular merger motivations. Those characteristics can act as a set of conditioning variables to be used in econometric analysis to sort banks according to the likely motivation of their mergers.

Therefore, average measured gains from consolidation—whether measured by stock price reactions or by performance improvements—are not reliable indicators of the true average gains. That is not to say, however, that merger optimists are free to ignore these pessimistic results. In addition to the questionable findings about averages, the literature on bank mergers has reported some important cross-sectional differences, and these cross-sectional differences suggest that not all mergers have been equally value maximizing for bank stockholders.

Cross-Sectional Differences and Managerial Incentives

As in other industries (Jensen 1988; Lang, Stulz, and Walkling 1989; Shleifer and Vishny 1990, 1992; Servaes 1991; Healy, Palepu, and Ruback 1992), some bank consolidations produced noncontroversial gains. Some types of bank consolidations are received with enthusiasm by the stock market and offer clear evidence of performance improvement. Acquisitions where acquirers and targets are geographically coincident and where cost-saving opportunities are often transparent, for example, tend to enjoy more favorable market reactions (Houston and Ryngaert 1996, 1997). Some mergers offer clear, visible cost savings in the form of branch closures and payroll savings, while the advantages from strategic mergers (where management stresses product and marketing synergies or diversification) have been harder to identify empirically.

Recent literature has stressed the importance of managerial incentives for determining the success of bank consolidations. This emphasis is particularly plausible in the banking industry. In their analysis of bank profitability and survival, Gorton and Rosen (1995) emphasize that the banking industry traditionally had suffered from regulatory limits on corporate governance that insulated managers from stockholder discipline. Regulations effectively prevented competing banks (or commercial enterprises) from acquiring inefficient banks. Gorton and Rosen argue that much of the exit from banking during the 1980s reflected inefficiency and overcapacity in bank lending resulting from the previous lack of discipline over management.

Gorton and Rosen's (1995) emphasis on tolerance for poor management has been echoed in many earlier studies of bank efficiency. That literature (summarized in Evanoff and Israelevich 1991; Berger, Hunter, and Timme 1993; and Peristiani 1996) finds that much of the cross-sectional variation among banks in efficiency is attributable to x-inefficiency (poor management) rather than to differences in scale, scope, or choice of inputs. The conclusion of these studies is that an important source of efficiency gain in mergers should come from taking banks away from inefficient managers and placing bank operations in the hands of efficient management.

Studies of the gains or losses from bank mergers and acquisitions lend support to the Gorton-Rosen view that entrenched management and regulatory protection from competition explain bank inefficiency in the 1980s.

Whether one measures success by an examination of changes in bank performance after mergers or by reactions of stock prices to consolidation announcements, there is enormous variation across banks, and some variation in the benefits of consolidation can be explained by the incentives and abilities of the acquiring institutions' management.

Allen and Cebenoyan (1991) contend that the combination of the ownership share of management and the concentration of nonmanagement ownership helps to predict which consolidation transactions are most successful. They argue that managers may pursue mergers for value-maximizing reasons or, alternatively, for selfish career objectives. Whether a merger deal will be beneficial to stockholders depends on whether the incentives of managers are aligned with the interests of stockholders (through a combination of the carrot of an ownership stake and the stick of stockholder discipline). Palia (1993) concludes that managers without a large stake in their banks tend to pursue non-value-maximizing mergers for their bank's stockholders, presumably because they seek private gains from the merger. Similarly, Cornett, Palia, and Tehranian (1997) find that the structure of bank CEO compensation is an important predictor of the stock market's reaction to consolidation announcements. If bank CEOs own large stakes in their banks and have highly sensitive pay-for-performance contracts, they tend to choose acquisition targets that inspire more confidence in the stock market.

Stories of the 1980s for the 1990s?

By relating the gains from consolidation to the incentives of management, these studies offer plausible explanations for why potential advantages from consolidation are not always realized. They also suggest a possible synthesis of the contrary evidence regarding average profitability of mergers. Perhaps the potential gains from bank consolidation are great (as suggested by cross-regime comparisons), but in many cases managerial incentives prevent those gains from being realized.

What is less clear is the applicability of the evidence of postmerger performance from 1980s consolidations to the current merger wave in banking. All the aforementioned inquiries that relate managerial incentives to bank efficiency and managerial consolidation decisions use pre-1992 data, and many use samples with an even earlier end date. The problem in applying these results to the post-1992 period is that the recent period is one of far greater competition, far fewer barriers to entry, and significant improvement in performance for the industry as a whole.

The possibility that the 1990s are different from the 1980s suggests the value of examining cases from the 1990s to see if efficiency gains resulting from mergers are larger than in the 1980s. Rhoades (1993b) reported preliminary findings of unusually high cost savings from his sample of nine case studies of mergers between 1986 and 1992, with many cases drawn from 1991 and 1992. While some of his evidence pertains to 1980s transactions, he picked those transactions because he believed they were illustrative of the sorts of transactions that characterize the new wave of mergers. The sample includes Wells-Crocker (1986), BONY-Irving (1988), First Union–Florida National (1989), Fleet/Norstar–Bank of New England (1991), Chemical–Manufacturers Hanover (1991), BankAmerica–Security Pacific (1992), Society-Ameritrust (1992), Comerica–Manufacturers National (1992), and Barnett-First Florida (1992).

As in any case analysis, one can question the representativeness of the sample. But, by selecting a set of cases that exemplify current transactions better than a representative sample of past mergers, Rhoades may actually have minimized selectivity bias for answering his question. His sample of cases was chosen according to the following criteria: large bank size (for both target and acquirer), large geographic overlap between acquirer and target, and explicitly stated motivations of cost cutting. Thus, while Rhoades's sample may have little to say about merger motivations other than cost cutting and while it may have little relevance for understanding the acquisition of small banks by large ones, it is well focused to answer the specific question of whether within-market consolidations between large banks are producing large cost savings in the 1990s. The answer seems affirmative.

The case studies we discuss below have little overlap with those studied by Rhoades (Comerica-Manufacturers is the one case common to both samples), and our cases capture a broader set of phenomena. Like Rhoades, we also provide evidence that the 1990s are different from the 1980s. In particular, we find that competitive pressures are lessening the latitude of managers and thus removing an important impediment to the realization of efficient consolidation.

2   Case Studies

In section 1 we reviewed the existing evidence on the efficiency gains from bank consolidation and pointed to several possible advantages from an examination of individual cases of recent transactions. We posed several questions that helped to motivate our case studies and which we address from the perspective of our nine examples.

To what extent does the consolidation wave reflect pure technological operating cost savings, as opposed to savings from increases in quasi rents (through improved relationship banking) or cost savings from improving the quality of management? Are mergers typically motivated by the same combination of goals, or do mergers typically reflect one goal more than others? Have the mergers of the 1990s produced efficiency gains? Do the circumstances of the cases suggest that the gains from the merger wave of the 1990s should exceed those of the 1980s? What are the lessons of these case studies for future econometric analysis? How important in practice are the methodological problems of performance studies discussed above (for example, realization lags, one-time charges, and difficulties of constructing reliable benchmarks)? Do the cases support the methodological criticisms of using stock price reactions to infer expected gains?

To shed light on these questions, we developed nine case studies, with the assistance of teams of MBA students from the 1994 commercial bank management course taught by one of us (Calomiris) at the University of Illinois. Those case studies were originally published by Calomiris and Karceski (1995). Here we summarize and update them. After describing the way cases were selected, we provide a brief overview and evaluation of each case.

Sample Selection and Performance Criteria

Unlike Rhoades (1993b), we did not target a particular set of banks for which we knew cost cutting, or any other motivation, was the stated objective of the merger. Rather, student teams were allowed to select cases based on their own interest, with the constraint that the merger be completed between 1992 and 1994. Our sample contains an unrepresentative proportion of Midwestern banks, as the location of these banks offered more convenient access for student interviews of management.

Our intent in not constraining the mergers by type was to pull together a somewhat representative sample of cases. As it turned out, our cases differ greatly from one another. The sizes of the banks involved, their locations, their lines of business, and the motivations behind the mergers are different. Technology- or location-driven cost reductions mattered in the stated motivations for many of these mergers, but so did relationship advantages or x-efficiency gains through better management.

Analysis of Cases

Why Merge?

While all our case studies of bank mergers and acquisitions reflect common competitive pressures, the most obvious lesson of the various case studies is the multiple motivations for combining banks. The characteristics of acquirers and acquirees and the nature of their deals reflect those differences. Some deals were primarily motivated by operating cost savings, while in one case there was no possibility of reducing operating costs at all. Market access to a particular client base or location was the most important motive in some cases, sometimes as a means to cross-sell products to customers when their preexisting intermediary lacked comparative advantage in delivering those products. In one case, the managerial inefficiency of the target provided the largest potential gains from acquisition.

The first two case studies—Harris (BMO)–Suburban and First Bank–

Boulevard—exemplify how different the motivations and circumstances of a bank acquisition can be. The Harris takeover of Suburban was, in essence, the acquisition of a reasonably successful suburban Chicago banking franchise by a large Chicago city franchise with an aggressive strategy to buy customer relationships. Harris and Suburban continued to operate independently after the takeover, and there was virtually no opportunity for cost reduction through operating cost savings, executive salaries, or x-efficiency gains. Executives and directors were not eliminated to save overhead costs. The two banks and their managers had worked with one another for many years in the context of a correspondent relationship. The acquisition was a friendly, unsolicited offer made at a high premium. Suburban was a family-owned bank in which the concentration of ownership and control was high. Concentration of control had been enhanced by the issuance of two classes of common stock. X-efficiency gains from improving managerial personnel were not anticipated.

Harris Bank's stock is not traded since it is a wholly owned subsidiary of Bank of Montreal. The stock price of Bank of Montreal showed a slight increase around the announcement date, although it would be inappropriate to attribute that change to such a small acquisition. What we can say, however, is that the Suburban acquisition and, more broadly, the first important implementation of BMO's Vision 2002 did not produce a negative reaction from the market.

In contrast, First Bank's acquisition of Boulevard followed Boulevard's managers' decision to sell an extremely inefficient bank to the highest bidder. Boulevard was the most inefficient bank in Chicago at the time of its acquisition. In a sample of forty-four banks in the Chicago area, Calomiris and Karceski (1994) found that Boulevard ranked at or near the bottom according to every performance measure, including ROE (forty-second), ROA (forty-second), net interest spread (thirty-sixth), and efficiency ratio (forty-fourth). Boulevard's management—which had long avoided takeover—decided in the summer of 1993 that its best option was to sell the bank. Management voluntarily placed the bank on the auction block two months after establishing lucrative golden parachutes. One way to interpret that decision is that Boulevard's management understood that its franchise value to an acquirer was on a declining path. If it did not sell, it would be out-competed by existing banks or de novo entrants and would face continuing losses of customers and charter value. Under those circumstances, entrenched management decided to exit (taking with it a significant share of the bank's existing charter value) rather than maintain a hold on a declining institution.

While Boulevard shareholders benefited from the deal, entrenched management clearly extracted enormous rents as the price for allowing the shareholders to profit from the merger. The winning bid for Boulevard contained a relatively small acquisition premium, and the winning bidder was a regional bank from a different city that specialized in trimming the costs of takeover targets. In the Boulevard deal, the acquirer looked to achieve significant cost cutting, partly through widespread layoffs. Not only did Boulevard's stock appreciate as the result of its placing itself on the auction block; First Bank also saw a modest increase in its stock price (1.1 percent absolutely and 1.7 percent relative to the Standard and Poor's financial index in the two days following the acquisition announcement).

The new competitive pressures of the 1990s encouraged both of these acquisitions, but the channels through which competition operated were different. While both deals were justified by anticipated synergies—cross-selling opportunities in the Harris-Suburban transaction and cost-cutting opportunities in the First Bank–Boulevard deal—those potential efficiency gains do not explain the timing of the acquisitions. In the case of Boulevard, the exit strategy of inefficient management, which determined the timing of the deal, had changed as the result of deregulation and competition. In the Harris-Suburban case, Bank of Montreal's aggressive Vision 2002 relationship-based strategy for Harris to seize market share, which was set in motion in 1992, was the determining factor.

The other seven deals reflect somewhat different motives and circumstances. Table 2-1 summarizes some salient features of each of the nine case studies, and a slightly more detailed summary of each case appears in separate "deal at a glance" exhibits (tables 2-2 through 2-10). Although common themes run through many of the cases, the variation across the cases is at least as striking as the similarities.

Two cases are virtually simultaneous acquisitions by Firstar. They share some important features. In both cases, the targets were mortgage specialists, and Firstar's motivation for acquiring them was expansion of market share in the important Chicago and Twin Cities areas. According to Firstar management, the choice of targets reflected some anticipated cost savings but also cross-selling opportunities. Especially in the case of the acquisition of Investors, management claimed that Investors had special skills in mortgage intermediation but could not realize its full potential because of limited financial resources. Firstar had both the capital and the customer network to allow a significant expansion of mortgage intermediation by Investors' mortgage group. In both acquisitions, Firstar expected to retain the management of the preexisting banks, which it regarded as capable.

Both of Firstar's acquisitions coincided with strong negative reactions in the stock market. The market's negative reactions seem surprising, given Firstar's positive track record of successful acquisitions in the years immediately before these deals, which had demonstrated its ability to realize cost savings and revenue gains from acquiring banks.

As noted in our critique of market reactions as measures of potential

Table 2-1   Key Aspects of Nine Case Studies

Acquirer-Target	In-Market or Across-Market Deal	Relative Size of Acquirer to Target	Motivation for the Deal		Who Initiated the Deal?	Were There Multiple Bidders?	Were There Managerial Parachutes?	Size of the Takeover Premium	Stock Market Reaction		
			Acquirer	Target					Acquirer	Target	Overall
Harris–Suburban	In	Much larger	Expansion according to Vision 2002	Could not turn down such a high premium	Acquirer	No	No	High	Slightly positive	Large positive	Slightly positive
First Bank–Boulevard	Across	Much larger	Entry into the Chicago market	Loan loss problems, entrenched management	Target	Yes	Yes	Low	Slightly positive	Large positive	Positive
Firstar–First Colonial	In and across	Much larger	Increased share in Chicago market	Concerned about the difficulty of keeping a small bank profitable	Target	Yes	No	Average	Negative	Negligible	Negative
Firstar-Investors	In	Much larger	Increased share in Minnesota market	Concerned about the difficulty of keeping a small bank profitable	Target	No	No	Average	Slightly negative	Large positive	Slightly negative
First Chicago–Lake Shore	In	Much larger	Increased share in affluent Chicago market	High takeover premium	Target	Yes	Yes	High	Slightly negative	Large positive	Slightly negative

(continued)

Table 2-1 (continued)

Acquirer–Target	In-Market or Across-Market Deal	Relative Size of Acquirer to Target	Motivation for the Deal — Acquirer	Motivation for the Deal — Target	Who Initiated the Deal?	Were There Multiple Bidders?	Were There Managerial Parachutes?	Size of the Takeover Premium	Stock Market Reaction — Acquirer	Stock Market Reaction — Target	Stock Market Reaction — Overall
Comerica–Manufacturers National	In	Same—merger of equals	Concerned about potentially hostile acquirer in the future, revenue and cost synergies	Concerned about potentially hostile acquirer in the future, revenue and cost synergies	Unknown	No	Yes	Negligible	Large positive	Large positive	Large positive
NationsBank–MNC	Across	Much larger	Entry into Northeastern U.S. market	Severe real estate loan losses	Target	Yes	Unknown	Low	Slightly positive	Positive	Slightly positive
Roosevelt Financial–Farm & Home	In	Slightly larger	Expand to remain independent in the long run	Problems containing costs; concerns over long-run profitability	Target	Yes	Yes	High	Slightly negative	Large positive	Positive
Mercantile–United Postal	In	Much larger	Increased share in Missouri market	Concerned about potentially hostile acquirer in the future	Unknown	No	Yes	Average	Slightly negative	Large positive	Slightly positive

Source: Authors.

Table 2-2   **Harris Bankcorp's Acquisition of Suburban Bancorp, 1994**

Nature of the Deal: Acquisition

Buyer: Harris Bankcorp, Inc., with the help of its parent, Bank of Montreal (BMO)

Headquarters:	Chicago
Total assets:	$13.1 billion (12/31/93), BMO—$102 billion (9/31/94)
ROA:	0.90% (year ended 12/31/93)
ROE:	12.31% (year ended 12/31/93)
Tier 1 capital:	9.00% (12/31/93)
Efficiency ratio:	75.29% (year ended 12/31/93)

Target: Suburban Bancorp, Inc.

Headquarters:	Palatine, Illinois (a Chicago suburb)
Total assets:	$1.47 biliion (9/31/94)
ROA:	1.18% (year ended 12/31/93)
ROE:	15.28% (year ended 12/31/93)
Tier 1 capital:	14.52% (12/31/93)
Efficiency ratio:	67.76% (year ended 12/31/93)
Announcement Date:	April 18, 1994
Completion Date:	October 1, 1994

Accounting Method: Pooling of Interests

Financial Terms: Stock swap—each share of Suburban Bancorp stock was exchanged for 3.9352 shares of Bank of Montreal. The total cost of the takeover was $224 million.

Motivation: Harris made an unsolicited offer for Suburban on March 23, 1994, to expand its presence in the Chicago market according to BMO's Vision 2002 plan. No synergies were created other than cross-selling to existing Suburban customers.

Other Notes: Harris paid a high premium for Suburban (2.42 times book value) and received a bank with a strong balance sheet and a similar organizational culture built around de-centralized management. The takeover was friendly, and there were no other bidders.

Market Reaction

BMO: There was little, if any, reaction because of the large difference in size between BMO and Suburban. BMO stock fell 1.94% to C$25.25 on April 18, 1994, while the Dow Jones Canadian Stock Index dropped 1.61% on the same day.

Suburban: Suburban shares jumped dramatically on news of the takeover. The stock closed at $66 on April 18, 1994, representing a 33% daily gain as well as a 65% eight-day gain (information about the deal may have been leaked during the previous week).

Source: Authors.

efficiency gains, one interpretation of a negative response to an acquisition announcement is that the announcement disappoints another market expectation. In this case, before Firstar's acquisition announcements, the market may have been expecting Firstar to position itself as an acquiree rather than as an acquirer. In the areas where Firstar operates, it suffers a size disadvantage relative to competing giants like Norwest and First Bank System in the Twin Cities and Harris (Bank of Montreal), BankAmerica, Lasalle (ABN Amro), and others in Chicago. As interstate branching becomes a reality, Firstar could suffer an increasing competitive disadvantage due to its limited size. Attempting to grow itself into the position to compete in the future may have been seen as an indication of an unwillingness to maximize its franchise value by allowing itself to be acquired.

Table 2-3   First Bank System's Acquisition of Boulevard Bancorp, 1994

Nature of the Deal: Acquisition

Buyer: First Bank System Inc. (FBS)

Headquarters:	Minneapolis
Total assets:	$26.4 billion (12/31/93)
ROA:	1.17% (year ended 12/31/93)
ROE:	13.8% (year ended 12/31/93)
Efficiency ratio:	59.8% (year ended 12/31/93)

Target: Boulevard Bancorp, Inc.

Headquarters:	Chicago
Total assets:	$1.6 billion (3/25/94)
ROA:	0.45% (year ended 12/31/93)
ROE:	6.44% (year ended 12/31/93)
Tier 1 capital:	6.91% (12/31/93)
Efficiency ratio:	83% (year ended 12/31/93)
Announcement Date:	August 16, 1993
Deadline for Bids:	September 22, 1993
Takeover Announcement Date:	September 30, 1993
Completion Date:	March 26, 1994

Accounting Method: Purchase

Financial Terms: Stock swap—each share of Boulevard stock was exchanged for 0.8132 shares of FBS stock. FBS repurchased and exchanged 6.2 million shares at a total cost of $206.2 million.

Motivation: Boulevard put itself up for sale, after establishing a lucrative $3.7 million golden parachute on June 21, 1993. First Bank submitted the highest bid, facilitating its entrance into the critical Chicago market.

Other Notes: FBS paid only a 10% premium above Boulevard's stock price. Boulevard was suffering from some commercial realty loan losses and inefficient operations. The low takeover premium may have been the result of other banks' inability or unwillingness to fix Boulevard's problems, as well as the golden parachutes.

Market Reaction

First Bank: Even with the large difference in size, FBS's stock went up 1.14% in the two days ended September 30, 1993, while the S&P 500 fell 0.56%. The combined market value of FBS and Boulevard declined less than the S&P financial index during the year ending March 25, 1994.

Boulevard: Boulevard's share price went up almost 31% from the end of June to mid-August 1993, including a 7.53% increase in the two days ending September 30, 1993.

Source: Authors.

First Chicago's acquisition of Lake Shore is a unique example of a large, local Chicago franchise acquiring a successful small bank catering to the affluent retail market around Michigan Avenue. Lake Shore's interest in becoming acquired was the result of a managerial shakeup that brought in a new CEO who felt that the value-maximizing strategy of the bank was to allow itself to become acquired. This suggestion was greeted initially with some alarm by Lake Shore's board of directors. But the board changed its view once the potential profitability to shareholders became apparent. Clearly, Lake Shore was not a bank with entrenched, inefficient management. It was a successful bank that decided that the best use of its

Table 2-4   **Firstar's Acquisition of First Colonial Bankshares, 1995**

Nature of the Deal: Acquisition
Buyer: Firstar Corporation
   Headquarters: Milwaukee
   Total assets: $15.1 billion (12/31/94)
   ROA: 1.51% (year ended 12/31/94)
   ROE: 17.0% (year ended 12/31/94)
   Tier 1 capital ratio: 8.20% (12/31/94)
   Efficiency ratio: 60.6% (year ended 12/31/94)
Target: First Colonial Bankshares Corporation (FCBC)
   Headquarters: Chicago
   Total assets: $1.8 billion (9/30/94)
   ROA: 0.96% (year ended 12/31/94)
   ROE: 11.0% (year ended 12/31/94)
   Overall capital ratio: 11.67% (12/31/93)
   Efficiency ratio: 74% (year ended 12/31/94)
Takeover Announcement Date: July 29, 1994
Approval Date: January 31, 1995
Accounting Method: Pooling of Interests

Financial Terms: Stock swap—each share of FCBC common stock was exchanged for 0.7725 shares of Firstar common stock, and each share of FCBC preferred stock was exchanged for one share of Firstar preferred stock. Firstar exchanged about 6.5 million shares of common stock, and the total cost of the deal was about $314 million.

Motivation: FCBC was less profitable and efficient than its peers in the early 1990s. Management felt it would be difficult for FCBC to remain independent and profitable over the long run. With its long tradition of expansion through acquisitions, Firstar wanted to expand significantly and consolidate its Chicago operations.

Other Notes: Firstar paid a premium of 1.90 times book value. There were multiple bidders, and the deal was friendly.

Market Reaction

Firstar: Firstar's common stock price fell significantly after the announcement. The stock dropped 3.6% on August 1, 1994, while the S&P 500 fell by less than 0.1%. From July 4 through August 12, Firstar declined 4.8%, though the S&P 500 was up 3.5%.

First Colonial: Surprisingly, FCBC's common stock price did not increase on news of the takeover. The stock dropped 1.6% on August 1, 1994, and was unchanged from July 4 through August 12.

Source: Authors.

franchise value—its highly desirable customer relationships—was to sell them to an acquirer. Many banks bid for Lake Shore, which was able to command a handsome premium from First Chicago. First Chicago claimed to see opportunities to both expand its retail market share and cut costs by combining its operations with its acquiree. The market's reaction to First Chicago's acquisition was slightly negative both for First Chicago and for the combined entity in the two days following the announcement.

The merger between Comerica and Manufacturers National is a unique case among the nine: it was a merger of equals. Both banks were in the

Table 2-5   Firstar's Acquisition of Investors Bank Corporation, 1995

Nature of the Deal: Acquisition

Buyer: Firstar Corporation

Headquarters:	Milwaukee
Total assets:	$15.1 billion (12/31/94)
ROA:	1.51% (year ended 12/31/94)
ROE:	17.0% (year ended 12/31/94)
Tier 1 capital ratio:	8.20% (12/31/94)
Efficiency ratio:	60.6% (year ended 12/31/94)

Target: Investors Bank Corporation

Headquarters:	Minneapolis/St. Paul
Total assets:	$1.4 billion (5/1/95)
ROA:	1.03% (year ended 12/31/94)
ROE:	21.6% (year ended 12/31/94)
Tier 1 capital ratio:	6.41% (12/31/93)
Efficiency ratio:	61.2% (year ended 12/31/94)
Announcement Date:	August 19, 1994
Completion Date:	May 1, 1995

Accounting Method: Pooling of Interests

Financial Terms: Stock swap—each share of Investors common stock was exchanged for 0.8676 shares of Firstar common stock, and each share of Investors preferred stock was exchanged for $27.50 in cash. The total cost of the takeover was $106 million.

Motivation: Investors started to consider putting itself up for sale in late 1993. The size and expertise of Investors mortgage banking division were particularly attractive to Firstar, which wanted to diversify its holdings. Management expects some cross-selling opportunities and eventual efficiency gains.

Other Notes: Piper Jaffray estimated the takeover premium at 21.8%, slightly above average for the takeover of a similarly sized Midwest thrift. The deal was friendly, and there were no other bidders.

Market Reaction

Firstar: Firstar's common stock price fell after the announcement. In the week after the announcement, Firstar's stock dropped 0.4%, while the S&P financial index was up 2.2%. From July 15 to August 19, the stock fell by 5.16% (S&P financial index rose 0.88%), though this was partially the result of the announcement of the Firstar–First Colonial deal on July 29, 1994.

Investors: Investors' share price drastically increased with the takeover. In the week after the announcement, Investors' stock climbed 3.06%, and from July 15 through August 19, the share price rose 30.67%.

Source: Authors.

middling size category, and their futures as independent franchises—like those of Firstar and First Chicago—were in doubt. Despite the fact that the merger can be understood partly as a defensive action against future acquisition, management argued that there were strong cost-saving opportunities and product complementarities between the two banking organizations that made the merger desirable. As the result of the acquisition, 1,800 jobs were eliminated (mainly through attrition and early retirement).

Product complementarities within the context of relationship building were also key to the motivations of management; management at both

Table 2-6   **First Chicago's Acquisition of Lake Shore Bancorp, 1994**

Nature of the Deal: Acquisition

Buyer: First Chicago Corporation (FCC)

Headquarters:	Chicago
Total assets:	$56.9 billion (12/31/93)
ROA:	1.50% (year ended 12/31/93)
ROE:	23.0% (year ended 12/31/93)
Tier 1 capital ratio:	8.80% (12/31/93)
Efficiency ratio:	54.2% (year ended 12/31/93)

Target: Lake Shore Bancorp

Headquarters:	Chicago
Total assets:	$1.3 billion (7/8/94)
ROA:	1.03% (year ended 12/31/93)
ROE:	10.04% (year ended 12/31/93)
Tier 1 capital ratio:	10.02% (12/31/93)
Efficiency ratio:	62.7% (year ended 12/31/93)
Announcement Date:	September 21, 1993
Takeover Announcement Date:	November 22, 1993
Completion Date:	July 8, 1994

Accounting Method: Pooling of Interests

Financial Terms: Stock swap based on FCC's twenty-day average closing share price just prior to the official completion date. Each share of LSB stock was exchanged for 0.625 shares of FCC stock. FCC issued about 6.2 million shares at a cost of $323 million.

Motivation: Lake Shore decided to put itself up for sale since its performance and the heated acquisition market afforded a high takeover premium. FCC won the bidding war and received a highly visible and consistently profitable bank in downtown Chicago.

Other Notes: FCC paid a high premium for Lake Shore (2.5 times book value), partially caused by bids from as many as fifteen other institutions. This was a friendly takeover. Some top LSB managers exercised golden parachutes.

Market Reaction

First Chicago: There was little, if any, reaction due to the large difference in size between FCC and LSB. The combined market value of FCC and LSB dropped slightly relative to the S&P Financial index from May 1993 to June 1994.

Lake Shore: LSB's share price rose dramatically in late August 1993 as word leaked out that Lake Shore was looking for a buyer. Over the three-month period beginning in mid-August 1993, LSB's shares went up by 30%.

Source: Authors.

banks viewed the development and maintenance of long-term relationships with customers as central to their strategies. An important product complementarity between the two banks that management expected to develop as the result of the merger was the cross-selling of trust services to the managers of corporate customers. Comerica had the better trust service division, while Manufacturers had the more valuable corporate relationships. The market reaction to the merger announcement was positive for both Comerica and Manufacturers. Stock prices of each entity, and thus of the combined entity, jumped nearly 16 percent in the two days following the announced merger.

Table 2-7   Comerica and Manufacturers National—A Merger of Equals, 1992

Nature of the Deal: Merger

Buyer: Comerica Inc.

Headquarters:	Detroit
Total assets:	$14.4 billion (12/31/91)
ROA:	1.06% (year ended 12/31/91)
ROE:	15.90% (year ended 12/31/91)
Tier 1 capital ratio:	6.60% (12/31/91)
Efficiency ratio:	71.1% (year ended 12/31/91)

Target: Manufacturers National Bank

Headquarters:	Detroit
Total assets:	$13.5 billion (12/31/91)
ROA:	1.02% (year ended 12/31/91)
ROE:	15.31% (year ended 12/31/91)
Tier 1 capital ratio:	6.68% (12/31/91)
Efficiency ratio:	64.0% (year ended 12/31/91)
Announcement Date:	October 28, 1991
Completion Date:	June 18, 1992

Accounting Method: Pooling of Interests

Financial Terms: Stock swap—each of the 31.2 million outstanding shares of Manufacturers common stock was exchanged for 0.81 shares of Comerica common stock.

Motivation: Both banks were concerned about being targets of future, possibly hostile takeover activity. Comerica and Manufacturers had similar corporate cultures that emphasized long-term customer relationships. The banks' areas of expertise complemented each other well, allowing for cross-selling and additional market share expansion opportunities.

Other Notes: There were no other interested parties involved in the negotiations, and the deal was friendly. About 1,800 jobs were cut, but most of this reduction in force was facilitated through early retirement and normal attrition.

Market Reaction

Comerica: In the five-day period ended November 1, 1991, Comerica's stock price jumped 15.5% compared with a corresponding increase in the S&P financial index of 3.4% over the same period.

Manufacturers: In the five-day period ended November 1, 1991, Manufacturers National's stock price increased 15.9%.

Source: Authors.

NationsBank's acquisition of Maryland National Corporation combined a large, high-performance bank with a struggling, middling-sized institution. Maryland National found itself in dire straits as a result of overexposure to local real estate loan losses. The main attraction for NationsBank was gaining a foothold in a region that it had targeted for expansion. Acquiring distressed institutions at low cost has been a key feature of NationsBank's strategy for interregional expansion; knowing how to structure and execute such acquisitions is considered a comparative advantage of NationsBank. Maryland National was not considered a desirable takeover for many banks because of its loan portfolio problems.

NationsBank's strong bargaining position allowed it to pay a small premium over book value and attach stringent conditions to its offer, giving it

Table 2-8   **Takeover of MNC Financial by NationsBank, 1993**

Nature of the Deal: Acquisition

Buyer: NationsBank Corporation

Headquarters:	Charlotte
Total assets:	$118.1 billion (12/31/92)
ROA:	1.00% (year ended 12/31/92)
ROE:	15.8% (year ended 12/31/92)
Shareholders' equity to total assets:	6.62% (12/31/92)
Noninterest expense to total assets:	3.36% (year ended 12/31/92)

Target: Maryland National Corporation (MNC)

Headquarters:	Baltimore
Total assets:	$16.5 billion (9/30/93)
ROA:	0.60% (year ended 12/31/92)
ROE:	7.8% (year ended 12/31/92)
Shareholders' equity to total assets:	7.84% (12/31/92)
Noninterest expense to total assets:	4.30% (year ended 12/31/92)
Announcement of Initial Agreement:	July 17, 1992
Exercise of the Full Purchase Option:	February 18, 1993
Completion Date:	October 1, 1993

Accounting Method: Pooling of Interests

Financial Terms: NationsBank initially paid $200 million for a 17% stake in MNC through preferred stock along with an option to acquire the remaining 83% within five years. Upon exercise of this option, MNC shareholders had the option to exchange each share of MNC stock for $15.17 in cash or 0.2985 shares of NationsBank common stock. This resulted in an extra cost to NationsBank of about $700 million, including the issuance of up to 13.6 million new shares.

Motivation: MNC initiated the deal, driven by an overexposure to real estate risk in the Maryland–Washington, D.C., area. NationsBank seized the opportunity to establish a stronghold in the Northeastern region of the United States.

Other Notes: NationsBank paid a low takeover premium (about 1.25 times MNC's book value). MNC was eager to be acquired, and other large banks were wary of potential hidden problems with MNC's real estate holdings.

Market Reaction

NationsBank: The reaction was positive. NationsBank stock rose 6.1% during the two days surrounding the bank's decision to purchase all of MNC.

MNC: The reaction was positive and remarkably noise free. MNC stock took a one-time jump of 9.7% between February 18 and 19, 1993, and increased just slightly thereafter.

Source: Authors.

the option to cancel the agreement if large, hidden loan problems became apparent. The low price of the acquisition and its locational advantage for NationsBank produced an unusually positive appreciation (6.1 percent) of the acquirer's stock over the two days following its announcement.

Mercantile's acquisition of United Postal Bancorporation saw the absorption of a small S&L by one of the dominant regional banks operating in the same market (St. Louis). The closing of overlapping branch facilities would provide some opportunity for operating cost savings. But United Postal was attractive to Mercantile primarily because of its comparative advantage in mortgage retailing, which reflected its innovative and effi-

Table 2-9   **Purchase of Farm & Home by Roosevelt Financial Group, 1994**

Nature of the Deal: Acquisition

Buyer: Roosevelt Financial Group, Inc. (RFG)

Headquarters:	St. Louis
Total assets:	$4.47 billion (12/31/93)
ROA:	0.90% (year ended 12/31/93)
ROE:	18.2% (year ended 12/31/93)
Tier 1 capital ratio:	2.73% (12/31/93)
Efficiency ratio:	36.86% (year ended 12/31/93)

Target: Farm & Home Financial Corporation (F&H)

Headquarters:	St. Louis
Total assets:	$3.57 billion (12/31/93)
ROA:	0.24% (year ended 12/31/93)
ROE:	4.83% (year ended 12/31/93)
Tier 1 capital ratio:	2.29% (12/31/93)
Efficiency ratio:	69.87% (year ended 12/31/93)
Takeover Announcement Date:	December 3, 1993
Completion Date:	June 30, 1994

Accounting Method: Pooling of Interests

Financial Terms: Stock swap—each share of F&H common stock was exchanged for 0.67 shares of RFG common stock. The total cost of the takeover was about $258 million, and RFG issued about 18 million common shares.

Motivation: Hired by F&H to provide advice on strategic alternatives, Bankers Trust recommended that F&H look for an acquirer. RFG was expanding its holdings rapidly to achieve a size that would allow it to remain independent over the long run. The deal was motivated more by cost-cutting opportunities than by prospects for revenue growth.

Other Notes: RFG paid a premium of 40% above current market value at the time of the announcement. The deal was friendly, and there was probably at least one other bidder.

Market Reaction

Roosevelt: There was little market reaction to the deal. In the two-week period from November 24 through December 8, 1993, RFG's stock price was unchanged, while the S&P financial index increased 3.76% over the same period.

Farm & Home: There was a large positive reaction to the takeover announcement. In the two-week period from November 24 through December 8, 1993, F&H's common stock price went up by 44.1%.

Source: Authors.

cient management. Mercantile hoped to see cross-selling opportunities, particularly between consumer credit and mortgage credit. Thus, the acquisition largely sought to combine Mercantile's existing customer network with the technical skills of United Postal's mortgage unit.

The capital gains enjoyed by United Postal's stockholders illustrate the magnitude of the potential gains to the skillful management of a retail mortgage business. Its stock-holders enjoyed a 600 percent capital gain on their investment over only eighteen months. Mercantile's stock price showed little or no relative decline on the announcement of the deal (its stock price remained unchanged, but other financial stocks rose by an

Table 2-10   **Mercantile's Takeover of United Postal, 1994**

Nature of the Deal: Acquisition

Buyer: Mercantile Bancorporation

Headquarters:	St. Louis
Total assets:	$12.2 billion (12/31/93)
ROA:	0.97% (year ended 12/31/93)
ROE:	13.0% (year ended 12/31/93)
Tier 1 capital ratio:	11.06% (12/31/93)
Efficiency ratio:	64.0% (year ended 12/31/93)

Target: United Postal Bancorporation, Inc. (UPBI)

Headquarters:	St. Louis
Total assets:	$1.3 billion (12/31/93)

No data are available for UPBI since the firm went public in 1992.

Takeover Announcement Date:	August 17, 1993
UPBI Shareholder Approval Date:	December 16, 1993
Completion Date:	February 2, 1994

Accounting Method: Pooling of Interests

Financial Terms: Stock swap—each share of UPBI stock was exchanged for 0.6154 shares of Mercantile stock. The total cost of the takeover was $177 million.

Motivation: Mercantile was engaged in a series of acquisitions in the early 1990s in response to regulatory changes that increased competition in Missouri banking. United Postal realized it was too small to remain independent and so chose to agree to the merger with Mercantile.

Other Notes: Mercantile paid a premium of 27% over UPBI's market value as of August 16, 1993. There were no other bids, and the deal was friendly.

Market Reaction

Mercantile: There was little market reaction to the deal, especially since the total market value of UPBI was only about 12% of Mercantile's total market capitalization at the time of the announcement. In the two-day trading period ending August 20, 1993, Mercantile's stock price was unchanged, while the S&P financial index was up about 2%.

United Postal: There was a large positive reaction to the takeover announcement. In the two-day trading period ending August 20, 1993, UPBI stock went up 18%. Original UPBI shareholders (those who purchased shares during the IPO in the middle of 1991) had a capital gain of about 600% over an eighteen-month holding period.

Source: Authors.

average of 2 percent over the two-day postannouncement window). The value of the combined entity increased slightly on the announcement of the merger.

The final case is the friendly combination of two Missouri thrift institutions of similar size, Roosevelt Financial (the acquirer) and Farm & Home Financial. The predicted gains from the merger were cost reductions. The acquiree was suffering high costs and poor earnings and was searching for a suitor that could provide cost savings and the resources to permit continuing growth. The acquirer was pursuing acquisitions to cut average cost. The stock market reaction to the announced acquisition was highly favorable. Roosevelt's stock price was essentially unchanged, while Farm

& Home's stock price rose 44 percent over the two weeks following the announcement. The value of the combined entity thus rose significantly.

Were Acquirers' Advertised Gains Real?

To evaluate these cases, we ask whether acquirers' claims of anticipated efficiency gains from the mergers were plausible ex ante and whether ex post results are consistent with those claims. Our perspectives on these questions are based on available public data. The availability of relevant information is not identical across cases. Nevertheless, we can address these questions reasonably well in most cases. In evaluating whether acquirers' claims were plausible ex ante, we look at the performance of acquirers at the time of the acquisition announcement. Were acquirers relatively efficient banks with relatively high franchise value (and thus likely able to realize potential gains), or were they struggling institutions attempting to expand their size to discourage would-be acquirers? Were acquisitions associated with improvements in relative performance?

Tables 2-11 through 2-17 examine pre- and postmerger performance for our list of acquirers and acquirees, sometimes at the bank holding company level and, where available and relevant, at the chartered bank level. In each case, we compare our list of banks with constructed benchmarks that provide the most relevant comparisons. We emphasize that our goal is not to prove the advertised benefits of these mergers but rather to ask whether acquirers' claims were plausible in light of available evidence and to investigate whether and to what extent our case studies confirm the broader methodological critiques of earlier studies, outlined previously.

Harris-Suburban

Harris's acquisition of Suburban provides a unique opportunity to gauge the potential value of cross-selling synergies as the motivation for bank mergers. This acquisition achieved virtually no cost reductions through the consolidation of operations or management since Harris's strategy with Suburban (and other acquirees) has been to preserve the independence and separateness of existing management. Furthermore, Harris acquired no other banks between 1990 and 1996 (in part because of regulatory pressures on Harris to improve its compliance with the Community Reinvestment Act before continuing its expansion plans). Thus, measured postmerger gains through 1996 are not complicated by additional acquisitions. (In 1997, Harris acquired Household Bank, adding fifty-four banking locations and bringing to fruition its Vision 2002 goal of a 140-branch distribution network five years ahead of schedule.)

The Harris-Suburban transaction is of particular interest given the natural suspicion with which many observers of corporate mergers greet the idea of revenue synergies. In other industries, acquisitions that lack visible opportunities for cost reduction—typically justified by revenue synergies

Table 2-11   Postmerger Performance of Harris-Suburban, 1992–1997 (percent)

Year and Bank	Asset Growth	Loans to Assets	Net Interest Margin	Noninterest Income to Assets	Noninterest Expense to Assets	Efficiency Ratio[a]	Return on Equity	Earnings per Share ($)
1992								
Harris (BHC)[b]	1.39	53.81	3.49	2.55	4.30	77.08	12.71	16.99
Harris banks[c]		53.86	4.16	2.75	4.89	70.90	14.01	NA
Suburban + 12[d]		52.89	4.22	1.00	3.11	64.88	14.04	NA
Suburban only		41.71	4.14	0.88	2.97	62.78	18.94	NA
Ten unaffiliated banks[e]		39.04	3.91	0.63	2.69	63.30	14.10	NA
Lasalle banks[f]		55.60	3.24	0.67	2.36	65.49	8.83	NA
Firstar Bank, Illinois[g]		55.63	4.54	1.70	4.10	70.93	14.27	NA
First National Bank of Chicago[h]		43.03	2.56	1.85	3.56	91.71	−17.10	NA
1993								
Harris (BHC)	−0.62	58.90	3.48	2.58	4.22	75.29	12.31	17.64
Harris banks	5.43	55.09	3.74	2.50	4.52	72.33	11.74	NA
Suburban + 12	5.35	51.89	4.11	1.06	3.12	65.21	13.89	NA
Suburban only	9.82	43.71	3.92	0.90	3.17	69.27	16.61	NA
Ten unaffiliated banks	10.94	39.73	4.05	0.71	2.78	62.24	15.28	NA
Lasalle banks	15.43	58.43	3.34	0.68	2.28	60.78	10.62	NA
Firstar Bank, Illinois	55.76	60.64	4.81	1.15	3.42	62.33	19.08	NA
First National Bank of Chicago	8.31	37.60	2.43	2.96	3.56	72.94	11.14	NA
Midwest banks[i]	14.86	61.49	4.57	2.15	4.18	66.37	14.70	NA

(*continued*)

Table 2-11   (continued)

Year and Bank	Asset Growth	Loans to Assets	Net Interest Margin	Noninterest Income to Assets	Noninterest Expense to Assets	Efficiency Ratio[a]	Return on Equity	Earnings per Share ($)
1994								
Harris (BHC)	8.70	57.88	3.52	2.21	4.25	80.60	9.70	14.60
Harris banks	13.48	52.71	3.57	2.20	4.42	76.74	11.21	NA
Suburban + 12	4.84	53.04	4.18	0.91	3.02	64.30	15.63	NA
Suburban only	12.32	44.11	3.93	0.82	2.88	64.72	18.82	NA
Ten unaffiliated banks	3.60	42.74	4.07	0.64	2.75	62.67	12.15	NA
Lasalle banks	15.32	59.48	3.49	0.61	2.21	58.13	10.94	NA
Firstar Bank, Illinois	95.96	56.65	4.66	1.09	3.27	61.25	15.25	NA
First National Bank of Chicago	23.34	35.88	2.12	1.43	2.51	83.16	5.24	NA
Midwest banks	42.92	60.66	4.19	2.05	3.79	64.67	15.10	NA
1995								
Harris (BHC)	9.13	61.35	3.39	2.18	3.61	70.42	13.60	22.13
Harris banks	5.75	58.14	3.53	2.03	3.79	68.11	13.71	NA
Suburban + 12	13.68	53.04	3.73	0.79	2.64	62.45	15.13	NA
Suburban only	17.70	46.32	3.44	0.72	2.45	62.16	16.13	NA
Ten unaffiliated banks	7.68	43.49	3.74	0.68	2.65	63.97	12.64	NA
Lasalle banks	28.07	61.23	3.30	0.53	2.29	63.87	8.07	NA
Firstar Bank, Illinois	194.28	51.10	4.35	0.88	3.81	78.35	3.90	NA
First National Bank of Chicago	16.03	32.64	2.14	1.50	2.52	82.73	5.12	NA
Midwest banks	11.20	61.87	3.96	2.12	3.61	63.19	14.60	NA
1996								
Harris (BHC)	10.72	62.55	3.34	1.92	3.46	71.78	11.50	19.10
Harris banks	14.11	58.71	3.41	1.76	3.47	67.08	10.46	NA

Suburban + 12	9.02	63.70	3.73	0.77	2.59	61.41	15.74	NA
Suburban only	9.71	59.36	3.57	0.70	2.37	58.60	16.26	NA
Ten unaffiliated banks	10.33	48.90	3.81	0.75	2.75	64.33	11.75	NA
Lasalle banks	11.60	62.67	2.98	0.58	2.13	63.43	8.95	NA
Firstar Bank, Illinois	−4.48	50.80	4.13	0.97	3.18	67.06	12.39	NA
First National Bank of Chicago	4.58	44.61	2.76	1.28	2.26	67.44	8.18	NA
Midwest banks	5.18	64.08	3.78	2.42	3.84	65.53	15.90	NA
1997 (estimated)								
Harris (BHC)	15.75	56.00	3.27	1.77	3.16	68.53	11.13	NA
Harris banks	17.04	56.11	3.39	1.78	3.45	66.70	11.48	NA
Suburban + 12	−0.10	65.49	3.99	0.80	2.55	56.69	19.15	NA
Suburban only	1.18	61.80	3.87	0.77	2.44	55.28	19.02	NA
Ten unaffiliated banks	9.50	49.74	3.45	0.69	2.50	64.66	10.21	NA
Lasalle banks	13.43	62.35	3.26	0.81	2.38	61.50	11.06	NA
Firstar Bank, Illinois	−5.87	51.62	3.94	0.75	2.86	65.22	13.18	NA
First National Bank of Chicago	19.12	42.51	2.50	1.23	2.17	68.91	8.88	NA
Midwest banks	14.28	59.85	2.89	2.63	3.43	65.28	16.00	NA

Source: Holding company data are taken from annual reports; chartered bank data are from Federal Reserve *Call Reports.* The 1997 statistics are estimates based on first-quarter results.

[a] Noninterest expense/(interest income + noninterest income − interest expense).

[b] Harris bank holding company.

[c] Includes all Chicagoland chartered banks within Harris (the parent bank, the twelve Harris independent banks, and Suburban).

[d] Same as note c but excludes parent bank.

[e] Aggregate of unaffiliated Chicago banks constructed by the authors as a nonconsolidation benchmark (see text for details).

[f] Aggregate of Lasalle's Chicagoland chartered banks (comparable to Harris banks).

[g] Illinois chartered bank of Firstar.

[h] Parent chartered bank of First Chicago.

[i] Value Line Midwest bank index from table 1-3.

Table 2-12   Postmerger Performance of First Bank and NationsBank, 1992–1996 (percent)

Year and Bank	Asset Growth	Loans to Assets	Net Interest Margin	Noninterest Income to Assets	Noninterest Expense to Assets	Efficiency Ratio[a]	Return on Equity	Earnings per Share ($)
1992								
First Bank[b]	4.20	71.76	4.54	2.97	4.32	64.70	16.40	3.26
NationsBank[b]	7.02	61.59	3.82	1.62	3.36	65.96	15.83	2.30
U.S. banks	1.86	57.30	4.42	1.95	3.87	66.15	12.66	NA
1993								
First Bank	11.63	72.99	4.69	2.84	3.93	59.80	13.80	2.47
NationsBank	33.57	58.35	3.23	1.33	2.72	63.71	15.00	2.89
Midwest banks[c]	14.86	61.49	4.57	2.15	4.18	66.37	14.70	NA
U.S. banks	3.60	56.25	4.42	2.13	3.94	65.23	15.34	NA
1994								
First Bank	4.21	73.20	4.74	2.82	4.02	64.00	17.60	2.14
NationsBank	7.56	60.95	3.38	1.53	2.91	63.29	16.10	3.06
Midwest banks	42.92	60.66	4.19	2.05	3.79	64.67	15.10	NA
U.S. banks	8.33	56.06	4.38	2.00	3.76	64.94	14.64	NA
1995								
First Bank	-1.96	80.28	4.91	2.38	3.67	53.90	21.30	4.11
NationsBank	10.43	62.48	3.20	1.64	2.76	60.56	17.10	3.56
Midwest banks	11.20	61.87	3.96	2.12	3.61	63.19	14.60	NA
U.S. banks	7.40	58.39	4.31	2.02	3.65	63.48	14.71	NA
1996								
First Bank	10.96	74.35	3.89	2.38	3.32	52.89	23.80	5.25
NationsBank	-0.80	66.00	3.75	1.96	3.05	56.79	17.95	4.00
Midwest banks	5.18	64.08	3.78	2.42	3.84	65.53	15.90	NA
U.S. banks	5.54	59.91	4.33	2.19	3.73	62.69	14.60	NA

Source: Holding company data are taken from annual reports; chartered bank data are from Federal Reserve *Call Reports.*

[a]Noninterest expense/(interest income + noninterest income − interest expense).

[b]Bank holding company.

[c]Value Line Midwest index from table 1-3.

Table 2-13   Postmerger Performance of Firstar, 1992–1997 (percent)

Year and Bank	Asset Growth	Loans to Assets	Net Interest Margin	Noninterest Income to Assets	Noninterest Expense to Assets	Efficiency Ratio[a]	Return on Equity	Earnings per Share ($)
1992								
Firstar (BHC)[b]	6.99	74.54	5.11	2.39	3.33	64.04	17.40	2.50
U.S. banks[c]	1.86	57.30	4.42	1.95	3.87	66.15	12.66	NA
Firstar Bank, Illinois[d]		55.63	4.54	1.70	4.10	70.93	14.27	NA
First Colonial (BHC)[e]	−3.30	63.00	4.45	1.38	4.09	75.41	8.73	1.08
Ten unaffiliated banks[f]		39.04	3.91	0.63	2.69	63.30	14.10	NA
1993								
Firstar (BHC)	4.75	78.48	5.04	2.56	2.67	62.56	18.60	2.99
Midwest banks[g]	14.86	61.49	4.57	2.15	4.18	66.37	14.70	NA
U.S. banks	3.60	56.25	4.42	2.13	3.94	65.23	15.34	NA
Firstar Bank, Illinois	55.76	60.64	4.81	1.15	3.42	62.33	19.08	NA
First Colonial (BHC)	1.45	59.98	4.44	1.38	3.95	73.04	8.83	1.15
Ten unaffiliated banks	10.94	39.73	4.05	0.71	2.78	62.24	15.28	NA
1994								
Firstar (BHC)	9.50	78.83	4.89	2.26	2.79	60.61	17.00	2.98
Midwest banks	42.92	60.66	4.19	2.05	3.79	64.67	15.10	NA
U.S. banks	8.33	56.06	4.38	2.00	3.76	64.94	14.64	NA
Firstar Bank, Illinois	95.96	56.65	4.66	1.09	3.27	61.25	15.25	NA
Ten unaffiliated banks	3.60	42.74	4.07	0.64	2.75	62.67	12.15	NA
1995								
Firstar (BHC)	26.93	65.89	4.55	2.18	3.24	61.5	15.11	3.00
Midwest banks	11.20	61.87	3.96	2.12	3.61	63.19	14.60	NA
U.S. banks	7.40	58.39	4.31	2.02	3.65	63.48	14.71	NA
Firstar Bank, Illinois	194.28	51.10	4.35	0.88	3.81	78.35	3.90	NA
Ten unaffiliated banks	7.68	43.49	3.74	0.68	2.65	63.97	12.64	NA

(continued)

Table 2-13 (continued)

Year and Bank	Asset Growth	Loans to Assets	Net Interest Margin	Noninterest Income to Assets	Noninterest Expense to Assets	Efficiency Ratio[a]	Return on Equity	Earnings per Share ($)
1996								
Firstar (BHC)	3.11	66.76	4.51	2.30	3.36	58.18	15.95	3.36
Midwest banks	5.18	64.08	3.78	2.42	3.84	65.53	15.90	NA
U.S. banks	5.54	59.91	4.33	2.19	3.73	62.69	14.60	NA
Firstar Bank, Illinois	−4.48	50.80	4.13	0.97	3.18	67.06	12.39	NA
Ten unaffiliated banks	10.33	48.90	3.81	0.75	2.75	64.33	11.75	NA
1997 (estimated)								
Firstar Bank, Illinois	−5.87	51.62	3.94	0.75	2.86	65.22	13.18	NA
Ten unaffiliated banks	9.50	49.74	3.45	0.69	2.50	64.66	10.21	NA
Midwest banks	14.28	59.85	2.89	2.63	3.43	65.28	16.00	NA

Source: Holding company data are taken from annual reports; chartered bank data are from Federal Reserve *Call Reports.* The 1997 statistics are estimates based on first-quarter results.

[a] Noninterest expense/(interest income + noninterest income − interest expense).

[b] Firstar bank holding company.

[c] Aggregate of all chartered U.S. banks from table 1-3.

[d] Firstar Bank, Illinois, an Illinois chartered bank.

[e] First Colonial bank holding company.

[f] Aggregate of all unaffiliated Chicago banks constructed by the authors as a nonconsolidation benchmark (see text for details).

[g] Value Line Midwest bank index from table 1-3.

Table 2-14   Postmerger Performance of First Chicago, 1992–1997 (percent)

Year and Bank	Asset Growth	Loans to Assets	Net Interest Margin	Noninterest Income to Assets	Noninterest Expense to Assets	Efficiency Ratio[a]	Return on Equity	Earnings per Share ($)
1992								
First Chicago Corp. (BHC)[b]	4.18	44.45	2.61	3.02	3.57	71.90	3.40	0.64
First National Bank of Chicago[c]		43.03	2.56	1.85	3.56	91.71	−17.10	NA
American National Bank[d]		64.83	4.36	1.60	2.99	55.37	11.26	NA
U.S. banks[e]	1.86	57.30	4.42	1.95	3.87	66.15	12.66	NA
Ten unaffiliated banks[f]		39.04	3.91	0.63	2.69	63.30	14.10	NA
1993								
First Chicago Corp. (BHC)	3.83	38.69	2.61	4.19	3.27	54.20	23.00	8.43
First National Bank of Chicago	8.31	37.60	2.43	2.96	3.56	72.94	11.14	NA
American National Bank	17.95	64.08	4.36	1.58	3.10	56.58	12.48	NA
Midwest banks[g]	14.86	61.49	4.57	2.15	4.18	66.37	14.70	NA
U.S. banks	3.60	56.25	4.42	2.13	3.94	65.23	15.34	NA
Ten unaffiliated banks	10.94	39.73	4.05	0.71	2.78	62.24	15.28	NA
1994								
First Chicago Corp. (BHC)	12.65	48.93	2.62	2.28	2.86	59.90	5.46	3.62
First National Bank of Chicago	23.34	35.88	2.12	1.43	2.51	83.16	5.24	NA
American National Bank	12.20	74.21	4.72	1.45	3.12	56.04	15.03	NA
Midwest banks	42.92	60.66	4.19	2.05	3.79	64.67	15.10	NA
U.S. banks	8.33	56.06	4.38	2.00	3.76	64.94	14.64	NA
Ten unaffiliated banks	3.60	42.74	4.07	0.64	2.75	62.67	12.15	NA
1995								
First Chicago Corp. (BHC)	90.33	52.81	2.63	2.12	2.90	56.35	14.30	3.45
First National Bank of Chicago	16.03	32.64	2.14	1.50	2.52	82.73	5.12	NA
American National Bank	6.11	78.28	5.06	1.19	3.17	55.94	14.69	NA
Midwest banks	11.20	61.87	3.96	2.12	3.61	63.19	14.60	NA

(*continued*)

Table 2-14   (continued)

Year and Bank	Asset Growth	Loans to Assets	Net Interest Margin	Noninterest Income to Assets	Noninterest Expense to Assets	Efficiency Ratio[a]	Return on Equity	Earnings per Share ($)
U.S. banks	7.40	58.39	4.31	2.02	3.65	63.48	14.71	NA
Ten unaffiliated banks	7.68	43.49	3.74	0.68	2.65	63.97	12.64	NA
1996								
First Chicago Corp. (BHC)	−14.25	62.14	2.76	2.44	3.11	59.87	17.00	4.32
First National Bank of Chicago	4.58	44.61	2.76	1.28	2.26	67.44	8.18	NA
American National Bank	24.05	81.09	4.46	1.09	2.72	53.84	15.51	NA
Midwest banks	5.18	64.08	3.78	2.42	3.84	65.53	15.90	NA
U.S. banks	5.54	59.91	4.33	2.19	3.73	62.69	14.60	NA
Ten unaffiliated banks	10.33	48.90	3.81	0.75	2.75	64.33	11.75	NA
1997 (estimated)								
First Chicago National Bank	19.12	42.51	2.50	1.23	2.17	68.91	8.88	NA
Midwest banks	14.28	59.85	2.89	2.63	3.43	65.28	16.00	NA
Ten unaffiliated banks	9.50	49.74	3.45	0.69	2.50	64.66	10.21	NA

Source: Holding company data are taken from annual reports; chartered bank data are from Federal Reserve *Call Reports.* The 1997 statistics are estimates based on first-quarter results.

[a]Noninterest expense/(interest income + noninterest income − interest expense).

[b]First Chicago's holding company.

[c]Main chartered bank within the holding company.

[d]FCC's specialist in middle-market business lending.

[e]Aggregate of all chartered U.S. banks from table 1-3.

[f]Aggregate of all unaffiliated Chicago banks constructed by the authors as a nonconsolidation benchmark (see text for details).

[g]Value Line Midwest bank index from table 1-3.

Table 2-15 Postmerger Performance of Comerica, 1992–1996 (percent)

Year and Bank	Asset Growth	Loans to Assets	Net Interest Margin	Noninterest Income to Assets	Noninterest Expense to Assets	Efficiency Ratio[a]	Return on Equity	Earnings per Share ($)
1992								
Comerica (BHC)[b]	0.55	65.81	4.73	1.51	4.07	76.90	12.10	1.99
Old Kent (BHC)[b]	4.97	60.06	4.81	1.44	3.53	64.00	16.25	2.57
U.S. banks[c]	1.86	57.30	4.42	1.95	3.87	66.15	12.66	NA
1993								
Comerica (BHC)	2.74	67.22	4.65	1.65	3.76	68.00	15.94	2.85
Old Kent (BHC)	5.62	56.37	4.82	1.46	3.73	62.70	16.65	2.90
Midwest banks[d]	14.86	61.49	4.57	2.15	4.18	66.37	14.70	NA
U.S. banks	3.60	56.25	4.42	2.13	3.94	65.23	15.34	NA
1994								
Comerica (BHC)	15.48	64.26	4.32	1.43	3.31	64.50	16.74	3.28
Old Kent (BHC)	10.73	59.15	4.63	1.35	3.74	63.60	16.04	3.02
Midwest banks	42.92	60.66	4.19	2.05	3.79	64.67	15.10	NA
U.S. banks	8.33	56.06	4.38	2.00	3.76	64.94	14.64	NA
1995								
Comerica (BHC)	12.78	66.43	4.19	1.46	3.06	60.09	16.46	3.54
Old Kent (BHC)	13.93	61.94	4.46	1.55	3.66	64.38	14.58	3.11
Midwest banks	11.20	61.87	3.96	2.12	3.61	63.19	14.60	NA
U.S. banks	7.40	58.39	4.31	2.02	3.65	63.48	14.71	NA
1996								
Comerica (BHC)	-3.56	76.62	4.54	1.48	3.39	64.21	15.98	3.55
Old Kent (BHC)	8.33	64.02	4.41	1.68	3.42	64.44	15.86	3.39
Midwest banks	5.18	64.08	3.78	2.42	3.84	65.53	15.90	NA
U.S. banks	5.54	59.91	4.33	2.19	3.73	62.69	14.60	NA

Source: Holding company data are taken from annual reports; chartered bank data are from Federal Reserve *Call Reports*.

[a] Noninterest expense/(interest income + noninterest income − interest expense).

[b] Bank holding company.

[c] Aggregate of all chartered U.S. banks from table 1-3.

[d] Value Line Midwest bank index from table 1-3.

Table 2-16 Postmerger Performance of Mercantile and Roosevelt, 1992–1996 (percent)

Year and Bank	Asset Growth	Loans to Assets	Net Interest Margin	Noninterest Income to Assets	Noninterest Expense to Assets	Efficiency Ratio[a]	Return on Equity	Earnings per Share ($)
1992								
Roosevelt (BHC)[b]	4.92	38.91	2.22	0.51	1.66	65.86	11.11	0.88
Mercantile (BHC)[b]	15.54	61.93	4.34	1.42	3.47	65.00	11.95	2.42
Boatmen's (BHC)[b]	8.45	52.93	4.35	1.86	3.47	66.37	14.20	2.42
U.S. banks[c]	1.86	57.30	4.42	1.95	3.87	66.15	12.66	NA
1993								
Roosevelt (BHC)	25.77	35.18	2.39	0.19	1.30	55.08	12.86	1.11
Mercantile (BHC)	5.01	60.03	4.55	1.52	3.56	64.00	13.00	2.79
Boatmen's (BHC)	9.27	54.55	4.46	1.92	3.69	68.98	15.42	2.78
Midwest banks[d]	14.86	61.49	4.57	2.15	4.18	66.37	14.70	NA
U.S. banks	3.60	56.25	4.42	2.13	3.94	65.23	15.34	NA
1994								
Roosevelt (BHC)	11.02	36.43	2.26	−0.13	1.37	71.27	5.85	0.48
Mercantile (BHC)	1.80	62.12	4.55	1.42	3.39	59.00	15.82	3.22
Boatmen's (BHC)	6.13	56.74	4.35	1.87	3.52	65.07	16.14	3.17
Midwest banks	42.92	60.66	4.19	2.05	3.79	64.67	15.10	NA
U.S. banks	8.33	56.06	4.38	2.00	3.76	64.94	14.64	NA

1995								
Roosevelt (BHC)	6.89	39.70	2.19	−0.29	0.97	57.17	4.60	0.56
Mercantile (BHC)	9.40	64.46	4.25	1.56	3.01	56.69	16.05	3.74
Boatmen's (BHC)	2.51	58.64	4.26	2.01	3.56	65.04	15.88	3.41
Midwest banks	11.20	61.87	3.96	2.12	3.61	63.19	14.60	NA
U.S. banks	7.40	58.39	4.31	2.02	3.65	63.48	14.71	NA
1996								
Roosevelt (BHC)	−13.50	55.13	2.49	−0.46	1.58	87.94	1.10	0.13
Mercantile (BHC)	19.42	67.27	4.20	1.58	3.36	62.88	11.90	3.10
Midwest banks	5.18	64.08	3.78	2.42	3.84	65.53	15.90	NA
U.S. banks	5.54	59.91	4.33	2.19	3.73	62.69	14.60	NA

Source: Holding company data are taken from annual reports; chartered bank data are from Federal Reserve *Call Reports.*

[a]Noninterest expense/(interest income + noninterest income − interest expense).

[b]Bank holding company.

[c]Aggregate of all chartered U.S. banks from table 1-3.

[d]Value Line Midwest bank index from table 1-3.

Table 2-17   Bank Stock Performance, 1990–1996

	One-Year Return (Dec.)						Two-Year Return (Dec.)	
	1990	1991	1992	1993	1994	1995	1992–1993	1994–1995
Suburban	−48.1	94.5	42.1	27.6			81.3	
First Bank	−17.4	92.2	21.2	13.0	11.6	54.4	37.0	72.3
Boulevard	−47.4	8.2	9.4	64.5			80.0	
Firstar	−8.9	77.5	33.9	0.6	−9.4	53.7	34.7	39.2
First Colonial	−39.5	54.6	0.0	28.4	9.5		28.3	
Investors	−25.0	150.0	31.1	94.2	−14.4		154.6	
First Chicago	−51.7	62.4	54.8	21.4	14.8	49.8	87.9	71.9
Lake Shore	−42.9	41.8	32.5	25.4			66.1	
NBD	7.9	40.1	13.7	−6.1	−4.4	51.6	6.8	45.0
Comerica	−7.1	29.3	23.7	−13.7	−4.1	70.9	6.8	64.0
Manufacturers	−9.5	94.1						
Old Kent	−13.2	55.9	51.4	−8.9	4.9	47.9	37.9	55.2
NationsBank	−48.3	84.8	30.6	−1.4	−4.4	59.8	28.7	52.7
MNC Financial	−84.0	50.0	164.1					
Mercantile	−14.0	87.1	32.5	−4.3	7.4	51.8	26.8	63.0
United Postal				73.5				
Roosevelt	−42.1	80.3	167.1	55.0	7.7	33.5	314.0	43.8
Farm & Home	−42.4	153.8	27.8	79.4			129.3	

| | Market-to-Book Value (End-of-April) | | | | | | |
	1990	1991	1992	1993	1994	1995	1996
Suburban	0.75	0.63	1.12	1.55	1.62		
First Bank	1.00	1.43	1.87	1.64	1.91	2.18	3.05
Boulevard	1.42	0.90	0.66	0.87			
Firstar	1.06	1.17	1.72	1.94	1.92	1.61	2.26
First Colonial	1.26	1.23	1.07	1.19	1.75		
Investors					1.36	1.62	
First Chicago	0.83	0.69	0.92	1.20	1.30	1.27	1.64[a]
Lake Shore	2.26	1.47	1.67	1.98	2.46		
NBD	1.27	1.53	1.68	1.72	1.46	1.49	
Comerica	1.00	1.20	1.00	1.73	1.57	1.40	1.98
Manufacturers	0.99	1.23	1.83				
Old Kent	1.13	1.14	1.67	1.94	1.61	1.55	1.74
NationsBank	1.30	1.28	1.82	1.56	1.42	1.26	1.87
MNC Financial	1.05	0.42	0.77	0.97			
Mercantile	0.97	1.11	1.53	1.44	1.76	1.55	1.94
Roosevelt	0.54	0.48	0.78	2.24	1.45	1.45	1.91
Farm & Home	0.26	0.27	0.63	0.69			

Source: Prices and shares are from Center for Research in Securities Prices (CRSP). Book values (which exclude preferred stock) are from annual reports and are prior December figures.

Note: Returns are defined in percentage terms. The use of April stock prices allows comparisons of book values and market values after book value statistics had been made public.

[a]For 1996, the market-to-book ratio for First Chicago is for First Chicago–NBD.

—often have performed poorly and may have been motivated more by managerial rent seeking than by profit maximization. Are cross-selling opportunities in banking real or just the newest justification for managerial empire building? Of our nine cases, Harris-Suburban provides the clearest window to view that question.

Harris's management regards the Suburban merger as a success story. According to Charles Tonge, the operating officer responsible for implementing Harris's takeover strategy in the Chicago area, revenue growth at Suburban (the key objective for the acquisition) has exceeded preacquisition expectations. The primary sources of revenue growth envisioned at the time of the merger were (1) combining Suburban's comparative advantage in access to low-cost deposits and customer relationships with Harris's other banking affiliates' comparative advantage in marketing and originating loans to increase Suburban's loan-to-asset ratio and the net interest margin for the new combined entity and (2) boosting fee income by bringing Harris's expertise in trust and asset management to Suburban's customers and by combining Harris's expertise in residential mortgage origination and resale with Suburban's mortgage origination opportunities. According to Tonge, home equity lending, asset management services, and other new products and services have permitted significant cross-selling and up selling (which he defines as moving existing customers up to longer-term, higher-margin products and services, in addition to simply selling them more products and services).

Tonge believes Harris's success reflected not only the types of revenue synergies that the bank planned to exploit, but the strategic decisions made about how to do so.

> In order of importance, the three key strategic decisions were, first, to target rapid growth to lock in customer relationships before other entrants had a chance; second, to set the right incentives for the bank presidents [of the acquired affiliates] by granting them separate accounting and managerial independence and rewarding high growth rather than simply current ROE; and third, to keep acquisition costs down by demonstrating a commitment to de novo branching as a potential alternative to acquisition. (Tonge 1997)

Tonge also emphasizes that the future profitability of Harris's Chicagoland operations will depend on its ability to cut costs by promoting PC (personal computer) banking, now in its infancy.

Harris's growth reflects not only its newly acquired customer base but the new customers that its expanded network has allowed it to attract. In terms of household contacts, the acquisition of Suburban coincided with a remarkable internal growth in Harris's customer base of roughly 30,000 households per year over and above those acquired directly in its acquisitions, according to internal bank calculations. With its recent acquisition of Household, Harris now serves over 800,000 households, or one-fifth of all Chicagoland households (compared with one-fourteenth in 1994).

Tonge sees the primary advantages from the acquisition as combining Suburban's customer contacts and deposit accounts with the lending expertise developed in Harris's pre-Suburban Chicagoland acquisitions (which we label the twelve Harris community banks). To investigate that claim, in table 2-11 we report performance measures for Harris in four different ways: for the holding company as a whole, for the Chicagoland chartered banks within the holding company taken together (the parent bank, plus the twelve independents, plus Suburban), for Suburban plus the twelve independents taken together, and for Suburban alone. Maintaining separate charters for its acquired banks permits this decomposition. Being a subsidiary of the Bank of Montreal, however, precludes the use of market-based benchmarks (stock returns or market-to-book value ratios).

For purposes of comparison, we report several performance benchmarks. One of those benchmarks is a composite of ten unaffiliated Chicagoland banks, each of which had assets in excess of $250 million in 1993 (with aggregate assets of $7.25 billion in that year) and remained independent from 1991 through 1996. While this constructed composite may have some survivorship bias, we found that the 1993 ROE for the composite equaled the median of Chicagoland banks in 1993. Thus, the intertemporal changes experienced by this group represent a reasonable counterfactual of what Suburban's changes would have been had it remained independent. The other benchmarks for comparison are the S&P Midwest banking industry composite and several individual Chicagoland banks. Of these individual banks, Lasalle is most like Harris—it is owned by Dutch giant ABN Amro and has pursued an aggressive strategy of seizing market share by acquisitions in recent years. Firstar Bank Illinois and First National Bank of Chicago are included for comparison because their primary business is retail banking in Chicago.

As table 2-11 shows, Suburban enjoyed rapid postacquisition loan and revenue growth during 1995 and 1996. Over those two years, total assets grew from $1.5 billion to $1.9 billion, while the loan-to-asset ratio rose from 44.1 percent to 59.4 percent. The comparable increases for the composite of Suburban and the twelve Harris independents were $5.7 billion from $4.6 billion in total assets and 63.7 percent from 53.0 percent in the loan-to-asset ratio. Compared with other banks, the loan growth of Harris's retail banking affiliates has been large. The composite of ten unaffiliated Chicagoland banks saw lower asset growth than Suburban (or Suburban plus the twelve Harris independents) and less increase in the loan-to-asset ratio. Only Lasalle Bank, which has pursued a similar revenue-oriented acquisition strategy, has seen higher asset growth than Suburban (or Suburban-cum-Harris independents) and has reached a comparably high loan-to-asset ratio.

The growth in assets and customers achieved by Harris's independent retail banking affiliates was achieved without sacrificing net interest margin and alongside reductions in the ratio of noninterest expenses to total assets. That is, loan growth has not been achieved by reducing the profitability of lending or by spending a lot of resources to attract low-cost deposits (through large noninterest expenses). The combination of high margins and high loan growth has resulted in high ROE and an improved (lowered) efficiency ratio.

While these facts seem to bear out Harris's claims for the profitability of its revenue-oriented acquisition strategy, the parent bank has not gained as much as its affiliates have, and one can question whether some costs of growing the affiliates may have been borne by the parent bank. Taken as a whole, Harris's Chicagoland banking operation (that is, the parent bank plus Suburban plus the twelve Harris independents) has shown ROE comparable to that of the ten unaffiliated banks, although Harris outperformed Lasalle and First National Bank of Chicago.

There are two ways to read the evidence on Harris. According to a sanguine view, Harris's rapid loan growth and the new customer relationships that it has captured will now set the stage for growth in total ROE through future growth in revenue per customer. According to that view, the low current profitability of Harris and of other banks based in Chicago (compared with the rest of the Midwest) reflects the aggressive competition for market share today to lock in valuable relationships for the future. An alternative, jaundiced view would point more skeptically to the low current ROE of Harris taken as a whole and question the future growth in the profitability of retail banking in Chicagoland and the desirability of having invested the Bank of Montreal's capital there. Whatever one's view, however, Harris seems to have achieved its short-term asset and revenue growth goals for its independents in the mid-1990s through its acquisition strategy. Whether those goals were wisely chosen remains to be seen.

First Bank–Boulevard and NationsBank-MNC

Because First Bank does not maintain a separate Illinois state bank charter, it is not possible to examine the postmerger performance of the Chicago operations of First Bank–Boulevard. By any measure, however, First Bank's expansion strategy is extremely successful. If Boulevard needed a high-performance acquirer to lower its costs and boost its revenue, First Bank seems to fit that description.

At the time of its acquisition of Boulevard in early 1994, First Bank had a market-to-book ratio of 1.91 (one of the highest in the industry). From

January 1994 through December 1995, First Bank's stockholders received a two-year return of 72.3 percent, and its market-to-book ratio rose to 3.05 by April 1996. As shown in table 2-12, First Bank's ROE in 1995 and 1996 are far above nationwide or Midwest benchmarks, and its earnings per share more than doubled from the end of 1993 to the end of 1996. This exceptional performance from the end of 1993 to the end of 1996 reflects a combination of a dramatic fall in noninterest expenses relative to assets, a persistently high net interest margin, and growth in noninterest income that has kept pace with asset growth.

First Bank continues to expand aggressively. In March 1997, it announced the acquisition of the Oregon-based U.S. Bancorp (in an \$8.8 billion stock swap), which was greeted favorably by the stock market (the stock of both banks rose on the announcement). This marks a new phase of westward expansion for First Bank.

Like First Bank, NationsBank does not maintain a separate charter that can be linked to the former operations of MNC. Instead, one has to gauge NationsBank's acquisition success by looking at its general performance. NationsBank has been one of the most aggressive acquirers in the country (see table 2-18). It has grown through acquisitions from \$118 billion in assets in 1992 to \$186 billion at the end of 1996. As table 2-12 shows, that growth has been accompanied by an unusually high ROE (17.95 percent in 1996), by a near doubling of its earnings per share, and by an impressive efficiency ratio of 56.95 percent.

NationsBank's market-to-book ratio in 1993 was 1.56, and it has remained below other banking system leaders since 1993 (as shown in table 2-17). The weakness in NationsBank's market-to-book value during the 1990s does not reflect declining profit or operating inefficiency but rather its willingness to pay high prices for some of its largest acquisitions. NationsBank paid 2.7 times book value (almost 50 percent more than the contemporaneous stock price) for Boatmen's Bank in August 1996 (at a time when 2 times book value was the norm for similar acquisitions), and in September 1997 NationsBank purchased Barnett Bank for 4 times book value. In the first transaction, its stock price declined roughly 8 percent when the acquisition was announced, and in the second case, its stock price declined nearly 6 percent on the announcement. NationsBank's management has defended these purchases and continues to disagree with skeptical market analysts in its projected cost savings and revenue growth from these acquisitions. In January 1997, for example, one market analyst forecasted roughly \$50 million dollars less in earnings growth and expense reduction for 1997 than NationsBank's management (*Wall Street Journal,* January 14, 1997, A3). In addition to disagreeing with these forecasts, NationsBank has been putting its money where its mouth is: in 1996, it repurchased over 17 million shares (a significant proportion of the 98 million shares issued in the Boatmen's acquisition), and it announced and followed through on plans to repurchase more than 11 percent of its outstanding common stock in 1997.

Some market analysts agree with NationsBank's view that these mergers will create more value than they have cost NationsBank's stockholders. The May 10, 1997, *Standard and Poor's Stock Reports* issued by a buy recommendation for NationsBank, based in large part on the perceived benefits from the Boatmen's acquisition. In its October 14, 1996, buy recommendation, Gerard Klauer Mattison & Co. argued that NationsBank's projections in its acquisition of Boatmen's were achievable for Nations-Bank but not for other would-be acquirers that lack its breadth and efficiency. It based that view largely on the opportunities for improved marketing and revenue growth from the purchase:

> We view NB as the most undervalued major bank stock. . . . Without question, one of the most controversial mergers in banking history, the NB/BOAT deal has many hidden positives. Thus, while many investors and other banking observers criticized the deal strongly, we applaud it. . . . Boatmen's is a "linchpin" strategic acquisition for NB. Its geographic fit is ideal, adding seven new states and deepening penetration in two others. The market shares are mostly very high, and the potential for cost cutting and cross-selling is very large. . . . We see a strong opportunity for NB to enhance revenues by selling products to the under-marketed BOAT customer base (1, 3, 9, 12).

Firstar's Acquisitions

Firstar's acquisitions in 1995 did not result in the dilution of earnings per share or in substandard performance in comparison with other Midwestern banks, as shown in table 2-13. While the negative market reaction to its expansion strategy resulted in a 9.4 percent stockholder return for 1994, Firstar's 1995 stock return was 53.7 percent. Firstar is not as highly prized a franchise as First Bank, but its April 1995 market-to-book ratio (1.61) still exceeded the nationwide average of 1.55, and its book-to-market ratio rose significantly in 1996, exceeding its value in April 1994 (before our two acquisition announcements).

The consequences of Firstar's acquisition of First Colonial can be gauged in greater detail. That acquisition resulted in a tripling of Firstar's Illinois operations during 1995, which is visible in its separately chartered Illinois bank. Data on that bank permit an evaluation of Firstar's ability to reap the cost savings that it had projected. One-time charges in 1995 raised noninterest expenses for that year, but noninterest expenses relative to assets have subsequently fallen faster than comparable benchmarks (from 3.3 percent of assets at the end of 1994 to 2.9 percent of assets in early 1997).

Thus, from the perspective of cost cutting, the First Colonial transaction seems to have resulted in improved efficiency. That conclusion is further supported by the fact that the decline in expenses did not coincide with a reduction in net interest margin (given the production complementarity between increases in net interest margin and increases in physical expenses). Firstar Illinois' first-quarter 1997 ROE of 13.2 percent is significantly higher that the 10.8 percent (size-weighted) ROE of the combination of Firstar Illinois and First Colonial in 1993.

The Firstar–First Colonial merger, however, did result in a decline in assets in 1996 and a slight decline in the loan-to-asset ratio. The acquisition of First Colonial produced surprising widespread defections of its loan officers, who moved to other banks and took many customers with them. Those reactions reflected the reduced autonomy of loan officers following Firstar's centralization of control over its acquiree's loan portfolio. Thus, while Firstar is posting a reasonable ROE in comparison with other Chicago-land banks and has achieved significant cost savings, it was blindsided by employee morale problems that hampered its revenue growth.

The Firstar Illinois experience reflects well on Harris Bank's approach to acquisition, which emphasizes preserving acquiree autonomy (at least during the initial postacquisition period). Someday Harris may choose to consolidate its acquirees (after having cemented customer relationships between customers and the parent through up-selling and cross-selling) at little cost to its loan portfolio. But the difference in the growth performance of Firstar and Harris acquirees suggests that the preservation of local autonomy may be crucial to maintaining postacquisition revenue growth.

Did the negative stock price reaction to Firstar's expansion strategy in 1994 reflect market anticipation of Firstar's postacquisition problems? Probably not. First, market reaction was negative for both acquisitions, while only the First Colonial acquisition resulted in stalled revenue growth. Second, it would be hard to argue that the market foresaw a personnel problem that the bank itself had not anticipated. It is more plausible that the negative reaction of the market to Firstar's expansion strategy in 1994 reflected market disappointment that Firstar had not positioned itself to be acquired, rather than concerns about Firstar's ability to achieve cost reductions or maintain above-average performance.

First Chicago–Lake Shore

First Chicago is probably the most obvious "suspect" acquirer. In six of our nine cases, price reactions were positive for the combined entity. In four of those six cases, price reactions were positive for both banks involved in the merger. The three cases of negative price reactions for combined entities were the two Firstar cases and First Chicago's acquisition of Lake Shore. While we have argued that Firstar's stock price decline did not reflect market views about the efficiency gains from its acquisitions, in the case of First Chicago it is easier to make an argument that the market reasonably doubted First Chicago's ability to create value through an acquisition.

In analyzing First Chicago's performance, it is important to distinguish the local banking operations of First Chicago's parent bank in Chicago (First National Bank of Chicago) from the operations of the rest of the holding company (which include major profit centers that operate as separate entities, such as its private equity affiliate, its middle-market lender—American National Bank—and its Delaware-based credit card bank). In 1994, 45 percent of First Chicago's net income came from credit card banking profits; American National and venture capital profits accounted for another 24 percent of holding company net income. While one could argue that some gains from the Lake Shore acquisition would show up in First Chicago's nonbank affiliates, the primary gains anticipated from the acquisition of Lake Shore entailed retail bank cost cutting, and thus it seems reasonable to ask whether First National Bank of Chicago (FNBC) was up to the task of enhancing the efficiency of Lake Shore.

At the holding company level, First Chicago has seen improvement in its market-to-book value over the 1990s, which largely reflected credit card profits, private equity earnings, and (in 1995 and 1996) its merger with National Bank of Detroit (NBD), which enjoyed a higher market-to-book ratio. The volatility of the holding company's profits indicates that the sources of holding company profitability have been dissimilar from many other banks. Moreover, the data in table 2-14 indicate that First Chicago's banking flagship—FNBC—was inefficient and unprofitable before the acquisition of Lake Shore. While First Chicago's holding company earned a 1993 ROE of 23 percent before acquisition, FNBC's ROE was only 11.14 percent in that year, and FNBC's 1992 ROE had been −17.10 percent. FNBC's efficiency ratio was extremely poor at 91.7 percent in 1992 and 72.9 percent in 1993.

In December 1995, First Chicago entered into a merger of equals with National Bank of Detroit (NBD) in an effort for its management to remain at least partly in control of its struggling franchise. Despite high ROE and improved efficiency and earnings per share after the FCC-NBD merger, FNBC performance has remained lackluster. There is little evidence to suggest that FCC's merger with NBD will lead to efficiency gains in First Chicago's core banking operations. Since 1994, ROE at FNBC has remained persistently below those of relevant benchmarks.

Thus, First Chicago's performance and consolidation history might be seen as evidence that it is pursuing a survival and acquisition strategy that favors managerial independence (and perquisites) over stockholder profits. While we do not claim to offer proof of that proposition, the facts for this case are at least consistent with many of the claims of the consolidation pessimists.

Comerica-Manufacturers

The 1992 merger of equals between Comerica and Manufacturers produced some one-time expenses in 1992, but subsequent growth and performance have been good. Table 2-15 presents data for Comerica-Manufacturers as a combined entity, from the year before the merger through 1996. We compare Comerica-Manufacturers' performance with that of Old Kent Bank, the other major bank holding company operating primarily in Michigan during this period. Old Kent has been a fast-growing and successful bank and has expanded through acquisition and de novo branching during the 1990s, both within Michigan and into Indiana and Illinois. Thus, it does not provide a counterfactual nonconsolidation benchmark against which to measure the effects of the merger of Comerica and Manufacturers. Nevertheless, the comparison with Old Kent is useful for gauging how disruptive the merger of equals has been. Some industry analysts are skeptical of the advantages of such mergers because of potential difficulties in integrating management and operations that can slow progress and reduce performance.

Comerica-Manufacturers and Old Kent have had similar experiences over the period 1993–1996. They have grown at similar rates and enjoyed similarly high net interest margins, high ROEs, and low efficiency ratios. The earnings-per-share growth has been high in both franchises. The market-to-book ratios of Comerica and Old Kent have been comparable over the past few years as well. We conclude from this comparison that the Comerica-Manufacturers merger of equals has successfully avoided potential problems of integrating management and operations.

Mercantile–United Postal and Roosevelt–Farm & Home

The two St. Louis 1994 acquisition cases are best considered together (see table 2-16), particularly because Mercantile ended up acquiring Roosevelt in 1997. Boatmen's Bank (which was acquired by NationsBank and thus filed no annual report for 1996) appears as a St. Louis banking benchmark against which to gauge the performance of these acquisitions. Boatmen's itself is not an ideal nonmerger counterfactual; it has been actively engaged in acquisitions over the past decade, particularly in the Southwest. We also include the Midwest regional benchmark.

Before reviewing Roosevelt's accounts, we point out that these accounts have changed dramatically from one annual report to the next: note the difference in reported 1993 ROE from the 1993 income statement (given in table 2-9) and the 1993 ROE reported in the 1996 annual report (in table 2-16). Given the dramatic changes in the way accounts have been reported, we suggest caution when using the balance sheet and income statement data that we report for Roosevelt in table 2-16. In particular, 1996 ROE was substantially reduced by one-time charges. Those charges included a regulatory charge (faced by all thrifts) to recapitalize the thrift deposit insurance fund and a payment to terminate certain swap transactions.

From the perspective of some of our indicators, Roosevelt's postacquisition performance during 1995 and 1996 was disappointing when compared with that of Mercantile and other U.S. banks. As with other thrifts, Roosevelt's net interest margin and fee income have remained low compared with those of banks. Roosevelt–Farm & Home's ROE, earnings per share, and noninterest income growth all declined after they were combined. Its stock returns for 1994 and 1995 were 7.7 percent and 33.5 percent, respectively (a two-year return of 43.8 percent). While in some absolute sense this two-year return is respectable, compared with other banks in our sample it was a bit low. The two-year return for Mercantile over 1994 and 1995, for example, was 63 percent. Compared with our list of acquirers (table 2-17), only Firstar had a comparably low two-year return (39.2 percent); two-year returns for other acquirers ranged between 52.7 percent (NationsBank) and 72.3 percent (FirstBank).

That is not to say, however, that the acquisition was a failure. Roosevelt had seen enormous growth in its market-to-book value before acquisition (from 0.48 in April 1991 to 2.24 in April 1993). While its market-to-book ratio declined to 1.45 in 1994 and 1995, it rebounded by April 1996. It is unclear whether the high market-to-book ratio in 1996 reflected greater efficiency at Roosevelt or market expectations of the takeover of Roosevelt (which subsequently took place). There is some evidence, however, that Roosevelt was beginning to turn the corner on its performance before being acquired. *Standard and Poor's Stock Reports* (April 23, 1997) noted improvements in net interest margin, in asset quality, and in fee income in the first quarter of 1997 and argued that the acquisition price per share of $22 (nearly $5 higher than the April 1996 price) offered by Mercantile was justified, given the 1997 improvements in Roosevelt's performance.

Mercantile has been an active acquirer throughout 1995 and 1996, as is apparent in table 2-18, and it would be virtually impossible to measure the contribution of United Postal to Mercantile's performance. Mercantile's many acquisitions (with accompanying transitory merger expenses) also make it difficult to gauge the long-term gains from its acquisitions. Nevertheless, in contrast to Roosevelt's weak postacquisition performance, Mercantile has done reasonably well. It has avoided dilution of earnings per share since the acquisition, has maintained above-average ROE and efficiency in 1994 and 1995 (relative to the Midwest benchmark), and has kept pace with Boatmen's Bank during those years. Its unusually high growth in assets of 19.4 percent in 1996, due to several acquisitions (table 2-18), produced some one-time noninterest expenses that depressed 1996 ROE, but long-run indicators of performance unrelated to these one-time charges (net interest margin, loans-to-assets, and noninterest income) all remain strong. Mercantile's market-to-book value remained high from 1992 to 1996.

Table 2-18 Mergers and Acquisitions, 1990–1997

Pretransaction Acquisitions		Transaction		Posttransaction Acquisitions	
		Harris Bankcorp			
4/27/90	Libertyville Savings and Loan	10/1/94	Suburban Bancorp	7/96	Household Bank
10/90	Frankfort Bankshares, Inc.				
		FirstBank			
12/18/90	Northern Cities Bancorporation, Inc.	3/26/94	Boulevard Bancorp, Inc.	4/29/94	First Financial Investors, Inc.
6/30/92	Siouxland Bank Holding Company			9/9/94	United Bank of Bismarck
12/18/92	Western Capital Investment Corp.			9/30/94	Green Mountain Corporation, Inc.
12/31/92	Bank Shares Incorporated			1/24/95	Metropolitan Financial Corporation
5/93	Colorado National Bankshares			3/16/95	First Western Corporation
6/28/93	Republic Acceptance Corporation			11/1/95	First Bank of Omaha
2/28/94	American Bancshares of Mankato			11/1/95	Southwest Bank
				2/6/96	FirsTier Financial
				3/20/97	U.S. Bancorp
		Firstar			
1/90	Bank of Park Forest	1/31/95	First Colonial Bankshares Corporation	1/29/96	Harvest Financial Corporation
7/90	First Western Bank of St. Louis Park	5/1/95	Investors Bank Corporation		
8/90	State Bank of Elkhorn				
4/91	Bank of Iowa, Inc.				
12/91	Northwestern State Bank				
6/92	First National Bank of Geneva				
8/92	Citizens National Bank of Lake Geneva				
9/92	Federated Bank				
2/93	DSB Corporation				
8/93	Bank of Athens				
10/94	First Southeast Banking Corporation				

(continued)

Table 2-18 (continued)

Pretransaction Acquisitions		Transaction		Posttransaction Acquisitions	
		First Chicago			
7/8/94	Lake Shore Bancorp			12/1/95	NBD Corporation
				6/6/96	Barrington Bancorp. Inc.
9/90	Purchase from RTC				
91	Purchase from RTC				
		Comerica			
6/18/92		Manufacturers National Corporation		11/92	Fortune Financial
9/28/90	Empire FSB of America			12/31/92	Hibernia National Bank of Texas
1/14/91	Plaza Commerce Bancorp			2/93	Sugar Creek National Bank
7/3/91	InBancshares			5/93	Nasher Financial Corporation
11/91	Midlantic National Bank & Trust Co.			5/93	NorthPark National Corporation
				7/93	Fidelity National Bank
				3/30/94	Pacific Western Bancshares
				8/4/94	Lockwood Banc Group, Inc.
				3/28/95	University Bank & Trust Company
				6/26/95	W.Y. Campbell & Company
				9/6/95	Professional Life Underwriters Services
				12/95	QuestStar Bank, N.A.
				1/96	Metrobank California
		NationsBank			
10/1/93		MNC Financial Inc.		12/7/93	U.S. WEST Financial Services Inc.
2/1/93	Chrysler First Inc.			11/7/94	Consolidated Bank, N.A.
7/2/93	Chicago Research and Trading			11/94	RHNB Corporation
				11/28/94	Corpus Christi NationalBank
				12/13/95	Intercontinental Bank
				12/21/95	North Florida Bank Corporation
				1/9/96	Bank South Corporation

Date	Company
3/19/90	Home Federal Savings
10/18/91	Hannibal Mutual Loan and Building
10/9/92	Conservative Bank
10/9/92	First Granite Savings and Loan
6/11/93	First Nationwide Bank of San Francisco
11/8/93	Home Savings of America
4/22/94	Home Federal Bancorp of Missouri, Inc.

Roosevelt Financial Group

Date	Company	Date	Company
6/30/94	Farm & Home Financial Corporation	10/20/95	WSB Bancorp Inc.
		12/29/95	Kirksville Bancshares, Inc.
		7/1/97	RFG taken over by Mercantile Banc.

Mercantile Bancorporation

Date	Company	Date	Company
2/2/94	United Postal Bancorp, Inc.	1/10/96	CSF Holdings, Inc.
		1/31/96	Sun World, N.A.
		5/29/96	Charter Bancshares Inc.
		1/7/97	Boatmen's Bancshares, Inc.
		8/30/97	Barnett Bank (announced)
12/5/91	Old National Bancshares, Inc.	1/3/95	UNSL Financial Corporation
4/30/92	Ameribanc, Inc.	1/3/95	Wedge Bank
6/92	American Bank of St. Louis	5/1/95	Central Mortgage Bancshares, Inc.
7/92	American Bank of Franklin County	5/1/95	TCBankshares, Inc.
1/4/93	MidAmerican Corporation	7/7/95	Plains Spirit Financial Corporation
1/4/93	Johnson County Bankshares, Inc.	8/1/95	Southwest Bancshares, Inc.
4/1/93	First National Bank of Flora	1/2/96	Hawkeye Bancorporation
9/1/93	Mt. Vernon Bancorp, Inc.	1/2/96	First Sterling Bancorp
1/3/94	Metro Bancorporation	2/9/96	Security Bank of Conway
		3/7/96	Metro Savings Bank
		4/25/97	Mark Twain Bancshares
		7/1/97	Roosevelt Financial Group

Source: Authors.

While Roosevelt's postacquisition performance was somewhat disappointing, its acquisition by a successful acquirer in 1997 (Mercantile) illustrates why the efficiency of bank mergers must be judged in a dynamic context. Inevitably, some mergers will be less successful than others. The important question for economic efficiency is not what proportion of mergers are successful, but rather whether unsuccessful franchises (including those that result from previous mergers) are quickly identified and absorbed by successful institutions. One lesson of our St. Louis cases is the speed with which a disappointing merger can turn an acquirer into a target.

3 Conclusion

What have we learned from our case studies of bank consolidation during the 1990s? What do our cases have to say about the efficiency of the recent bank consolidation wave, and what lessons do they offer for future empirical work?

Four lessons about the recent wave of bank consolidation should be stressed. First, our nine cases largely support the view that bank mergers in the 1990s have created value. For the most part (with the exception of First Chicago and possibly Roosevelt), acquirers seem to have achieved gains that they claimed they could achieve ex ante. In the case of Roosevelt, a weak acquirer rapidly became the target of a successful acquirer. First Chicago's use of consolidation as a tool to retain managerial independence (possibly at the expense of stockholders) is the exception rather than the rule.

Second, not all the remaining mergers were pure success stories. Firstar's acquisition of First Colonial achieved the gains that it expected, but it suffered from losses in revenue growth due to the unexpected defection of loan officers. The lesson of that merger is that the single-minded pursuit of physical cost savings may be an inadequate strategy. A bank's resources are almost entirely its staff; successful relationship banking depends on the careful management of the bank's human resources.

Third, while First Chicago's case illustrates that managerial incentives may still limit efficiency gains for some mergers, the behavior of the management of our targets (notably those of Boulevard and Lake Shore) illustrates how competition has changed managerial incentives in the 1990s. In the case of Boulevard, highly inefficient, previously entrenched management surrendered the franchise in the face of increased competition. In the case of Lake Shore, the new CEO's first action was to convince his board of directors that the value-maximizing strategy for the bank was to put itself on the market.

Fourth, our study of Harris's acquisition of Suburban illustrates that revenue synergies can be legitimate motivations for consolidation. That is, even mergers that offer no opportunities for cost savings can lead to significant improvements by means of cross-selling and up-selling to boost loan growth, net interest margin, and fee income.

Our case studies offer three additional lessons from a methodological standpoint. First, stock price reactions to consolidation announcements (which tended to be positive for combined entities in our cases) do not offer a reliable guide to expected or actual productivity gains from consolidations. In our two Firstar cases, cost-saving acquisitions undertaken by a bank with a track record of successful similar acquisitions were greeted with negative stock price reactions. As we have argued, those reactions are better viewed as market disappointment that Firstar itself was not placed on the market rather than as market skepticism over value creation from acquisition.

Not only do stock price reactions have multiple interpretations; in a rapidly changing environment, the profitability estimates that underlie market reactions are much more prone to error. The strong positive reaction to Roosevelt's acquisition of Farm & Home, for example, and the rapid appreciation of Roosevelt's stock in the year before the merger announcement were followed by somewhat disappointing postmerger performance. NationsBank's open disagreement with some market analysts in the past two years (and its aggressive stock repurchase program) illustrates the potential for significant disagreement in the midst of dramatic change.

A second methodological lesson for empirical studies of the productivity gains from mergers is that they should focus on the dynamics of the consolidation process, rather than add up the numbers of failed and successful mergers that occur. If disappointing mergers are quickly corrected by subsequent transactions (as in the case of Roosevelt–Farm & Home), empirical work that focuses on the relative frequency of failed and successful mergers may substantially overstate the costs of consolidation and thus understate the net long-run productivity benefits from such transactions.

A final methodological lesson from our cases is the practical difficulty of constructing useful nonconsolidation benchmarks for panel data analysis of the gains from consolidation. In our critique of existing empirical work in section 1, we argued that there were many potential pitfalls in constructing counterfactual benchmarks to measure the gains from consolidation. In our case analyses, some of those pitfalls became apparent. Should postmerger performance be analyzed at the level of the holding company or the chartered bank? Should the comparison be restricted to the local acquired bank or to the wider franchise, which may operate throughout a state or across state lines? How does one perform comparisons when some banks choose to consolidate bank charters within states and across states lines (such as NationsBank and First Bank), while others (such as Harris) choose not to do so? How can one isolate the effects of mergers in an environment where so many mergers are occurring, where the size of one-time (as opposed to permanent) costs is unclear, and where the time-lag of implementing cost savings may be several years? We hope that future microeconometric work will worry more about these questions. Future work should also follow Jayaratne and Strahan's (1997) example of broadening the measurement of efficiency changes in banking to encompass consumers' gains from increasing competition, which may lower bank profitability in the midst of deregulation. In the meantime, the overarching lesson from our cases is that when gauging the productivity gains from bank consolidation, one should attach less weight to panel studies of stock price reactions or postmerger performance and more weight to the relatively sanguine cross-regime studies of the benefits of consolidation.

References

Akhavein, Jalal D., Allen N. Berger, and David B. Humphrey. 1997. "The Effects of Megamergers on Efficiency and Prices: Evidence from a Bank Profit Function." *Review of Industrial Organization* 12 (February): 95–139.

Allen, Linda, and A. Sinan Cebenoyan. 1991. "Bank Acquisitions and Ownership Structure: Theory and Evidence." *Journal of Banking and Finance* 15 (April): 425–48.

Bankers' Roundtable. 1997. *Deposit Insurance Reform: Partnering for Financial Services Modernization.* Washington, D.C.: Bankers' Roundtable.

Beatty, R., A. Santomero, and M. Smirlock. 1987. "Bank Merger Premiums: Analysis and Evidence." Monograph Series in Finance and Economics. Solomon Center, Stern School of Business, New York University.

Berger, Allen N. 1997. "The Efficiency Effects of Bank Mergers and Acquisitions: A Preliminary Look at the 1990s Data." In *Mergers of Financial Institutions,* edited by Y. Amihud and G. Miller. Homewood, Ill.: Business One-Irwin.

Berger, Allen N., and David B. Humphrey. 1992. "Megamergers in Banking and the Use of Cost Efficiency as an Antitrust Device." *Antitrust Bulletin* (fall): 541–600.

Berger, Allen N., William C. Hunter, and Stephen G. Timme. 1993. "The Efficiency of Financial Institutions: A Review and Preview of Research Past, Present, and Future." *Journal of Banking and Finance* 17 (April): 221–49.

Berger, Allen N., Anil Kashyap, and Joseph M. Scalise. 1995. "The Transformation of the U.S. Banking Industry: What a Long, Strange Trip It's Been." *Brookings Papers on Economic Activity* 2:55–218

Berger, Allen N., and Loretta J. Mester. 1997. "Inside the Black Box: What Explains Differences in the Efficiencies of Financial Institutions?" Finance and Economics Discussion Series, working paper 1997-10, Federal Reserve Board.

Berger, Allen N., Anthony Saunders, Joseph M. Scalise, and Gregory F. Udell. 1997. "The Effects of Bank Mergers and Acquisitions on Small Business Lending." Working paper, Federal Reserve Board (May).

Best, R., and H. Zhang. 1993. "Alternative Information Sources and the Information Content of Bank Loans." *Journal of Finance* 48 (September): 1507–22.

Billett, M. T., Mark J. Flannery, and J. A. Garfinkel. 1995. "The Effect of Lender

Identity on a Borrowing Firm's Equity Return." *Journal of Finance* 50 (June): 699–718.

Booth, James R. 1991. "Contract Costs, Bank Loans, and the Cross-Monitoring Hypothesis." *Journal of Financial Economics* 31 (February): 25–41.

Boyd, John, and Mark Gertler. 1994. "Are Banks Dead? Or Are the Reports Greatly Exaggerated?" *Quarterly Review,* Federal Reserve Bank of Minneapolis (summer): 2–23.

Brewer, Elijah. 1989. "Relationship between Bank Holding Company Risk and Nonbank Activity." *Journal of Economics and Business* 41 (November): 337–53.

Calomiris, Charles W. 1993. "Regulation, Industrial Structure, and Instability in U.S. Banking: An Historical Perspective." In *Structural Change in Banking,* edited by M. Klausner and L. J. White. Homewood, Ill.: Business One-Irwin, 19–115.

———. 1995. "The Costs of Rejecting Universal Banking: American Finance in the German Mirror, 1870–1914." In *The Coordination of Activity within and between Firms,* edited by N. Lamoreaux and D. Raff. Chicago: University of Chicago Press, 257–315.

Calomiris, Charles W., and Mark S. Carey. 1994. "Loan Market Competition between Foreign and U.S. Banks: Some Facts about Loans and Borrowers." *Proceedings of the Thirtieth Annual Conference on Bank Structure and Competition.* Chicago: Federal Reserve Bank of Chicago, 331–51.

Calomiris, Charles W., and Jason Karceski. 1994. *Competing Bank Strategies in Chicago: An Illinois MBA Project Report.* Champaign, Ill.: Office for Banking Research, University of Illinois, Urbana-Champaign.

———. 1995. *The Bank Merger Wave of the 90s: Nine Case Studies.* Champaign, Ill.: Office for Banking Research, University of Illinois, Urbana-Champaign.

Calomiris, Charles W., and Carlos D. Ramirez. 1996. "The Role of Financial Relationships in the History of American Corporate Finance." *Journal of Applied Corporate Finance* 9 (summer): 52–73.

Calomiris, Charles W., and Berry Wilson. 1997. "Bank Risk and Portfolio Management: The 1930s Capital Crunch and Scramble to Shed Risk." Working paper, Columbia University.

Cornett, Marcia M., Darius Palia, and Hasan Tehranian. 1997. "CEO Compensation and Acquiring Bank Returns." Working paper, Columbia Business School.

Cornett, Marcia M., and Hasan Tehranian. 1992. "Changes in Corporate Performance Associated with Bank Acquisitions." *Journal of Financial Economics* 31 (April): 211–34.

Crook, Clive. 1992. "Fear of Finance." *Economist,* September 19: 5–18.

Dubofsky, D., and D. Fraser. 1988. "Regulatory Change and the Market for Bank Control." In *Bank Mergers: Current Issues and Perspectives,* edited by B. Gup. Boston: Kluwer Academic, 121–39.

Evanoff, Douglas. 1988. "Branch Banking and Service Accessibility." *Journal of Money, Credit and Banking* 20 (May): 191–202.

Evanoff, Douglas, and Philip Israelevich. 1991. "Productive Efficiency in Banking." *Economic Review,* Federal Reserve Bank of Chicago, 15 (July): 11–32.

Gorton, Gary, and Richard Rosen. 1995. "Corporate Control, Portfolio Choice and the Decline of Banking." *Journal of Finance* 50 (December): 1377–420.

Greenspan, Alan. 1988. "An Overview of Financial Restructuring." *Proceedings of the Twenty-fourth Annual Conference on Bank Structure and Competition.* Chicago: Federal Reserve Bank of Chicago, 1–9.

———. 1990. "Subsidies and Powers in Commercial Banking." *Proceedings of the Twenty-sixth Annual Conference on Bank Structure and Competition.* Chicago: Federal Reserve Bank of Chicago, 1–8.

————. 1992. "Putting FDICIA in Perspective." *Proceedings of the Twenty-eighth Annual Conference on Bank Structure and Competition.* Chicago: Federal Reserve Bank of Chicago, 1–7.

Healy, P. M., K. G. Palepu, and R. S. Ruback. 1992. "Does Corporate Performance Improve after Mergers?" *Journal of Financial Economics* 31 (April): 135–75.

Hoshi, Takeo, Anil Kashyap, and David Scharfstein. 1990a. "The Role of Banks in Reducing the Costs of Financial Distress." *Journal of Financial Economics* 27 (September): 67–88.

————. 1990b. "Bank Monitoring and Investment: Evidence from the Changing Structure of Japanese Corporate Banking Relationships." In *Asymmetric Information, Corporate Finance, and Investment,* edited by R. G. Hubbard. Chicago: University of Chicago Press, 105–26.

————. 1991. "Corporate Structure, Liquidity, and Investment: Evidence from Japanese Industrial Groups." *Quarterly Journal of Economics* 106 (February): 33–60.

Houston, Joel F., and Michael D. Ryngaert. 1994. "The Overall Gains from Large Bank Mergers." *Journal of Banking and Finance* 18 (December): 1155–76.

————. 1996. "The Value Added by Bank Acquisitions: Lessons from Wells Fargo's Acquisition of First Interstate." *Journal of Applied Corporate Finance* 9 (summer): 74–82.

————. 1997. "Equity Issuance and Adverse Selection: A Direct Test Using Conditional Stock Offers." *Journal of Finance* 52 (March): 197–219.

James, Christopher. 1987. "Some Evidence on the Uniqueness of Bank Loans." *Journal of Financial Economics* 19 (December): 217–35.

James, Christopher, and Joel F. Houston. 1996. "Evolution or Extinction: Where Are Banks Headed?" *Journal of Applied Corporate Finance* 9 (summer): 8–23.

James, Christopher, and Peggy Wier. 1987. "Returns to Acquirers and Competition in the Acquisition Market: The Case of Banking." *Journal of Political Economy* 95 (April): 355–70.

————. 1988. "Are Bank Loans Different? Evidence from the Stock Market." *Journal of Applied Corporate Finance* 1:46–54.

Jayaratne, Jith, and Philip E. Strahan. 1997. "Entry Restrictions, Industry Evolution, and Dynamic Efficiency: Evidence from Commercial Banking." Staff report 22, Federal Reserve Bank of New York, March.

Jensen, Michael. 1988. "Takeovers: Their Causes and Consequences." *Journal of Economic Perspectives* 2 (winter): 21–48.

Kaen, F., and Hasan Tehranian. 1988. "New Hampshire Bank Mergers: The Returns to Acquiring Bank Shareholders." In *Bank Mergers: Current Issues and Perspectives,* edited by B. Gup. Boston: Kluwer Academic, 141–55.

Kashyap, Anil, and Jeremy C. Stein. 1995. "The Impact of Monetary Policy on Bank Balance Sheets." Carnegie-Rochester Series on Public Policy 42 (June): 151–95.

Keeley, Michael C. 1990. "Deposit Insurance, Risk, and Market Power in Banking." *American Economic Review* 80 (December): 1183–200.

Lang, L. H. P., R. Stulz, and R. A. Walkling. 1989. "Managerial Performance, Tobin's Q, and the Gains from Successful Tender Offers." *Journal of Financial Economics* 24 (September): 137–54.

McCoy, John B., Larry Frieder, and Robert Hedges. 1994. *Bottom Line Banking: Meeting the Challenges for Survival and Success.* Chicago: Probus Publishing.

Mengle, David. 1990. "The Case for Interstate Branch Banking." *Economic Review,* Federal Reserve Bank of Richmond 76 (December): 3–17.

Myers, Stewart C., and Nicholas Majluf. 1984. "Corporate Financing and Investment Decisions When Firms Have Information That Investors Do Not Have." *Journal of Financial Economics* 13 (June): 187–221.

Nolle, Daniel E. 1994. "Are Foreign Banks Out-Competing U.S. Banks in the U.S. Market?" Working paper, Office of the Comptroller of the Currency, Washington, D.C.

Palia, Darius. 1993. "Recent Evidence on Bank Mergers." *Financial Markets, Institutions, and Instruments* 3 (December): 36–59.

Peristiani, Stavros. 1996. "Do Mergers Improve the X-Efficiency and Scale Efficiency of U.S. Banks: Evidence from the 1980s." Research paper 96-23, Federal Reserve Bank of New York.

———. 1997. "Do Mergers Improve the X-Efficiency and Scale Efficiency of U.S. Banks?" *Journal of Money, Credit and Banking* 29 (August): 326–37.

Petersen, Mitchell A., and Raghuram Rajan. 1994. "The Benefits of Firm-Creditor Relationships: Evidence from Small Business Data." *Journal of Finance* 49 (March): 3–37.

Rajan, Raghuram. 1992. "Insiders and Outsiders: The Choice between Relationships and Arms-Length Debt." *Journal of Finance* 47 (September): 1367–400.

Rhoades, Stephen A. 1993a. "The Efficiency Effects of Horizontal Bank Mergers." *Journal of Banking and Finance* 17 (April): 411–22.

———. 1993b. "The Efficiency Effects of Bank Mergers: Rationale for a Case-Study Approach and Preliminary Findings." *Proceedings of the Twenty-ninth Annual Conference on Bank Structure and Competition.* Chicago: Federal Reserve Bank of Chicago, 377–400.

Servaes, Henri. 1991. "Tobin's Q and the Gains from Takeover." *Journal of Finance* 46 (March): 409–19.

Shaffer, Sherrill. 1993. "A Test of Competition in Canadian Banking." *Journal of Money, Credit and Banking* 25 (February) 49–61.

Shleifer, Andrei, and Robert W. Vishny. 1990. "The Takeover Wave of the 1980s." *Science* 249 (August): 745–49.

———. 1992. "Liquidation Values and Debt Capacity: A Market Equilibrium Approach." *Journal of Finance* 47 (September): 1343–65.

Slovin, Myron B., Marie E. Sushka, and John A. Polonchek. 1993. "The Value of Bank Durability: Borrowers as Stakeholders." *Journal of Finance* 48 (March): 247–66.

Spindt, Paul A., and Vefa Tarhan. 1992a. "Are There Synergies in Bank Mergers?" Working paper, Tulane University, New Orleans.

———. 1992b. "An Empirical Examination of the Market for Corporate Control in the Banking Sector." *Proceedings of the Twenty-eighth Annual Conference on Bank Structure and Competition.* Chicago: Federal Reserve Bank of Chicago, 568–601.

Srinivasan, Aruna, and Larry D. Wall. 1992. "Cost Savings Associated with Bank Mergers." Working paper, Federal Reserve Bank of Atlanta.

Sushka, Marie, and Y. Bendeck. 1988. "Bank Acquisitions and Shareholder Wealth." *Journal of Banking and Finance* 12 (December): 551–62.

Toevs, Alden L. 1992. "Under What Circumstances Do Bank Mergers Improve Efficiency?" *Proceedings of the Twenty-eighth Annual Conference on Bank Structure and Competition.* Chicago: Federal Reserve Bank of Chicago, 602–28.

Tonge, Charles, interview with Charles W. Calomiris, August 14, 1997.

Wall, Larry, and Benton Gup. 1988. "Market Valuation Effects of Bank Acquisitions." In *Bank Mergers: Current Issues and Perspectives,* edited by B. Gup. Boston: Kluwer Academic, 107–20.

Comment   Christopher James

Introduction

The academic literature on the value gains from bank mergers creates a troubling paradox. Empirical studies examining the stock market reaction to merger announcements and the performance of banks after acquisitions find, on average, no significant gain in value or improved operating performance. On average the empirical evidence indicates that acquired firms gain at the expense of the acquiring firm. Moreover, there appears to be little in the way of improved operating performance for the merged firms relative to industry peers following the acquisition. However, despite any apparent value gains, mergers in banking continue at a rapid pace. The lack of econometrics evidence of efficiency gains is even more troubling in light of the fact that an important impetus for consolidation has been the removal of geographic and product market entry restrictions that are generally believed to impede operating efficiency and bank profitability.

The paper by Calomiris and Karceski attempts to reconcile these conflicting facts through an in-depth analysis of nine bank mergers in the 1990s. Case studies, the authors argue, can uncover value gains that are difficult to estimate and identify using standard large sample econometrics tools. Specifically, they argue that average measured gains from mergers—whether measured by stock price reactions or performance improvements—are not reliable measures of the true gains from acquisitions. Part of the problem lies in the data used in large sample studies. For example, ex post performance gains are often measured using accounting data. However, accounting measures of performance may not capture the economic gains from mergers. Moreover, mergers often involve restructuring costs that can mask operating gains that may take a considerable amount of time to be achieved.

An alternative measure of performance is the stock returns of the bidder and target around the time the acquisition is announced. The change in the combined market value of the acquired and acquiring bank, the argument goes, provides a measure of the expected gains from the acquisition. However, studies using stock returns have their own set of problems. Important among them is that stock returns only measure the value of *new* information revealed at the time the merger is announced. However, to the extent that the merger is anticipated, the stock price reaction to the merger will provide a downward biased estimate of the value created (or destroyed) by the acquisition.

A second reason large sample studies may fail to identify value gains is that there may be important cross-sectional differences in the source of

Christopher James is the William H. Dial/SunBank Professor of Finance at the Graduate School of Business of the University of Florida.

merger gains that are difficult to identify or estimate using standard econometric tools. Specifically, the literature suggests that the motives for bank mergers are quite varied—ranging from cost savings to revenue enhancement to so-called managerial hubris. Failure to condition on these differences may lead to average measures of performance providing unreliable measures of the actual gains from acquisitions.

Given these problems with large sample studies, Calomiris and Karceski argue that to understand the gains from mergers requires a case-by-case analysis. Their goal is to document that the source of merger gains varies cross sectionally and through time. Moreover, they argue that, by conditioning on the motive for the merger and by examining performance changes in the context of the different motives, the real efficiency effects of the merger wave of the 1990s can be uncovered.

While I am extremely sympathetic to a case study approach, the lessons learned from the authors' nine case studies are quite limited. As I discuss below, the primary benefit of case studies is their ability to reconcile the contradictory finding of large sample empirical studies. Are the performance measures used misleading or are the real efficiency gains simply not there? In particular, the goal should be to explain why, in the face of what the authors believe to be significant efficiency gains from mergers, large sample studies provide such weak evidence of efficiency gains. The challenge here is to structure clinical studies in a way that allows the researcher to go from the specific to the general (or at least learn more about the shortcomings of large sample studies). For example, clinical studies have the potential to identify conditioning variables that can be used in large sample studies to sort mergers based on their motivation and likely sources of gains. Alternatively, clinical studies may permit us to better understand the timing of performance gains from acquisitions and the circumstance in which accounting measures of performance are misleading.

In my discussion I focus on why the large sample empirical studies fail to find significant value gains from mergers. I also discuss how clinical studies might be used to provide evidence to improve large sample econometric studies. Finally I discuss some of the lessons that can be learned from the cases Calomiris and Karceski study.

Measuring the Gains from Bank Acquisitions

Academic studies of merger-related gains in banking follow one of two approaches. The first approach compares accounting performance of the merged banks to a benchmark of either premerger performance or a group of comparable banks that were not involved in merger activity. In these studies, mergers are assumed to result in improved performance if the postmerger performance of the combined banks exceeds the performance of either comparable banks or the pro forma performance of the merging banks before the merger. Studies based on accounting data focus on three measures of performance: operating income, cash flows, and operating costs.

The second approach to analyzing merger gains examines the stock price performance of the bidder and the target firm around the announcement of an acquisition. A merger is assumed to be value enhancing if the combined value of the bidder and the target increase following the merger announcement. However, with the exception of several recent papers, most studies examine the abnormal returns of the bidder and the target separately, making an assessment of the overall gains from the acquisition difficult.

What do these studies show? Looking first at the studies that examine stock returns, there is little evidence that mergers are value enhancing. Specifically, all studies find a significant increase in the value of the target (on the order of 15 percent in the two days around the merger announcement) and most find a decrease in the value of the bidder (of about 2 percent). Since the acquiring banks are on average significantly larger than the acquired bank, the combined value of the bidder and target declines slightly on the announcement of the merger. Overall the studies based on stock returns suggest no increase in value resulting from the merger.[1]

As Calomiris and Karceski point out, there are several reasons why measures of gains based on stock returns may be flawed. First, merger announcements mix information concerning the proposed acquisition with information concerning the financing of the acquisition. Since most bank acquisitions are financed with stock and since stock issues are, in general, associated with a negative stock price reaction for issuers, the returns to bidding firms may understate value gains anticipated from the merger. Consistent with this view Houston and Ryngaert (1997) find that the returns to bidders are significantly greater in mergers financed with cash or debt than in mergers financed with stock. However, even for cash offers, bidders continue to earn negative abnormal returns, suggesting that the adverse consequences of using stock to finance the acquisition do not offset positive returns to bidders associated with acquisitions.

A second reason abnormal return studies may not accurately reflect the value gains is that acquisitions are largely anticipated so that the positive effects on bank value do not show themselves on the announcement date. This problem may be particularly important for bank acquisitions in the late 1980s and the 1990s because many banks clearly expressed a strategy to grow through acquisitions. It seems unlikely, however, that the negative stock price performance of bidding firms can be explained by the acquisition being anticipated. Pre-announcement leakage is likely to attenuate the announcement day returns but not change what would be positive

---

1. See for example Houston and Ryngaert (1994), Cornett and De (1991), James and Wier (1987), Cornett and Tehranian (1992), and more recently DeLong (1998).

returns to bidders into negative announcement day returns. Pre-announcement leakage may also effect target returns since there is considerable speculation concerning potential targets prior to an acquisition. This attenuation bias together with the attenuation of bidder returns may result in positive though insignificant abnormal returns for the combined banks on the announcement day. Unfortunately this issue has not been addressed in the literature.[2] This may be a fruitful area for future research where the results of clinical studies may be particularly helpful.

A final problem with event studies is that the negative stock market reaction of bidding firms may reflect disappointment with the announced transaction because it conveys information that the bidding firm is less likely to be acquired in the future. This clearly has been a factor in several acquisitions (most notably the recent acquisition by SunTrust of Crestar Financial Corporation, which led to a decline of about 10 percent in the value of SunTrust shares). However, it is unlikely that the market's disappointment with a few potential targets' becoming acquirers can explain the negative average returns to bidding firms.

Overall it seems unlikely that these problems are important enough to mask a significant increase in the average value of acquired and acquiring firms resulting from mergers. However, this conclusion does not imply that efficiency gains are limited or that a number of acquisitions may not create value for bank shareholders. As Calomiris and Karceski point out, efficiency gains from acquisitions may accrue to bank customers in a competitive market. If this is the case, then the small positive return to the combined entity may simply reflect the fact that the bank captures only a small fraction of the gains. More important, cross-sectional studies of the abnormal returns from acquisitions reveal significant differences in the combined returns to bidders and targets across mergers. For example, Houston and Ryngaert (1994) find the value weighted returns to bidder and target is increasing in the degree of market overlap between the acquired and the acquiring banks, the percentage of the acquisition financed with cash or conditional stock, and the profitability of the bidder prior to the acquisition.[3] In a recent paper, DeLong (1998) finds that a positive and statistically significant return for mergers involves both geographic focus (where acquiring and acquired bank are headquartered in the same state) and activity focus (where the stock returns of the acquired and acquiring firms

---

2. Several studies attempt to control for this by measuring the abnormal returns of target firms from the date it is announced that a bank is a potential target (see, e.g., Houston and Ryngaert 1994). Controlling for pre-announcement leakage, the combined value gain of the bidder and target is not significantly different from zero.

3. Conditional stock offers involve financing the acquisition with common stock, but making the number of shares issued a function of the future price of the bidder's stock. Conditional stock issues may be a way for bidders to communicate that good news may be revealed before the deal is closed (or warrant that bad news will not be revealed).

are highly correlated in the twelve months preceding the merger). In contrast, DeLong finds that diversifying mergers destroy value.

The cross-sectional variation in abnormal returns suggests that there may be a number of "good" acquisitions (at least from the standpoint of bank shareholders). For example, the fact that returns are increasing in the degree of market overlap suggests that mergers involving cost savings or the creation of market power add value for shareholders. Unfortunately, without detailed information concerning the anticipated gains from the merger, it is impossible to distinguish between these two alternatives.

Given the inability of stock price performance studies to determine whether mergers create real economic value and the sources of such value gains, researchers have turned to examining postmerger performance using accounting data.[4] However, studies of postmerger performance also provide weak evidence of an overall improvement in performance. For example, Cornett and Tehranian (1992) find a small but significant increase in postmerger operating cash flows compared with the performance of banks not engaged in merger activity. However, their results appear to be sensitive to the banks used as a benchmark. Specifically, Cornett and Tehranian use as a benchmark a group of publicly traded banks that did not engage in any merger activity during the comparison period. However as Pilloff (1996) points out, a more appropriate benchmark is the performance of banks that are located in the same region as the merging banks. Accounting for regional differences in performance, Pilloff finds no significant improvement in operating performance.

Methodological problems may partly explain why performance studies provide little evidence of performance gains. The most important among these is the difficulty in constructing a good benchmark and the timing of performance gains. As Calomiris and Karceski point out, there is selectivity bias in the sample of comparable banks. Banks that do not merge may be doing so for good reason. For example nonmerging banks may have chosen internal growth or may have been involved in prior merger activity. The problem of finding a suitable benchmark is particularly important in banking during the last decade precisely because the industry was involved in a merger wave.

Even if mergers result in improvements in performance, the lags between the completion of mergers and the realization of operating improvements may be long and varied. Moreover, restructuring and consolidation costs may lead to a deterioration in short-term performance even though long-term performance is expected to improve. This problem is particularly important if there is cross-sectional variation of the source of merger gains. For example, mergers motivated by anticipated cost savings may result in faster improvements in operating performance than mergers mo-

---

4. See for example Berger (1997), Cornett and Tehranian (1992), and Pilloff (1996).

tivated by revenue synergies or diversification opportunities. This fact may lead to a significant understatement in the gains (or losses) arising from mergers.

Consistent with the results from stock price studies, performance studies suggest that there is considerable cross-sectional variation in the performance of merged banks. For example, Pilloff (1996) finds that low target profitability and high target and bidder expenses are correlated with subsequent performance improvements. Pilloff also finds, however, that although both performance changes and abnormal returns are related to premerger expenses and operating performance, the significant variables differ between the two measures. For example, performance gains are related to high target and bidder expenses, while abnormal returns are related to the difference between bidder and target expense measures. More troubling, variables that explain cross-sectional differences in abnormal returns—such as the mode of financing or the degree of market overlap—do not explain cross-sectional differences in postmerger performance. In addition, there is no consistent evidence that abnormal returns are significantly related to postmerger performance.

What can we conclude from the studies of merger gain? First, the gains from mergers appear to be significantly related to the motive behind the merger. Specifically, mergers motivated by cost savings appear to generate greater gains to bank shareholders than mergers motivated by revenue enhancement or diversification benefits. The failure of performance-based studies to provide confirming evidence on the importance of cost savings may arise from differences across mergers in the timing of cost savings. Second, gains to shareholders appear to be significantly related to how the merger is financed, suggesting that abnormal stock returns may not provide an accurate measure of the value gains associated with the merger. Finally, there appears to be significant variation in the pricing of deals and the motive for mergers over time. For example, Houston and Ryngaert (1994) provide some evidence of an improvement in bidder returns and an increase in the overall gains from acquisitions in the 1990s. For example, they find that the combined returns to bidders and targets since 1989 are positive. In contrast, the combined returns were negative in the 1980s.

Additional evidence, consistent with an improvement in the returns from mergers comes from an analysis of deal pricing in the 1980s and 1990s. For example, table 3C.1 provides summary statistics for large bank acquisitions (where the acquired bank has over $250 million in market value in 1982 constant dollars) during the period 1982–97. Notice that since 1992 there has been a decline in the premium paid over market for the acquired firm. Moreover, recent mergers are much less dilutive of earnings than mergers in the 1980s. Finally, notice that the percentage of overhead reduction needed for the deal to break even (in terms of being nondilutive of earnings per share) is much less in the 1990s than it was in the

Table 3C.1   Bank Mergers since 1982

	1982	1983	1984	1985	1986	1987	1988	1989	1990	1991	1992	1993	1994	1995	1996	1997
Total number of transactions	18	37	30	46	67	37	26	29	12	29	38	54	71	58	79	32
Number of intermarket transactions	2	7	2	15	28	17	16	9	4	10	9	13	24	23	17	7
Percentage of intermarket transactions	11	19	7	33	42	46	62	31	33	34	24	24	34	40	22	22
Accounting treatment																
Total number of purchases	11	27	24	28	20	10	13	13	7	11	6	9	28	13	27	7
Total number of poolings	7	10	6	18	47	27	13	16	5	18	32	45	43	45	52	25
Premium paid over market price (%)																
One day prior to announcement	46.9	33.1	33.4	29.6	19.6	27.2	28.3	33.2	41.2	30.2	33.7	17.8	20.9	23.2	18.4	20.6
One month prior to announcement	59.3	43.2	38.2	39	30.5	38	34.4	39.6	38.6	48.4	39	34.5	30	32.7	30.3	28.2
Transactions medians																
Median deal value (in millions of dollars)	72.9	76.6	52.9	82.9	55.3	102.9	92	74	49	187	105	75	52	68	56	63
Mean deal value (in millions of dollars)	92.2	130.9	99.8	156.1	172.8	290.7	229.7	192.6	99.8	539.8	253.8	192.6	123.7	630.5	390.6	615.4
Price/earnings multiple	10.4	11.8	12.3	13.2	16	16.4	15.3	14.4	13	15	15.9	15.9	16.1	17	17.9	19.4
Price/book value multiple	1.4	1.42	1.41	1.88	2.2	2.31	1.71	1.89	1.68	1.59	1.8	2.09	2.03	2.14	2.17	2.5
Price/tangible book value multiple	1.45	1.42	1.49	1.88	2.25	2.36	1.79	1.89	1.8	1.65	1.91	2.14	2.18	2.22	2.25	2.55
Fully diluted earnings-per-share dilution (%)	-6.4	-5.4	-5.5	-4.7	-4.4	-4.4	-2.5	-3.6	-1.4	-1.8	-1.7	-2.1	-1.4	-2.9	-1.9	-1.8
Premium to total deposits	4.14	3.16	4.37	7.36	10.96	10.94	5.4	8.3	8.1	6.02	7.17	10.81	10.46	11.65	12.26	16.39
Percentage of overhead to breakeven	25.3	14.7	16.9	20.7	21.6	25.7	21.7	23.7	9.8	12.6	5.2	18.2	22.4	19.7	22.1	15.7

Source: Salomon Brothers Industry Report: "Shop Til You Drop" August 1997.

1980s. Whether the improvement in deal pricing is a result of an improvement in the market for corporate control in banking (as Calomiris and Karceski argue) or a change in the motivation for mergers (cost reduction versus revenue enhancement) is an issue that deserves further research.

What Can Be Learned from Case Studies?

As discussed earlier, the primary benefit of case studies of bank mergers is to better our understanding of the source of merger gains (or losses) so as to resolve the conflicting results of large sample empirical studies. The case studies presented by Calomiris and Karceski assist us in understanding how acquisitions might add value. In particular, the main finding of their paper is that the motives for mergers in banking are quite varied. As a result, failure to condition on the motive for the acquisition may obscure performance improvements arising from the acquisition. Unfortunately the nine case studies do not enable us to go from the specific to the general. In particular, they do not identify new easily quantifiable conditioning variables that can be used in large sample studies to empirically test whether mergers add value. As a result, the conclusions one can draw from the nine case studies are similar to the conclusions one can draw from the large sample studies: certain types of acquisitions are more likely to generate value gains than others.

The next step in this area should be to undertake an in-depth analysis of a larger number of acquisitions and then use the results to test whether refined measures of the reason for the merger and a better understanding of the timing of performance changes can resolve the conflicting results of abnormal stock returns and performance studies. In this regard, analyst research reports on the anticipated gains from mergers and their forecasts of cost savings and revenue gains may be particularly useful. In a project currently underway, Joel Houston, Mike Ryngaert, and I use analyst research reports obtained through INVESTEXT together with bank annual reports and news releases to sort mergers based on what analysts believe to be the motive for the merger and the likely source of value gain (or in some cases value loss). These reports also provide a detailed description of the anticipated timing of performance changes resulting from the merger (in many cases by expense and revenue item). This examination allows us to then condition the analysis of actual performance on the stated motive for the merger and the anticipated changes in performance at the time of the merger.

Structuring clinical analysis in this way allows one to go from the specific to the general. In particular, we use our clinical studies to identify conditioning variables that can be used in large sample studies to sort mergers based on their motivation and likely sources of gains. Moreover, we are able to assess whether the failure of large sample performance studies to identify merger gains results from the failure to control for timing differences among mergers, inappropriate classification of mergers by objective, or simply because these acquisitions have no significant effect on performance.

In addition to permitting a more refined classification of the anticipated source of merger-related gains, many of the analyst research reports provide detailed valuations of the anticipated merger gains. These valuations in turn can be related to the premium paid by the acquiring bank to evaluate the circumstances in which bidders appear to overpay. The difference between the premium paid and the value of merger-related gains can be compared to the abnormal stock price performance of the bidder to assess whether bidder returns are related to the degree of overpayment.

Our preliminary analysis indicates that analysts classify mergers into four categories: (1) cost savings arising from shared overhead expenses, (2) revenue enhancement from cross selling, (3) diversification, and (4) managerial entrenchment (mergers as an antitakeover device). Analyst assessments of the gains from acquisitions appear to be closely related to motive for the acquisition and the degree to which the merger is expected to be dilutive of earnings per share. Specifically, anticipated value gains are greatest for intramarket mergers where anticipated expense reductions are greatest. Moreover, these acquisitions tend to be the least dilutive, with earnings accretion expected within eighteen months. These acquisitions are also expected to generate the greatest earnings improvements (through both expense reduction and increases in revenue arising from cross-selling opportunities). We also find evidence of significant changes in deal pricing and the nature of acquisition in the 1990s. For example, we find a significant decline in the earnings-per-share dilution and in the percent of overhead reduction needed to recover the merger premium for acquisitions in the 1990s. In addition, the frequency of "in market" mergers increased in the 1990s (partly as a result of the completion of regional and interstate banking pacts in the late 1980s).

Conclusion

Over the past fifteen years, there has been a dramatic consolidation in the U.S. banking system. A combination of deregulation, globalization, and changing technology has induced a large number of bank mergers over this time period. Not surprisingly, this widespread consolidation has been the impetus for a large number of academic studies. While this literature has provided a number of insights, a number of important questions concerning both the motivation for bank mergers and the estimated value added from these mergers remain unanswered.

In many respects, because of the lack of detailed data, the existing literature has had a difficult time classifying the motivation for mergers and estimating the ex ante and ex post gains from bank mergers. Case studies provide important insights into merger-related gains. The challenge, however, is to structure the case studies in a way that bridges the gap between individual case studies and the existing large sample studies. In this regard, the study by Calomiris and Karceski is an important first step.

References

Berger, Allen N. 1997. The efficiency effects of bank mergers and acquisitions: A preliminary look at the 1990s data. In *Mergers of financial institutions*, ed. Y. Amihud and G. Miller. Homewood, Ill.: Business One–Irwin.

Cornett, Marcia Millon, and Sankar De. 1991. Common stock returns in corporate takeover bids: Evidence from interstate bank mergers. *Journal of Banking and Finance* 15:273–95.

Cornett, Marcia Millon, and Hassan Tehranian. 1992. Changes in corporate performance associated bank acquisitions. *Journal of Financial Economics* 31 (April): 211–34.

DeLong, Gayle L. 1998. Domestic and international bank mergers: The gains from focusing versus diversifying. Working paper, New York University, Stern School of Business.

Houston, Joel F., and Michael D. Ryngaert. 1994. The overall gains from large bank mergers. *Journal of Banking and Finance* 18 (December): 1155–76.

———. 1997. Equity issuance and adverse selection: A direct test using conditional stock offers. *Journal of Finance* 52 (March): 197–219.

James, Christopher, and Peggy Wier. 1987. Returns to acquirers and competition in the acquisition market: The case of banking. *Journal of Political Economy* 95 (April): 355–70.

Pilloff, Steven J. 1996. Performance changes and shareholder wealth creation associated with mergers of publicly traded banking institutions. *Journal of Money, Credit, and Banking* 28, no. 3 (August): 294–309.

Comment   Anil K Kashyap

Charles Calomiris and Jason Karceski are to be congratulated for bringing some new evidence to the debate over the fallout from bank mergers. As they stress in their paper, there is little consensus in the literature over the impact of mergers on operating efficiency, profitability, or shareholder wealth. Given this state of affairs I expect that most researchers interested in banking will find the paper valuable and well worth reading.

In my comments, I try to accomplish three things. First, because the paper contains a wealth of data and a number of interesting conjectures

Anil K Kashyap is professor of economics at the Graduate School of Business of the University of Chicago, a consultant at the Federal Reserve Bank of Chicago, and a research associate of the National Bureau of Economic Research.

The author thanks Jennifer Francis for helpful conversations. The views expressed below are not necessarily those of the Federal Reserve Bank of Chicago or the Federal Reserve System.

about the direction of the industry, I start by laying out what I see as the main arguments of the paper. While I am sympathetic to many of the authors' claims, there are a couple of areas where I disagree. In the second part of my review I identify these points. Finally, I step back and offer some thoughts on how case studies can be used along with more traditional types of research. To keep things concrete these suggestions are couched in terms of the paper, but I hope it is clear how these principles could be applied to any research-oriented case work.

The Core of the Argument

As mentioned above, the motivation for this paper is the observation that, using conventional research techniques, it is hard to find evidence that mergers cut costs or raise shareholder value. I share the concern of Calomiris and Karceski that this result is troubling in light of the massive amount of consolidation that has taken place and the widespread view among practitioners that mergers are beneficial.

The authors argue that this tension is even worse than is commonly thought because there is another line of research to support the practitioners' view. Specifically, they point to the literature that looks at the efficiency of banks across regimes. These studies look both at cross-state evidence from the United States and comparisons of different countries. Calomiris and Karceski read the results as showing that consolidation is useful if it helps banks expand their diversification either through enhanced branching or expanded product lines. I suspect that skeptics will doubt the cross-country studies because they are not ceteris paribus comparisons. But the domestic evidence, particularly the comparison of the fate of banks headquartered in North Carolina and Illinois, seems harder to dismiss. Thus, I am inclined to agree with their contention that the cross-regime research suggests that there are likely to be gains from consolidation.

Against this backdrop, the authors tackle the obvious question of why conventional merger analysis provides such weak evidence regarding the gains from consolidation. They offer separate explanations for why stock price reaction studies and postmerger performance analyses might not accurately capture the gains from mergers. I review some of the details of their arguments below, but I believe it is fair to summarize their view as saying that mergers are complicated transactions in several important respects. In particular, they are difficult to analyze because they are taking place throughout the banking industry, during a period when the fundamental business of banking may be changing, and (perhaps as a result) individual organizations may have very different motivations for undertaking mergers. Because of these factors, Calomiris and Karceski believe that correctly executing any econometric work is very challenging.

Since the authors are particularly concerned about the changing aspects of the whole industry, one theme they repeatedly stress is that data from the 1980s may not be a reliable guide about what to expect regarding later mergers. Given this view it is natural to look for data on the most recent mergers to see if it tells a different story than past studies. Moreover, the objections they raise about conventional work lead them to adopt a case study approach. Implicitly this strategy presumes that by carefully and thoroughly looking over a small number of representative cases, a clear set of patterns should emerge.

The paper's main conclusion is that seven of the nine mergers they analyze are clear success stories. In these seven cases, Calomiris and Karceski argue that the acquiring banks seem to have accomplished their (publicly) stated goals. Importantly, two of the seven ex post successful mergers were subject to negative stock price reactions at the time they were announced. Another one of these successful cases (Harris and Suburban) involved a combination of two banks that were not trying to cut costs but were seeking to boost revenue through cross selling. Turning to the two less successful cases, the authors find that one (involving First Chicago and Lake Shore Bancorp) might be well described as reflecting a preference for managerial gains at the expense of shareholders. The other unsuccessful case is complicated by the fact that the acquiring institution was itself soon taken over.

Calomiris and Karceski also offer some observations on the lessons they believe their work offers for traditional econometric analysis. They begin this discussion by saying "that stock price reactions to consolidation announcements (which tended to be positive for combined entities in our cases) do not offer a reliable guide to expected or actual productivity gains from consolidation." Next, the authors point to the importance of considering the dynamics of the consolidation process, whereby a poor acquisition may be unwound in a subsequent transaction. Finally, they highlight the difficulty of getting a control sample that can be used as a benchmark for gauging the impact of mergers.

Disagreements

On the most important point of their paper—that most of the mergers in their sample were successful—I agree with Calomiris and Karceski. However, my process for reaching this conclusion differs slightly from theirs and I also have a somewhat different vision than they do about how to build on the case research in this paper. I begin by explaining my interpretation of their results and then trace that reasoning through to draw lessons for further work.

I agree with the authors' conclusion that the postmerger performance analysis using only publicly available data is very difficult to conduct. As they emphasize, most organizations in this industry have been in a nearly constant state of flux, so that tracing out the dynamic effects of a single transaction can be quite difficult. On the other hand, as I explain below, I am much more confident that the stock market reaction provides a reasonable measure of the deals that they are analyzing. Therefore, I believe that in assessing these deals we should put much more weight on the stock market reactions than on the postmerger performance.

Judging by the simple metric of what happened to adjusted returns, six of the nine deals in this paper were desirable. But, as Calomiris and Karceski convincingly argue, there can be problems with the event studies. I find three of the objections they highlight to be potentially serious. A first potential problem is that the stock market value of a combined entity may drop because consumers (rather than the shareholders) capture the gains from the merger. A second serious problem is that in a merger wave similar to what we have seen in the U.S. banking industry, it is hard to construct a reasonable benchmark portfolio. Finally, the market reaction might be unfavorable because even though a merger is expected to lower costs or raise revenues, the merger undertaken may not be the best option for a bank to pursue. Let's consider whether each of these complicating considerations might be important for the nine cases analyzed by Calomiris and Karceski.

The possibility that consumers rather than shareholders gain from a transaction is interesting, but we have no particular reason to believe that this possibility is important in these cases. Moreover, if consumers are benefiting from a merger, that means that the shareholder gains would understate the overall efficiency gains from the transactions. Since most of the stock market responses are already favorable, any unmeasured gains to consumers would only strengthen the presumption that these were mostly good deals. For the stock market signals to be a misleading indicator of overall efficiency, one must fear that the mergers permit banks to exercise market power in an untoward fashion. Given the characteristics of the organizations and banking markets involved in these cases, we have also no indication that this is a problem. So for these nine cases I see no reason to believe that the market reactions are significantly affected by these possibilities.

The potential biases created because of the lack of suitable benchmark banks to use for comparisons are more problematic. On the one hand, if the best organizations decide that consolidation is the only way to survive, while the industry laggards avoid being taken over and eventually fail, then merging banks will appear to outperform their peers. On the other hand, if there are different long-run strategies that are viable, so that only the best banks steer clear of mergers and pursue different options, then merging institutions will appear to underperform.

The cases in this paper suggest that management entrenchment may make things even more complicated. For instance, Boulevard was a poorly performing institution that probably deserved to be acquired or shut down before First Bank acquired it. As Gorton and Rosen (1995) persuasively argue, such entrenchment is more likely in banking than in other industries. If the Boulevard pattern is at all typical, then there will be periods when the sample of nonmerging firms will be dragged down by banks that ought to be acquired. However, once the acquisition occurs, a quick turnaround may be difficult so that it would be hard to determine the full impact of entrenchment on the comparison of merging and nonmerging institutions.

All these possibilities lead me to agree with Calomiris and Karceski that finding comparable benchmarks is not an easy task. Nevertheless, I believe that the benchmark nonmerging institutions that they have assembled are fairly representative. For the nine mergers, therefore, the benchmarking concerns do not lead me to doubt the basic stock market reports.

Finally, we must consider what to make of situations where the market assessment is negative because a merger announcement signals that other options are being forsaken. Since I agree with the authors' assessment that this is a plausible explanation for the Firstar market reactions, settling this issue is important. To this end, it may be helpful to rephrase the question to ask how we should interpret a situation where the market prices reflect the sentiment that management has simply made a suboptimal decision.

One view is that the decision is reversible (because the merger can be cancelled or the acquired bank can later be spun off), so that investors with a long horizon may not see any wealth destroyed. By this logic one might favor waiting to see the impact on operating performance of the combined institution before deciding on the ultimate impact. This is one interpretation of Calomiris and Karceski's view, since they advocate checking whether cost savings or revenue enhancements can be identified. However, they are also willing to entertain the possibility that the market simply misunderstands the nature of some transactions—a point I discuss further in the next section. Either way, the authors favor downplaying the market reactions.

An alternative view is that once the proposed merger is announced, Firstar forecloses the option to be taken over, thereby extinguishing an option and destroying value. Since there are likely to be nonnegligible transactions costs to unwinding the merger if it is consummated, it may be impossible to recover the option. In this case, one could conclude that although the merger may lead to a local improvement, from a more comprehensive perspective the merger would not be efficient.

We do not have enough information to sort out these competing hypotheses. Absent evidence that the market systematically misprices such transactions my preference is to give the benefit of the doubt to the market. Thus, I conclude that it is possible that the Firstar mergers were ill advised, even if they did subsequently lead to cost cutting and some revenue enhancement.

Overall, it seems to me that the basic fact that market reactions were positive in six of the nine cases is fairly compelling evidence that these deals were attractive. We have no reason to believe that this finding is an artifact of problems with benchmarking the stock returns. The fact that consumer windfalls are omitted from the analysis only strengthens this view. Similarly, if one accepts the authors' view of the two Firstar deals, the outlook is even more favorable. Moreover, the other negative stock price reaction was associated with the First Chicago–Lake Shore merger. All the supporting evidence corroborates the view that this market reaction was justified.

Integrating Case Research and Conventional Research

This study offers an interesting window into nine specific deals. I suspect, however, that most banking scholars will wait for more studies before drawing any firm conclusions. Nevertheless, in the meantime, I believe that there two further contributions that could be made by further exploring the data from these nine cases.

One path worth pursuing is to flush out new hypotheses that others can test. Calomiris and Karceski already develop several interesting hypotheses from looking at these cases. For instance, they point out that Nations-Bank (prior to its subsequent merger with Bank of America) was planning to buy back some of its stock because the management believed that the market did not fully appreciate their acquisition strategy. As discussed above, it is also plausible to argue that the management at Firstar and market participants disagreed over which options to pursue. Obviously, one cannot develop hypotheses by scrutinizing a set of data and then test the hypotheses on the same data set. However, the possibility that the market systematically misprices certain types of transactions is interesting and merits further study.

I encourage the authors to see if they can pick out some characteristics that might predict which types of transactions are most difficult to price. For instance, they provide some evidence that there was considerable heterogeneity among the professional analysts that were following Nations-Bank. It is well documented in the accounting literature that analysts' sentiment is systematically overly optimistic about firms' earnings per share. It would be interesting to know more about whether analyst heterogeneity has any predictive value or whether the typical bias is less pronounced during periods of high heterogeneity.

Calomiris and Karceski also stress the idea that relationship financing and cross selling are becoming increasingly important to successful banks. This view has strong support among practiners. For instance, cross-selling opportunities are commonly cited by bank analysts that believe the Travellers and Citibank merger will be a success. While the authors find some support for the existence of synergies, I would like to see if we could use the cases to refine our predictions regarding the success of synergy-motivated mergers. For instance, one could try to develop such predictions by systematically contrasting the Harris-Suburban and the First Chicago–Lake Shore deals.

In addition to generating and formalizing new hypotheses, more work on critiquing existing methods would be desirable. Many of the basic parameters of these deals that are described in table 2-1 are typically unavailable to researchers who are using standard public data sources. It would be very useful to see if augmenting the conventional analysis with the type of data in that table makes a difference. For instance, one could use a standard cost function approach to generate the predicted savings from the mergers. After calculating the difference between predicted and realized savings, one could check whether the unexplained cost variation is systematically related to any variables of the sort in table 2-1.

The basic idea that case studies can help generate new hypotheses and refine standard methodology is not controversial. Following through on these goals, however, is not easy. It is essential that the data are collected and organized in a systematic fashion so that comparisons across studies are possible. There is a natural temptation when one gets deep into details of particular cases to base explanations on the qualitative information that often is available from company insiders and press accounts. Progress will depend on aggregating across many studies and such aggregation depends on having tangible information that can be compared. Calomiris and Karceski have done a good job of avoiding this temptation and collecting lots of valuable data. I hope that subsequent researchers who seek to build on their work will do the same.

Reference

Gorton, Gary, and Richard Rosen. 1995. Corporate control, portfolio choice, and the decline of banking. *Journal of Finance* 50 (December): 1377–1420.

4

A Clinical Exploration of Value Creation and Destruction in Acquisitions
Organizational Design, Incentives, and Internal Capital Markets

Steven N. Kaplan, Mark L. Mitchell, and
Karen H. Wruck

4.1 Introduction

This paper attempts to further our knowledge of the sources of value creation and destruction in acquisitions. Prior work by economists consists primarily of large sample studies that provide mixed, incomplete, and sometimes conflicting evidence. Furthermore, these studies typically do not attempt to identify the organizational mechanisms and management practices that affect changes in productivity and performance.

In this paper, we ask two questions. First, when, how, and why is value created or destroyed in mergers and acquisitions? Second, how well do large sample performance measures reflect the underlying economics of acquisitions? To answer these questions, we present clinical analyses of two acquisitions: Cooper Industries' acquisition of Cameron Iron Works in 1989 and Premark's acquisition of Florida Tile (formally known as Sikes Corporation) in 1990. These acquisitions were selected because they received very different stock price responses at the time of their announce-

Steven N. Kaplan is the Neubauer Family Professor of Entrepreneurship and Finance at the Graduate School of Business of the University of Chicago and a research associate of the National Bureau of Economic Research. Mark L. Mitchell is associate professor of business administration at Harvard Business School. Karen H. Wruck is associate professor of finance at the Fisher College of Business Administration of the Ohio State University.

The authors especially thank Shel Erikson, Thomas Hix, William Berger, Michael Grimes, and Joseph Chamberlain of Cooper Cameron, John Deakins of Cameron Iron Works, and James Ringler and Larry Skatoff of Premark for talking with them and making this study possible. The authors thank Steven Hoffman, Sherry Roper, and Bradley Thompson for excellent research assistance. Comments from Larry Berlin, Derrick Deakins, Marc Knez, Toby Stuart, G. William Schwert, René Stulz, and seminar participants at the National Bureau of Economic Research and the University of Chicago were very helpful. This research has been supported by the Sloan Foundation through a grant to the National Bureau of Economic Research, and by a Merrill Lynch grant to Mitchell to study mergers and acquisitions.

ment—Cooper Industries' acquisition was viewed positively, while Premark's acquisition of Florida Tile was viewed negatively. Despite the different market reactions, neither acquisition ultimately created value. In exploring the reasons for these negative outcomes, we rely primarily on interviews with managers and on internally generated (and nonpublic) performance data. We compare the results of these analyses to those from analyses of postacquisition operating and stock price performance traditionally applied to large samples.

Taken together, our analyses of these two acquisitions suggest the following. First, it is very difficult to implement a value-creating acquisition strategy (and run an effective internal capital market). In both cases, postacquisition difficulties resulted from three circumstances:

1. Managers of the acquiring company did not deeply understand the target company. Despite the fact that Cooper Industries had operations in Cameron Iron Work's industry (the petroleum equipment business), Cooper's management did not understand that its expertise in manufacturing technology and internal control would not translate into success for Cameron. As Cameron managers described it, Cooper did not understand that "Cameron was not a manufacturing business. It was a service business with a manufacturing component." Similarly, Premark managers recognized only after the fact that they did not have sufficient expertise in Florida Tile's business. At the time of the acquisition, they viewed Florida Tile as an expansion of their decorative products division. As Premark's chief executive officer (CEO) Jim Ringler noted, "[W]hat we learned [from the Florida Tile acquisition] is that no matter how simple a business appears, it is complex in its execution."

2. An inappropriate organizational design was imposed on the target as part of the postacquisition integration process. After the acquisition, Cooper implemented its standard organizational structures and control procedures at Cameron. This process has been lionized as "Cooperization" in the popular press and in a widely taught corporate strategy case on Cooper (Collis and Stuart 1991; Collis 1991). Cooperization was inefficient for Cameron's business and, we hypothesize, ultimately for Cooper as a whole. For Cameron, it created an overcentralized, highly bureaucratic organization that stifled innovation and motivation. In July 1995, Cooper split off its energy-related businesses, including Cameron, creating a new firm called Cooper Cameron. Following the split, Cooper Cameron's new management team redesigned the organization and implemented new control procedures and incentive compensation plans. Many of these changes effectively undid Cooperization and appear largely responsible for the split-off's outstanding performance. Premark made Florida Tile part of its decorative products division and then essentially managed Florida Tile from headquarters. Premark also made no major changes in Florida Tile's organizational design. The distance between Premark headquarters and

Florida Tile's operations was responsible for Premark's slow response to production problems at Florida Tile.

3. Inappropriate management incentives existed at both the top management and division levels. After Cameron was acquired, Cooper implemented its standard incentive compensation system. Described by Cameron executives as "mysterious," divisional executives asserted they did not know what determined their compensation. Similarly, Premark's compensation system did not tie compensation to performance in any significant way. In fact, Premark's governance process and capital budgeting system actually encouraged managers to spend free cash flow rather than return it to shareholders.

It is worth emphasizing that in both cases, managers of acquiring firms expected synergies from the acquisition because the businesses were seen as related. While there is considerable disagreement as to whether mergers create value in general (which we describe below), there is something of a consensus that combinations of related companies can realize synergies and are, therefore, more valuable than unrelated combinations. These two cases, however, provide counterexamples that illustrate the difficulty of realizing synergies even when managers have the best of intentions. We hypothesize that potential synergies are often illusive and sometimes mythical in organizations; they appear as possibilities but never materialize either because they are difficult to achieve or because they never actually existed.

A second conclusion we draw from our analyses is that standard measures of operating performance used in large sample studies are weakly, if at all, correlated with actual postacquisition operating performance. Standard large sample measures of operating performance—company changes in operating margins and operating return on assets—indicate incorrectly that both the Cooper and Premark acquisitions were successful.

We argue that while neither acquisition created value, the initial stock market reaction to the acquisitions at the time were arguably reasonable. The market reacted positively to Cooper's acquisition of Cameron because the two firms appeared to operate in the same industry and there was an expectation that overlapping functions could be eliminated. Moreover, Cooper had a multidecade-long track record of making successful acquisitions (see Collis and Stuart 1991). In contrast, the market reacted negatively to Premark's acquisition of Florida Tile because the market understood that Premark had substantial free cash flow from its Tupperware division, and management provided no concrete explanation of how Florida Tile would add value to the organization. In addition, the acquisition would divert management's attention from Tupperware, its primary business, which was deteriorating.

We also discuss the biases that our research design uncovered and that are likely to affect most clinical or case-based research projects. We asked four candidate acquisitions to participate in this study. Two turned us down immediately—one was a poor performer, the other had a long-standing nondisclosure policy. Another firm agreed to participate and then was only mildly cooperative. Only one candidate participated, and even their participation was limited to target management. In this sense, our sample is selected or biased.

We believe that such selection bias is unavoidable in clinical research and teaching case studies. Thus, it is important to place clinical evidence in the context of the large sample literature. While clinical research likely suffers from some bias, its strength is that it facilitates the study of phenomena that cannot be examined through large sample approaches, for example, research into the structural models underlying the phenomenon in question. It also has the potential to identify important factors that might then be studied in large sample contexts. Thus, the two lines of empirical work are complementary.

The paper proceeds as follows. In section 4.2, we both summarize the existing (large sample) evidence on mergers and acquisitions and discuss the omissions in that literature. In section 4.3, we discuss our research design and sample selection. In this section, we also illustrate some of the biases that affect clinical or case-based research. In section 4.4, we analyze Cooper Industries' acquisition of Cameron Iron Works. In section 4.5, we analyze Premark's acquisition of Florida Tile. For both acquisitions, we discuss the motivations for the acquisitions, detail the acquisitions' effects on operating performance and the sources of value creation and destruction, and perform both a traditional operating performance analysis and longer-term stock performance analysis. In section 4.6, we discuss our conclusions, the generalizability of those conclusions, and their implications for future research.

4.2   Existing Evidence on Mergers and Acquisitions (and Lack Thereof)

The existing evidence on the effects of mergers and acquisitions comes from two basic types of large sample studies: event studies and performance studies. Event studies consistently find positive average combined returns to acquirer and target stockholders around the announcement of an acquisition. This suggests that the market anticipates that acquisitions will create value on average. These studies (and reactions) do not, however, provide deep insight into the sources of value changes in mergers, or whether those market expectations are ultimately realized. Furthermore, the combined returns cover a broad range of responses from very positive to very negative.

Cross-sectional analyses of event-period returns provide some evidence that the broad range of combined announcement-period returns reflects the market's ability to forecast an acquisition's success. For example, both

Mitchell and Lehn (1990) and Kaplan and Weisbach (1992) find that there is a relation between (1) acquirer and combined returns and (2) the ultimate outcome of the acquisition. Mitchell and Lehn find that acquirers earning low returns are subsequently more likely to become the target of a hostile takeover bid. Similarly, Kaplan and Weisbach find that both low acquirer and combined returns are associated with an increased likelihood of subsequent divestiture at a loss to the acquirer. Morck, Shleifer, and Vishny (1990) find that acquirer returns are greater in acquisitions in which the acquirer and the target are in the same line of business. Other studies examine a number of different determinants of the cross-sectional variation in returns associated with acquisitions (e.g., Lang, Stulz, and Walkling 1991; Maloney, McCormick, and Mitchell 1993; and Servaes 1991).

While cross-sectional analyses of event-period returns provide insight into the nature of the market reaction to acquisition announcements, they do not examine whether the anticipated value creation or improved productivity materializes. Nor do they have a great deal to say about the organizational mechanisms and management practices that drive acquisition success or failure.

Performance studies attempt to measure the longer-term implications of mergers and acquisitions. These studies use both accounting and stock return data to measure performance. Independent of the type of data analyzed, these studies fail to find consistent evidence of improved performance or productivity gains. For example, Healy, Palepu, and Ruback (1992) study the postmerger operating performance of fifty large mergers completed in the early 1980s. Although they document an increase in return on the market value of assets, Healy et al. find no evidence of changes in operating margins or capital expenditures. Similarly, Ravenscraft and Scherer (1987) find no evidence of margin improvements in a large sample of acquisitions completed in the 1960s and 1970s. In contrast, Lichtenberg (1992) reports evidence of productivity improvements at the plant level for a sample of acquisitions in the 1970s. Studies that focus on acquirers' long-term stock performance also find mixed results: abnormally negative stock returns after the acquisition (Agrawal, Jaffe, and Mandelker 1992), no abnormal returns (Franks, Harris, and Titman 1991), and negative abnormal returns only for stock mergers (Mitchell and Stafford 1996). Like the announcement-period event studies, longer-term performance and event studies document substantial cross-sectional variation in performance. But again, they do not provide deep insight into the sources of value changes in mergers and acquisitions.

Also relevant to this paper is a growing literature that attempts to explain overall merger activity by documenting aggregate, institutional, and industry trends in acquisitions (see e.g., Jensen 1993; Comment and Jarrell 1995; Mitchell and Mulherin 1996; and Andrade and Stafford 1999).

While these studies link acquisition activity to legal, regulatory, industry, or technological changes, they do not study whether these acquisitions achieve their objectives or meet the market's expectations.

We also surveyed the relevant literature in the field of corporate strategy and discussed that literature with our strategy colleagues. Again, we found no study that examined the link between the outcomes of acquisitions and organizational strategy and structure.

In sum, the voluminous economics, finance, and strategy literatures on takeovers during the past twenty years offer little insight to practitioners or academics on what managers do to influence whether mergers succeed or fail. Prior clinical work, such as Baker and Wruck (1989) and Wruck (1994), documents a connection between value creation and the nature of a firm's governance structure, organizational design, and compensation systems. However, these studies examine firms undertaking highly leveraged transactions, not mergers and acquisitions.

4.3 Research Design and Sample Selection

We chose candidate sample firms from a sample of mergers and acquisitions created by the Center for Research in Security Prices (CRSP) at the University of Chicago. The sample includes all firms delisted from the CRSP database between 1955 and 1995. We restricted our sample to acquisitions that were completed between 1987 and 1994. We began with 1987 because we wanted the acquisition to be sufficiently fresh in the minds of the executives we interviewed. We ended with 1994 to ensure that at least two years had elapsed since the acquisition. Because we were interested only in acquisitions by nonfinancial firms, we eliminated acquisitions by financial firms.

We then ranked acquisitions based on the market's announcement-period response. We classified the reaction as positive if the combined value of the acquirer and target increased by more than 5 percent (net of the return on the S&P 500) over the eleven days around the announcement. In these cases, the market anticipated that the value of the two companies in combination exceeded their stand-alone values. We classified the reaction as negative if the bidder's stock declined by more than the increase in the target's stock. In these cases, the market anticipated that the combination would destroy value.

This ranking process generated thirty-four positive candidates and fourteen negative candidates. We then approached two positive and two negative candidates, based on geographical proximity and school connections to executives at the acquirer. We approached each of the four companies by telephoning and/or writing a letter to the CEO or other top manager to explain our project and ask if they would participate. In each letter, we mentioned the contact who had referred us to the company. These contacts included two directors, the development office at one of the author's schools, and an alumnus of one of the author's schools. The acquisitions are

1. American Home Products' 1994 acquisition of American Cyanamid. The acquisition had announcement-period returns (three- and eleven-day) of −$122 million and −$108 million to American Home Products, and $2.65 billion and $2.81 billion to American Cyanamid. The combined value increase was $2.53 billion and $2.70 billion from an initial value of American Cyanamid of $5.52 billion.

2. Cooper Industries' 1989 acquisition of Cameron Iron Works. The acquisition had announcement period returns (three- and eleven-day) of $113 million and $207 million to Cooper, and −$13 million and −$8 million to Cameron. The combined value increase was $100 million and $199 million from an initial value of Cameron of $703 million.[1] Cooper Industries also acquired Champion Spark Plugs in 1989. This acquisition had announcement period returns (three- and eleven-day) of −$34 million and $5 million to Cooper, and $166 million and $254 million to Champion. The combined value increase was $132 million and $259 million from an initial value of Champion of $556 million.

3. Maytag's 1988 acquisition of Chicago Pacific. The acquisition had announcement period returns (three- and eleven-day) of −$175 million and −$195 million to Maytag, and $165 million and $167 million to Chicago Pacific. The combined value change was −$10 million and −$28 million from an initial value of Chicago Pacific of $518 million.

4. Premark International's 1990 acquisition of Sikes Corporation. Sikes Corporation's primary operating unit was Florida Tile. The acquisition had announcement period returns (three- and eleven-day) of −$48 million and −$183 million to Premark, and $29 million and $30 million to Sikes. The combined value change was −$19 million and −$153 million from an initial value of Sikes of $103 million.

American Home Products turned us down immediately. The vice president we contacted explained that American Home Products has a longstanding policy of not participating in such projects. This outcome is consistent with the experience of several colleagues who have attempted to study this company.

Cooper Industries made two acquisitions we were interested in studying. Cooper Industries, however, did not want to participate. As mentioned above, in 1995 Cooper Industries split off Cooper Cameron, which

---

1. This understates the value increase in this acquisition. As described in section 4.4, Cameron's share price had risen substantially several months earlier when its largest shareholder announced that its shares were for sale.

included the remaining assets of Cameron Iron Works. Cooper Industries' CEO suggested that we contact Cooper Cameron and Cooper Cameron's top management agreed to participate.

Maytag turned us down immediately. An assistant to the CEO stated that the acquisition of Chicago Pacific had been an extremely painful chapter in Maytag's history. Maytag had spent years undoing the damage that had been done by the acquisition. Subsequently, we learned that the *Wall Street Journal* had written an extremely critical front-page story on the acquisition (31 January 1991).

Premark agreed to participate. We met with the CEO and the chief financial officer (CFO) for one afternoon at Premark's headquarters. At that time, they agreed to proceed with the project and provide us with more detailed information. Several weeks after this meeting, Premark's CFO informed us that the company did not wish to continue its participation. Accordingly, our analysis of this acquisition relies on publicly available data and our one on-site meeting. Although we were unable to conduct as detailed an analysis as we originally anticipated, our findings are of interest and lend support to our conclusions.

To ensure the integrity of the research, we asked the firms to agree that they would not dictate the analysis or conclusions, but would have the right to review the information we published for factual accuracy and for sensitive competitive information.

Our experience in obtaining the sample makes clear that clinical and case-based research is subject to selection biases. We strongly suspect that firms with negative performance, such as Maytag, are less likely to participate. Even Cooper Industries, whose CEO was extremely helpful to us, did not want to participate directly. Both these organizations cited the counterproductive effects of revisiting the past as important factors in reaching their decision. In addition, firms with nondisclosure or nonparticipation policies are not potential research sites even when they do well, as was the case with American Home Products. Finally, we found that our access to firms was easier when we (as individuals or through our institution) had management contacts.

Although we are not sure what the effect of these biases is on our paper, we feel it is important to report them. It is also important to point out that biases arose in spite of the fact that we attempted to minimize them through our sample selection method. As stated earlier, a critical part of the value of clinical work is to identify important phenomena that are unlikely to emerge from large sample studies. Once identified, it is possible to study those phenomena more broadly in a larger sample context. However, the potential for biases in clinical work makes it essential that these biases be identified so that particular firms and transactions can be grounded in the context of the large sample literature.

4.4   Cooper Industries' Acquisition of Cameron Iron Works

4.4.1   Company Descriptions

In 1988, the year before the Cameron acquisition, Cooper Industries had sales of $4.25 billion and operating cash flow (also referred to as earnings before interest, taxes, depreciation, and amortization, or EBITDA) of $610 million. The company operated in three segments. The largest—electrical and electronics—generated more than half of Cooper's sales and operating profits. Its products included power transmission and distribution systems, lighting products, wire and cable, and protective electrical equipment. Cooper entered this segment with its 1981 acquisition of Crouse-Hinds. The second segment—Cooper's commercial and industrial segment—included hand tool, window treatment, and automotive businesses. It generated roughly 30 percent of sales and operating profits. The third segment—compression, drilling, and energy equipment business—generated roughly 20 percent of sales and 10 percent of operating profit. This segment's performance was the most highly variable and had been hurt by the collapse of the energy market in the early 1980s. As recently as 1981, it had generated more than half of Cooper's sales and operating profits.

Based on reported SIC codes, this acquisition would be considered unrelated using Compustat primary SIC codes, CRSP primary SIC codes, and Value Line industry classifications, but related at the three-digit level using the primary and secondary SIC codes listed in Dun and Bradstreet's Million Dollar Directory. Compustat lists Cooper Industries' primary four-digit SIC code as 3640 (electrical wiring and lighting equipment). In contrast, CRSP assigns Cooper a four-digit SIC code of 3511 (steam, gas, and hydraulic turbines). In the year before the Cameron acquisition, Dun and Bradstreet's Million Dollar Directory listed Cooper with a primary SIC code of 3469 (metal stamping), and secondary SIC codes of 3646 (commercial and industrial electric lighting fixtures), 3643 (current-carrying wiring devices), 3613 (switchgear and switchboard applications), 3679 (electronic components), and 3625 (relays and industrial controls). The Value Line Investment Survey includes Cooper in the electrical equipment industry.

Cameron Iron Works had two operating divisions. The larger of the two, the Oil Tool Division, manufactured "pressure control equipment used at the wellhead in the drilling for and production of oil and gas, both onshore and offshore."[2] The Oil Tool Division had sales of $428.7 million and EBITDA of $50.7 million in 1989. The smaller division, Forged Prod-

---

2. See Cameron Iron Works Annual Report, 1989.

ucts, made forged and extruded metal products, some of which were sold to the Oil Tool Division. The Forged Products Division had sales of $182.3 million and EBITDA of $19.3 million in 1989.

Compustat assigns Cameron a primary four-digit SIC code of 3533 (oil and gas field machinery and equipment). Again, in contrast, CRSP assigns Cameron a four-digit SIC code of 3462 (iron and steel forging). Dun and Bradstreet's Million Dollar Directory lists Cameron with a primary SIC code of 3533, and secondary codes of 3462, 3494 (values and pipe fittings), and 5084 (wholesale industrial machinery and equipment) in the year prior to the acquisition. Value Line includes Cameron in the oilfield services industry.

4.4.2   Acquisition Motivation and Events

At the time of the acquisition, Cooper's Energy Services division manufactured large compressors that pushed natural gas through pipelines and pumped oil out of the ground. Cameron had operated in related businesses since its founding in 1921. The potential for synergies with Cooper's energy businesses and the opportunity to improve efficiency through consolidation and cost-cutting made Cameron an attractive takeover target to Cooper. Cooper and Cameron sold to many of the same customers, and Cameron had a strong brand name and a reputation for technological excellence and high quality products.

Cameron became a likely acquisition candidate on 3 March 1989, when Cameron Iron Works' largest shareholder, the Robinson Family Trusts, announced its intention to sell its interests in Cameron or sell the company as a whole. The trusts, which were owned and controlled by the family of Cameron's founder, held 47.5 percent of Cameron's common stock. The founder's daughter owned an additional 7.5 percent of the company. On 16 March 1989, Cameron announced that it had held a special board meeting and had authorized its financial advisors to consider alternatives that included selling the company.

Cameron's investment bankers, First Boston and Goldman Sachs, contacted 126 potential buyers for Cameron.[3] Ultimately, 5 of these buyers submitted bids. The bids were discussed and evaluated by Cameron's board of directors and Cooper's was chosen as the winner. On 24 July 1989, the *Wall Street Journal* reported that Cameron and Cooper had entered into negotiations concerning a merger of the two companies. On 1 August 1989, Cooper and Cameron announced that they had signed a merger agreement.

The acquisition of Cameron by Cooper Industries was completed on 28 November 1989. The acquisition was structured as a tax-free exchange

---

3. This section is based on conversations with John Deakins, Cameron's CFO before the acquisition, and his son Derrick.

of Cooper Industries' preferred stock for Cameron's common stock. In addition to acquiring Cameron's equity, valued at $710 million, Cooper also assumed $257 million of Cameron debt resulting in a total transaction value of $967 million.

Cooper Industries' firm value at the end of the year before the acquisition was $2.7 billion. Thus the acquisition increased Cooper's size by over one-third. In its 1989 annual report, Cooper provided this optimistic assessment of the acquisition: "[The Cameron oil tool business] operations complement Cooper's existing valve and wellhead business. There are many opportunities to combine marketing and distribution and to reduce costs even further, although Cameron's management had done an excellent job of cutting operating costs. This acquisition puts Cooper in a very strong position to benefit from an expected upturn in the energy markets."

4.4.3   Cooper's Acquisition Strategy and Cooperization

This section and those that follow rely on both publicly available information—particularly Collis and Stuart (1991), Collis (1991), and Keller (1983)—and out interviews with William Berger, vice president of finance and administration, the Cameron division of Cooper Cameron; Joe Chamberlain, Cooper Cameron's corporate controller; Shel Erikson, Cooper Cameron's CEO; Thomas Hix, Cooper Cameron's CFO; and James Deakins, Cameron Iron Works' CFO. The four Cooper Cameron executives worked for Cooper Cameron at the time of the interviews in August 1996. Both Berger and Chamberlain had worked for Cooper Industries for many years before the acquisition. John Deakins was Cameron's CFO at the time of the acquisition and had joined Cameron in the 1970s.

The Evolution of Cooper's Acquisition Strategy

For Cooper, Cameron Iron Works was the latest in a long series of acquisitions resulting from an acquisition program that began in the 1960s and accelerated in the late 1970s and early 1980s. Table 4.1 presents a history of Cooper's profitability and size from 1960 to 1995. In 1960, Cooper's firm value was $36.8 million; sales were $61.4 million. Over the next three decades, Cooper made more than forty acquisitions (as well as over thirty divestitures) of firms in related industries. Its value increased 213-fold, while revenues climbed 99 times and operating profit increased 173 times.

Cooper's substantial increase in size was in large part due to its aggressive acquisition strategy, which was rooted in its history. Since its founding, the company had maintained a strong presence in the manufacture of heavy equipment for energy-related applications. The high volatility of cash flows from these energy-related applications led to what managers described as "low quality" earnings. To address this "problem," Cooper's management decided to use acquisitions both as a source of growth and

Table 4.1   Cooper Industries' History of Profitability, Sales, and Assets, Fiscal Years 1960–1995 (in millions of dollars)

	1960	1965	1970	1975	1980	1985	1990	1991	1995
Sales	61.4	118.5	225.7	478.1	1,836.7	3,061.8	6,206.2	6,155.3	4,848.7
Operating profit before depreciation	6.2	17.5	32.1	76.9	347.0	437.4	1,065.2	1,080.5	810.6
Net income	3.0	7.0	31.1	12.4	146.7	135.1	361.4	393.2	94.0
Earnings per share[a]	0.35	0.56	0.35	0.76	1.07	0.70	2.81	3.04	2.51
Total assets	45.9	61.6	183.9	369.2	1,613.4	3,635.9	7,167.5	7,148.6	6,063.9
Intangible assets			6.4	NA	238.3	863.5	2,609.5	2,543.8	2,226.0
Firm value	36.8	90.8	173.7	310.4	1,880.6	3,051.1	6,196.1	7,902.8	5,829.8
Five-year increase in firm value (%)		146.7	91.3	78.7	505.9	62.2	103.1		−26.2
Five-year stock return (%)		103.6	50.1	84.5	433.0	−2.93	129.9		4.0
Five-year return to S&P 500 (%)		86.3	17.8	17.1	92.1	98.6	85.4		98.7

Note: NA = not available. Data items are taken from Compustat and Cooper Industries Annual Reports.

[a]Adjusted for subsequent stock splits. Between 1960 and 1995, Cooper Industries had four 2-for-1 splits occurring on 4 November 1966, 26 March 1976, 21 April 1980, and 10 April 1989.

to provide a hedge against the operating risk associated with Cooper's large investment in the energy sector. This strategy was articulated in a late 1950s memo from Gene Miller, the first nonfamily president of Cooper, to corporate officers and division managers:

> Over the long term, our basic corporate objective is growth. Specifically, it is a rate of growth that will increase earnings per share (before tax) at a compound annual rate of 11 percent. Growth by itself, however, will not be sufficient. We must also improve the quality of earnings by reducing the fluctuations of income that have characterized our company in the past. Stability of earnings, therefore, represent a collateral objective. This objective implies a careful examination of opportunities in less cyclical and countercyclical areas as well as a continuing effort to expand our current businesses. We will have achieved stability along with growth when our earnings in any one year never fall below those of the previous year.
>
> There are two reasons why the achievement of these objectives is essential. First, the resulting earnings performance will ensure an above-average return on shareholders' investment, in terms of dividend income and increased market value of Cooper shares. Second, the growth inherent in this performance is necessary to provide the opportunities for individual growth and development that will enable us to attract and hold high talent personnel. (Keller 1983, 140)

Robert Cizik, who became Cooper's CEO in 1969 and led the company as chairman and CEO until 1996, refined Cooper's acquisition strategy. The company established three criteria for identifying potential acquisitions: (1) the companies should be in industries in which Cooper could become a major player; (2) the companies should be in relatively stable, low-tech manufacturing industries; and (3) only companies with leading market positions should be considered. Cooper looked for companies with strong brand name recognition and strong marketing programs. Family owned and operated businesses were often attractive candidates because they offered the possibility of value creation through an infusion of capital and the addition of Cooper's management expertise. Cooper pursued both complementary business acquisitions that would build upon established product lines and diversifying acquisitions that would put "another leg on the stool" of the company.

In a 1977 address, Cizik described the principles underlying Cooper's diversification program (which remained an integral part of the firm's strategy well into the 1990s):

> In general, our diversification program has been very selective, carried out at a methodical and deliberate pace. . . . My point is that on every occasion, top corporate management controlled each major move. No move was made unless it offered Cooper the opportunity to become a principal factor and potential leader in a major and growing market.

New diversifications were never attempted until earlier ones were thoroughly understood and under control.

. . . Diversification is the means by which an organization is preserved and temporal resources are replaced. As management strives to strengthen and adapt the organization to changing economic conditions, markets and environments, untapped talents and capacities will emerge, creating opportunities for expansion into new areas. By diversifying into new products and subsequently exploiting new markets, acquiring new facilities, and infusing new blood into its organization, a company can restore depleting resources. Diversification is the natural outcome of foresight and the instinct to survive in a changing world, and it is made possible through the wise use of financial assets, or more specifically, cash.

. . . Throughout its existence, an organization must deal with the challenge created by the cash flow cycle—that is, cash into the business and cash out of the business. It must continually search for sources of funds and opportunities for investment. In a very real sense, its health and survival depends on its success in these searches. If a company cannot finance its growth, financially stronger competitors will relegate it to the corporate backwaters. Similarly, a mature company that fails to translate today's cash into tomorrow's profits will decay. The latter problem can be solved in part through diversification. When businesses are combined, those with cash flow surpluses can feed those with a need for cash. Later, as investments made in one line of business come to fruition and opportunities emerge in another, their roles can be reversed.

. . . In my opinion, it is not a question of whether diversification should occur, but rather how much and in what direction. (Keller 1983, 242)

Through the late 1970s, Cooper's acquisitions were relatively small. The company concentrated on building what it called its "toolbasket," making a series of acquisitions in the hand tool industry that included Ken-Tool Manufacturing, Lufkin Rule, Cresent Niagara, Nicholson File, Xcelite, and J. Wiss & Sons (Keller 1983). The firm also assembled an aircraft services segment in addition to its petroleum-related compression and drilling segment.

With its May 1979 acquisition of Gardner-Denver, however, Cooper's acquisition strategy changed. Gardner-Denver was about the same size as Cooper, with revenues of $642 million versus Cooper's $780 million. In addition, Gardner-Denver operated in the cyclical energy business, manufacturing machinery for petroleum exploration and mining. Because Gardner-Denver was perceived to be poorly managed and in a related business, Cooper management saw it as an attractive target.

Less than two years later, in November 1980, Cooper made a white knight tender offer for Crouse Hinds, which was in the midst of a takeover contest. Crouse Hinds had 1980 revenues of $754 million, making it roughly equal in size to both Cooper and Gardner-Denver prior to the acquisitions. Crouse-Hinds produced electrical plugs, receptacles, and industrial lighting, and was itself in the process of acquiring Belden, an electrical wire, cable, and cord producer. The acquisition of Crouse-Hinds represented a new business segment for Cooper. After 1980, Cooper continued acquiring both smaller and larger companies. McGraw-Edison (acquired in 1985 for $1.1 billion) and Champion Spark Plug (acquired in 1989 for $800 million) were the two largest of these.

Integrating Acquisitions: Cooperization

In conjunction with its acquisition strategy, Cooper's management had developed a systematic approach for absorbing newly acquired companies that became known both internally and externally as "Cooperization." Cooper and Cooperization became the subject of two well-known teaching cases. The earlier of the two, Piper (1974), focuses on Cooper's 1972 acquisition of the Nicholson File Company, which was part of its strategy to assemble a strong presence in the nonpowered hand tool industry. The latter, Collis and Stuart (1991), addresses Cooper's acquisition strategy and its purchase of Champion Spark Plug and Cameron Iron Works. Both cases present Cooper as a successful acquirer and strong performer. In fact, Collis (1991) goes so far as to say that for the only time in his course, he is willing to make a normative statement: "Cooper is a great company." Collis also notes that "Cooper is a wonderful example of a large, successful and diversified company which has grown through acquisition, but remains fundamentally an operating company." He bases this conclusion on the fact that Cooper's stock price performance cumulated over several decades outperforms the S&P 500 and on his assessment that Cooper's strategy is internally consistent. As we show later, analysis utilizing more appropriate performance measures and our qualitative organizational evidence provides strong evidence to the contrary for the Cameron acquisition.

Overview of Cooperization. Following an acquisition, Cooper implemented its manufacturing practices and accounting and control systems at the target firm. Cooper did not become heavily involved in the strategy or marketing aspects of acquired businesses. Instead, they selected target firms based in large part on the strength of target management teams in these areas. In our visit to Cooper Cameron, William Berger, formerly with Cooper Industries, now vice president of finance and administration for the Cameron division of Cooper Cameron, described Cooperization as follows:

> In my view, Cooperization was comprised of the following: (1) leave the best managers in the acquired business in place and bring in a few key

Cooper managers; (2) revamp the financial reporting structure; and (3) put in Cooper's fundamental management and control policies and procedures. The Cooperization process was a process of internalizing management control systems and accounting systems. It was not intended to change product market strategies or even to understand them at first. That knowledge came over time.

Cooper would always find ways to get cash out of a company. They implemented new working capital management practices; found market niches; implemented better product pricing structures; stripped out product lines that had become fixtures in the organization, but weren't carrying their weight; consolidated fragmented businesses when part of an acquired business fit with something they already owned—they put the two together and reduced administrative and overhead costs.

The impetus didn't come because Cooper management was expert in the businesses they acquired. It came from taking a fresh look at the acquired business, a willingness to infuse capital, and asking management a lot of questions about why things were the way they were. For example, why do we make this product? Why are we in this business?

This characterization of Cooperization is consistent with the one in Collis and Stuart (1991) and with our readings of analyst reports.

Manufacturing Services. Manufacturing improvement was an important part of Cooperization. To this end, Cooper headquarters maintained a manufacturing services group of roughly fifteen professionals to provide management and consulting services to new acquisitions as well as to existing units of the firm. Furthermore, the manufacturing services group oversaw Cooper's capital budget (Collis and Stuart 1991). Cooper invested heavily in the companies it acquired both to improve manufacturing processes and to bring financial reporting and control practices up to speed.

Manufacturing services focused on eliminating weak "old fixture" product lines, improving product pricing structures, consolidating operations where it found synergies with existing businesses, and reducing spending on perquisites. The slogan "Cash is king" became an integral part of each target's working vocabulary. In addition to being held accountable for profitability, managers were encouraged to utilize working capital efficiently through a system that charged them interest on its use.

Joe Chamberlain, who had worked on Cooper's acquisitions and divestitures as a controller at Cooper, elaborated: "Cooper bought businesses where they manufactured something. It was the job of the senior vice-president of the manufacturing services group to oversee the implementation of modern manufacturing technology in acquired firms. Cooper invested in businesses that hadn't had a whole lot invested in them. They put lots of money into businesses that couldn't afford it. Cooper also put in modern control systems. The idea was that the combination of modern manufacturing practices and modern management control would generate tremendous cash flow that would repay the debt from the acquisitions. Then they could do it all over again."

Because of this heavy involvement with and investment in manufacturing, Cooper became known as one of the leaders of American manufacturing. For example, Cizik was named outstanding chief executive in the machinery industry in both 1980 and 1981, and was president of the National Association of Manufacturers in 1993.

Accounting and Control Systems. Following an acquisition, Cooper invested in the target's accounting and control systems to make them consistent with Cooper's systems. In addition, as part of its implementation of the purchase method of accounting for acquisitions, Cooper headquarters established and managed reserve accounts for each target firm. Consistent with purchase accounting, Cooper routinely estimated liabilities that would be incurred as part of the Cooperization process. These included anticipated expenditures required to revamp facilities, shut down parts of operations, and perform necessary maintenance. The anticipated liabilities were credited to "other long-term liabilities." The offsetting debit was to "goodwill." Because goodwill is amortized over forty years, this accounting treatment allowed Cooper to spend heavily on improvements soon after the acquisition without a concomitant reduction in reported earnings. Berger commented: "Cooper was on the leading edge of technology with respect to acquisition accounting. For example, in 1990, after the Cameron acquisition they set up reserves for people who were on the payroll today that would be terminated under restructuring. Their salaries from January 1 through their termination were put in the reserve." Both Berger and Chamberlain viewed Cooper's purchase accounting practices as motivated by management's desire to deliver consistent growth in earnings per share to shareholders.

Cooper's aggressive approach to purchase accounting is reflected in the growth of intangible assets on the firm's balance sheet from $6.4 million in 1970 to $238.3 million in 1980 and $2,609.5 million in 1990. The offsetting entries are reflected in the growth of liability accounts (not presented in table 4.1). As intangible assets increased, so did split-adjusted earnings per share (EPS) from $0.35 in 1970 to $1.07 in 1980. EPS did dip to $0.70 in 1985, a poor year for the energy business, but bounced back, reaching $2.81 in 1990.

Evaluating the Success of Cooperization before the Cameron Acquisition. Based on Cooper's stock performance, Cooper's acquisition strategy was arguably a success through the time of the Cameron acquisition. Figures 4.1 and 4.2 present Cooper's stock performance (including dividends) from 1970 to 1995 and from 1980 to 1995, respectively. Figure 4.1 compares the returns to strategies of buying and holding Cooper Industries

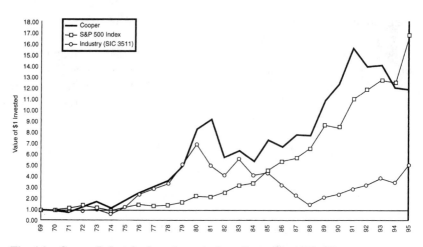

Fig. 4.1   Cooper Industries long-term stock performance, 1970–95

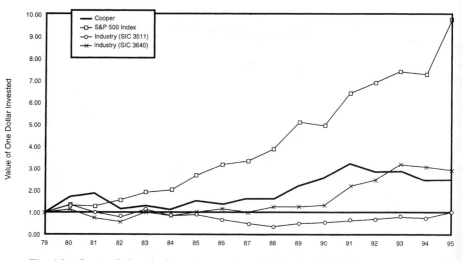

Fig. 4.2   Cooper Industries long-term stock performance, 1980–95

stock, the S&P 500, and an equal-weighted portfolio of stocks listed on CRSP as having an SIC code of 3511, Cooper's primary SIC code at the start of the period. The figure indicates that from 1970 to 1989—the year of the Cameron acquisition—Cooper outperformed both its industry and the S&P 500.[4]

Figure 4.2 measures Cooper's performance from the beginning of 1980 to 1995 relative to the S&P 500, and to an equal-weighted portfolio of

---

4. We use the term *arguably* at the start of the paragraph because these comparisons and the ones that follow are not based on statistical tests.

stocks listed by CRSP as having SIC codes of 3511 and 3640. (Crouse-Hinds had a CRSP SIC code of 3640.) The beginning of 1980 is chosen because it marks the start of the period in which Cooper began to make substantially larger acquisitions. The figure indicates that from 1980 to 1989, Cooper underperformed the S&P 500. This underperformance, however, appears to have been driven by the poor performance of Cooper's two primary industries. During this period, Cooper outperformed both industry indices by a substantial margin.

4.4.4 Initial Market Reaction to the Cameron Acquisition

Table 4.2 presents the stock price response of Cooper and Cameron shareholders to events associated with the merger for a three-day window centered on the announcement date and the corresponding eleven-day window. Performance is based on market-model abnormal returns and their associated abnormal dollar value. Both companies' market value increased at the merger announcement. Our estimate of the market's expectation of the total value created by Cooper's acquisition of Cameron is $300 million based on the three-day window and $352.8 million based on the eleven-day window.

For Cameron's shareholders, the abnormal dollar value across all events totals $188.2 million measured during the three-day window and $146.1 million measured during the eleven-day window. Most of this value increase occurred around the first indications that the firm would be sold, both when the Robinson Family trusts announced their intention to sell and when Cameron's board held its special meeting on 16 March 1989. It is worth adding that these abnormal returns imply that Cameron's capital value without the acquisition would have been roughly $800 million, $779 million, or $821 million, based on Cameron's capital value in the acquisition of $967 million.

For Cooper's shareholders, the abnormal dollar value across all events totals $112.8 million measured during the three-day window and $206.7 million measured during the eleven-day window. Most of this value accrued when the two companies signed a merger agreement. For the three days around 24 July 1989, when Cooper and Cameron announced they were negotiating, Cooper's share price fell by a significant 4.42 percent; the corresponding value decline was $148.1 million. Roughly one week later, on 1 August 1989, when the merger agreement was signed, Cooper's abnormal return was a significant 8.04 percent for the three-day and 10.92 percent for the eleven-day window. The corresponding abnormal dollar values were $260.9 million and $356.1 million, respectively.

The market's positive reaction is consistent with the hypothesis that investors expect the past success of Cooper's acquisition strategy to continue. In fact, several analyst reports at the time describing the acquisition made this argument.

Table 4.2   Stock Price Response to Events Associated with Cooper Industries' Acquisition of Cameron Iron Works (millions of dollars)

	Days −1 through 1					Days −5 through 5				
	Cooper Industries Common Stock		Cameron Iron Works Common Stock		Total Abnormal Dollars	Cooper Industries Common Stock		Cameron Iron Works Common Stock		Total Abnormal Dollars
Event Description (Date)	% Abnormal Return	Abnormal Dollars	% Abnormal Return	Abnormal Dollars		% Abnormal Return	Abnormal Dollars	% Abnormal Return	Abnormal Dollars	
Robinson Family Trust files a 13-D discussing the possibility of selling their shares (3/3/89)			15.97	85.0	85.0			15.29	77.8	77.8
Cameron holds special board meeting to consider alternatives, including selling the company (3/16/89)			13.25	81.0	81.0			8.39	49.4	49.4
Cameron's board authorizes financial advisors to explore alternatives (4/5/89)			4.94	34.2	34.2			9.03	60.1	60.1
Cameron and Cooper announce they have entered into negotiations (7/24/89)	−4.42	−148.1	2.19	15.1	−133.0	−0.31	−10.2	1.23	8.7	−1.5
Cameron and Cooper sign a merger agreement (8/1/89)	8.04	260.9	−1.26	−28.1	232.8	10.92	356.1	−3.89	−15.4	340.7
Total abnormal dollars		112.8		188.2	300.0		206.7		146.1	352.8

Note: Abnormal returns are computed based on market models estimates from days −200 through −21 prior to the first announcement for both Cooper Industries and Cameron Iron Works. Abnormal dollars for eleven-day windows are not additive because of window overlap.

4.4.5   Clinical Analysis of Postacquisition Outcome

All of the measures of productivity change associated with Cooper's acquisition of Cameron that we consider indicate that the combination was unsuccessful. As mentioned earlier, a little over five years after the acquisition, Cooper divested Cameron and three other energy-related divisions through a tax free split-off transaction/exchange offer in which Cooper's shareholders could exchange Cooper shares for shares in the new Cooper Cameron. The new company, Cooper Cameron Corporation, consisted of Cameron (Cooper Oil Tools), Cooper Energy Services (Cooper's original energy-related business), Cooper Turbocompressor, and Wheeling Machine Products. In connection with the split-off, Cooper recognized a $313 million (accounting) charge or write-down. Immediately after the split-off, Cooper Cameron wrote down an additional $441 million. In accounting terms, therefore, the Cameron acquisition is associated with $441 million to $754 million in write-downs of a total purchase price of $967 million. To the extent that the write-downs reflect real losses, they imply realized capital values for Cameron of $213 to $526 million. These values are consistent with a substantial deterioration in Cameron's value following the acquisition and/or substantial overpayment by Cooper.

As we discuss below, the qualitative and quantitative evidence we have collected strongly corroborates the write-off data. We find that the acquisition destroyed $400 to $500 million in value (relative to the initial value of $800 million). The Cooperization process failed to function effectively in integrating Cameron. In giving us his assessment of the Cameron acquisition, Shel Erikson, CEO of Cooper Cameron, argued: "The thing that hurt Cooper in its acquisition of Cameron was the lack of success of the 'Cooperization' process." In fact, given that Cooper is no longer an active acquirer, it appears that Cooperization might have failed not only in Cameron's case, but more broadly as well.

Our evidence in this section comes from one manager of (the preacquisition) Cameron Iron Works and from several managers of Cooper Cameron. They provided us with a perspective on the preacquisition Cameron, the Cameron acquisition, the Cameron operations as a part of Cooper, and on the actions taken following the split-off to create value. The post-split-off actions are associated with outstanding stock performance for Cooper Cameron shareholders. Figure 4.3 indicates that from the split-off date, 19 July 1995, through 1 October 1996, Cooper Cameron's stock returned 160.3 percent. The corresponding return to the S&P 500 was 25.1 percent. Cooper Cameron's stock return also exceeded the return to other companies in its industry. Over the same period, firms in the Dow Jones Oil Equipment Services Index returned 37.2 percent. The return to Cooper Cameron's stock represents value creation of $388 ($890) million in 1989 (1995) dollars, adjusted for industry performance. (This value cre-

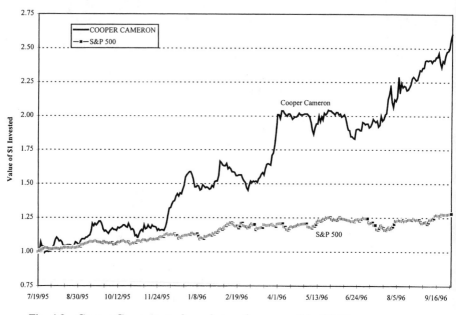

Fig. 4.3   Cooper Cameron stock market performance, July 1995 to September 1996

ation includes both Cameron and Cooper Energy Services.) Thus, Cooper's decision to split off Cooper Cameron allowed shareholders that chose to retain the Cooper Cameron shares to recover some, but not all, of the value destroyed following the acquisition.

The actions that led to Cooper Cameron's stock performance provide indirect evidence on how value was destroyed while Cameron was part of Cooper: what the split-off managers choose to do differently when running a free-standing organization provides insight into how Cooper could have managed Cameron more effectively.

As we describe below in detail, the story we heard from the Cooper Cameron managers was that the Cooperization process and organizational structures were inappropriate for Cameron. In addition, an increasing number of acquisition and divestiture transactions per year took more and more of top management's time at Cooper, so less time was spent on operating and strategic management issues. As this occurred, Cooper's management systems were ineffective in addressing fundamental problems with leadership or strategy at Cameron. Finally, Cooper's compensation system, which Cameron's managers described as "mysterious," failed to provide strong incentives. We hypothesize that Cameron's experience is consistent with the Cooperization process moving from an initially effective system to an overly centralized and bureaucratic process that inhibited management decisionmaking.

Organizational Design

Overcentralization and Bureaucratic Creep. Cooper's organization of Cameron (and Cooper Energy Services) was overly centralized. As Shel Erikson, Cooper Cameron's CEO, explained, "Cooper organized Cameron functionally out of Houston as one profit center. The president of Cameron was accountable for those profits. This doesn't put profit responsibility where it is best managed. Roughly two-thirds of Cameron's business was outside the U.S. Yet under Cooper, people in the field had to get OKs from Houston. Obviously this was very time consuming."

Michael Grimes, president of Cooper Cameron's Energy Systems Division who had recently joined the firm from General Electric Power Systems, concurred with Erikson's assessment. He noted that Cooper had organized Cameron and Cooper Energy Services as "very tall functional chimneys with lots of layers within each chimney." This centralization made it difficult for sales executives in the field to obtain cooperation from operations executives in Houston.

John Deakins, Cameron's preacquisition CFO, provided independent corroboration of the view that Cooper was overly centralized relative to Cameron: "Cooper was forms oriented, while Cameron was people oriented. Cameron sold big ticket items with multi-million-dollar prices where personal relationships mattered while Cooper sold more commodity-type products. Cooper's style and culture were completely the opposite of Cameron's."

Consistent with the excessive centralization, immediately after the split-off, Cooper Cameron's new management reorganized both Cameron and Cooper Energy Services. According to Erikson, "We toyed with different organization concepts. We came up with a matrix. We had three regions. . . . These regions were matrixed against products. . . ." This new organization put decisionmaking closer to the customer and allowed Cameron to manage regionally and by product.

At the same time that Cooper became overly centralized, it also appears to have become overly bureaucratized. As Berger explained:

Part of the Cooperization process is to establish a consistent methodology of reporting financial performance. The idea was to gain management control/internal control over the business. This became an end unto itself rather than an effective way to run a business.

In the final analysis, the Cooperization process went too far. By the time Cooper had digested Champion and Cameron, managers were so concerned about control that it was difficult for divisions to make decisions. The internal control process was overbearing. The amount of time we spent on bureaucratic administration versus running the business was unbelievable. The internal controls were taken to a point where they hamstrung businesses and kept them from making decisions. That has changed under Cooper Cameron. We are making significant changes without the bureaucracy associated with heavy internal control. We had to unravel the bureaucracy that we had established through the Cooperization process.

Grimes added, "The management control system in this organization [was] unbelievable. It was one of the first things I encountered. When I put in a $3,000 request for a laptop computer, it required ten signatures. This is a very control-oriented culture. . . . The first thing I did was to get the bureaucracy out by delayering. I didn't want to redefine the processes to get the job done. We took reports out and layers out, but we didn't want to confuse people about the fundamentals of the business."

Chamberlain gave this story as an example of how the system took on a life of its own:

One year, Cizik said to each of his seven direct reports that he wanted a monthly report on how their business was doing. So each of them requested a monthly report of their direct reports and so on. On average, one or two days a month were spent generating a report telling us what we were doing all month. Each month, Cizik got a 70–80 page report from each of his direct reports. In the treasury department, they kept logs of our activities so we could accurately report what we'd done. This is the kind of thing that happened. It's the kind of thing that happens in big companies when one man at the tops says "give me this." There was a fear of asking the boss, "Is this what you want? Do you want this to happen?"

Cooper's Manufacturing Services Group evaluated capital requests. All of the requests went through an extensive process. To spend $600,000 for a machine tool you had to fill out a request that was 25 pages long. It would be reviewed by a bunch of people. Then finally approved. The approval process took several weeks. We [the new Cooper Cameron] are trying to get it down to 2 to 3 pages, including a summary of the expected return. We want to emphasize that the return is the most important thing. The new process takes two days at most.

Preoccupation with Acquisition and Divestiture Transactions. As Cooper increased the size and number of acquisition and divestiture transactions, they became an increasingly large part of activity at corporate headquarters. It appears that completing transactions successfully became as important as or more important than whether the transactions were strong ones. Chamberlain explained:

As viewed in hindsight, Cooper became too involved in acquisitions and divestitures—they were doing seven to eight a year. Headquarters was focused on doing acquisitions and not on the process of managing businesses. Acquisitions and divestitures chew up a tremendous amount of resources. Cooper tended to do all of the work internally. All aspects of the corporate office were involved in each acquisition and divestiture. Acquisitions were fun, more fun than running the business. At the end of the year kudos would go to the general manager who suggested we acquire XYZ business and we acquired it. What a great acquisition! Success was measured by making acquisitions and divestitures. They didn't have to be good. It was a failure if something we wanted was for sale and we didn't get it. We started worrying about the next one before we had figured out what to do with this one. We did conduct postacquisition reviews, but the numbers were really soft because we would often be absorbing a new business and new products into our existing product lines.

At Cooper Cameron, I feel like I see a lot more attention to what's going on with the businesses.

Inability to Understand Business and Confront Strategy and Leadership Problems. As described earlier, part of Cooper's acquisition strategy was to acquire manufacturing businesses in related areas, invest resources to improve efficiency, cut costs, and implement modern management control systems. According to Cooper Cameron managers, this approach proved particularly unsuitable for Cameron. In Erikson's view, Cooper misunderstood the importance of manufacturing versus service and marketing in Cameron's businesses. He explained:

> Cameron didn't fit the Cooper style. There was a lack of understanding of what the oil field market was all about. Cooper was a manufacturing company. Bob Cizik was president of the National Association of Manufacturers. But this is not a manufacturing business. It is a service business with an equipment manufacturing component. Cooper missed the marketing and service side of the business, and the changes in this direction that were taking place in the market.
>
> Cooper had an effective business strategy that was manufacturing oriented. It was not focused on the customer (and most of their products were sold through distributors). When it was running Cameron, Cooper was constantly trying to improve the manufacturing processes.
>
> Here is an example of a mistake they made. Cameron was a franchise business when Cooper bought it. They changed its name to Cooper Oil Tools. This was wasteful. We changed back to Cooper Cameron. Cooper did this because it was part of their strategy to call everything Cooper, and because they didn't understand that our business was a service business.

John Deakins also questioned whether Cooper understood what it was buying in Cameron. "Not only did the nature of Cooper's and Cameron's businesses differ, but Cameron had already spent the greater part of the 1980s improving quality and wringing out costs. I had worked for Cooper briefly in 1973 and greatly respected what they did in the area of quality and cost management. During the 1980s downturn, we instituted a quality management program and worked on reducing costs. Employment declined to 5,500 from 14,000 and we wrung out 20 percent of our costs. I do not know that Cooper understood that we had done that."

Cameron's problems were exacerbated by a slump in the oil industry that began in 1992. Its poor performance during this period significantly affected Cooper's earnings. Management hired outside consultants to assess Cameron's market position. Their report was unfavorable, stating that the division was losing market share. Cameron's president disagreed, claiming that the performance was to be expected in light of business conditions, but that they were not losing share. Top management accepted the division manager's analysis. Berger described the situation:

> The two years following the acquisition were great. Around the time of the Gulf War, business started to fall off dramatically. In August 1992, orders fell away. They did not recover until early to mid-1995. But in 1992, we were still profitable. In 1993 we broke even. In 1994, we lost significant dollars. It was virtually a disaster. In response, we did a lot of consolidation. We went from 6,500 employees in 1991 to 4,200 employees in 1995.
>
> Cooper knew there were problems. Cameron was in a cycle headed into a trough and it was affecting Cooper's earnings and stock price. At the 1993 annual meeting, Cizik talked about the company's weak outlook. The stock price fell from $51 to $43 in a day. The rest of Cooper's businesses were doing fine.
>
> Booz Allen was hired to do a market analysis of Cameron. In their report, Booz Allen concluded that we were losing market share. The president of Cameron was able to discredit the Booz Allen report and convince Cizik and other top managers [incorrectly] that we hadn't lost market share. There was no management or organizational response to the data from Booz Allen. But their data shouldn't have been necessary. Our own financial statements provided us with data that there was a problem.
>
> Cameron's management knew the market so well that we [Cooper's managers] had convinced ourselves that we could not find someone who knew the business like they did. They were always saying that performance was going to improve and they seemed to be taking the right actions. They convinced us that when the market rectified itself the performance was going to be there. All of us had the arrogance of the dominant competitor in the industry. We let competitors penetrate the low-tech end of the business. We couldn't respond as they were able to respond. We weren't focused on our competitors—we were losing market share.
>
> Nine days after the split-off, Cameron's president was let go. Following its split-off, Cooper Cameron changed its organizational structure to focus on customers and marketing rather than manufacturing.

Compensation and Incentives

Cooper used the Hay system of job classifications to set salary levels (Collis and Stuart 1991, 13). Under the Hay system, each job is assigned a number of points based on measures of job size, including number of persons managed and size of the budget under a manager's control. The objective of the system is to allow cross-job comparisons that help the firm pay similar salaries to managers with similar jobs. At Cooper, management felt that the uniform pay scales resulting from the Hay system allowed managers to move easily between divisions. Unfortunately, the Hay system also creates incentives for managers to increase personnel and resources under their control. Taken in combination with Cooper's strategy of growth through acquisition, managers arguably had a strong incentive to grow the firm beyond its optimal size.[5] While empirically establishing the optimal size of an organization is not possible, our findings are consistent with the hypothesis that Cooper destroyed value, in part, by becoming "too large."

Cooper also paid bonuses that could reach 20 to 40 percent of base salaries. The bonuses were determined by executives at headquarters. Collis and Stuart (1991) emphasize Cooper's Management Development and Planning (MD&P) system for evaluating key managers. Under MD&P, managers developed detailed goals for the forthcoming year and then were evaluated on their attainment of those goals. "The program uncovered existing or potential management gaps and identified people worthy of succession" (Collis and Stuart 1991).

In fact, the managers we spoke with did not understand Cooper's compensation and incentive system and were critical of it. They felt Cooper's bonus allocations were largely independent of performance—theirs or the company's—and therefore provided little motivation for performance. A sample of comments concerning compensation at Cooper include the following:

> Cooper described bonuses as discretionary, subject to a maximum— and they were. They were whatever they wanted to pay any individual.

> There is one word that best describes Cooper's compensation system: mystery. It was an absolute mystery. I never knew why my salary was what it was. Bonuses were even more mysterious. There were two years where I got no bonus. I never knew why. One year, I was managing a small part of the business and we had turned around performance from a $750 thousand loss to a $3 million gain. My incentive bonus that year was $6,500; I thought it should have been triple that. I scratched my head forever on the compensation issue.

> Cooper paid bonuses, but no one knew why they got what they got. It was kind of like getting a Christmas turkey.

> We commiserated about it all the time. We would cry on each other's shoulders, we didn't understand it. We put trust in the division president to get us a decent bonus.

---

5. This issue is related to the more general problem of the trade-off between using promotions for incentives and to place individuals in the appropriate job, discussed in Baker, Jensen, and Murphy (1988) and Baker (1990).

It is difficult to argue that these comments are those of disgruntled employees because the executives who made them did well at Cooper and were consistently promoted.

Immediately after the split-off from Cooper, Cooper Cameron adopted a very different compensation philosophy that relied heavily on bonuses tied to objective performance goals (known by employees) and equity-based compensation. Upon taking control, Erikson and Hix tied the compensation of their managers to EBITDA. Moreover, Erikson and Hix arranged to be paid entirely in stock options. Erikson explained that "before Cooper Cameron was split off, Cooper did a search for someone to run the division. That was in October of 1994. I joined Cooper in January of 1995. At that time I was still the CEO of a publicly traded company [The Western Company of North America] that we were in the process of selling. Tom Hix also came from The Western Company. When we talked about compensation, I told them I wanted all options, no salary. That's what I got. That's Tom's arrangement as well. Our board also takes only options for compensation." Hix explained his compensation philosophy succinctly: "Compensation is the single most important thing in business. People will follow whatever path you've laid out. If you have a weak compensation system, you get what you deserve."

It is also possible to see the different emphases on incentives before and after the split-off by comparing the equity ownership of top management at Cooper Industries and at Cooper Cameron. At the time of the split-off in 1995, Cooper's directors and executive officers as a group owned directly or through options approximately 0.76 percent of the company's stock. In contrast, Cooper Cameron directors and executive officers as a group owned stock and options for 4.87 percent of Cooper Cameron— 1.89 percent directly or through vested options and an additional 2.98 percent in options that would vest by the year 2000.

Informed Operating Performance

In this section, we analyze the success of Cooper's acquisition of Cameron using financial data provided to us by Cooper Cameron management. It is difficult, if not impossible, to measure the performance of Cooper's acquisition of Cameron using publicly available data for two reasons. First, data are unavailable for 1990 and 1991 because Cooper did not report Cameron's results separately. Second, while Cooper Cameron does report EBITDA (and capital expenditures) for Cameron's segment from 1992 to 1995, those data do not include Cooper's expenditures out of "acquisition reserves."

Table 4.3 presents our analysis of Cameron's operating performance before and after the acquisition. It indicates that EBITDA to assets and EBITDA to sales declined significantly after the acquisition, both nominally and adjusted for industry performance. It is worth emphasizing that

Table 4.3   Informed Operating Performance for Cameron Acquisition

	EBITDA Assets	EBITDA Sales
A. Normal Operating Performance		
Preacquisition		
1984	0.025	0.041
1985	0.084	0.127
1986	0.081	0.112
1987	0.042	0.066
1988	0.034	0.051
1989	0.093	0.113
Postacquisition		
1990	0.089	0.091
1991	0.088	0.081
1992	0.103	0.080
1993	−0.011	−0.010
1994	−0.064	−0.071
Average	0.041	0.034
B. Industry-Adjusted Operating Performance		
Preacquisition		
1984	−0.074	−0.119
1985	−0.010	0.006
1986	0.142	0.237
1987	0.166	0.209
1988	−0.003	−0.025
1989	0.007	0.021
Postacquisition		
1990	0.008	−0.042
1991	−0.055	−0.020
1992	0.027	0.000
1993	−0.103	−0.129
1994	−0.180	−0.212
Average	−0.061	−0.081

Note: Changes and industry-adjusted changes in operating income before depreciation (EBITDA) to sales and assets for Cameron Iron Works and Cooper Oil Tools only, using information provided by Cooper Cameron. Industry-adjusted performance based on median performance of firms in Cameron's Compustat primary SIC code of 3533.

the industry-adjusted results are insensitive to the type of industry adjustment. Table 4.3 reports industry-adjusted results using the median performance of Compustat firms in Cameron's primary Compustat SIC code of 3533. We obtain similar, albeit slightly more negative, results using firms in the same Value Line industry. We also obtain similar results when we restrict the industry controls to firms similar in size (as measured by assets) to Cameron.

Given the interim cash flow data, it is also possible to analyze the over-

Table 4.4   **Market Value of Remaining Assets of Cameron as of 19 July 1995**

	Market Value (Cooper Cameron)		
Total debt	375		
Equity	625		
Total	1,000		

	Petroleum Production Equipment (Cameron)	Compression and Power Equipment (Cooper Energy Services)	% Cameron
EBITDA	10.6	90.2	10.5
Sales	562.7	546.0	50.8
Assets	1,286.7	379.9	77.2

Note: Calculated using Cooper Cameron prospectus and CRSP stock prices. Values are in millions of dollars.

all impact of the Cameron acquisition on Cooper's shareholders. To do this, we perform an analysis similar to that performed by Kaplan (1989a, 1989b, 1994). The analysis is presented in tables 4.4, 4.5, and 4.6.

Table 4.4 reports that Cooper Cameron had an initial market value of total capital of $1 billion on 19 July 1995 when it was split off from Cooper Industries. It is not possible to assign a precise value to Cameron at this time because Cooper Cameron included Cameron as well as the assets of Cooper Energy Services. Table 4.4 also reports the EBITDA, sales, and assets of Cooper Cameron's two segments for fiscal year 1994. The petroleum production equipment (PPE) segment consisted largely of Cameron. As a percentage of the entire company, the PPE segment contributed 11 percent of EBITDA, 51 percent of sales, and 77 percent of assets. Based on these percentages, we assume, in what follows, that Cameron contributes 50 percent of the value of Cooper Cameron. In other words, we assume Cameron has a capital value of $500 million on 19 July 1995. Because Cameron's (book value) assets are the least reliable of these figures, 50 percent may overstate Cameron's true value.

Table 4.5 reports the cash flows generated by the assets of Cameron from January 1990 through June 1995. The cash flows are measured as EBITDA less capital expenditures less the increase in net working capital plus the proceeds of asset sales. These cash flows differ from those that would be produced from Cameron's (or Cooper's) financial statements because they include expenditures associated with the acquisition that Cooper capitalized at the time of the acquisition and did not run through the income statement. It also is worth noting that these cash flows are before tax and, therefore, likely overstate the cash flows that would have been available to Cameron investors.

Table 4.6 presents the estimated postacquisition market value of Cam-

Table 4.5   **Cameron Interim Cash Flows**

	Period Ending					
	12/90	12/91	12/92	12/93	12/94	6/95
EBITDA	68.6	68.5	63.0	(6.6)	(38.4)	8.6
Capital expenditures	(52.1)	(88.4)	(40.3)	(39.6)	(39.6)	(9.4)
Cash flow in noncash working capital	10.2	10.0	74.9	(6.8)	6.3	40.5
Asset sale proceeds	34.8	0.0	0.0	0.0	81.3	0.0
Total interim cash flow	61.5	(9.9)	97.6	(53.0)	9.6	39.7

Note: Interim cash flow equals EBITDA less purchases of property, plant, and equipment, plus the estimated cash from (used in) noncash working capital, plus asset sale proceeds. These cash flows include expenditures that Cooper capitalized at the parent level. The interim cash flows were provided from internal records by William Berger of Cooper Cameron. All values are in millions of dollars.

Table 4.6   **Postacquisition Value of Cameron Compared to Purchase Price**

	Nominal Cash Flows	Industry-Adjusted		Market-Adjusted	
		Nov. 1989	July 1995	Nov. 1989	July 1995
Cameron's postacquisition market value					
Interim cash flows[a]	145.5	92.8	212.6	120.3	230.1
Value of remaining assets[b]	500.0	218.2	500.0	261.4	500.0
Total	645.5	311.0	712.6	381.7	730.1
Price paid by Cooper for Cameron[c]	967.4	967.4	2,217.2	967.4	1,850.6
Implied premerger value of Cameron[d]	821.3	821.3	1,882.4	821.3	1,571.1
Value destroyed by Cooper[e]	175.8	510.3	1,169.8	439.6	841.0
Overpayment by Cooper[f]	321.9	656.4	1,504.6	585.7	1,120.5

Note: Nominal, industry-, and market-adjusted values of Cameron Iron Works postacquisition compared to acquisition value. Postacquisition value equals the sum of asset sales, interim cash flows, and the value of remaining Cameron assets. All values are in millions of dollars.

Nominal value equals actual value. Industry-adjusted (market-adjusted) values in November 1989 equal the actual values discounted from the month in which they occur to 30 November 1989 by the return on the equal weighted index of firms in Compustat with Cameron Iron Works SIC code of 3533 (S&P 500). The industry- (or market-) adjusted values in July 1995 equal the actual values adjusted from the month in which they occur to July 1995 by the return on the equal-weighted industry index (S&P 500) over that period.

[a] Interim cash flows and asset sales are from table 4.5. Interim cash flows equal EBITDA less capital expenditures less the increase in net working capital plus the proceeds from asset sales.

[b] The value of the remaining assets is based on table 4.4 and assumes that the Cameron assets constituted 50 percent of the market value of Cooper Cameron.

[c] Purchase price paid by Cooper is the sum of the market value paid for the equity and the book value of Cameron debt outstanding in November 1989.

[d] Implied premerger value of Cameron is the purchase price paid by Cooper less the abnormal return earned by Cameron shareholders of $146.1 million over the eleven-day window described in table 4.2.

[e] Value destroyed by Cooper equals Cameron's implied premerger value less Cameron's postacquisition value.

[f] Overpayment by Cooper equals the price paid by Cooper less Cameron's postacquisition vlaue.

eron and compares it to both the value paid by Cooper ($967 million) and the implied premerger value of Cameron ($821 million, which excludes the increases in Cameron's stock price from announcements related to the acquisition using the eleven-day window). The table presents these values in nominal terms, industry-adjusted to November 1989 and July 1995, and market-adjusted to November 1989 and July 1995. The industry- and market-adjusted values are calculated by discounting (or growing) the interim cash flows and the value of the remaining assets by the returns on, respectively, an equal-weighted index of firms in Compustat with Cameron's SIC code and the S&P 500.

Table 4.6 indicates that in November 1989 dollars, Cooper realized a value of only $382 million market-adjusted, or $311 million industry-adjusted, from its acquisition of Cameron. Relative to the $967 million capital value that Cooper paid in November 1989, this represents an overpayment by Cooper of $586 to $656 million. If we use the implied premerger value, taking into consideration the $146 million premium Cooper paid to Cameron's shareholders, we estimate that the acquisition lost or destroyed $440 to $510 million in value.

The results in table 4.6 accurately reflect the value realized by Cooper from its investment in Cameron as of the date of the split-off. These results also reflect the effects of Cooperization on Cameron. They do not reflect the total value or returns realized by Cooper because Cooper retained a 20 percent stake in Cooper Cameron after the split-off. As we reported earlier, Cooper Cameron's shares substantially outperformed the market after the split-off. Through 1 October 1996, Cooper Cameron's stock increased in value by an industry-adjusted $388 million in 1989 dollars ($890 million in 1995 dollars). Assuming that Cooper Energy Services and Cameron contributed equally to this increase in value, Cameron increased in value by $194 million in 1989 dollars ($445 in 1995 dollars). Under this assumption, Cooper's 20 percent stake increased Cooper's value by $39 million in 1989 dollars, or less than 10 percent of the overall loss to Cooper's shareholders.

4.4.6 Traditional Operating Performance

As noted earlier, researchers typically measure performance using the ratios of EBITDA to both assets and sales. Healy, Palepu, and Ruback (1992) introduce an additional performance measure that deflates by the market value of the firm's capital (the sum of market value of equity and book value of debt) rather than assets or sales. Before the acquisition, we obtain these ratios by adding the relevant variables for both the acquirer and the target. After the acquisition, we use the values for Cooper Industries as a whole.

We adjust for industry performance using the median performance of Compustat firms in Cameron's primary Compustat SIC code of 3533 and Cooper's primary Compustat SIC code of 3640. We weight overall industry performance by the appropriate relative amount of Cooper and Cameron assets, sales, or value.

Panel A of table 4.7 presents operating performance variables for the combination of Cooper Industries and Cameron Iron Works from 1984 to 1994. Panel B presents the industry-adjusted results. The industry-adjusted results are qualitatively similar using Value Line industry control

Table 4.7   Traditional Operating Performance for Cameron Acquisition

	EBITDA Assets	EBITDA Sales	EBITDA Value
A. Nominal Operating Performance			
Preacquisition[a]			
1984	0.112	0.124	0.127
1985	0.113	0.140	0.264
1986	0.129	0.136	0.151
1987	0.116	0.130	0.158
1988	0.124	0.134	0.154
1989	0.114	0.149	0.189
Postacquisition[a]			
1990	0.149	0.172	0.159
1991	0.151	0.176	0.185
1992	0.127	0.154	0.125
1993	0.141	0.161	0.147
1994	0.116	0.163	0.114
Average	0.137	0.165	0.146
B. Industry-Adjusted Operating Performance[b]			
Preacquisition[a]			
1984	−0.023	0.013	−0.020
1985	−0.014	0.029	0.118
1986	−0.002	0.053	0.044
1987	−0.011	0.042	0.071
1988	−0.028	0.029	0.021
1989	−0.034	0.042	0.049
Postacquisition[a]			
1990	0.027	0.072	0.043
1991	0.032	0.087	0.073
1992	−0.013	0.055	−0.010
1993	−0.004	0.064	0.007
1994	−0.017	0.063	−0.041
Average	0.005	0.068	0.014

Note: Changes and industry-adjusted changes in operating income before depreciation (EBITDA) to sales, assets, and value for Cooper Industries' acquisition of Cameron Iron Works using publicly available data.

[a]Preacquisition performance is measured by combining the performance of Cooper and Cameron. Postacquisition performance is measured based on data from Cooper's financial statements.

[b]Industry-adjusted performance based on median performance of firms in Cooper's and Cameron's Compustat primary SIC codes.

firms and for industry- and size-matched control firms. The table indicates that EBITDA to assets and EBITDA to sales increased after Cooper's acquisition of Cameron, both nominally and adjusting for industry. This is completely at odds with the actual acquisition outcome described above. The EBITDA to value measure, in contrast, rises and then declines after the acquisition, successfully matching the pattern of actual acquisition results.

It is worth adding here that our analysis uses EBITDA reported by Cooper Industries after the acquisition. As we noted earlier, this EBITDA overstates true EBITDA by a substantial amount because Cooper created liability accounts at the time of the acquisition for expenses that would otherwise have reduced EBITDA. For example, Cooper Cameron's financial statements report changes in other assets and liabilities of $-\$48.6$ million and $-\$56.2$ million in 1992 and 1993. Our internal data are consistent with this order of magnitude.

4.4.7 Longer-Term Stock Performance

From the time Cooper acquired Cameron until the split-off, as shown in fig. 4.2, Cooper's stock underperformed both the S&P 500 and its two primary industries. Subsequent to the split-off (through 1 October 1996), Cooper continued to underperform the S&P 500. This deterioration in stock performance coincides with the Cameron Iron Works acquisition and is consistent with the internal deterioration in organizational practices described earlier.

Furthermore, following a downturn in oil prices in 1991, Cooper reported poor earnings due largely to the performance of Cameron and Cooper's other oil tools businesses. These announcements generated an extremely strong, negative response from the market, the press, and financial analysts. Cooper's announcement that its 1991 earnings and sales in its petroleum and industrial segment would be off was greeted with a return 17.8 percent below the S&P 500 over the eleven surrounding days. Cizik's announcement on 26 January 1994 that 1993 earnings would drop substantially because of a slump in the oil industry coincided with a Cooper stock price decline of 21.2 percent relative to the S&P 500. Both declines are statistically significant.

4.4.8 Summary of Sources of Value Creation and Destruction

Based on our clinical and quantitative analyses, we conclude that Cooper's acquisition of Cameron destroyed value rather than increasing it. Although Cameron operated in the same industry as one of Cooper's divisions, Cameron's business was substantially different from Cooper's. The imposition of Cooper's centralized organizational design and incentives was particularly inappropriate for Cameron. Although the stock market initially responded positively to the acquisition of Cameron, in large part because of Cooper's past acquisition successes, Cooper's stock price ultimately declined, reflecting the failure of the Cameron acquisition.

We suspect that Cooperization failed more generally and that Cooper's stock price decline has reflected that failure. While proving this suspicion or hypothesis is beyond the scope of this paper, it seems hard to argue that Cooper's acquisition strategy did not ultimately fail.

4.5   Premark's Acquisition of Florida Tile

4.5.1   Company Descriptions

In 1989, the year before the Florida Tile acquisition, Premark had sales of $2.6 billion and EBITDA of $231 million. Premark operated in three business segments: (1) The Tupperware division produced plastic food storage and serving containers, and generated 40 percent and 56 percent, respectively, of Premark's sales and operating profit in 1989. (2) The Food Equipment Group manufactured commercial food equipment, and generated 36 percent and 12 percent, respectively, of Premark's sales and operating profit in 1989. The Food Equipment Group consisted of the Hobart and Vulcan-Hart Corporations. (3) The Consumer and Decorative Products segment consisted of the Decorative Products Group and the Consumer Products Group, and generated 24 percent and 32 percent, respectively, of Premark's sales and operating profit in 1989. The Decorative Products Group included Ralph Wilson Plastics, which made decorative plastic laminates under the Wilsonart label, and Tibbal Flooring, which manufactured and sold oak flooring under the Hartco name. The Consumer Products Group included West Bend and Precor, which sold small electric appliances under the West Bend trademark and home physical fitness equipment under the Precor, West Bend, and Total Gym trademarks. West Bend also manufactured bathroom scales under the Borg trademark.

Premark's primary SIC code is listed as 3089 (plastic products) by Compustat, CRSP, and the Million Dollar Directory. The Million Dollar Directory also lists Premark as operating in industries with SIC codes of 3944 (games, toys, children's vehicles, excluding dolls), 3589 (service industry machinery), 3556 (food products machinery), 3596 (scales and balances, excluding laboratories), and 3565 (packaging machinery). Value Line assigns Premark to its diversified industry classification.

Florida Tile (Sikes Corporation) engaged "primarily in the business of manufacturing and selling glazed ceramic wall and floor tile for residential and commercial uses."[6] The company's products were marketed under the Florida Tile brand name. In the fiscal year ending February 1989, Florida Tile had EBITDA of $23.9 million.

---

6. Sikes Corporate 1989 10-K, p. 2.

Florida Tile's primary SIC code is listed as 3250 (structural clay products) by Compustat and as 3253 (ceramic wall and floor tile) by both CRSP and the Million Dollar Directory. The Million Dollar Directory also lists Sikes as operating in industries with SIC codes of 5032 (brick and related construction material, wholesale) and 3544 (special dies, tools, and die sets). Florida Tile was not listed in Value Line.

The SIC code listings indicate that this acquisition would be considered unrelated using the primary SIC codes in Compustat and CRSP. Using the Million Dollar Directory and the secondary SIC codes, the acquisition would be considered related at the two-digit level.

4.5.2   Acquisition Motivation and Events

Before the Florida Tile acquisition, Premark made one successful and two unsuccessful attempts to acquire firms in the decorative products industry. Management viewed acquisitions in this area as synergistic with its prosperous laminate business, which was a part of Wilson Plastics. In 1988, Premark completed its first acquisition in this area when it acquired Hartco (Tibbal Flooring). In 1989, Premark attempted to buy American Olean, one of the leading companies in the wall and floor tile business, but was outbid by Armstrong World Industries. In 1990, another tile company, Dal Tile, was put up for sale. Again, Premark was unsuccessful in buying the company, losing out to a private equity fund, AEA.

After missing out on two opportunities, Premark's management told us they felt strongly at the time that they could not miss out again when Florida Tile put itself up for sale. James Ringler, Premark's current CEO, recalled that "there was an organizational momentum that we had to do something. The momentum rolled right over the top of that thing."

On 12 September 1989, Florida Tile announced that it had received an informal and unsolicited expression of interest from a foreign company in the $190 to $200 million dollar range. On 16 October 1989, Florida Tile announced that it was seeking a buyer. In December, Florida Tile announced that it was still in the process of seeking a buyer. In February, a Lebanese investor group, Cerabati, acquired a 5.4 percent stake in Florida Tile. Also in February, Florida Tile considered and turned down an offer from a French ceramic company. On 23 April 1990, Florida Tile announced an agreement to be acquired by Premark. Premark paid $201 million for Florida Tile's equity and assumed $14 million in debt for a total price of $215 million. Premark's firm value at the end of the year prior to the acquisition was $1.5 billion. The acquisition, therefore, increased Premark's firm value by only 14 percent.

4.5.3   Premark's Acquisition Strategy

This section and those that follow rely on publicly available information as well as on interviews with James Ringler, Premark's current CEO, and

Larry Skatoff, Premark's current CFO. At the time of the transaction, James Ringler had just been hired as an executive vice president to run the non-Tupperware businesses. Larry Skatoff joined the firm in 1991. At the time of the transaction, Warren Batts served as Premark's CEO.

As was the case with Cooper, it seems that Premark's acquisition strategy was strongly influenced by its history. Premark was created in 1989 through a spin-off by Dart and Kraft. It comprised a hodgepodge of businesses that did not fit with one another or with Dart and Kraft's remaining businesses. According to Dart and Kraft's 8-K describing the spin-off, the "lines of business to be assigned to Premark have not fully developed their potential" (see Schipper and Smith 1988). So rather than being the result of a conscious diversification strategy, Premark's combination of businesses was the result of happenstance. At the time of the Florida Tile acquisition, according to Ringler, "Premark was a conglomerate with no specific focus." As we detail below, Premark's acquisition strategy lacked focus as well.

Premark's acquisition strategy was to be a smart, opportunistic buyer. Ringler explained, "Tupperware was Premark's cash cow. The issue was how to redeploy the cash." Inside the organization, distributing cash to shareholders either as a dividend or share repurchase was not viewed as a viable option. In fact, one or two years *after* the Florida Tile acquisition, Larry Skatoff made a presentation to the board of directors concerning a possible share repurchase. He felt his presentation "was not well received." In his view, "the board viewed a repurchase as a cop out. It was something a weak management did when they could not think of anything else to do." This description of Premark's approach to internal resource allocation parallels the arguments by Jensen (1986) concerning the potential for value-destroying investment by organizations with free cash flow.

Also as in the case of Cooper, Premark's managers felt that growth was critical to the success of their organization. Ringler explained, "Our real issue is where to get growth in a mature industry. Managers are not interested in empire building or being bigger. To me, I don't care whether my company is $2 million in sales, $2.5 billion in sales, or even $5 billion in sales. The real issue is that managers live in constant fear that by not growing or investing in the business it will stagnate and ultimately you will lose it. You don't want to lose the attributes that make you successful because the other guy does something and you don't and that hurts you."

At the request of top managers, executives in the corporate strategy area evaluated potential acquisitions and investments. After detailed research, the strategy group and Premark's top management determined that additional investment in the decorative products business would be attractive. This decision was reached at headquarters with little input from division managers but with strong support from an outside consulting firm.

Table 4.8   Stock Price Response to Events Associated with Premark's Acquisition of Sikes/Florida Tile (millions of dollars)

| | Days −1 through 1 | | | | | Days −5 through 5 | | | | |
| | Premark International Common Stock | | Sikes/Florida Tile Common Stock | | Total Abnormal Dollars | Premark International Common Stock | | Sikes/Florida Tile Common Stock | | Total Abnormal Dollars |
Event Description (Date)	% Abnormal Return	Abnormal Dollars	% Abnormal Return	Abnormal Dollars		% Abnormal Return	Abnormal Dollars	% Abnormal Return	Abnormal Dollars	
Premark agrees to acquire Florida Tile for $201 million (4/23/90)	−5.95*	−48.4	28.50*	29.1	−19.3	−19.24*	−182.9	29.16*	30.1	−152.8
Total abnormal dollars		−48.4		29.1	−19.3		−182.9		30.1	−152.8

Note: Abnormal returns are computed based on market models estimates from days −200 through −21 prior to the first announcement for both Premark and Sikes/Florida Tile. Returns based on the excess of firm returns over the S&P 500 yield similar results.

*Abnormal return is significantly different from zero at the 5 percent level, two-tailed test.

4.5.4   Initial Market Reaction to the Acquisition

Table 4.8 presents the stock price response of Premark and Sikes/Florida Tile shareholders to the merger for a three-day window from days -1 to 1, and an eleven-day window from days -5 to 5. Again, performance is based on market-model abnormal returns and their associated abnormal dollar value.[7] As a result of the merger, combined value decreased by $19.3 million based on the three-day window and by $152.8 million based on the eleven-day window. Value increased for Florida Tile shareholders, while it declined for Premark's shareholders. For Florida Tile shareholders, the abnormal dollar value totals $29.1 million measured during the three-day windows and $30.1 million measured during the eleven-day windows. The corresponding total value decreases for Premark's shareholders are $48.4 million and $182.9 million.

According to Ringler, the acquisition and concomitant decline in Premark's market value was not well received by investors and analysts. Shortly after the acquisition, he and Warren Batts, then CEO of Premark, went to New York to meet with a group of equity analysts. Ringler described their experience: "There were about 75 to 100 people there. They were incredibly angry. They were personally insulting to Warren. They asked questions like, 'Are you as dumb as you look?' It was as ugly a business session as I have ever been to. We decided that the primary Premark shareholder was a Tupperware-oriented person. They were buying because they liked Tupperware. The other businesses were background pains that they had to tolerate."

The strong investor reaction ($183 million decline for a $215 million acquisition) is consistent both with (1) their expectation that the Florida Tile would be unsuccessful, and (2) their mounting frustration over Premark's decision not to distribute free cash flow to its shareholders and an expectation that Premark would continue to make poor decisions concerning how to allocate that free cash flow. Large sample evidence in Lang, Stulz, and Walkling (1991) also finds that acquirer shareholders react negatively to acquisitions by acquirers with high free cash flow. In the eyes of Premark executives, the market reaction to the Florida Tile acquisition was unpleasantly negative, but it had an underlying rationale that in retrospect seemed reasonable.

4.5.5   Clinical Analysis of Postacquisition Outcome

Premark's top management do not view the Florida Tile acquisition as a success. Motivated by the possibility of synergies, Premark bought Florida Tile only to learn that it did not have as much in common with its

---

7. The estimation period runs from 200 to 21 days prior to the first announcement of Florida Tile's possible sale.

preexisting businesses as it had anticipated. According to Ringler, "we did not know the decorative products business, we knew laminates." Wilson Plastics had produced attractive returns for Premark, but Florida Tile "was a laminates company and it served a different market." In retrospect, they felt that Premark had "no skills on the acquisition side, but we acted as if we did. We jumped in and then were stuck. If we were going to go down this road and do acquisitions, we had to commit more resources and more money. We were not an acquisition factory. What we learned is that every business is complex in its execution. We had no expertise and no synergies."

Another problem arose because acquisition decisions were made centrally at headquarters. Managers of related divisions did not participate and their input was not actively sought. This made it unlikely that potential synergies, if they existed, would be realized.

Organizational Design

After the acquisition, Premark managed Florida Tile as it managed its other businesses. Each operating unit had a division president who was local. None of Premark's businesses was in Chicago where Premark was headquartered, and there were no operating people in headquarters. The division presidents typically reported to the operating executive vice president (then Ringler) who reported to the CEO (then Batts).

The president of Wilson Plastics was made the group president of Decorative Products. In this role, he oversaw Wilson Plastics, Hartco, and Florida Tile. This was somewhat unusual in that he was both a division president and a group president. Ringler recalled that "in anticipation of Premark's increased emphasis on decorative products, we thought about moving him up to headquarters from Texas, but he didn't want to come."

To monitor its divisions, Premark had formal quarterly review sessions. These were one- or two-day meetings between (1) the division president and CFO, and (2) the corporate CEO, chief operating officer (COO), CFO, and roughly twelve other corporate staff people. According to Ringler, "This wasn't an enjoyable process for anyone, but particularly for the division people. A root canal without anesthesia would have been more enjoyable. At these meetings we talked about strategic issues, not financial performance. It was issue-oriented as opposed to looking at the numbers."

Over the course of the year, Ringler also would visit all of the individual units. The time Ringler spent at each division "was about proportional to the size of and problems at the division." The distance between Premark headquarters and Florida Tile's operations made it more difficult for Premark's management to know when Florida Tiles was experiencing problems. This was particularly important in Premark's slow response to production problems at Florida Tile.

Compensation and Incentives

It does not appear that Premark/Florida Tile took an innovative or thoughtful approach to compensation or to capital allocation. According to Ringler, "The division presidents were compensated based on financial performance that was essentially profit after tax relative to budget. We had a few other bells and whistles in there like working capital charges, but it boiled down to after tax net income." In addition, the company decided which projects to do in the coming year at a two-day strategic budgeting meeting that was attended by corporate and division officers. Again according to Ringler, "[T]he context of the company was that we were cash rich and so cash was not a scarce resource that had to be allocated. Often we encouraged division presidents to spend more rather than less. We'd ask them, 'Why don't you try this or spend on that?'" Thus, Premark did not measure cash flow relative to any cost of capital either in compensating its executives or in choosing capital projects.

Informed Operating Performance

Ringler claims that Florida Tile (and Hartco) never performed well:

The acquisition momentum turned out to be at corporate and nowhere else in the organization. We controlled it, the divisions sat back. No one at Wilson Plastics cared about it. We began to have to manage it out of headquarters.

About a year after the Florida Tile acquisition, we realized we were in trouble. We realized that we had overpaid and that we were not committed to ten more acquisitions in decorative products. And that the whole idea of a decorative products business didn't make strategic sense.

Entry is pretty easy in the tile business. It's pretty much controlled by the Italian tile equipment manufacturers and what they are willing to sell. For $20 million to $40 million, you can order the equipment and within 12 months have a new state of the art plant up and running. For example, take Siam Cement (a Thai company); they did exactly that. Also, imports came in to the U.S. market from Mexico, Spain, and Italy.

In 1992–93 we realized that Florida Tile was more poorly run than we thought. Then we fired the president and cleaned house. We were afraid to do anything before that because we didn't know the business. We thought the management knew what they were doing. As we learned more about the business we became less satisfied with their responses. We started to think that they didn't know what they were doing and we knew enough that we felt comfortable with their leaving. Also, although Florida Tile has been a problem, it's a small business and its problems quickly got put on the back burner. Especially when Tupperware's cash flow swamped its monthly losses. When Tupperware was in trouble, turning its performance around was our top priority.

Because Hartco's performance had deteriorated so badly over the two years after we bought it, we almost congratulated ourselves that Florida Tile, although it did poorly, didn't do as horribly. Right now, its performance is about where it was when we bought it.[8]

Although this is what management said, analyst reports indicate that Florida Tile generated substantially less in operating profits in 1995 than the $16 million it generated in the fiscal year ending February 1989. According to a May 1996 analyst report from Advest Inc., "[T]hese two acquisitions (Florida Tile and Hartco) were mistakes in our opinion. Premark paid too much for them, they have been largely unprofitable and have held back the company's overall returns. By last year, the two businesses had at least reached break-even and we are not presuming they will do any better in the foreseeable future."

Other Premark Operations

At about the same time that Premark acquired Florida Tile, its Tupperware and Food Equipment businesses began to experience difficulties. By the fiscal year ending December 1990, Tupperware's operating income had declined to $64.9 million from $115.7 million in fiscal year 1988, and the Food Equipment Group's had declined to $26.9 million from $57.8 million. In large part because of these declines, Premark's stock price fell from $30.75 per share at the start of 1990 to $13 per share by the fall of 1990. Ringler explained:

The biggest factor behind the decline (at Tupperware) was that Premark made two major mistakes. First, we went after the microwave cooking product to the exclusion of other products. This was a product intended to go from freezer to a 400-degree oven. It worked great, except it shattered into thousands of pieces when you dropped it. When you offer a lifetime guarantee, this poses a real problem.

Second, we started a new distribution program called Tupperware Express which shipped the product directly to the customer. Before we started Tupperware Express, orders would be taken at a Tupperware party and then ordered from the company by the salesperson. The order would be delivered to the hostess who would see that the order was given to the person who ordered it. Under Tupperware Express, the orders would be shipped directly to the customer. We built a $100 million warehouse to handle this program. It worked great for a while. Then UPS told us they weren't making money on delivering our product and that they would have to raise the rates $2 to $3 per package. This wiped out our profits. The problem was that most people ordering Tupperware didn't live somewhere that you could just drop off the package and not worry about it being stolen. That meant it had to be delivered to a person and that meant multiple trips to the home by UPS. That's

---

8. The company would not release figures that were any more detailed than this.

what made it so expensive. Last year [1995] we pulled out of Tupperware Express completely.

Analyst reports at the time bear this out. For example, a report from PNC Institutional Investor Service dated 19 December 1989 described Tupperware Express and noted that "start-up costs have been high and implementation is running 18 months behind schedule. . . . As a result, sales have declined in markets where the program has been introduced. Market research has revealed that dealers have found it difficult to adapt to the shift. . . ."

In 1992, Premark focused on the three most important businesses it owned—Tupperware, Food Equipment, and Wilson Plastics. According to Ringler, "the company became better at managing what it had. The company stopped making acquisitions and decided to fix what we had." Premark brought in new presidents to run both Tupperware and the Food Equipment Group. Premark also eliminated the strategic function at headquarters and reduced headquarters employment from 300 to 150.

By 1994, Tupperware had recovered, obtaining an operating profit of $200 million. In November 1995, Premark announced it was spinning off Tupperware to shareholders. Ringler explained the reason behind the spin-off: "We realized that our shareholders were never going to let us do anything with the cash but repurchase shares. The market would unleash the wrath of God on us if we acquired anything with Tupperware's cash flow. We also felt we were two-thirds of the way up the hill on improving the operations of all our businesses. It was like two people at a picnic in a sack race. We could each run fine on our own. Why were we each putting one of our legs in a bag and trying to run together? It didn't make sense. Also, we wanted to do it in our own time, not the market's. We knew we would have to do it eventually. Why not now?"

It is worth noting that the Tupperware spin-off immediately reduced Premark's free cash flow problem. By eliminating the firm's major source of internally generated cash, it imposed a discipline on the remaining businesses to become self-sufficient. Ringler believed that Premark would have been forced to do the spin-off several years earlier by the external capital markets if the takeover and junk bond markets had not declined in the early 1990s.

4.5.6 Traditional Operating Performance

Table 4.9 presents the traditional accounting performance measures for the combination of Premark and Florida Tile from 1986 to 1994. We use 1989, the last preacquisition fiscal year, as the reference year. We adjust for industry using the median performance of Compustat firms in Florida Tile's primary Compustat SIC code of 3253 and Premark's primary Compustat SIC code of 3089. We weight overall industry performance by the

Table 4.9   **Traditional Operating Performance of Florida Tile Acquisition**

	EBITDA Assets	EBITDA Sales	EBITDA Value
A. Nominal Operating Performance			
Preacquisition[a]			
1986	0.138	0.100	N.A.
1987	0.136	0.099	0.216
1988	0.170	0.119	0.274
1989	0.145	0.094	0.179
Postacquisition[a]			
1990	0.124	0.093	0.171
1991	0.151	0.109	0.260
1992	0.156	0.103	0.180
1993	0.169	0.116	0.209
1994	0.190	0.130	0.155
Average	0.158	0.110	0.193
B. Industry-Adjusted Operating Performance[b]			
Preacquisition[a]			
1986	−0.008	−0.010	N.A.
1987	−0.018	−0.007	0.036
1988	0.004	0.012	0.096
1989	0.032	0.018	0.049
Postacquisition[a]			
1990	0.007	0.005	0.047
1991	0.056	0.024	0.143
1992	0.021	−0.003	0.048
1993	0.030	−0.001	0.054
1994	0.031	0.003	0.014
Average	0.029	0.006	0.061

Note: Changes and industry-adjusted changes in operating income before depreciation (EBITDA) to sales, assets, and value for Premark's acquisition of Florida Tile.

[a]Preacquisition performance is measured by combining the performance of Premark and Florida Tile. Postacquisition performance is measured based on data from Premark's financial statements.

[b]Industry-adjusted performance based on median performance of firms in Premark's and Florida Tile's Compustat primary four-digit SIC code.

appropriate relative amount of Florida Tile and Premark assets, sales, or value. Again, the industry-adjusted results are qualitatively similar using industry and size-matched control firms.

Despite the fact that the acquisition of Florida Tile was not successful, panel A of table 4.9 indicates that all three measures using EBITDA exceed their 1989 values from 1991 onward. Adjusting for industry, panel B finds essentially no postacquisition change in performance. In contrast to the Cooper Cameron acquisition where the EBITDA to value measure was the only one that tracked the acquisition success by declining, the EBITDA to value measure registers the largest increase in performance.

It also is worth looking more closely at the patterns generated by deflating by the market value of a firm's capital. This method shows a substantial improvement in Premark's performance in 1991 as EBITDA to value increases from 0.179 to 0.260 (unadjusted for industry) and from 0.049 to 0.143 (adjusted for industry). The method then shows a substantial decline in 1994, when the ratio declines to 0.155 and 0.014 (unadjusted and adjusted for industry). The explanation for this pattern is straightforward. Operating performance appears to improve because Premark's stock price declines substantially and the denominator declines substantially. Operating performance appears to decline because Premark's stock price increases substantially and the denominator increases substantially. This pattern suggests that the measure of operating performance developed in Healy, Palepu, and Ruback (1992) may be inappropriate for evaluating acquisition success.

4.5.7   Longer-Term Stock Performance

Figure 4.4 details the performance of Premark's stock versus the S&P 500 and an equal-weighted index of firms in Compustat with Premark's primary SIC code (3089). The chart indicates that Premark's stock declined substantially from late 1989 to late 1990 as the difficulties at Tupperware became apparent. From late 1990 to the end of 1995, as the company fixed the problems at Tupperware, Premark's stock improved substantially, increasing by more than a factor of seven (with dividends reinvested).

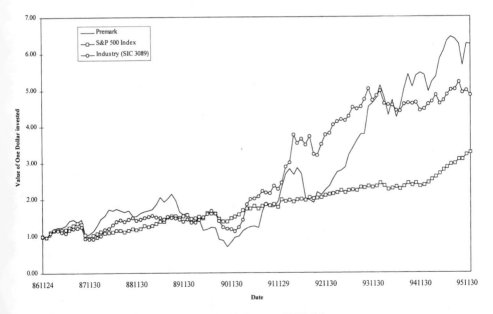

Fig. 4.4   Premark long-term stock performance, 1986–96

Premark's stock performance from the acquisition through 1995 is substantially better than that of the S&P 500 and approximately the same as the industry.

4.5.8 Summary of Sources of Value Creation and Destruction

Based on our analysis and conversations with Premark top management, we conclude that Premark's acquisition of Florida Tile reduced value overall and to Premark's shareholders, consistent with the market's initial assessment. We think that Premark's experience illustrates the pressures excess cash flow places on top managers and the difficulties in using that cash flow to make successful acquisitions in unrelated businesses. Partially because the company had no focused acquisition strategy, Premark overpaid for a target firm that had no synergies with its existing businesses.

Furthermore, shortly after the Florida Tile acquisition, Tupperware's performance began to deteriorate. Management turned its attention toward resolving problems in that business, and only when those problems were resolved did they have the time to devote to problems at Florida Tile.

4.6 Discussion and Implications

While our findings are based on only two acquisitions, they suggest three hypotheses or conclusions concerning the determinants of acquisition success or failure. These analyses and hypotheses illustrate the strengths of clinical research in that large sample studies have been relatively silent on this important issue. Given the limited research on what organizations do following acquisitions, we also believe that our hypotheses can serve as a guide to developing large sample studies of those determinants.

First, it is important for an acquirer to have a deep understanding of the target's business and industry when the acquirer begins to negotiate. While it seems obvious that an acquirer should know its target well, the facts suggest this is often not the case. In both acquisitions we studied, the managers of the acquirers based their acquisition decisions on potential synergies that never materialized. Premark did not understand Florida Tile nor, surprisingly, did Cooper understand Cameron.

A possible challenge to this hypothesis is that it relies on hindsight, that it is not obvious whether the acquirers could have known more ex ante. For example, in Cooper's acquisition of Cameron, perhaps it was reasonable ex ante for Cooper to acquire Cameron and attempt to "Cooperize" it. According to this view, the outcome was a surprise. While we cannot reject this view with certainty, we believe it is implausible. It should have been clear that Cameron's products and markets were substantially different from those of Cooper. And even if this was not clear at the time of the acquisition, it is difficult to understand why the problems progressed to become as severe as they did following the acquisition. Furthermore, at the time of the acquisition, Cameron's managers and some financial analysts knew that Cameron had spent the last decade reducing costs. Thus, Cooperization-type measures were an unlikely source of postacquisition value creation. In our view, it seems likely that more careful and intensive research, including a willingness to critically test the potential for synergies, would help acquirers avoid bad outcomes.[9]

Our findings also suggest that measures of relatedness based on SIC codes are poor measures of an acquirer's understanding of a target's businesses. Future research would do well to develop better measures to reflect that understanding.

Second, organizational design and structures are important sources of value in acquisitions. For Cooper Industries, appropriate design and structure was probably a source of value creation in early acquisitions while inappropriate design was a source of value destruction in the Cameron acquisition. Although not fully developed in this paper, we suspect that organizational design and structure issues are highly related to corporate culture and its influence on decisionmaking. Indeed, we believe that an acquirer should analyze the organizational design not only of the target but also of itself in light of the changes that a particular acquisition may bring. Future research would be strengthened by the development of measures of the extent to which the acquirer places the appropriate organizational structure on the target and the combined company.

Third, incentives matter a great deal in determining the success of an acquisition. Neither Cooper nor Premark utilized high-powered incentives after their acquisitions. In contrast, after the split-off, Cooper Cameron introduced high-powered incentives—equity-based and EBITDA-based compensation—and experienced substantial performance improvements. This suggests that such incentives were particularly appropriate for Cameron. Future research that studies postacquisition incentives would be of great interest and value.

The second and third hypotheses in the context of Cooper and Cameron suggest an additional question or puzzle. By 1995, the management of Cooper Industries recognized the problems at Cameron and hired Erikson (and Hix) to repair them. Despite this recognition, Cooper decided to split off Cameron (and Cooper Energy Services) as a separate entity rather than keep them as divisions of Cooper. But why could Erikson not have run Cameron under Cooper's ownership, changed the organizational design, and introduced high-powered incentives? We suspect that the answer to this question will inform the debate on the costs and benefits of corporate diversification and focus.

9. Anecdotally, we have heard this recommendation in conversations with senior consultants at several consulting firms. We also are personally aware of a number of other acquisitions in which this recommendation was not followed.

References

Agrawal, A., J. Jaffe, and G. Mandelker. 1992. The post-merger performance of acquiring firms: A reexamination of an anomaly. *Journal of Finance* 47:1605–21.

Andrade, G., and E. Stafford. 1999. Investigating the economic role of mergers. Graduate School of Business, University of Chicago.

Baker, G. 1990. Pay for performance for middle managers: Causes and consequences. *Journal of Applied Corporate Finance* 3 (3): 50–61.

Baker, G., M. Jensen, and K. Murphy. 1988. Compensation and incentives: Practice vs. theory. *Journal of Finance* 43:593–616.

Baker, G., and K. Wruck. 1989. Organizational changes and value creation in leveraged buyouts: The case of O. M. Scott & Sons Company. *Journal of Financial Economics* 25:163–90.

Collis, D. 1991. *Cooper Industries' corporate strategy teaching note.* Publishing Division, Harvard Business School.

Collis, D., and T. Stuart. 1991. *Cooper Industries' corporate strategy (A).* Publishing Division, Harvard Business School.

Comment, R., and G. Jarrell. 1995. Corporate focus, stock returns and the market for corporate control. *Journal of Financial Economics* 37:67–88.

Franks, J. R., R. Harris, and S. Titman. 1991. The post-merger share price performance of acquiring firms. *Journal of Financial Economics* 29:81–96.

Healy, P., K. Palepu, and R. Ruback. 1992. Do mergers improve corporate performance? *Journal of Financial Economics* 31:135–76.

Jensen, M. 1986. Agency costs of free cash flow, corporate finance and takeovers. *American Economic Review* 76:323–29.

———. 1993. The modern industrial revolution. *Journal of Finance* 48:831–80.

Kaplan, S. 1989a. The effects of management buyouts on operations and value. *Journal of Financial Economics* 24:217–54.

———. 1989b. Campeau's acquisition of Federated: Value created or value destroyed? *Journal of Financial Economics* 25:191–212.

———. 1994. Campeau's acquisition of Federated: Post-bankruptcy results. *Journal of Financial Economics* 35:123–36.

Kaplan, S., and M. Weisbach. 1992. The success of acquisitions: Evidence from divestitures. *Journal of Finance* 47:107–38.

Keller, D. N. 1983. *Cooper Industries: 1833–1993.* Athens: Ohio University Press.

Lang, L., R. Stulz, and R. Walkling. 1991. A test of the free cash flow hypothesis: The case of bidder returns. *Journal of Financial Economics* 29:315–35.

Lichtenberg, F. 1992. *Corporate takeovers and productivity.* Cambridge, Mass.: MIT Press.

Maloney, M., R. McCormick, and M. Mitchell. 1993. Managerial decision making and capital structure. *Journal of Business* 66:189–217.

Mitchell, M., and K. Lehn. 1990. Do bad bidders become good targets? *Journal of Political Economy* 98:372–98.

Mitchell, M., and H. Mulherin. 1996. The impact of industry shocks on takeover and restructuring activity. *Journal of Financial Economics* 41:193–229.

Mitchell, M., and E. Stafford. 1996. Managerial decisions and long-term stock price performance. Working Paper, University of Chicago, November.

Morck, R., A. Shleifer, and R. Vishny. 1990. Do managerial motives drive bad acquisitions? *Journal of Finance* 45:31–48.

Piper, T. 1974. *Cooper Industries, Inc.* Publishing Division, Harvard Business School.

Ravenscraft, D., and F. M. Scherer. 1987. *Mergers, selloffs and economic efficiency.* Washington, D.C.: The Brookings Institution.

Schipper, K., and A. Smith. 1983. Effects of recontracting on shareholder wealth: The case of voluntary spin-offs. *Journal of Financial Economics* 12:437–67.

———. 1988. Restructuring in the food industry. In *Corporate reorganization through mergers, acquisitions, and leveraged buyouts.* Greenwich, Conn.: JAI Press.

Servaes, H. 1991. Tobin's Q and the gains from takeovers. *Journal of Finance* 46: 409–19.

Wruck, K. 1994. Financial policy, internal control, and performance: Sealed Air Corporation's leveraged special dividend. *Journal of Financial Economics* 36: 157–92.

Comment   G. William Schwert

Introduction

My understanding is that the theme of this NBER conference is to study a small number of acquisitions intensively with the goal of developing new insights into the market for corporate control. By interviewing managers, examining internal corporate records, and otherwise focusing attention on the details of a few transactions, we hope to learn the reasons why bidders are willing to pay large premiums to acquire target firms and whether their expectations at the time of the transaction are borne out by subsequent performance. One goal of this research is to develop hypotheses, methods, or data that could be applied to larger scale empirical analyses of the corporate control market. The goals for this conference are similar to the motivation for the Clinical Studies section of the *Journal of Financial Economics,* pioneered by Michael Jensen and Richard Ruback in 1989 (Jensen et al. 1989).

From this perspective, clinical studies are a good example of inductive inference, which is defined by Jeffreys (1961, 1) as "making inferences from past experience to predict future experience." Zellner (1971, 5) describes reductive inference as a process whereby science develops new hypotheses: "unusual and surprising facts often trigger the reductive process to produce new concepts and generalizations." Perhaps in some circumstances

G. William Schwert is Distinguished University Professor of Finance and Statistics at the William E. Simon Graduate School of Business Administration of the University of Rochester and a research associate of the National Bureau of Economic Research.

The Bradley Policy Research Center, William E. Simon Graduate School of Business Administration, University of Rochester, provided support for this research. The views expressed herein are those of the author and do not necessarily reflect the views of the National Bureau of Economic Research.

we will observe phenomena in detailed clinical studies that cause us to postulate new theories or hypotheses about economic behavior.

What Is Success or Failure in Mergers and Acquisitions?

Large sample studies have frequently shown substantial changes in wealth for stockholders of target and (sometimes) bidder firms. These changes are usually measured around the announcement of the first public bid. Targets generally benefit, bidders often lose, but the net gains are usually positive, so the target gains are not just overpayment by the bidder. Figure 4C.1 shows the distribution of takeover premiums for 2,003 exchange-listed targets and 1,110 exchange-listed bidders from 1975 to 1994. The premiums are measured as market-model adjusted stock returns accumulated from three months before to six months after the first bid announcement (similar to the method used in many papers that study takeovers, including Schwert 1996). The average premiums are 23.7 percent for targets and 0.6 percent for bidders, with standard deviations of 43.0 percent and 26.8 percent, respectively. The large standard deviations mean that

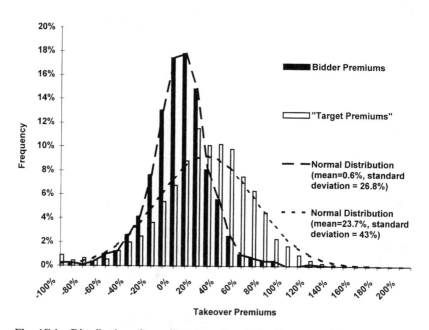

Fig. 4C.1   Distribution of premiums to exchange-listed target and bidder firms from 1975 to 1994, adjusted for market movements

Note: CRSP value-weighted market model residuals cumulated over trading days (−63, 126) around the first offer announcement date. Model estimated using days (−316, −64). Premiums are measured from three months before to six months after the announcement of the first public bid.

many realized premiums are negative. Figure 4C.1 also shows normal distributions with the same means and standard deviations represented as dotted and dashed curves. These approximate the histograms of target and bidder premiums well.

The message that I get from figure 4C.1 is that there is a lot of "noise" in the cross-sectional distribution of premiums. Focusing on differences in average premiums can miss the point that there are many idiosyncratic differences across cases. Of course, the other side of this argument is that any small sample of cases is not likely to be representative of the complex population represented in the figure.

Kaplan, Mitchell, and Wruck looked at one deal that the market thought would be profitable and one that the market thought would be unprofitable. They focused on exchange-listed nonfinancial firms that completed deals from 1987 to 1994. Ex ante success was defined as an eleven-day abnormal return greater than 5 percent, while failure was defined as an eleven-day abnormal return less than 0 percent, based on a weighted average of announcement returns for targets and bidders, using equity capitalization as weights. There were thirty-four possible successes and fourteen possible failures. Next, they looked for cases where personal or institutional contacts or geographic proximity made it more likely that management would share private information. They pursued four firms as possible candidates and received favorable responses from two initially, although one later withdrew support.

Selection Biases

Kaplan, Mitchell, and Wruck point out several biases that cause the selection of cases for detailed clinical study to be nonrandom. Selection biases may be (1) performance-related, in which case firms that experience poor performance are less likely to want to publicize their story; (2) privacy-related, where the choice of nondisclosure policies by firms is probably not random but is likely to be related to the value of information about the firm's investment opportunities; or (3) institution-related, where the question may be asked whether, if personal or institutional contacts are necessary to conduct clinical research, this somehow slants the results. Is there an incentive to pull punches in describing corporate behavior to increase the likelihood of access to other companies in the future? All of these factors could limit the generalizability of clinical analysis and they are likely to be important in any clinical study.

There is evidence in the authors' paper that managers are reluctant to criticize themselves. Most of the information about poor performance of Cooper comes from Cooper Cameron managers after they had been spun off from Cooper, and even they are reluctant to seem critical of former colleagues. Premark withdrew its cooperation early in the project, forcing Kaplan, Mitchell, and Wruck to rely on public sources of information, rather than management interviews and internal records, to enrich the analysis of the Premark–Florida Tile transaction.

Confounding Events

In measuring the ex post performance of these transactions, the authors track accounting and stock price performance for many years after the deal was announced. An obvious difficulty, which they discuss in detail, is to abstract from the many other factors that influence the performance of the merged firm.

Besides acquiring Cameron Iron Works, Cooper also took over Champion Products in 1989. This was part of a strategy of acquisitions that began in the 1960s. In fact, this strategy, called "Cooperization," is often taught in strategy courses using Harvard cases (Collis 1991; Collis and Stuart 1991). Thus, the success or failure of the Cameron acquisition has to be viewed in the context of a long-term strategy that involved many acquisitions. In July 1995, Cooper spun off Cameron. Kaplan, Mitchell, and Wruck point out that Cooper Cameron increased focus, decreased bureaucracy, and increased incentive compensation after it split from Cooper's control. The authors argue that Cooper Cameron has been much more successful than Cameron was as a wholly owned subsidiary inside a highly bureaucratic Cooper organization.

In Premark's acquisition of Florida Tile, the authors argue that Premark was spending the cash generated by its Tupperware division to finance the acquisition in 1990. Shortly afterward, the Tupperware market was adversely affected by factors unrelated to the acquisition. The authors argue that solving the Tupperware problem probably distracted Premark management from focusing on Florida Tile, which contributed to the failure of this transaction.

Ex Ante Profitability—Stock Market Reaction to Bids

Kaplan, Mitchell, and Wruck use the initial stock market reaction as a measure of whether the transaction was likely to be successful. I have much sympathy with this approach, but there are also some potential limitations. As noted by the authors, part of the change in the bidder's stock price can be a reaction to information about the bidder's alternative uses for capital. For example, the Florida Tile transaction might have been a neutral deal for Premark (i.e., it could have been a zero net present value investment), but if the market had expected a better alternative, Premark's stock price would fall.

As another example, the strong negative reaction to Kodak's "white knight" takeover of Sterling Drug in 1988 was likely to be more than overpayment because the loss in value for Kodak exceeded the premium offered to Sterling by a substantial amount. The market probably inferred something negative about the future profitability of Kodak's main line of business (chemical photography) from the eagerness with which Kodak pursued Sterling.

Thus, the use of initial stock market reaction as a basis for identifying successful or unsuccessful deals has some difficulties.

Ex Post Profitability—Stock and Accounting Returns

Kaplan, Mitchell, and Wruck measure profitability after the deal using both accounting and stock returns. Accounting returns (EBITDA relative to sales, assets, and value) based on private data show poor performance for the Cameron division in table 4.3. In contrast, the public data based on the consolidated performance of Cooper hide the poor performance of Cameron in table 4.4. This is an important example where the methods of clinical studies, including access to internal records and information from companies, provides substantially different information from the publicly available data.

Nevertheless, the problem of identifying abnormal accounting performance over long time periods is difficult. Barber and Lyon (1996) provide simulation evidence that shows the difficulties and imprecision associated with testing for unusual accounting performance.

A similar problem arises in measuring abnormal stock returns over long time periods. Barber and Lyon (1997) and Kothari and Warner (1997) use different simulation methods to show the difficulties and imprecision associated with testing for unusual stock price performance. Mitchell and Stafford (1998) also show the wide dispersion of abnormal stock return measures when calculated over multiyear horizons.

The linkage between the expected net benefits from an acquisition based on announcement period stock returns and the realized benefits based on accounting performance is likely to be weak, simply because there is much noise in both measures. If the correlation is small, it would be difficult to measure in a large sample of cases. It would be unlikely to see a relation between these measures in a small sample of cases (e.g., two), except by chance.

Finally, in an efficient market one would not expect a correlation between the abnormal stock return at the time of the acquisition announcement and the abnormal return measured over subsequent periods. Thus, if the Cooper and Premark stock returns are disappointing after the acquisitions, this can be viewed as a reflection of new negative information, but not as confirmation or contradiction of initial market reactions (to the extent that markets are efficient). This point is worth reiterating, not so much because Kaplan, Mitchell, and Wruck interpret it incorrectly, but because much of the discussion at the conference for many of the papers often overlooked this point.

Conclusions and Implications for Future Research

The authors conclude that both of these deals failed. Cooper's acquisition of Cameron failed because they were in a different business (despite SIC code similarities) and because Cooper's centralized organization and incentives were inappropriate. Premark's acquisition of Florida Tile failed because they were in different businesses, because Premark overpaid (spending free cash flow), and because other divisions had problems.

One lesson the authors advocate is that bidders must understand their targets. It is hard to argue with this conclusion, but it is also hard to implement it. It seems clear that SIC codes are not helpful, because different sources at different times yield different answers. On the other hand, no suggestions are offered for alternative methods of identifying target companies that are similar to the bidders.

Kaplan, Mitchell, and Wruck argue that organizational design or corporate cultures are important, but they offer few guidelines for identifying problems. The challenge here is to develop a measurable, implementable, replicable method that could be used in large samples.

The authors also argue that incentives are important. They point to the "high powered" equity incentives used by Cooper Cameron after the spinoff, but not by Cooper or Premark. On the other hand, my sense is that this is typical of the distinction between "focus-increasing" going private or recapitalization transactions versus acquisitions. I doubt that Kaplan, Mitchell, and Wruck would conclude that acquisitions would fail unless such incentive compensation is part of the transaction.

Another question that concerns many of the clinical studies in this conference was whether bidding firms were making mistakes. Roll (1986) hypothesizes that managers often become carried away with the bidding process and overpay. Jensen (1986) argues that firms with abundant free cash flow often waste it, perhaps by overpaying in acquisitions. From this perspective, negative stock price reactions for bidders could reflect systematic free cash flow mistakes that are recognized by the outside world at the time. This raises the question of whether managers have better information about the likely success of a possible acquisition than security analysts. It would be interesting to augment the retrospective analysis by managers with reports of securities analysts (or other disinterested parties) at the time of the transaction. This would give clinical studies an additional dimension of information beyond the usual public databases without the problem of translating through the "20/20 hindsight" of managers who were involved in the transaction.

References

Barber, Brad M., and John D. Lyon. 1996. Detecting abnormal operating performance: The empirical power and specification of test statistics. *Journal of Financial Economics* 41:359–99.

———. 1997. Detecting long-run abnormal stock returns: The empirical power and specification of test statistics. *Journal of Financial Economics* 43:341–72.

Collis, D. 1991. *Cooper Industries' corporate strategy teaching note.* Publishing Division, Harvard Business School.

Collis, D., and T. Stuart. 1991. *Cooper Industries' corporate strategy (A).* Publishing Division, Harvard Business School.

Jeffreys, Harold. 1961. *Theory of probability.* 3d ed. Oxford: Clarendon.

Jensen, Michael C. 1986. Agency costs of free cash flow, corporate finance, and takeovers. *American Economic Review* 76:323–29.

Jensen, Michael C., Eugene F. Fama, John B. Long, Richard S. Ruback, G. William Schwert, Clifford W. Smith, and Jerold Warner. 1989. Clinical papers and their role in the development of financial economics. *Journal of Financial Economics* 24:3–6.

Kothari, S. P., and Jerold B. Warner. 1997. Measuring long-horizon security price performance. *Journal of Financial Economics* 43:301–39.

Mitchell, Mark L., and Eric Stafford. 1998. Managerial decisions and long-term stock price performance. Working paper, University of Chicago, Graduate School of Business.

Roll, Richard. 1986. The hubris hypothesis of corporate takeovers. *Journal of Business* 59:197–216.

Schwert, G. William. 1996. Markup pricing in mergers and acquisitions. *Journal of Financial Economics* 41:153–92.

Zellner, Arnold. 1971. *An introduction to Bayesian inference in econometrics.* New York: John Wiley.

Comment   René M. Stulz

The paper by Kaplan, Mitchell, and Wruck provides an extremely detailed and careful analysis of two acquisitions, Cooper Industries' acquisition of Cameron Iron Works in 1989 and Premark's acquisition of Florida Tile in 1990. The paper argues that neither acquisition was successful in creating value. The lack of value creation is attributed to several causes, but one surprising conclusion is that the managers of the acquiring companies did not understand the characteristics of the target well. The other reasons uncovered by the authors for the lack of success of the acquisitions are more commonly emphasized in the literature. They are the inappropriate

René M. Stulz holds the Everett D. Reese Chair of Banking and Monetary Economics at the Ohio State University and is a research associate of the National Bureau of Economic Research.

incentives of managers and the poor organizational design of the merged firms.

In this discussion, I address three issues in turn. First, I consider the difficulty in assessing whether a specific acquisition decision was the right one as opposed to whether acquisitions in general create wealth. Second, I argue that the difficulties documented in the study may have more to do with growth through diversification in general than with acquisitions per se. Third, I point out that we cannot judge the shareholder wealth impact of a business strategy without knowing what management would have done instead.

What Can We Learn from a Sample of Two?

Over recent years, there has been renewed interest in studies that emphasize the institutional context of business activities. Typically, such studies are limited to small samples when proper care is taken to understand the institutional context. An analysis based on few data points cannot draw on the formal statistical tools available for hypothesis testing in large sample studies. As a result, interpreting the evidence of small sample studies is particularly difficult. This problem is quite clear in the context of this study. The authors find that both acquisitions failed. The important question they would like to answer, however, is whether these acquisitions were positive net present value projects for the firms that undertook them. In other words, were these acquisitions failures ex ante or good acquisitions that failed because bad things happened? In a large scale study of takeovers, the idiosyncrasies of individual takeovers average out and the net effect of takeovers should be positive for shareholders if takeovers create wealth in general. Yet, it would be perfectly possible for some individual takeovers to have bad outcomes when all takeovers are positive net present value projects when undertaken. The number of bad outcomes in a large scale study would help us assess the hypothesis we are trying to test. Here, we have bad outcomes but do not know whether they result from acquisitions that would have destroyed wealth if they worked out as expected. If the outcome of a takeover is the expected value creation of the takeover plus random noise that is the product of idiosyncrasies specific to that particular takeover, we cannot separate the noise from the expected value creation with two observations and hence cannot tell whether the expected value creation is positive or not. Takeovers are bad for shareholders in general only if the expected value creation is negative.

The authors make a gallant effort to convince the reader that the acquisitions were poor ones ex ante. Their arguments are persuasive, but their information differs from the information that was available to management when it decided to make the acquisition. Once one knows that an acquisition has been unsuccessful, it is only natural to look for possible explanations of failure and uncover issues that management neglected or misunderstood. Here, it would appear that an ex ante source of failure is that management did not know enough about the target. Again, this may be true, but how do we know that management made its decision inefficiently? There are many demands on management's time and, in the case of these acquisitions, management may have felt that it had enough information to make its decision. Obviously it was surprised after the acquisition when it discovered some unexpected target attributes. Based on two observations, it is difficult to understand what these surprises imply. Suppose that managers always allocate the same amount of time to make acquisition decisions. To place the surprises observed in these two acquisitions in context, we would have to know how often such surprises occur. If they occur rarely, then management is probably spending the right amount of time on acquisitions. If they happen often, then one has to wonder about the incentives of managers to make decisions with insufficient information.

While it is difficult to calculate generally what to make out of two data points, it should be stressed that these two data points are the basis for a study that is extremely useful in at least two ways. First, it should be required reading for students because it shows precisely what can happen in acquisitions and how problems could be avoided. There is no way that a large scale study could be as informative for a manager-to-be. A manager does not worry whether acquisitions in general create wealth but wants to know how to ensure that the next acquisition she makes fulfills her objectives. If the manager's objective is to create wealth, then she wants to know how to make it more likely that this will happen. Second, this study should lead researchers to address some questions that they have not addressed in large scale studies. The existing literature has documented that many takeovers fail, but a systematic investigation of why they fail and how prevalent failure is should be conducted; this paper shows what such an investigation should focus on.

Why the Failure?

Why did these acquisitions fail? One can think of two different explanations that have dramatically different implications for the theory of the firm. The first possible explanation is that it is always difficult to integrate the activities of two firms, so that in general it is difficult to make acquisitions work. In other words, acquisitions could be positive net present value projects, but they would have a high rate of failure because they are difficult to carry out. The difficulty with this hypothesis is that in the case of the acquisition of Cameron, the acquisition seems to have destroyed value of Cameron as a stand-alone firm. Hence, it is not as if nothing was added by the takeover and the gains of the potential combination were not realized. The evidence suggests that what happened is that something was taken away from Cameron and that what was taken away represents a substantial fraction of the premerger value of Cameron. This means that the value destroyed is much larger than the synergy that did not happen.

The evidence in the study is quite consistent with the alternative explanation that the acquisitions did not work out because diversification and growth through diversification destroy wealth on average. As evidenced in the literature, diversified firms are valued less than comparable portfolios of specialized firms. Here, the targets lost value being part of a larger firm because their management did not have the appropriate incentives and the more complex organization was not as nimble in reacting to changes in investment opportunities. Viewed from this perspective, it is not clear that it is important that Cameron and Florida Tile were acquired. Had these divisions been grown internally, value would still have been lost because the same problems would have been present. Acquiring these divisions was more costly for the shareholders of the acquirers than internal growth because they paid a premium. However, at the level of the economy as a whole, this premium does not correspond to value destruction but rather to value transfer.

If what destroys value is growth through diversification, acquisitions are just an easy way to implement a strategy of growth through diversification. If acquisitions were not feasible, management would still engage in growth through diversification and value would still be destroyed if the incentives that lead management to choose such business strategies remain unchanged. These considerations make it even harder to assess the two takeovers discussed in this study. In both firms, management had resources to grow the firm but lacked investment opportunities in the existing core business. The best outcome from the perspective of shareholders would have been for management to pay out these resources to shareholders. Management did not want to do that because it would have been an admission of failure or because management felt that it could do better for the shareholders. Had therefore management not been allowed to make acquisitions, it is not at all clear that shareholders would have been better off. What if, instead, management had chosen to invest in core activities? It might be that more corporate resources would have been wasted that way. This problem suggests a difficulty with many studies that assess takeovers. If takeovers that do not create wealth are undertaken by management, the proper comparison of the gains and losses of takeovers is not with what management would do if it maximized shareholder wealth but rather with what it would do if it did not undertake the takeover being considered.

While it is true that the acquisitions of Cameron and Florida Tile destroyed wealth, they might have accomplished management's objectives of growth through diversification at lower cost to shareholders than the alternatives management was contemplating. Hence, when the market reacts to acquisitions, it is quite difficult to know how to interpret the stock price reaction. If management maximizes shareholder wealth, acquisitions that have negative announcement returns are either managerial mistakes or acquisitions that reveal information about the acquirer that the market did not have. If management pursues its own objectives and the market knows these objectives, an acquisition with a negative announcement return reveals that management destroyed more wealth than expected. In this case, acquisitions with no abnormal returns for the acquirer could still destroy wealth because the wealth destruction is anticipated.

Based on the considerations just discussed, one should be quite cautious in evaluating announcement abnormal returns associated with single transactions. The authors chose their sample by selecting one acquisition with a positive abnormal return and one with a negative abnormal return. Our discussion suggests that such a strategy would yield a sample of one positive net present value and one negative net present value acquisition only if managers maximize shareholder wealth and if the abnormal returns of acquisitions only reveal information about whether management made the right or wrong decision. If these assumptions are not met, a positive net present value takeover could have a negative abnormal return because it reveals adverse information about the bidder's investment opportunities, and a negative net present value takeover could have a positive abnormal return because its managers wasted less shareholder wealth than expected.

Conclusion

This study and the other papers in the volume show how little we know about takeovers and about managerial incentives. Why is it that managers make all these acquisitions when so few of them appear to be successful? Here we have authors who initially sought to discuss successful acquisitions only to find, after all was said and done, that the acquisitions were not successful. If successful acquisitions are so hard to find, why is it that shareholders approve mergers as often as they do?

Workforce Integration and the Dissipation of Value in Mergers
The Case of USAir's Acquisition of Piedmont Aviation

Stacey R. Kole and Kenneth Lehn

> Somewhere along the line a strong carrier, instead of
> becoming stronger by acquisition, is going to merge itself into
> weakness, and maybe this [USAir transaction] is going to be it.
> —Edmund Greenslet, Merrill Lynch (19 February 1987)

5.1 Introduction

In November 1987, USAir Group acquired Piedmont Aviation for $1.6 billion in a cash tender offer. The acquisition, which remains the largest airline merger in history, transformed USAir from a regional airline into a major national airline. Comparably sized, USAir and Piedmont had the two highest profit rates in the industry and reputations as strong regional airlines that had thrived under deregulation. Following the integration of the two carriers, the new USAir incurred huge operating losses, became the least profitable major airline, sustained a large reduction in its stock price, eliminated its dividend, and came close to bankruptcy. We examine USAir's acquisition of Piedmont and its postmerger performance to address the following question: How can the combination of two highly profitable firms dissipate so much value?

Figure 5.1 shows USAir's stock price performance from 1978 through 1995. From 1979 to 1986, the first eight years of airline deregulation,

Stacey R. Kole is associate professor of economics and management at the William E. Simon Graduate School of Business Administration of the University of Rochester. Kenneth Lehn is the Samuel A. McCullough Professor of Finance at the J. M. Katz School of Business of the University of Pittsburgh.

The authors gratefully acknowledge the many individuals from USAir, the Department of Transportation, and Goldman Sachs who spoke with them and provided information for this project. These individuals include Dwain Andrews, Michael Armellino, Paul Bowser, Edwin Colodny, Glenn Engel, Robert Gaudioso, John Harper, Randall Malin, General Robert Oaks, Larry Phillips, and Seth Schofield. The authors also thank Severin Borenstein, Harry Evans, Marc Knez, Michael Spiro, Bill Schwert, and Karen Wruck for comments on an earlier draft; Bill Schwert for data on merger and takeover activity; and Tom Bates for research assistance. Financial support was provided by the John H. Olin Foundation (Kole) and the National Bureau of Economic Research.

Fig. 5.1 USAir's cumulative monthly net-of-market returns, 1978–95

USAir experienced a cumulative net-of-market return of roughly 75 percent. In February 1987, USAir announced its bid for Piedmont. Although Piedmont was acquired in November 1987, integration was delayed for regulatory and labor-related reasons until August 1989. Almost immediately thereafter, USAir's costs rose, productivity and customer service deteriorated, and in the year following August 1989, USAir's stock price fell from $54 to $21.375. Within five years of the completion of the Piedmont merger, USAir had destroyed more than $2.5 billion of shareholder value.

We conclude that the major source of USAir's value destruction was the strategy it used to integrate the Piedmont and USAir workforces. This integration was further complicated by USAir's acquisition of PSA, a smaller California airline, for $400 million at roughly the same time. Before the acquisitions, the workforces at the three airlines had different pay scales, work rules, and cultures. After the acquisitions, USAir faced a choice: maintain these differences within the firm or standardize the labor contracts and cultures of the three organizations.

USAir opted for the latter. Attempting to buy labor peace, it brought the Piedmont and PSA employees under the more generous pay scales and work rules of USAir's collective bargaining agreements. This raised labor costs substantially and lowered the productivity of the newly acquired airlines. In addition to adopting uniform labor contracts for the three workforces, USAir used a "mirror image" strategy to homogenize the operations of the acquired airlines in order to expedite Federal Aviation Administration (FAA) certification of the acquired carriers. However, the policy extended beyond regulatory requirements and "turned out to be an irritant to everyone—PSA and Piedmont employees and their customers."[1]

The USAir case, and perhaps airline mergers more generally, provides evidence consistent with Williamson's (1985) conjecture that the boundaries of the firm are limited in part by considerations of "internal equity." Williamson raises the oft-asked question, "why can't a large firm do everything that a collection of small firms can do and more?" (131). He suggests that one large (merged) firm may be unable to sustain desirable differences in compensation plans across separate units because of the disharmony it creates among the firm's lower paid workers. Even though synergies may exist in the merger of two firms, these benefits can be more than offset by the costs of integrating disparate workforces. United Airlines' highly public analysis of a bid for USAir is a good example. Although United's management acknowledged substantial operating synergies between the two airlines, United cited the carrier's high labor costs and the expected difficulties combining the two workforces in its decision not to acquire USAir.

Our analysis of the USAir-Piedmont case reveals the thorny labor relations issues that exist in airline mergers more generally. While these issues exist in varying degrees in other industries as well, we conjecture that they are especially challenging in the airline industry for several reasons. First, labor costs account for a larger proportion of operating expenses for airlines (especially for carriers that predate deregulation) than they do in most industries. Second, labor unions, especially the pilots' and mechanics' unions, have considerable hold-up power in the airline industry since flight crews and mechanics develop skills that are specific to aircraft and costly to replace. Third, since the airline industry is a service industry, worker disharmony can substantially damage an airline's brand name. Finally, airlines face unique regulations, such as the Railway Labor Act, that affect the integration of workforces. Later, we present evidence showing that the long-run stock price performance of acquiring airlines is highly negative.

This paper is organized as follows. Section 5.2 provides background information on USAir and Piedmont, describes the rationale and structure of the merger, and discusses the regulatory and organizational issues that delayed the implementation of the Piedmont-USAir merger for almost two years. We also present premerger financial data for the airlines and document a substantial difference in the labor costs of Piedmont and

---

1. Seth Schofield, former chairman and chief executive officer at USAir, interview by authors, Pittsburgh, Pa., 7 October 1996.

USAir in section 5.2. Section 5.3 shows that the stock market did not view the Piedmont acquisition as unwise during 1987, when the acquisition was initially announced and approved. Section 5.4 describes the decline in USAir's performance after the integration of Piedmont and documents that the principal source of the decline is the increase in USAir's labor costs. In section 5.5, we discuss factors that contributed to USAir's poor performance after the merger, including the integration and organizational policies it adopted. Section 5.6 provides concluding comments.

5.2   USAir's Acquisition of Piedmont

Before examining the effect of the Piedmont acquisition on USAir's performance, it is useful to describe some background information on USAir and Piedmont, the strategy behind the acquisition, and the takeover process that led to the acquisition.

In retrospect, USAir's acquisition of Piedmont had several elements that might have predicted the postmerger problems that USAir experienced. First, before the merger, USAir was generating substantial cash flow but had low growth opportunities in its existing markets. Given that USAir management owned a small percentage of stock, it had the profile of a firm that suffered from the agency costs of free cash flow (Jensen 1986). Second, the acquisition came on the heels of a major consolidation of the airline industry—ten airline mergers had occurred in the two years prior to the Piedmont acquisition. USAir management felt that it had to acquire or be acquired, and hastily proceeded to acquire PSA and Piedmont. Third, and relatedly, USAir placed the survival of the organization ahead of the interests of shareholders. Fourth, USAir management had a track record for avoiding confrontation with employees, which might have suggested a substantial increase in its postmerger labor costs. Finally, as a regional airline, USAir did not have the infrastructure to seamlessly digest an acquisition as large as Piedmont.

Notwithstanding these considerations, as we show below, the market generally did not anticipate the postmerger problems that USAir would experience. Hence, while it is tempting to criticize the strategy behind the acquisition, there were few negative signals conveyed to USAir management at the time.

5.2.1   Background Information on USAir and Piedmont

USAir

USAir began in 1939 as All American Aviation providing mail service in isolated communities throughout Appalachia. It changed its name to Allegheny Airlines in 1953 upon offering passenger air travel on short-haul routes in the Northeast. Between 1939 and 1978, USAir's predecessor company acquired two smaller regional airlines—Lake Central Airlines in 1968 and Mohawk Airlines in 1972. By the time price and entry regulations were lifted in 1978, Allegheny Airlines had a reputation as a marginally profitable regional airline.

In 1979, shortly after deregulation, Allegheny Airlines changed its name to USAir, Inc., to reflect its growing service network and to signal its intention to expand nationally. Like most major airlines, the company established a holding company structure after deregulation. In 1983, USAir Group was formed as the holding company for USAir, Inc., which became the wholly owned subsidiary through which USAir Group conducted its airline business. Shortly thereafter, USAir Group acquired two small commuter airlines—Pennsylvania Commuter Airlines in 1985 and Suburban Airlines in 1986. By the end of 1986, USAir Group owned four subsidiaries: USAir, Inc., the two commuter airlines, and U.S. Leasing and Services, a small aircraft leasing company. By the end of 1986, USAir offered service to more than one hundred cities and seventy-seven airports within the United States.

Piedmont

Piedmont Aviation was founded in 1940 as a small regional airline providing passenger air travel in the Southeast. Like Allegheny Airlines, its counterpart in the Northeast, Piedmont concentrated its operations on short-haul markets.

In early 1986, Piedmont Aviation acquired Greensboro High Point Air Services, a small commuter airline with operations in North Carolina and Virginia. After deregulation, Piedmont acquired two other small airlines—Henson Aviation, a regional airline with operations in the Southeast, and Empire Airlines, which operated in upstate New York. Piedmont also acquired Aviation Supply Corp. in 1983, which sold and distributed aircraft parts and equipment. By 1986, Piedmont Aviation consisted of Piedmont Airlines, its principal division, and two wholly owned subsidiaries engaged in aviation sales and services, though Piedmont, like USAir, earned 95 percent of its consolidated revenues from passenger sales. By the end of 1986, Piedmont provided service to one hundred U.S. cities and seventy-five airports.

USAir and Piedmont's Performance, 1979–86

During the early years of deregulation, the major trunk airlines withdrew from many of the short-haul markets served by USAir, Piedmont, and other regional airlines. Under regulation, trunk lines were encouraged to serve short-haul markets by a fare structure that provided cross-subsidies from travelers on long-haul routes to those on short-haul routes. With the elimination of cross-subsidization, the major airlines largely conceded the short-haul routes to regional airlines with fleets of smaller aircraft.

By 1986, USAir and Piedmont dominated the short-haul markets in the Northeast and Southeast, respectively. USAir developed a hub in Pittsburgh through which it provided frequent passenger service to smaller cities in the Northeast, such as Allentown, Bethlehem, Albany, Syracuse, and Rochester. Piedmont maintained its principal hub in Charlotte through which it provided frequent air service to smaller cities in the Southeast, such as Asheville, Fayetteville, and Columbia, South Carolina. Piedmont also operated smaller hubs in Dayton, Ohio, and at Baltimore/ Washington International Airport. Both airlines maintained fleets of smaller planes (e.g., DC-9s and Boeing 727s and 737s) allowing them to achieve high load factors in the smaller markets that fed traffic into their hub operations. "Fortress" hubs and route structures provided USAir and Piedmont with a major strategic advantage in the deregulated environment—both were considered to be less vulnerable to the intense fare competition that prevailed on other routes in the early 1980s.[2] It was perceived that the traffic on the USAir and Piedmont routes was sufficiently light to deter substantial entry by other airlines (Rotbart 1984; Stevens 1984).

Both USAir and Piedmont enjoyed unusually high profit rates during the early years of deregulation. Figure 5.2 shows the annual ratio of operating income to operating revenue for both airlines and an industry portfolio from 1978 to 1986.[3] The figure shows that throughout the period, USAir and Piedmont consistently outperformed the industry with operating margins of 8.6 percent and 8.0 percent for USAir and Piedmont, respectively, versus an operating margin of 1.6 percent for the industry portfolio. In fact, USAir and Piedmont typically ranked among the most profitable airlines. The revenues of both airlines also grew rapidly during this period. From 1978 to 1986, the operating revenues of USAir and Piedmont grew by 224 percent and 812 percent, respectively, compared with 67 percent for the industry portfolio. By the end of 1986, the two former regional carriers were among the ten largest airlines in the country.

The stock prices of both companies increased substantially during the years 1979 to 1986. Figure 5.1 shows that USAir's cumulative net-of-market stock return for the period was 75 percent; figure 5.3 shows a corresponding return of 130 percent for Piedmont. Whereas Piedmont's cumulative returns had been highly negative during the first few years of deregulation, they increased sharply in 1981. In contrast, USAir's returns had generally been positive from the outset of deregulation. A *Wall Street Journal* article (Byrne 1983) discussing the winners and losers of deregula-

---

2. Rotbart (1984) quotes an official of a mutual fund that specializes in airline stocks as saying that "Piedmont and USAir get competition occasionally on point-to-point routes, but you can't compete with their hub and spoke systems."

3. The industry portfolio consists of nineteen airlines that were publicly traded in 1978. It includes Alaska, Aloha, American, Braniff, Continental, Delta, Eastern, Frontier, Hawaiian, Northwest, Ozark, Pan Am, PSA, Republic, Southwest, Texas, TWA, United, and Western.

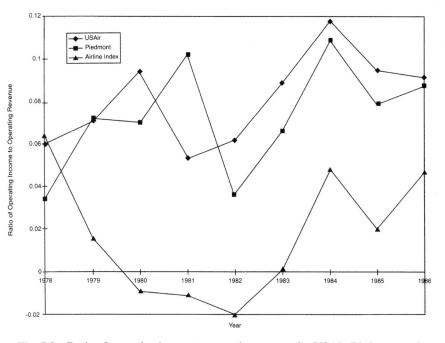

Fig. 5.2   Ratio of operating income to operating revenue for USAir, Piedmont, and an airline index, 1978–86

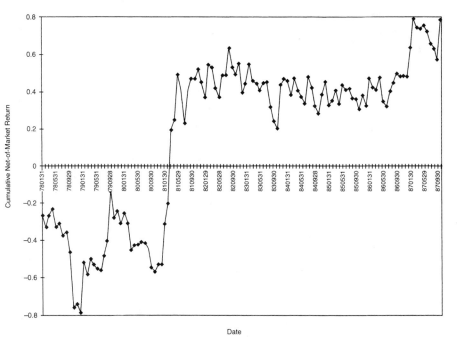

Fig. 5.3   Piedmont's cumulative monthly net-of-market return, 1978–87

tion referred to USAir and Piedmont as two of three "notable successes" in the industry, with Southwest being the third.

Notwithstanding the similarities in their strategy, size, and performance, USAir and Piedmont differed greatly in their cost structures. Bailey, Graham, and Kaplan (1985) document that USAir had the highest cost per available seat mile (ASM) in the industry in 1982, even controlling for its relatively short flight length.[4] The major source of USAir's higher costs was its high labor costs, and while other airlines began reducing their labor costs around deregulation, USAir did not.

5.2.2   Rationale behind USAir's Acquisitions

In the mid-1980s the airline industry experienced a rapid consolidation of assets through merger and acquisition activity. Figure 5.4 shows little activity among NYSE and AMEX traded airlines during the first few years of deregulation, followed by a large spike in mergers from 1985 to 1987.[5] Former USAir chairman Edwin Colodny attributes this pattern to the fact that airlines grew simply by flying where they wanted during the early years of deregulation.[6] By the mid-1980s, he argues, the cumulative growth of established airlines and the entry of new airlines led to excess capacity that was rationalized through a flurry of mergers. From March 1985 through November 1986, the airline industry experienced ten mergers involving seventeen airlines, including the major trunk airlines and regional carriers such as TWA, Ozark, Northwest, and Republic.

In a May 1986 speech to the American Institute of Aeronautics and Astronautics, USAir chairman Colodny expressed skepticism about "merger mania" in the airline industry, stating that the "consolidation trend is thought by many to be the logical follow-on phase of deregulation, with the larger carriers gobbling up the small, weak, and vulnerable. . . . The assumption that bigger is better should not be blindly accepted." Colodny went on to discuss the implications of the merger trend for USAir: "[M]any financial commentators and others keep talking about the need for 'critical mass,' suggesting that a carrier must be some preordained size in order to survive. When I hear critical mass, I recall what it really means. Critical mass is 'the amount of a given radioactive material necessary to sustain a chain reaction at a constant rate.' Does this mean an airline could reach critical mass and explode? *If so, perhaps USAir should continue as a profitable, northeast niche carrier*" (italics added).

Colodny's skepticism about airline mergers was based on both his own experience and the problems that other airlines were experiencing with

---

4. Bailey et al. (1985, 92) report USAir's cost per ASM (10.5 cents) exceeds Piedmont's (8.6 cents) by more than 20 percent.

5. We refer the reader to Comment and Schwert (1995) for a discussion of the data.

6. Edwin Colodny, former chairman and chief executive officer of USAir, interview by authors, Washington, D.C., 9 October 1996.

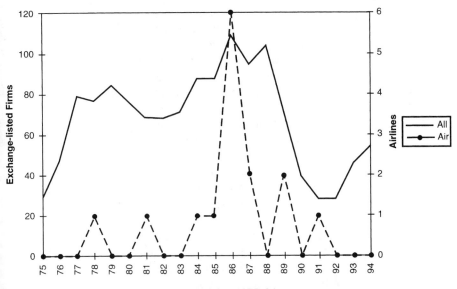

Fig. 5.4   Merger and tender offer activity, 1975–94

deregulation-era mergers. Colodny was executive vice president for legal affairs at Allegheny Airlines when USAir's predecessor company acquired Lake Central and Mohawk before deregulation. Although he acknowledges that both acquisitions contributed to the development of the Pittsburgh hub, there were the difficulties of integrating the acquired companies' labor agreements with Allegheny's.[7] A critical issue was the integration of pilot seniority lists. For example, is a Mohawk captain with twenty years of experience on Mohawk's small aircraft senior to an Allegheny captain with ten years of experience on Allegheny's more sophisticated fleet? These difficulties led to a codification of regulations referred to as the "Allegheny-Mohawk" labor protective provisions (LPPs) which protect the interests of airline employees in a merger. These provisions, in combination with the Railway Labor Act, became the industry standard for integrating labor agreements in airline mergers.

Colodny also observed the problems that other airlines experienced after mergers. For example, in 1979, almost immediately after deregulation, Pan Am acquired National in an attempt to build a domestic airline to complement its international routes. Rather than operate National as an independent subsidiary with its own labor agreements, Pan Am merged National into Pan Am. Martin Shugrue, a former senior executive at Pan Am, believes that decision "cost Pan Am its future" (Peterson and Glab 1994, 90). By merging National's labor contracts into Pan Am's more gen-

7. Ibid.

erous labor agreements, Pan Am's costs increased dramatically.[8] In addition to increasing the compensation levels of the former National employees, Pan Am extended its restrictive union work rules to National, further increasing its costs and lowering the productivity of the new employees. Since deregulation, other acquiring airlines including Republic, Texas, and Northwest have experienced problems associated with the integration of an acquired airline's workforce.

Despite his reservations about acquisitions, Colodny ultimately came to the view that USAir had to "acquire or be acquired" (Payne 1989). With its strong franchise in the Northeast and as one of the few remaining independent regional airlines, USAir was an attractive target. Carl Icahn, then chairman of TWA, had acquired a 4.9 percent stake in USAir early 1986 and, in Colodny's words, was "making noise about an acquisition of US-Air."[9] Furthermore, the Department of Transportation (DOT) approved every merger proposed postderegulation, making it unlikely that DOT would oppose another airline's acquisition of USAir. In 1986, USAir added a poison pill to antitakeover amendments it had adopted, revealing that it viewed itself as a viable takeover target.

In 1986, Colodny initiated preliminary discussions with several airlines about a possible combination. He had been interested in expanding US-Air's operations in California for some time based on the size of the California market.[10] USAir had direct flights from Pittsburgh to San Francisco, Los Angeles, and San Diego, but it had few routes serving other cities on the West Coast. USAir saw expansion into California as an opportunity to enhance the productivity of its resources.[11] Since planes could not fly back from California to Pittsburgh after 10 P.M., USAir's planes and crew often lay idle in California. If USAir had additional routes on the West Coast, it could make more efficient use of these resources by flying up and down the coast.

In 1985, United acquired Pan Am's Pacific routes, which immediately gave it a large presence in California. Speculation grew that other airlines would follow suit by acquiring one of the three major regional airlines serving California—AirCal, Western, and PSA (Harris 1986). USAir approached AirCal, arguably the most compatible of the three because of its small fleet of Boeing 737s. However, USAir and AirCal could not agree on an acquisition price, and shortly thereafter AirCal was acquired by American for $225 million. Delta acquired Western in September 1986,

8. Peterson and Glab (1994) quote another former executive at Pan Am as stating "basically what happened is that Pan Am ended up capitulating and paying all the National people at the higher Pan Am rates—which was suicide. That ensured they could never, ever run a successful domestic system" (90).

9. Interview with Colodny, see note 6.

10. Ibid.

11. Randall Malin, former senior vice president of marketing at USAir, interview by authors, 25 September 1996.

leaving PSA as the only remaining independent regional airline with substantial operations in California.

Colodny turned his attention to PSA. As an intrastate airline not subject to regulation by the Civil Aeronautics Board (CAB), PSA offered air service within California at fares below those of interstate airlines. It was known as a "fun" airline that adorned its planes with a smile, served granola cookies, and clad flight attendants in hot pants during the 1970s. Once a highly successful carrier, PSA experienced financial difficulties after deregulation as low-cost entrants and its established competitors began to compete on price. Colodny "quickly reached an agreement" with Paul Barkley, the chairman of PSA and PS Group (the holding company for PSA), whereby USAir would acquire PSA for $17 per share, or about $400 million. The two airlines announced the agreement on 8 December 1986, subject to the provision that USAir could agree with PSA's unions over the terms of their employment at USAir.

At the same time that Colodny pursued PSA, he was holding talks with William Howard, the chairman of Piedmont Aviation, about a possible merger of USAir and Piedmont. Colodny and Howard had talked about a merger in early 1986, but could not agree on a management structure for the new company. Colodny's interest in a combination with Piedmont was renewed after a September meeting with Carl Icahn in which Icahn expressed interest in acquiring USAir. Attracted by USAir's high labor costs, Icahn intended to reduce USAir's labor expenses by imposing TWA's lower pay scales and more demanding work rules on USAir employees in a merger of the two companies.[12] Colodny resolved to maintain USAir's independence, in part because of his concern about the implications of a TWA takeover for USAir employees and the communities USAir served.

Piedmont was always the most desirable merger partner for USAir, according to Seth Schofield, who was executive vice president of operations in 1987 and later became Colodny's successor as chairman and CEO of USAir.[13] Piedmont had "tremendous consumer loyalty in the Southeast and was just a terrific airline," according to Schofield.[14] Its routes were contiguous to USAir's with little overlap. A combination of USAir and Piedmont would blanket the entire eastern part of the United States and provide USAir with strong routes in Florida, where it had been expanding. The two airlines also had the same unions and similar aircraft fleets, which, it was thought at the time, would facilitate integration of the two airlines.[15]

By the end of 1986, USAir management concluded that to survive as

12. Interview with Colodny, see note 6.
13. Interview with Schofield, see note 1.
14. Ibid.
15. Interview with Malin, see note 11.

an independent company it would have to make a large acquisition. This assessment was based on the increasing importance of frequent flier programs and the perceived need to offer an expanded route structure to retain the loyalty of USAir customers. Intent on being a survivor, Colodny viewed Piedmont as its most attractive target. The timing was tricky, since USAir was focusing on the integration of PSA. Nonetheless, USAir management felt an urgency to proceed—they were convinced that if USAir and Piedmont did not combine, both would become targets.[16]

5.2.3   Structure of the Piedmont Merger

A decision to make a bid for Piedmont was prompted in January 1987 when Norfolk Southern, which owned almost 20 percent of the equity in Piedmont, disclosed in a 13-D filing that it would explore a possible acquisition of Piedmont. Colodny contacted the chairmen of both Piedmont and Norfolk Southern to indicate USAir's interest in acquiring Piedmont. On 13 February, USAir made an unsolicited bid for Piedmont. It submitted two alternative proposals to the Piedmont board: either a pure stock swap consisting of $71 in USAir stock (consisting of no less than 1.55 and no more than 1.9 USAir shares) for each Piedmont share, or a mixed cash/ stock offer consisting of $34 in cash and $34 in USAir stock (consisting of no less than 0.74 and no more than 0.91 USAir shares) for each Piedmont share. On 17 February 1987, a special committee of the Piedmont board recommended that the full board accept a $65 per share cash offer from Norfolk Southern and reject the proposals submitted by USAir. USAir sweetened the bid on the next day, to $71 per share in cash for the first 50.1 percent of the Piedmont shares and $73 per share in stock (consisting of no less than 1.55 and no more than 1.9 USAir shares) for each remaining Piedmont share. The following day, 19 February, the special committee of Piedmont's board withdrew its support for Norfolk Southern's offer and stated that it would invite other bids for the company.

USAir's bid for Piedmont was complicated on 21 February, when Carl Icahn contacted Colodny to indicate his interest in a TWA-USAir combination. Colodny rebuffed Icahn and continued to discuss a merger with Piedmont. On 3 March, Colodny and Howard reached tentative agreement on a merger agreement, which they presented to their respective boards the next day. On the day of the two board meetings, TWA disclosed that it had a 9.9 percent stake in USAir and was proposing to acquire USAir for $52 per share. In a letter to USAir, TWA chairman Icahn stated that "we believe that your other shareholders would prefer our cash merger proposal for USAir over USAir's proposed acquisition of Piedmont" (Agins and Cohen 1987). Icahn also raised the possibility of a

---

16. Dwain Andrews, vice president of labor relations at USAir, interview by authors, Washington, D.C., 9 October 1996.

merger of all three airlines—USAir, Piedmont, and TWA. He indicated that if USAir rejected his proposal, he might make a tender offer directly to the USAir shareholders. On 4 March, USAir's board rejected TWA's offer, stating that it is "grossly inadequate and not in the best interests of USAir Group or its shareholders, employees or passengers."[17] Colodny stated that TWA's offer was "nothing more than an attempt by Carl Icahn to disrupt at the 11th hour" USAir's acquisition of Piedmont.[18]

Two days later, on 6 March 1987, the Piedmont and USAir boards unanimously approved a restructured merger agreement in which Piedmont would be acquired by USAir for $69 per share in a cash offer valued at $1.59 billion on a fully diluted basis. USAir restructured its offer from a mixed cash/stock offer to a pure cash offer in order to expedite the acquisition of Piedmont—a cash offer avoids the delays associated with SEC registration requirements and shareholder votes in stock deals. Restructuring the offer as a pure cash deal required USAir to arrange a credit facility to provide the cash for the offer. Within three weeks, USAir reached agreement with a syndicate of commercial banks, led by Manufacturers Hanover, for a $2 billion credit facility. Meanwhile, a federal court temporarily blocked TWA from buying more USAir shares. Shortly thereafter, TWA dropped its bid for USAir. Subject to regulatory approval, USAir's bid for Piedmont was successful.

5.2.4   Regulatory Approval

Under section 408 of the Federal Aviation Act of 1958, acquisitions of federally certificated airlines must be approved by the DOT.[19] The DOT is required to use the "public interest" criteria, which is defined in section 102 of the Act to include the effect of an acquisition on competition and the quality of services in the airline industry. In addition, section 102 defines the public interest to include the "need to encourage fair wages and equitable working conditions for air carriers." Parties wishing to acquire an airline must file an application with the DOT, which then conducts an investigation of whether the proposed acquisition is in the public interest. Concurrently, the DOT invites the public to comment on the proposed transaction. As an artifact of airline deregulation, an administrative law judge (ALJ) within DOT makes a recommendation to the assistant secretary for policy and international affairs, who has final authority for approving the acquisition.[20]

---

17. USAir rejects TWA's takeover proposal of $52 a share, or more than $1.6 billion, *Wall Street Journal,* 6 March 1987, p. 4.

18. Ibid.

19. This authority originally resided with the CAB. It was transferred to the DOT when the CAB was abolished in 1984.

20. Prior to deregulation, an ALJ at the CAB would make a recommendation to the board, which had final authority for approving the acquisition.

On 22 March 1987, the DOT restricted USAir from acquiring more than 51 percent of Piedmont's common stock, pending its approval of the acquisition. USAir proceeded with its cash tender offer of $69 per share for 50.1 percent of Piedmont's shares, which would be held in a voting trust until the DOT approved the deal. On 6 April, USAir announced that 92 percent of the Piedmont shares had been tendered and that the offer would be prorationed, as required by the Williams Act of 1968. Pending DOT approval, USAir would acquire the remaining 49.9 percent of Piedmont's shares at the same $69 price plus interest.

In an order relating to USAir's application, the DOT indicated that USAir would provide standard labor protective provisions to USAir and Piedmont employees. In late April, USAir confirmed formally that generous labor protective provisions, which had been standard in airline mergers during the period of CAB regulation, would be offered to the two sets of employees. At that point, all affected labor parties, except the International Association of Machinists and Aerospace Workers (IAM), waived further participation in the regulatory proceeding. This effectively rendered labor issues moot in the regulatory process.

The DOT's investigation of USAir's proposal centered on the competitive effects of a USAir-Piedmont merger. America West Airlines had filed an objection to the merger on grounds that it would provide USAir with market power in the East and allow it to preclude entry, especially at La-Guardia and Washington National Airports. The states of Massachusetts, New York, and West Virginia initially opposed the transaction, but withdrew their objections after receiving assurances about the levels of fares and services from USAir. After investigating the effects of a USAir-Piedmont combination on competition, the Department of Justice and the DOT's public counsel independently chose not to oppose the merger.

On 21 September 1987, administrative law judge Ronnie Yoder recommended that the DOT reject the merger on grounds that it "would substantially reduce competition" in some short-haul markets in the east. Colodny described the decision as "incomprehensible" and stated that the merger had been "carefully planned to avoid the consumer and labor problems" that had been experienced in other airline mergers (McGinley and Valente 1987). On 30 October, assistant secretary Matthew Scocozza rejected the ALJ's recommendation and approved the USAir-Piedmont merger without condition, paving the way for the integration of Piedmont into USAir.

5.2.5   Integration of Piedmont into USAir

At the time of its initial bid for Piedmont, USAir indicated that it planned to operate Piedmont as a wholly owned subsidiary for at least nine months after DOT approval of the acquisition. During the nine months, it would develop a strategy for merging Piedmont's personnel, assets, and operations into its own and "seek to identify . . . operating efficiencies" between the two airlines, such as rationalizing schedules and redeploying aircraft.[21] After the transition period, Piedmont would be merged into USAir and the Piedmont name would cease to exist.

After receiving DOT approval, Colodny reiterated USAir's plan to operate Piedmont as an independent subsidiary for at least nine months. He indicated that this was intended to avoid the labor and service problems that other airlines had experienced after hastily integrating the workforces and operations of acquired airlines. In a 1988 speech at a Salomon Brothers conference, Colodny stated that "we do not rush headlong into combining companies . . . you have all seen what happens when airlines do not take enough time."[22] Colodny's strategy was endorsed by many, including the *Wall Street Journal*, which stated in an editorial that "part of the public's dissatisfaction with air travel stems from the highly publicized service problems that resulted from some recent mergers. Efforts to integrate work forces were poorly handled, and the proposed USAir-Piedmont merger would benefit from those mistakes. . . . *integration problems would be minimized by an agreement that the merger would not take place for at least nine months after the approval by DOT*" (italics added).[23]

Perhaps the most challenging task during the transition period was the integration of the Piedmont and USAir workforces, which included the integration of seniority lists, pay scales, and work rules. As required by collective bargaining agreement, the integration of pilot seniority lists was left to the USAir and Piedmont Master Executive Councils of the Air Line Pilots Association. This process alone took roughly five months and ultimately involved the use of arbitration.[24] In addition, USAir had to reach transition agreements with each group of employees to reconcile the Piedmont collective bargaining and employment agreements with those of USAir.

To facilitate FAA approval of the integration, USAir adopted a "mirror image" strategy developed for the PSA acquisition. Prior to the merger, USAir and Piedmont had been regulated by the eastern and southern districts of the FAA, respectively. Colodny recalled that the two districts had different regulations, which in part accounted for the different operating procedures at the two airlines.[25] Since USAir was the acquiring airline, the merged entity would be regulated by the FAA's eastern district. Hence, USAir could either extend its procedures to Piedmont's operations or it

21. Piedmont Aviation Schedule 14d-1, Securities and Exchange Commission, 9 March 1987, p. 20.
22. Remarks by Edwin I. Colodny, chairman & president, USAir Group, Inc., Salomon Brothers Transportation Conference, New York, 10 November 1988.
23. Merger myopia. *Wall Street Journal,* 19 October 1987, p. 30.
24. Interview with Malin, see note 11.
25. Interview with Colodny, see note 6.

could seek FAA approval to use a mix of Piedmont and USAir procedures. Since Colodny perceived that the latter might jeopardize FAA approval, USAir chose to blanket the newly acquired airline with USAir's operating procedures, which were already approved by the FAA's eastern district.

In a 1989 interview, Schofield stated that the mirror image strategy was devised to "make the two operations look alike in every aspect so that the competency was then transferable from one operating certificate to another" (Ott-Washington 1989). This required extensive retraining of Piedmont employees, including pilots, flight attendants, and mechanics. By the summer of 1989, an estimated eight hundred thousand hours of such training had occurred (Ott-Washington 1989).

Twenty-two months after receiving DOT approval, the integration of Piedmont into USAir was complete. The Piedmont planes were painted with the USAir logo, and on 5 August 1989, the Piedmont name ceased to exist.

5.2.6   Comparative Premerger Data on USAir, Piedmont, and PSA

Table 5.1 presents premerger data that highlight the similarities and differences between Piedmont, PSA, and USAir before the two acquisitions.[26] The size data in table 5.1 show the USAir-Piedmont union to be a merger of equals and that both of these airlines were substantially larger than PSA. USAir and Piedmont had comparable profit rates that were higher than PSA and the two airlines had similar investment rates, capital structures, load factors, and revenue yields. In contrast with USAir and Piedmont, PSA had a lower investment rate, load factor, and revenue yield, and a higher ratio of debt to value.

The data also reveal some significant premerger differences between USAir and Piedmont. As mentioned in subsection 5.2.1, the cost structures of the two airlines differed. Labor costs represented a larger percentage of USAir's higher operating expenses while nonlabor components of costs—fuel, rentals and landing fees, travel agency commissions, and maintenance—accounted for similar percentages of operating expenses at USAir and Piedmont. Except for rentals and landing fees, which are substantially higher at PSA, these costs accounted for comparable percentages of operating expenses at PSA.

Another notable difference between USAir and Piedmont shown in table 5.1 is their premerger stock price performance—USAir's was substantially worse than Piedmont's. From January 1984 through October 1986 (i.e., two months before the first announcement of USAir's bid for PSA), USAir's cumulative net-of-market return was −29.8 percent versus 1.1 percent for Piedmont and 6.7 percent for PSA. Figure 5.5 plots stock

---

26. Unless otherwise noted, we list the mean value of each variable from 1984 to 1986, the last three years that Piedmont and PSA were independent entities.

Table 5.1   **Summary Financial and Firm Characteristics Data for Piedmont, PSA, and USAir, 1984–86**

	Piedmont	PSA	USAir
Size			
Operating revenues ($millions)	1,559	647	1,743
Book value of assets ($millions)	813	514	1,347
Market value of assets ($millions)	924	550	1,319
Number of employees	16,448	4,597	13,763
Cost structure			
Operating expenses ($millions)	1,417	617	1,567
Percentage of operating expenses accounted for by:			
Personnel costs	32	32	41
Fuel costs	18	17	19
Travel agency commissions	7	6	7
Rentals and landing fees	5	10	5
Maintenance costs	5	6	4
Performance			
Operating income as a percentage of operating revenue	9.1	4.7	10.1
Net income as a percentage of market value of common	11.0	−1.8	12.7
Cumulative net of market stock returns (%), January 1984–October 1986	1.1	6.7	−29.8
Investment policy			
Operating working capital as a percentage of revenue	4.3	5.2	7.4
Net investment as a percentage of revenue	10.4	1.3	11.6
Liquidity			
Current ratio	1.119	1.056	1.541
Quick ratio	0.666	0.531	1.292
Cash ratio	0.236	0.152	0.952
Rates of networking capital to total assets	0.025	0.014	0.095
Growth opportunities			
Annual revenue growth rate, 1984–86 (%)	26	18	9
Value Line's projected long-run revenue growth (%)	8	6	7
Market to book ratio	1.13	1.05	0.98
Market to gross equipment ratio	1.11	1.02	1.01
Capital structure			
Percentage of market value accounted for by:			
Long-term debt	32	57	33
Preferred stock	5	11	0
Common stock	63	33	67
Operating statistics			
Revenue passenger miles (millions)	8,392	3,692	9,692
Available seat miles (millions)	15,020	6,614	16,262
Passenger load factor (%)	55.5	55.7	59.5
Break even load factor (%)	51.8	57.1	54.1
Revenue yield (%)	16.6	15.3	16.7
Cost per available seat mile (cents)	8.7	8.6	9.4

Note: All variables are computed as average values over the period 1984–86, except as otherwise noted.

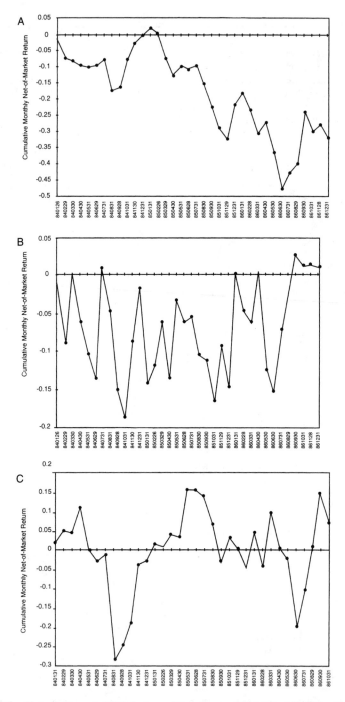

Fig. 5.5 Cumulative net-of-market monthly returns, 1984–86: *A*, USAir; *B*, Piedmont; *C*, PSA

returns during this period for the three airlines, revealing two sharp declines in USAir's stock price—a decline of more than 20 percent during August–November 1985 and one of almost 30 percent during February–July 1986.

The first decline is difficult to explain with USAir-specific news announcements; the only announcements in the *Wall Street Journal* report increases in passenger traffic, an agreement to buy Fokker jet airliners, and an earnings announcement in October. The second decline has more obvious explanations. In early March 1986, USAir had announced selective fare cuts in response to cuts by People Express and Eastern, signaling that USAir increasingly would be involved in fare wars. Later in March, Texas Air announced a proposed acquisition of Eastern, with the intention of lowering Eastern's labor costs. USAir's stock price fell by 3 percent on the announcement of the bid,[27] suggesting that the market viewed the Texas-Eastern combination as a viable threat to USAir's market dominance in northeastern markets. During the month of March, USAir's return was −7 percent. Its market-adjusted stock price fell another 20 percent in May–June, a period in which it had a near collision and announced a decline in May's passenger traffic. The substantial decline in USAir's stock price during mid-1985 through 1986 reveals growing pessimism about USAir's fortunes immediately prior to its acquisitions of PSA and Piedmont.

Data on the liquidity and growth opportunities for the three airlines indicate that USAir had the most cash and the lowest growth opportunities. Combined with its high profitability, these data suggest that USAir had the profile of a firm with substantial free cash flow. USAir's cash ratio was more than four times higher than Piedmont's. At the end of 1986, USAir had $336 million (15 percent of total assets) in cash versus $65 million (4 percent of total assets) for Piedmont. Similar, albeit less dramatic, patterns exist for the other liquidity measures listed in table 5.1. PSA was substantially less liquid than USAir and Piedmont.

Using several proxies for growth options, we find that Piedmont had more growth potential than USAir at the time of the merger. During the years 1984 to 1986, its operating revenue grew at almost three times USAir's annual rate (i.e., 26 percent versus 9 percent). Value Line's five-year projection of annual revenue growth was higher for Piedmont, as were its market-to-book and market value to gross equipment ratios. These data suggest that USAir was more likely than Piedmont to suffer from the agency costs of free cash flow, given its lower growth opportunities, higher liquidity, and high profit rates.

27. USAir's net-of-market return over the three days surrounding the first announcement of Texas Air's bid for Eastern was −3.1 percent. The NYSE Composite was used as the market index for this exercise.

5.3   Market Assessment of USAir's Acquisitions

During most of the period spanning USAir's agreement to acquire PSA and final DOT approval of the Piedmont acquisition, USAir's stock price performed well. Figure 5.6 shows USAir's cumulative daily abnormal returns from November 1986 through December 1987, a period that includes the October stock market crash. Careful inspection of USAir's stock price reaction around key events during this period suggests that the market was skeptical of the PSA acquisition, but not the Piedmont merger. Table 5.2 lists key announcement dates during the period and the corresponding abnormal returns on those dates.

On 8 December 1986, the date that USAir announced the agreement to acquire PSA, USAir experienced a statistically significant abnormal return of −4.6 percent; the cumulative abnormal return (CAR) over the three days surrounding the announcement was −9.4 percent, representing a loss of roughly $100 million in shareholder value. Consistent with the view that the market was skeptical of a USAir-PSA combination, USAir sustained negative abnormal returns on the days that the shareholders of PSA and PS Group (PSA's parent company) approved the transaction (−3

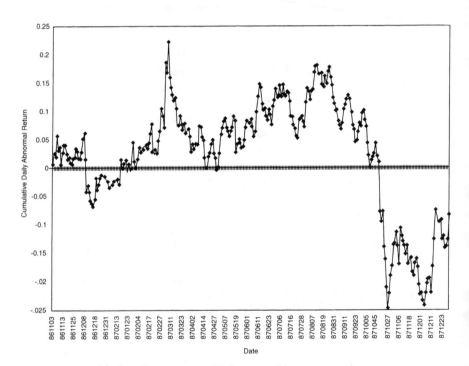

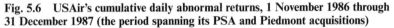

Fig. 5.6   USAir's cumulative daily abnormal returns, 1 November 1986 through 31 December 1987 (the period spanning its PSA and Piedmont acquisitions)

Table 5.2   Chronology of Events Concerning USAir's Acquisitions of PSA and Piedmont and the Corresponding Abnormal Daily Stock Return for USAir on These Event Dates

Date	Event	USAir's Abnormal Stock Return (%)
12-8-86	USAir agrees to acquire PSA for $400 million	−4.6***
1-28-87	DOT approves USAir's acquisition of PSA	4.7***
2-13-87	USAir proposes merger with Piedmont	1.0
2-17-87	Special committee of Piedmont's board recommends that Piedmont accept Norfolk Southern's bid and reject USAir's bid	1.7
2-18-87	USAir sweetens its bid for Piedmont	1.7
2-19-87	Piedmont's board rejects both Norfolk Southern's and USAir's bids and invites other bids for the company	−4.9***
2-21-87	TWA contacts USAir about a possible TWA-USAir combination	0.5
3-3-87	Chairmen of USAir and Piedmont reach tentative agreement on merger of the two companies	−2.2
3-4-87	TWA discloses a 9.9% stake in USAir and announces a proposal to acquire USAir for $52 per share	11.5***
3-6-87	Piedmont and USAir announce that they have reached agreement for USAir to acquire Piedmont for $69 per share	5.4***
3-9-87	Federal judge issues temporary restraining order prohibiting TWA from buying more shares in USAir, pending further ruling	−6.2***
3-10-87	TWA announces that it is "reassessing" its bid for USAir	−1.8
3-16-87	TWA calls off its bid for USAir	−1.8
3-17-87	Shareholders of PSA and PSGroup approve USAir's acquisition of PSA for $400 million	−3.0
3-23-87	DOT announces it will restrict USAir from acquiring Piedmont, pending its approval; TWA says it will not interfere with USAir's acquisition of Piedmont	−1.0
3-25-87	TWA sells its stake in Piedmont	−1.8
3-31-87	USAir reaches agreement with banks for $2 billion credit line to finance acquisitions of PSA and Piedmont	−2.7
4-6-87	USAir says its offer for Piedmont is oversubscribed	0.3
4-15-87	DOT denies USAir's request for expedited approval of its Piedmont acquisition	−1.9
4-16-87	USAir's acquisition of PSA is jeopardized by Teamsters union local	0.0
5-18-87	USAir reaches agreement with Teamsters, clearing way for PSA acquisitions; USAir also announces $400 million offering of common stock	−5.7***
9-18-87	USAir's acquisition of Piedmont is running into opposition at DOT	−2.4
9-21-87	Administrative law judge recommends that DOT reject USAir's acquisition of Piedmont	−0.7
9-22-87	USAir may have to modify its acquisition of Piedmont to gain DOT approval	−2.2
10-5-87	USAir takes hard line and states it won't restructure the Piedmont deal	−2.9
10-19-87	Stock market crash	−5.8***
10-29-87	DOT expected to approve USAir's acquisition of Piedmont with modification	3.1*
10-30-87	DOT approves USAir's acquisition of Piedmont without modifications	1.7

***Significant at the 1 percent level.

*Significant at the 10 percent level.

percent on 17 March 1987) and the Teamsters union local approved some changes in its collective bargaining agreement to clear the way for the acquisition (-5.7 percent on 18 May 1987). The inference to be drawn from the abnormal return on the latter date is complicated by the fact that USAir announced a $400 million equity offering on the same day, an event normally associated with significant stock price declines. Further clouding the issue, USAir enjoyed a 4.7 percent abnormal return on 28 January 1987, the day that the DOT approved the PSA acquisition. Taken together, the abnormal returns on the four announcements suggest at least some market skepticism about the PSA acquisition.

The evidence on the Piedmont acquisition is much clearer—there were no signals that the market thought this was a foolhardy acquisition. Perhaps most convincingly, USAir's market-adjusted stock price fell by more than 6 percent during 17–22 September, a period spanning initial reports that the Piedmont acquisition was running into trouble at DOT. Similarly, USAir's stock had a large positive CAR of 11 percent from 28 October through 2 November, when contrary to expectations the DOT approved the Piedmont acquisition without condition.

In fact, it is hard to read any skepticism about the Piedmont deal from USAir's stock returns during its initial bidding for Piedmont. From 12 February through 18 February, USAir's stock had a CAR of 4.5 percent. During this period, USAir submitted its initial merger proposal to Piedmont, had it rejected, and then sweetened the bid. On 19 February, the day that Piedmont's board rejected USAir's bid and announced it would invite additional bids, USAir's abnormal return was -4.9 percent (significant at the 1 percent confidence level). On 6 March, the day that Piedmont and USAir announced that they had reached agreement on a restructured deal, USAir's abnormal return was a significant 5.4 percent. These data, combined with the evidence on the reaction of USAir's stock price to the DOT decisions, suggest that the market looked favorably on a USAir-Piedmont combination.

The steep increase and subsequent decline in USAir's stock price in March reflects the effect of TWA's merger proposal and the ultimate withdrawal of its proposal. On 4 March, the day TWA announced both its stake in USAir and the merger proposal, USAir's abnormal return was 11.5 percent. On 9 March, the day a federal judge issued a temporary restraining order against further stock purchases by TWA, USAir sustained a -6.2 percent abnormal return. These data indicate that the market believed at the time that USAir's shareholders would be better served by a TWA acquisition of USAir than by a USAir acquisition of Piedmont. Based on the evidence above, however, it favored a Piedmont acquisition over doing nothing.

The stock price evidence generally conforms with comments in the press and analysts' reports about the benefits of a USAir-Piedmont combination. Analysts praised USAir's move: "the USAir-Piedmont combination will form one of the most powerful and profitable competitors in the industry" (Ross and McGinley 1987); "you now have a presence that can compete effectively east of the Mississippi and build competition in the transcontinental markets to cities on the West Coast" (Ross and McGinley 1987); "USAir will cover the eastern U.S. like Sherwin-Williams paint, and they will have enormous marketing clout" (Agins and Morris 1987). Edmund Greenslet of Merrill Lynch, whose opinion of the acquisition is quoted on the first page of this paper, was a lone dissenting voice.

5.4   USAir's Postmerger Performance

USAir's performance began to deteriorate immediately after the integration of Piedmont in August 1989. In the subsections that follow, we document the decline in USAir's profitability and the component cost and revenue trends.

5.4.1   Profitability

Table 5.3 lists performance data for a simulated USAir-Piedmont-PSA combination during 1984–86, hereafter referred to as USAir*, and the actual combination during the years 1989 to 1995. Data for USAir* during 1984–86 are computed simply by adding the relevant data for the three companies. Ratios are computed on a value-weighted basis. We exclude the intervening years of 1987 and 1988 when PSA (1987) and Piedmont (1988) were neither independent nor fully integrated into the USAir system.

As seen in panel A of the table, the ratio of operating income to revenue for USAir* ranges from 8 percent to 11 percent during the years 1984 to 1986. This ratio falls to 0.3 for the newly merged company in 1989 and is followed by five years of operating losses. A similar pattern emerges with data on the ratio of operating income to book asset value.

The deterioration in net income, shown in panel B, is considerably worse. From 1984 to 1986, USAir* had aggregate net income of $522 million, ranging between $166 and $184 million. From 1989 to 1994, USAir accrued over $3 billion in losses. Net income expressed as a percentage of the book value of common stock was −4 percent in 1989, −3 percent in 1990, and −28 percent in 1991. Thereafter, the book value of common stock becomes negative, rendering this percentage meaningless. Net income expressed as a percentage of the market value of common stock varies from −266 percent to −4 percent during 1989–94. The extraordinary value of net income in 1992 includes a charge of $982 million related to grounded aircraft and USAir's accounting for postretirement benefits under the Financial Accounting Standards Board's FAS 106.

Table 5.3   **Profitability Measures for Simulated Merged Company Consisting of USAir, Piedmont, and PSA (USAir*), 1984–86, and USAir, 1989–95**

A. Operating Income ($millions)

Year	Operating Income	Operating Income as a Percentage of:	
		Operating Revenue	Book Value of Assets
1984	362	10.5	15.6
1985	322	8.2	11.2
1986	360	8.0	12.7
1989	21	0.3	0.6
1990	−501	−7.6	−12.5
1991	−168	−2.6	−4.4
1992	−331	−4.9	−12.4
1993	−75	−1.1	−2.5
1994	−491	−7.0	−17.8
1995	322	4.3	12.2

B. Net Income ($millions)

Year	Net Income	Net Income as a Percentage of:	
		Book Value of Common Stock	Market Value of Common Stock
1984	175	14.2	13.9
1985	184	11.4	11.3
1986	166	9.0	7.9
1989	−63	−4.1	−4.1
1990	−454	−3.3	−63.9
1991	−305	−27.6	−54.5
1992	−1,229	n.m.f.	−204.5
1993	−393	n.m.f.	−51.6
1994	−685	n.m.f.	−266.1
1995	119	n.m.f.	14.4

C. Economic Value Added

Year	Return on Invested Capital (%)	Cost of Capital (%)	Economic Value Added ($millions)
1984	17.1	13.6	35
1985	16.2	12.6	40
1986	12.6	10.4	31
1989	2.2	10.8	−491
1990	−5.3	12.0	−1,085
1991	−2.2	12.4	−1,012
1992	−2.9	10.1	−955
1993	0.4	9.1	−622
1994	−2.9	9.4	−926

Note: n.m.f. = not a meaningful figure.

Table 5.4   **Operating Profit as a Percentage of Operating Revenue**

Year	USAir	Industry
1989	0.3	4.4
1990	−7.6	1.1
1991	−2.6	−2.6
1992	−4.9	−3.4
1993	−1.1	−1.3
1994	−7.0	0.1
1995	4.3	2.5
1989–95	−2.6	0.0

Panel C of table 5.3 presents measures of USAir's economic profits, including Stern Stewart's estimates of USAir's return on invested capital, cost of capital, and "economic value added" (EVA).[28] It shows that USAir (i.e., not USAir* since the database did not include data for Piedmont and PSA) generated returns in excess of its cost of capital in each year from 1984 to 1986. However, during the years 1989 to 1994, USAir's annual economic returns range from −5.3 percent to 2.2 percent, and in each year USAir fell short of earning its cost of capital.

By every measure, USAir's performance plummeted after the merger. Part of this decline is related to generally poor industry conditions in 1990–92. Iraq's invasion of Kuwait in August 1989 and the subsequent war in the Persian Gulf increased oil prices, and concurrently, fears of terrorism dampened passenger demand. In addition, a recession (1991–92) and a new wave of low-cost entrants eroded the profitability of airlines generally during this period. To adjust for this, we compute operating profits as a percentage of revenues for a portfolio of established airlines that survived as public companies during the entire period from 1989 to 1995.[29] This value-weighted profit measure for the industry versus USAir is shown in table 5.4. In contrast to the premerger period, when Piedmont and USAir had profit rates that were 6–7 percentage points higher than the industry average, USAir's profit rate was 2.6 percentage points less than the industry average over the postmerger period.

5.4.2 Cost Changes

A principal reason for USAir's sharp decline in performance after the merger is a large increase in its costs. Table 5.5 shows that from 1984 to 1986 USAir*'s cost per ASM ranged from 8.8 to 9.1 cents then jumped to 10.5 cents following implementation of the merger and increased

28. *The Stern Stewart Performance 1000,* Stern Stewart Management Services, New York, 1995. EVA is a registered trademark of Stern Stewart.
29. The portfolio includes Alaska, American, Delta, Southwest, and United.

Table 5.5   Cost Data for Simulated Merged Company Consisting of USAir, Piedmont, and PSA (USAir*), 1984–86, and USAir, 1989–95

Year	Cost per ASM (in cents)	Operating Expenses (in $billions)	Costs Expressed as a Percentage of Operating Revenues				
			Personnel	Fuel	Travel Agency	Rentals and Landing Fees	Maintenance
1984	9.1	3.1	33	19	6	4	4
1985	9.0	3.6	32	18	7	5	4
1986	8.8	4.1	33	13	7	7	5
1989	10.5	6.2	36	12	7	10	6
1990	10.8	7.1	40	15	8	10	6
1991	10.8	6.7	39	12	8	11	6
1992	10.8	7.0	39	11	9	14	6
1993	11.0	7.2	40	10	8	13	5
1994	11.0	7.5	41	10	8	14	6
1995	11.4	7.2	39	8	8	11	5

Table 5.6   **Personnel Cost Data for Simulated Merged Company Consisting of USAir, Piedmont, and PSA (USAir*), and USAir, 1989–95**

Year	Actual Personnel Costs (in $billions)	Simulated Personnel Costs (in $billions)	Difference (in $millions)	Present Value of Difference (in $millions)
1989	2.277	2.045	232	192
1990	2.617	2.145	472	354
1991	2.521	2.130	390	267
1992	2.624	2.187	437	271
1993	2.841	2.317	524	296
1994	2.890	2.289	601	309
1995	2.887	2.445	442	206

monotonically thereafter.[30] Among the components of costs, labor costs increased substantially after the merger. In addition to mandating some more labor-intensive procedures companywide, usually high turnover among employees added to USAir's large training expenses and further reduced labor productivity (Payne 1989). Table 5.5 shows that the ratio of personnel costs to operating revenues increased from 0.33 in 1984–86 for USAir* to 0.39 in 1989–95 for USAir.

The increase in personnel costs has a large effect on the value of USAir. To estimate this effect, we first compute the difference between USAir's actual personnel costs and what personnel costs would have been if US-Air had maintained its premerger ratio of personnel costs to revenues (equal to 0.327). This difference is listed in table 5.6 on an annual basis, along with present value calculations as of 1987 that assume a discount rate of 10 percent (i.e., Stern Stewart estimates USAir's 1986 cost of capital is 10.4 percent). The sum of the present value of the difference in personnel costs over the period 1989–95 is $1.9 billion, representing more than two-thirds of the shareholder value lost after the acquisition.

Table 5.5 reveals that nonlabor costs changed as well after the merger. Fuel costs declined dramatically, reflecting generally lower energy prices during the postmerger period. Maintenance costs increased during the first few years after the merger but thereafter declined to premerger levels. Rentals and landing fees increased substantially from the premerger to postmerger period, presumably reflecting a substitution of aircraft leasing for aircraft ownership. Travel agency commissions increased slightly over the period.

30. Although not a perfect substitute for controls that account for inflation and industry trends, there is other evidence that shows USAir continues to have the highest cost per ASM in the industry. A 1996 Goldman Sachs airline report finds that in 1995 USAir's cost per ASM was 11.48 cents versus an industry average of 9.02 cents. In early 1996, USAir's cost per ASM increased to 13.23 cents versus an industry average of 9.34 cents.

Table 5.7   **Revenue and Revenue Growth Data for Simulated Merged Company Consisting of USAir, Piedmont, and PSA (USAir*), 1984–86, and USAir, 1989–95**

Year	Operating Revenue (in $millions)	Annual Revenue Growth Rate (%)	Value Line Long-run Projected Annual Revenue Growth Rate (%)
1984	3.5	—	10
1985	3.9	14	7
1986	4.5	14	5
1989	6.3	—	13
1990	6.6	5	7
1991	6.5	−1	1
1992	6.7	3	1
1993	7.1	6	3
1994	7.0	−1	−2
1995	7.5	7	−10

5.4.3   Revenue Growth

In addition to incurring substantially higher costs after the merger, USAir revenue growth slowed. As table 5.7 shows, USAir* enjoyed an annual revenue growth rate of about 14 percent in 1984–86, while USAir's revenue growth rate in the postmerger period ranged from only −1 percent to 7 percent. Analysis of the 1989–95 period suggests reversion to the mean: revenue growth for the seven-year period is 19 percent for USAir and 20 percent for the industry as a whole.

In addition to showing USAir's actual revenue growth rate, table 5.7 lists Value Line's projected revenue growth for USAir* in the premerger period and USAir in the postmerger period. It shows a substantial decline in USAir's projected revenue growth, from 13 percent in 1989 to as low as −10 percent by 1995, which is the lowest projected growth rate of any U.S. airline covered by Value Line. As discussed later, possible reasons for the decline in revenue growth are service problems experienced immediately after the merger and some high profile crashes of USAir planes.

5.5   Discussion

5.5.1   Transition from a Regional to a National Airline

USAir's name change from Allegheny in 1979 was intended to signal the transformation of a regional airline into a national carrier with an extensive network of routes across the United States. In the early years of deregulation, USAir fortified its Pittsburgh hub, acquiring commuter airlines in Pennsylvania and expanding cautiously into new markets including Florida and Arizona, though with limited service. A map of

USAir's route structure in its 1985 annual report reveals a mass of short-haul routes in the Northeast and scattered spokes reaching west and south.

A reasonable question to ask is whether the USAir organization was prepared in 1986 to step into the shoes of a national airline. Examination of the successful players in the national market at that time—American, United, Delta—reveals a set of management teams with increasingly large marketing and pricing groups, significant investments in information technology, and deep benches of individuals ready to assume management responsibility.

At USAir, the organizational infrastructure appeared somewhat frail. Closely managed by a small team of individuals with little experience at major airlines, middle and upper-level managers had limited decisionmaking rights. The hierarchical organization that thrived in the early years of deregulation had failed to produce a large pool of management talent. This limited USAir's ability to manage the near tripling of size generated by the PSA and Piedmont acquisitions.

When USAir extended itself to the west with the PSA acquisition and to the south with Piedmont, its information systems were outmoded. On more than one occasion post-1989, the firm's payroll process broke down and secretaries at USAir headquarters were assigned to manually type paychecks.[31] As an indication of how far behind USAir was in the area of information technology, an estimated five hundred man-years of resources were devoted to information technology coordination between 1989 and 1991.[32]

USAir also was late in offering its customers a frequent flier program. At a time when other airlines were exploring alliances with other carriers and travel-related businesses to enrich the attractiveness of their programs, USAir was just introducing a program. Edwin Colodny strongly opposed the development of a frequent flier program, believing that there were better ways of building brand loyalty. "I thought they were one of the worst developments in the industry," Colodny stated, adding that he was "hoping that they would go away."[33] This may help explain USAir's failure to recognize the cost of discarding the valuable Piedmont and PSA brand names.

At the time of the PSA and Piedmont acquisitions, USAir did not have access to a major computer reservations system. USAir's participation in the purchase of the Apollo reservation system gave the airline an 11.3 percent stake in that system but did not alter the fact that USAir's sched-

---

31. Interview with Schofield, see note 1.
32. John Harper, chief financial officer at US Airways, interview by authors, Washington, D.C., 1 April 1996.
33. Edwin Colodny, former chairman and chief executive officer of USAir, telephone conversation with author (Lehn), 17 March 1997.

ules and ticket pricing were presented to travel agents via a shared system. Consequently, USAir relied more heavily on financial incentives for travel agents to generate business than did other airlines.

Finally, the procedures relating to labor management that were ultimately extended to the more than fifty thousand employees of USAir postmerger were designed for a small airline. One example that illustrates the mismatch between the firm's size and its procedures pertains to the replacement requirement. At most airlines, if a flight crew wants to drop a flight from its schedule, the crew (or crew member) must find a substitute. At USAir, management is obligated to locate the replacement. What this means is that scheduling for six thousand pilots on any given day is not finalized until 4:00 P.M. on the day prior to the travel date. While the management at USAir would like to rewrite outgrown policies, such as the replacement requirement, they can only alter such practices with the agreement of labor.

From the history of the Piedmont merger presented in subsection 5.2.3, it is clear that this defensive acquisition was hastily arranged. If, as was stated in 1979, USAir intended to expand into a nationwide carrier, they neglected to develop the firm's organizational infrastructure to support such growth.

5.5.2   USAir's Postmerger Labor Policy

Prior to industry deregulation, labor protective provisions or LLPs (financial accommodations extended to the employees of an acquired carrier) were invoked in all airline mergers. For example, employees who remain employed but are "placed in a worse position with respect to compensation" were entitled to monthly differential payments for four years. Acquiring airlines were required to pay dismissed workers an allowance equal to 60 percent of average monthly compensation in the employee's last year of employment for between six and sixty months depending on the employee's tenure. Provisions also required generous relocation packages for transplanted workers. To satisfy the requirement of "fair and equitable" integrating of seniority lists, management typically turned this process over to representatives of the Air Line Pilots Association (ALPA), the International Association of Machinists and Aerospace Workers, and the Association of Flight Attendants (Green 1986).

Although the requirement that airlines offer financial protection to workers in a merger was relaxed with deregulation, these costly provisions did not disappear. The DOT's stated position was that such issues were best left to the collective bargaining process.[34] However, DOT's "concern

---

34. In a 1987 internal memorandum to the Department of Transportation's secretary and deputy secretary entitled "Recent Airline Acquisitions: A Preliminary Analysis," Michael V. Scocozza, assistant secretary for policy and international affairs, cited the NWA-Republic acquisition case (Order 86–7–81) stating the agency would impose LPPs only if "necessary

that a merger or acquisition not lead to unnecessary service problems" left open the possibility that the DOT would oppose a combination "if the merging parties did not reach some accommodation with organized labor."[35] At the same time, support for LPPs was growing on Capitol Hill: a measure requiring their imposition was approved by the House of Representatives in the fall of 1986, only to lose by a one-vote margin in the Senate. In practice, some acquiring airlines voluntarily offered LPPs (e.g., Pan Am's acquisition of National, Delta's merger with Western) and many others negotiated LPPs in their union contracts (e.g., United's acquisition of Pan Am's Pacific Division).

The costs of these protections are large. In addition to direct outlays for "displacement" allowances and pay differentials, the process of integrating seniority lists could impose substantial time costs on airlines. Seniority lists are an essential input in assigning crews to aircraft via bidding for work schedules. In the case of USAir, the five-month delay of the integration process forced the acquiring carrier to maintain separate work crews and priority systems for matching aircraft with crews and forestalled the efficient utilization of an expanded route structure and fleet.

Throughout its history, USAir maintained labor peace. Recognizing the hold-up potential of each union, management actively sought to avoid strikes. Cost minimization was not a priority during regulation and US-Air's dominance in northeastern short-haul markets during the early years of deregulation perpetuated management's conciliatory stance at the bargaining table. Management believed that despite its high cost, a cooperative labor-management relationship was a key rather than an impediment to profitability.

Talks with PSA's unions began prior to the merger agreement. USAir came to the bargaining table in a position of strength. In 1985, PSA employees agreed to accept some compensation in the form of equity rather than cash and USAir's offer to reinstate certain wages dominated the existing pay scheme. In uncharacteristic fashion, USAir sought and obtained an agreement to gradually raise the wages of PSA workers to USAir's more generous levels.

The Piedmont acquisition unfolded much more rapidly than did the purchase of PSA, leaving little time for preliminary discussions with labor. In fact, it is unclear what estimates of labor expense USAir used in its valuation of Piedmont.[36] Once the deal was struck, the unions balked at

---

to prevent labor strife that would disrupt the national air transportation system or unless special circumstances of an acquisition show that LPPs are necessary to encourage fair wages and equitable working conditions."

35. Larry Phillips, economist at the DOT, email correspondence with author (Kole), 20 March 1997.

36. Regrettably, we have been unable to obtain the analysis of the merger conducted by Lehman Brothers for USAir.

USAir's plan to run Piedmont as a subsidiary with separate labor contracts. This arrangement would have allowed USAir to preserve Piedmont (and PSA's) lower labor cost as well as provide a valuable option to leverage the separate unions off one another (e.g., Piedmont's ALPA and USAir's ALPA). While such an arrangement would have been unpopular with labor, and probably would have ended up in litigation, the potential cost savings of the separate subsidiary plan was large.

In the end, USAir agreed to an immediate step-up in wage and work rules to bring Piedmont workers into the organization as equals with USAir employees. Demanding equal treatment, USAir surrendered the phase-in arrangement struck with former PSA employees. Given the existence of multiyear union contracts, the decision to standardize pay and the concurrent decision to homogenize operating procedures institutionalized higher costs at the acquired units.[37] Whereas USAir may have intended to identify and implement the most efficient methods of production from among PSA, Piedmont, and USAir practices after satisfying FAA competency requirements, the codification of higher pay and more generous work rules in collective bargaining agreements created entitlements that still plague USAir's cost structure. We conclude that the cost of preserving internal equity at USAir was huge.

5.5.3   Was the Increase in Labor Costs a Surprise?

The stock price evidence discussed in section 5.3 suggests that at the time of the merger the market did not anticipate the USAir's labor costs would increase by as much as they did. The data suggest that the market's approval of the merger was predicated on maintaining Piedmont's labor costs at roughly their premerger level. To examine this, we contrast USAir's actual postmerger financial data with projections made by Goldman Sachs in July 1988, more than one year before the integration of Piedmont into USAir. The actual and predicted data for 1989 are shown in table 5.8.

The data show that USAir's operating income in 1989 fell short of Goldman Sachs' estimate by $448 million. The reason for the difference is that USAir's actual operating expenses exceeded Goldman Sachs' expectations by $590 million. Goldman had projected labor costs of $2.07 billion in 1989, representing 32 percent of projected revenues. This estimate is almost identical to the simulated personnel costs discussed in section 5.4, which assumed that the relation between Piedmont's (and PSA's) revenues

---

37. The standardization of departure procedures, as an example, led to the hiring of an estimated one thousand additional mechanics (at $18 per hour plus benefits) to "push back" aircraft on the tarmac at Piedmont gates, a job that had been performed by part-time gate crews (college kids earning $6.75 an hour without benefits). In-flight staffing also increased at Piedmont as a result of mirroring USAir's teams of four flight attendants; for comparable aircraft, Piedmont flight attendants had worked in teams of three.

Table 5.8   Comparison of USAir's Actual and Projected Results for 1989

	Actual 1989 Results	Projected 1989 Results[a]
Revenue ($millions)	6,252	6,110
Operating expense ($millions)	6,230	5,640
Operating income ($millions)	22	470
Interest expense ($millions)	104	145
Net income ($millions)	−63	206
Available seat miles	55,609	54,000
RPM	33,697	31,525
Load factor (%)	60.5	58.4
Cost per seat mile (cents)	10.47	9.95
Break even load factor (%)	60.4	53.6
Labor expense ($millions)	2,277	2,070
Compensation per employee ($)	n.a.	46,206
Fuel expense ($millions)	776	685
Rentals and landing fees ($millions)	605	550
Agents' commissions ($)	434	410

Note: n.a. = not available.
[a]Goldman Sachs projection, 28 July 1988.

and labor costs would be maintained under USAir ownership. In reality, USAir's actual labor expense turned out to be $2.3 billion or 36 percent of operating revenue in 1989, and it increased to 40 percent of revenue thereafter. If the Goldman Sachs estimate is representative of market sentiment at the time, the data suggest that the labor policies adopted by USAir in 1988–89 were largely unanticipated by the market. The Goldman Sachs estimates also reveal that USAir's cost per ASM and its nonlabor costs exceeded expectations. USAir's revenue and load factor actually exceeded Goldman's projections, further suggesting that the major source of USAir's postmerger problems were related to unexpectedly high costs.

5.5.4   Corporate Culture and the Mirror Image Strategy

Although economists typically sidestep the issue of corporate culture (a notable exception is Kreps 1990), in every interview, whether with union leaders or management, we were implored to take this notion seriously. The "stuff you can't see on paper, the attitudes that are hard to measure," Colodny told us, "can have an amazing impact."[38]

The acquisition and integration of PSA's workforce challenged USAir's more conservative management. Known for its playful manner, even customer safety briefings were tongue-in-cheek at PSA: "For those of you who have not been in an automobile since 1962, this is a seat belt. . . ." To a carrier noted for its smiling nose cones and in-cabin games, assimilation into USAir's stricter procedures and rules meant the loss of a style of

38. Interview with Colodny, see note 6.

customer service that PSA viewed as a strength. However, for the struggling carrier whose employees held a 15 percent equity stake, USAir's acquisition was a windfall and an opportunity to earn increased wages. This undoubtedly lessened the sting of losing PSA's identity.

In the case of the Piedmont acquisition, both Piedmont and USAir successfully survived the early years of deregulation. However, Piedmont's rate of postderegulation expansion in number of employees, operating revenue, and ASMs during this period far outpaced USAir's growth. In 1985, Piedmont was honored as the Airline of the Year by Air Transport World magazine, an award usually bestowed upon larger airlines. Piedmont was touted as having the most sophisticated pricing staff among the regionals, a flexible workforce loyal to Piedmont's founder and still active board member, Thomas Davis, and a valuable brand name in the South that was synonymous with quality service. Positioned for continued expansion, the USAir acquisition was resented by many Piedmont employees who viewed theirs as the superior airline.

USAir's "mirror image" whitewash of PSA and Piedmont practices required the employees of the acquired units to relearn their jobs the USAir way. While this certainly imposed personal costs on workers, it is difficult to assess how great these costs were and how they were manifested. Customer satisfaction provides some clue to the extent of the problem. If a culture clash did exist, one likely manifestation is lower quality of operations: increased absenteeism would create scheduling problems, more lost baggage, and less satisfied customers.

USAir had "one of the worst records in the industry (for on-time performance and baggage service) most of 1989 and part of 1990" (Nomani and Valente 1990). Data on consumer complaints filed with the CAB and its predecessor agency echo these problems. Complaints rose from 1.4 complaints per 100,000 travelers in 1986 to 3.6 in 1987 and remained above premerger levels until 1990.[39]

Another, extremely crude, measure of quality of operations in the airline industry is the frequency of accidents. Postmerger, USAir experienced a number of incidences, the most serious of which involved flight 5050 which crashed into Flushing Bay soon after taking off from New York's LaGuardia Airport on 20 September 1989, killing two passengers. A lengthy FAA investigation pointed to a minimally trained crew and raised concerns about crew pairings and the preparation of pilots following the Piedmont merger.

Rather than list the numerous testimonials rich in Civil War analogies and regional stereotypes, we have attempted to demonstrate the impact of

---

39. In and of itself, this consumer complaint data is not strong evidence of a culture clash at USAir. Customer satisfaction deteriorates industrywide at this time suggesting either the existence of merger-related problems throughout the industry following a wave of mergers or a crankier traveling public.

a clash of cultures at the integrated USAir. While not definitive, they are suggestive of real integration problems that adversely effected USAir's performance postmerger.

5.5.5 Reversability of Mergers

USAir's acquisition of Piedmont raises an issue that, to our knowledge, is largely unexplored in the economics and finance literature: What determines the ease with which acquirers can reverse "bad" acquisitions? Research has found that the probability of divesting acquired firms or assets is inversely related to the effect of the acquisition on the acquiring firm's stock price (Kaplan and Weisbach 1992; Mitchell and Lehn 1990). Notwithstanding the central tendency, however, some value-reducing acquisitions, such as USAir's acquisition of Piedmont, do not result in subsequent divestitures. This raises a natural question: Why not?

Despite a general recognition that USAir's acquisition of Piedmont has had a large negative effect on USAir's value, to our knowledge investors have not placed pressure on USAir management to reverse the acquisition through a divestiture of the Piedmont assets. We asked analysts and USAir officials about the feasibility of a divestiture; the uniform response was that it was infeasible, since the Piedmont and USAir assets are now so integrated that it would be impractical to undo the merger. Michael Armellino, managing director and former airline analyst at Goldman Sachs, states that you can't "unscramble this egg."[40] This suggests an inverse relation between the probability that a bidder divests itself of an unsuccessful acquisition and the degree to which it has integrated the acquired firm into its own operations.[41]

5.5.6 Generalization to Other Airline Mergers

The evidence presented in this paper shows that USAir dissipated huge amounts of value after its acquisitions of Piedmont and PSA, largely because it was unable to maintain labor costs at their premerger levels. While the problems encountered by USAir are more dramatic than most, industry experts have commented on the general difficulty of integrating workforces in airline mergers. For reasons discussed above, we conjecture that the integration of labor is more problematic in airline mergers than it is in less heavily unionized, less regulated mergers. This leads us to the following question: Is postmerger performance different for acquiring airlines than it is for acquiring firms in other industries?

Anecdotally, much has been written about problems encountered by large acquirers in the airline industry, including Pan Am, TWA, and Texas,

---

40. Michael Armellino, managing partner and former director of research, Goldman Sachs, interview by authors, New York, N.Y., 16 July 1996.

41. This discussion also suggests that the option to reverse an acquisition should be considered in the valuation of takeover targets.

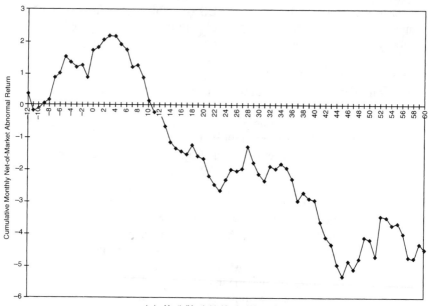

Index Month (Month 0 is Month of Merger Announcement)

Fig. 5.7   Cumulative monthly net-of-market returns for acquirers in eighteen airline mergers, 1979–91, from twelve months before the acquisition announcement

each of which filed for bankruptcy. It is worth noting that there has been little merger activity in the airline industry since the mid-1980s. To our knowledge, the only merger involving an established airline during this decade is United's acquisition of West Air Holdings' Air Wisconsin in 1991. The paucity of recent merger activity is consistent with learning—after the acquisitions of the mid-1980s, managers of airlines are opting to buy routes, gates, and slots rather than suffer the integration of two work-forces.[42]

Much of the existing work on airline mergers focuses on the impact of mergers on airfares (Borenstein 1990; Slovin, Suskha, and Hudson 1991; Kim and Singal 1993; Singal 1996). We are unaware of any systematic evidence on the relation between mergers and long-run performance in the airline industry. Preliminary results on long-term stock returns for acquiring airlines appear in figure 5.7.[43] The figure plots cumulative monthly net-of-market returns for a portfolio of eighteen acquirers of airlines during 1978–91 from twelve months prior to the acquisition announcements

42. The decline in merger activity in the airline industry also is consistent with the argument that antitrust policy became more stringent during the Bush and Clinton administrations than it was during the Reagan years. We thank Severin Borenstein for pointing this out.

43. Two recent papers discuss estimation problems associated with the measurement of long-run stock returns. See Kothari and Warner (1997) and Barber and Lyon (1997).

through sixty months after the announcements.[44] It shows highly negative returns several years beyond the acquisition. Cumulative returns are negative three years after the acquisition for eleven of the fifteen surviving acquirers (three did not survive three years postmerger) and twelve of fourteen acquirers had negative cumulative returns five years after the acquisition (four acquirers failed within five years of the acquisition).

To control for size and industry effects, we estimate the long-run abnormal return for each acquiring airline in the following way. For each acquiring airline, we identify the airline that had the closest market value of equity at the end of the calendar year immediately preceding the year of the acquisition. We then check to make sure that the matched airline did not make an acquisition itself during the five years before through five years after the acquiring airline's acquisition announcement; if it did, we exclude it, and go to the next airline that is closest in size to the acquiring airline. We continue this process until we identify a size-matched airline for each acquiring airline. We then compute the abnormal return for each acquiring airline as the difference between its buy-and-hold return and the corresponding return for the matched airline.

Table 5.9 lists the results on long-run buy-and-hold abnormal returns for acquiring airlines over periods of one, two, three, four, and five years after the acquisition announcements. Panel A, which reports the results for the entire sample, shows an average buy-and-hold abnormal return of −14.76 percent during the first year following the acquisition announcement and −47.16 percent during the first five years after the announcement. The average returns for two, three, and four years after the announcement lie somewhere between the two numbers. The only return that differs significantly from zero is the five-year return.

Panel B replicates panel A for the twelve acquiring airlines that were not themselves acquired after they made their acquisitions. The inclusion of the six acquirers who subsequently became targets themselves is likely to bias against finding negative long-run returns, since acquisitions are associated with significant positive returns for target firms. The results in panel B demonstrate the effect of the bias—the buy-and-hold abnormal returns become substantially more negative and significant. The average return is −23.25 percent, −30.26 percent, −49.7 percent, −44.13 percent, and −40.32 percent, during the one, two, three, four, and five years, respectively, after the acquisition announcement. With the exception of the

---

44. The eighteen mergers include the following (the acquiring airline is listed first): North Central–Southern (1979), Pan Am–National (1979), Republic-Hughes (1980), Texas-Continental (1981), Southwest-Muse (1985), People Express–Frontier (1985), Piedmont-Empire (1985), Texas–People Express (1986), Texas-Eastern (1986), Northwest-Republic (1986), TWA-Ozark (1986), Alaska–Jet America (1986), Delta-Western (1986), American-AirCal (1986), Alaska-Horizon (1986), USAir-PSA (1986), USAir-Piedmont (1987), and United–Air Wisconsin (1991).

Table 5.9   Buy-and-Hold Stock Returns for Eighteen Acquiring Airlines versus a Control Sample of Other Airlines with Equity Values Closest to the Acquiring Airline at the End of the Calendar Year Immediately Preceding the Acquisition

Number of Months after Acquisition	Average Buy-and-Hold Return (%) (t-statistic)	Number of Observations (number negative)
A. Buy-and-Hold Returns for All Eighteen Airlines		
12	−14.76	18
	(−0.77)	(10)
24	−12.40	17
	(−0.74)	(8)
36	−27.70	16
	(−1.14)	(9)
48	−30.47	15
	(−1.29)	(10)
60	−47.16	14
	(−2.21)	(9)
B. Buy-and-Hold Returns for Twelve Airlines That Are Not Themselves Subsequently Acquired		
12	−23.25	12
	(−1.04)	(9)
24	−30.26	12
	(−1.62)	(7)
36	−49.70	12
	(−1.82)	(8)
48	−44.13	12
	(−2.53)	(9)
60	−40.32	12
	(−2.01)	(8)

one-year return, all are significant at the 10 percent level. In addition, at least eight of the twelve airlines experienced negative returns in four of the five post-announcement intervals.

The evidence on long-run returns is consistent with the argument that airline mergers are especially hard to manage relative to other mergers. Agrawal, Jaffe, and Mandelker (1992) document long-run returns of about −10 percent for a large sample of acquiring firms over a five-year post-merger period, which is substantially less negative than the returns we find for acquiring airlines. We conjecture that the postmerger problems experienced by acquiring airlines may account for the large reduction in airline merger activity since the mid-1980s. An alternative explanation for the reduction in airline activity is that antitrust policy has become more binding, given changes in antitrust policy. Also, because of the existence of estimation errors associated with measurement of long-run stock returns, additional analysis comparing postmerger accounting profits, economic profits, and labor costs for acquiring and nonacquiring airlines would be informative.

One other piece of evidence consistent with the conjecture that the integration of workforces discourages airline mergers can be seen in data on the frequency of asset sales in the airline industry over time. Asset sales usually involve the sale of routes or planes, with no accompanying employees. If the integration of workforces is an impediment to mergers, one might expect to find a substitution of asset sales for mergers over time.

To examine this, we collected data on asset sales in the airline industry for each year during 1980–94 from Securities Data Company's Financial Database System. The data indicate that asset sales were infrequent during the period of high merger activity in the airline industry. During the eight-year period from 1980 to 1987, thirteen asset sales occurred, or roughly 1.5 per year. Since 1987, there has been little airline merger activity but a large increase in asset sales. During the seven-year period from 1988 to 1994, forty-three asset sales (twenty-eight of the asset sales occurred in 1990 and 1991) occurred, or roughly six per year. While there may be other explanations for the increase in asset sales, the evidence is consistent with the argument that it is easier for airlines to integrate routes and aircraft than it is to integrate workforces.

5.6 Conclusion

In 1987, USAir's acquisition of Piedmont Aviation was praised as a perfect match. The combination of two strong airlines with contiguous route structures would improve the utilization of aircraft, maintenance facilities, and crews. The more extensive route structure would appeal to Piedmont and USAir frequent travelers. Indeed, USAir's rationale for the merger—that the sum is more valuable than the parts—rang true at the time. However, as General Robert Oaks, executive vice president of operations at USAir, aptly states, "[I]t's easier to get accountants to integrate balance sheets than it is to combine people who must work together."[45] USAir stumbled in the implementation process and its present cost structure bears the legacy of those missteps.

References

Agins, Teri, and Laurie Cohen. 1987. TWA proposes to buy USAir for $51 a share. *Wall Street Journal,* 2 March, p. 57.

Agins, Teri, and Betsey Morris. 1987. USAir intensifies war for Piedmont by its raising bid. *Wall Street Journal,* 19 February.

Agrawal, Anup, Jeffrey F. Jaffe, and Gershon N. Mandelker. 1992. The post-merger performance of acquiring firms: A re-examination of an anomaly. *Journal of Finance* 47:1605–21.

Bailey, Elizabeth E., David R. Graham, and Daniel P. Kaplan. 1985. *Deregulating the airlines.* Cambridge, Mass.: MIT Press.

Barber, Brad M., and John D. Lyon. 1997. Detecting long-run abnormal stock returns: The empirical power and specification of test-statistics. *Journal of Financial Economics* 43, no. 3 (March): 341–72.

Borenstein, Severin. 1990. Airline mergers, airport dominance, and market power. *American Economic Review* 80:400–404.

Byrne, Harlan S. 1983. Airline industry faces another bid loss but some carriers weather the storm. *Wall Street Journal,* 25 January, p. 56.

Comment, Robert, and G. William Schwert. 1995. Poison or placebo? Evidence on the deterrence and wealth effects of modern antitakeover measures. *Journal of Financial Economics* 39:3–43.

Green, Gary. 1986. Labor protective provisions in the airline industry 1950–1985. Unpublished manuscript provided by D. Andrews, USAir.

Harris, Roy J., Jr. 1986. Western takeover rumors may portend move of carrier consolidation toward Pacific. *Wall Street Journal,* 10 March.

Jensen, Michael C. 1986. Agency costs of free cash flow, corporate finance and takeovers. *American Economic Review* 76:323–29.

Kaplan, Steven N., and Michael S. Weisbach. 1992. The success of acquisitions: Evidence from divestitures. *Journal of Finance* 47:107–38.

Kim, E. Han, and Vijay Singal. 1993. Mergers and market power: Evidence from the airline industry. *American Economic Review* 83:549–69.

Kothari, S. P., and Jerold B. Warner. 1997. Measuring long-horizon security price performance. *Journal of Financial Economics* 43, no. 3 (March): 301–39.

Kreps, David. 1990. Corporate culture and economic theory. In *Perspectives in positive political economy,* ed. James E. Alt and Kenneth A. Shepsle, 90–143. Cambridge: Cambridge University Press.

McGinley, Laurie, and Judith Valente. 1987. USAir, Piedmont shouldn't merge, agency judge says. *Wall Street Journal,* 22 September.

---

45. Robert Oaks, executive vice president of operations, USAir, interview by authors, Washington, D.C., 7 October 1997.

Mitchell, Mark, and Kenneth Lehn. 1990. Do bad bidders become good targets? *Journal of Political Economy* 98:372–98.

Nomani, Asra Q., and Judith Valente. 1990. Delayed takeoff: Strong as a loner, USAir loses its magic after two acquisitions. *Wall Street Journal,* 28 August, p. 1.

Ott-Washington, James. 1989. USAir prepares to complete acquisition of Piedmont. *Aviation Week & Space Technology,* 17 July, p. 94.

Payne, Seth. 1989. A promising plan—if no raiders show. *Business Week,* 14 August.

Peterson, Barbara Sturken, and James Glab. 1994. *Rapid descent.* New York: Simon and Schuster.

Ross, Robert, and Laurie McGinley. 1987. USAir merger with Piedmont cleared by U.S. *Wall Street Journal,* 2 November.

Rotbart, Dean. 1984. Regional airlines are suggested as alternatives when big boys get into fare wars downdraft. *Wall Street Journal,* 21 August, p. 53.

Singal, Vijay. 1996. Airline mergers and competition: An integration of stock and product price effects. *Journal of Business* 69:233–68.

Slovin, Myron, Marie Suskha, and Carl Hudson. 1991. Deregulation, contestability, and airline acquisitions. *Journal of Financial Economics* 30:231–51.

Stevens, Charles W. 1984. USAir shaking from its "agony air" past, profits from routes others avoid. *Wall Street Journal,* 28 February.

Williamson, Oliver E. 1985. *The economic institutions of capitalism.* New York: Free Press.

Comment   Severin Borenstein

Kole and Lehn have done an excellent job describing the challenges that an airline faces in integrating workforces as part of a merger. These problems, of course, exist in any merger, but as the authors point out, there are good reasons to think that difficulties are particularly acute in the airline industry. The great hold-up power of pilots' and mechanics' unions along with the service orientation of this industry—in which worker attitude can have a tremendous effect on customer satisfaction—make it likely that workforce integration will be a central challenge of any airline merger.

While the evidence that Kole and Lehn present makes it clear that these labor issues were critical in the disappointing outcome of the USAir–Piedmont–PSA merger, I think that the proportion of the value loss that labor costs explain might be overstated. The authors have attempted to separate the impact of the merger from the many other events that occurred in the industry around that time, which is an extremely difficult task. Three factors in particular make it difficult to parse the causes: (1) a

Severin Borenstein is professor of business at the Haas School of Business of the University of California, Berkeley, director of the University of California Energy Institute, and a research associate of the National Bureau of Economic Research. He was an expert witness for America West Airlines in its opposition to the USAir-Piedmont merger during the U.S. Department of Transportation administrative law hearing in 1987.

crash in the price of oil in early 1986 changed substantially the relative costs of inputs around the time of the merger; (2) with the exception of United, every major airline was involved in a merger between 1985 and 1988, thus making interfirm comparisons difficult to interpret; (3) the recession and Persian Gulf conflict in the early 1990s harmed the entire industry, but each firm in the market was affected differently.

Furthermore, the cost and inefficiencies of integration that the authors document in this case probably overstate the degree of the problem in a typical airline merger. Notwithstanding its profitability in the early 1980s, USAir was not viewed by most in the industry as a well-managed airline, and certainly not as one that was able to control worker compensation. Edwin Colodny, the CEO of USAir, was thought by workers to be one of the nicest and most generous executives in the industry, a reputation dating from before airline deregulation. It is telling that the quotes from analysts in support of the merger (at the end of section 5.3) refer to the merged carrier's power, presence, and marketing clout, not to production synergies, streamlining, or cost efficiency. Thus, the costs that USAir faced in integrating the Piedmont and PSA workforces were probably greater than other management teams are likely to encounter.

The primary approach that Kole and Lehn use to estimate the effect of labor force costs on USAir's postmerger performance is to extrapolate the share of revenue that was attributed to labor costs. They take the deviation from the earlier share after the merger as indicative of the costs due to workforce integration. Yet it is unclear why one would expect this ratio to stay constant, particularly through big swings in demand—the 1990–92 recession—and the costs of other inputs—the oil price crash in 1986 and the upward shock following the August 1990 invasion of Kuwait by Iraq. To illustrate this, one can recalculate the percentages in table 5.5 under the assumption that real fuel prices remained constant at their 1984 level for the following decade and that this change was fully reflected in revenues. The resulting increase in the personnel costs as a share of total revenue would have been substantially smaller than Kole and Lehn find and would explain about 45 percent of the value change following the merger. This is still a substantial share, but it points out that the authors' estimates come with significant margins of error. The decline in the real cost of fuel—which averaged about 20 percent lower during 1989–95 than during 1984–86—also partly explains why all other categories increased as a share of revenues.

A similar argument could be made regarding the 1990–92 recession. As demand slackens, fixed expenses will naturally rise as a share of total revenues. Because of union strength in this industry generally, for all the reasons the authors point out, labor costs are relatively fixed, particularly compared to fuel, airport fees, travel agent commissions, and a number of other expenses that exhibit virtually no stickiness. That, of course, does not explain why the percentage later stayed so high when the economy rebounded, demand increased, and the shadow value of capacity grew once again. Overall, while this approach to measuring the integration costs is sensible, it would be more useful if it could in some way account for the industrywide shocks that occurred during this time. It would be interesting, for instance, to see how the rise in labor cost share of revenue compares to the rest of the industry over the same time.

In general, it would be valuable to compare many of the premerger and postmerger changes with similar measures for other carriers or for the industry as a whole. Even these results, however, would have to be interpreted with caution. Most important is the fact that nearly every major airline experienced a merger between 1985 and 1987.[1]

The scarcity of nonmerging airlines also makes it difficult to compare the performance of merging and nonmerging carriers. In figure 5.7, Kole and Lehn demonstrate that mergers tend to be followed by negative abnormal returns. While provocative, the result may also be attributed to the fact that airline mergers seem to be leading indicators of recessions.[2] Nearly all mergers in the sample occur just prior to the 1981–82 recession or a few years prior to the 1990–92 recession. Recognizing this, the authors attempt to do a matched-pair analysis, but given the (reasonable) criteria they use for choosing matches, the only available airlines for comparing the 1985–87 mergers are United, and possibly Midway and Pan Am. Thus, the results of this comparison could be quite idiosyncratic.

Nonetheless, while Kole and Lehn's analysis of the adverse effects of airline mergers probably should not be taken as precise estimates, they convincingly show that the USAir–Piedmont–PSA merger was not a success, that labor costs were a significant part of the reason, and that the stock market was surprised by this failure. This latter insight is particularly surprising given USAir's reputation for poor management. Furthermore, while one can quibble with the analysis of overall returns to mergers in this industry, it is fairly clear that mergers have not had the beneficial impact that was suggested by managers and analysts at the time.

The authors' treatment of conflicts of corporate culture is also a refreshing addition to the economic study of mergers. They do not quantify these effects—it is not clear how one could—but they do recognize that such conflicts play a serious role. In light of the fact that every merger faces these issues, and that corporations spend significant sums studying how to overcome them, integrating issues of culture conflict into the analysis of mergers may very well yield new insights.

1. See authors' note 44. Only United resisted the urge to merge, but only so far as other airlines were concerned. It was during this period that United diversified into a number of other travel-related industries, including hotels.

2. Put differently, airline mergers appear to take place when firms possess substantial free cash flow, not when the airlines are weathering macroeconomic downturn.

My own discussions with former Piedmont and USAir employees reinforce Kole and Lehn's conclusions. The manager of pricing and yield management at Piedmont left the company shortly after the merger and before the workforce integration to work for America West. She reported that many others also chose to leave the company rather than work for USAir, which had the reputation of being stodgy and rule-bound and of failing to reward initiative.[3] During the 1987 DOT hearing on the USAir–Piedmont merger, testimony from USAir managers revealed that the carrier's pricing and seat management system lacked many of the capabilities of those used by American, United, and even Piedmont. The fact, that, immediately after it acquired PSA, USAir painted over the famous PSA smiles on their aircraft is consistent with this view of USAir management. It is worth noting that despite the high wages USAir paid and its reputation for very friendly relations with labor, most workers at Piedmont did not support the merger, and cheers were heard among Piedmont workers on 21 September 1987 when Judge Yoder recommended that DOT reject the merger.

The virtual absence of mergers in the 1990s may very well be a result of airlines' coming to recognize the realities that Kole and Lehn present, though antitrust policy probably plays a role as well. Many nonmerger cooperative arrangements between airlines have developed or spread in the decade since the airline merger wave. Though code-sharing existed in the 1980s as a way that jet carriers could exchange passengers with commuter airlines while maintaining a single brand, code-sharing is now also used between jet carriers.[4] Likewise, airlines are collaborating in their loyalty programs. Reno Air, for instance, took over many of American's West Coast routes out of San Jose in 1993. Even before it was purchased by American in November 1998, Reno distributed points on American's frequent flier program and shared codes with American, and the two carriers coordinated the timing of their flights.

It seems quite likely that these are attempts to gain the advantages of coordination and reduction of horizontal rivalry without bearing the costs of workforce integration.[5] With growing evidence of the pitfalls that mergers present, including the studies in this volume, further experimentation with forms of nonmerger coordination seems assured. Studying these mechanisms for nonmerger coordination, and contrasting them with mergers, will be a fruitful area for further research.

3. Personal communication with Marilyn Hoppe, July 1988.

4. Many of these arrangements are between U.S. and foreign airlines that cannot merge because of legal restrictions, but they also now occur between U.S. jet carriers such as Continental and America West.

5. The difficulty of workforce integration was highlighted again in February 1999, when American's pilots staged a sickout to protest the pay (too low) and seniority (too high) that was to be given to Reno's pilots as part of the American purchase of Reno Air.

Comment   Marc Knez

The literature on mergers and acquisitions suffers from an almost complete absence of careful empirical examinations of the organizational factors that influence successful or unsuccessful merger implementation. This paper, along with the other papers in this volume, represents the first significant step in filling this void.

As I see it, there are three principal points of interest in this paper. First, the authors provide powerful evidence that the postmerger losses incurred by USAir were driven in large part by their decision to raise Piedmont wages to the level of USAir's. Second, they provide powerful evidence that the market all but completely ignored this possibility. Finally, the description of the events leading up to USAir's decision to purchase Piedmont suggests that the management of USAir were less concerned about the potential for value creation through the merger than they were about their own survival in a consolidating industry. Each of these points (and others) is of significant interest to those of us attempting to develop a broader understanding of the factors facilitating and inhibiting the success of mergers.

One difficulty is the reconciliation of the first two points taken together. Is it the case that USAir made an "obvious" mistake when it raised Piedmont wages to USAir's levels and the market did not believe they would make such an obvious mistake? Or instead, is it the case that USAir had to raise Piedmont wages and the market simply missed this point? In other words, is this a case about mistakes that get made during merger implementation, or a case about the market's ignorance about merger implementation? Answering this question requires knowing whether USAir had to raise Piedmont wages. The authors provide a rather mixed view on this difficult question. In subsection 5.2.4, which describes the regulatory approval process, we are left with the impression that federal approval of the merger (nearly) required raising Piedmont wages. On the other hand, they conclude that the "decision" to raise wages was a mistake, and that USAir "stumbled" in the implementation process. To reconcile this issue we would need to evaluate the set of alternative actions that USAir could have taken. For example, what were the implications of not raising Piedmont wages; would it have significantly jeopardized regulatory approval? If not, would it have led to a strike? How costly would a strike have been?

If, for the moment, we accept the conclusion that the management of USAir stumbled, there is still the question of why they made such an "obvious" mistake. The scant literature on merger implementation suggests that CEOs tend to be overconfident about their ability to create value in

Marc Knez is associate professor of strategy at the Graduate School of Business of the University of Chicago.

a merger (see, e.g., Haspeslagh and Jemison 1991; Hayward and Hambrick 1997). In this case, USAir management may have been overconfident about the value created through increased market power emanating from the combined route structure, as well as about their ability to reduce costs despite the increase in Piedmont wages.

Beyond the wage issue, the authors also suggest that USAir's "mirror image" strategy of homogenizing operations of the two airlines was a mistake. This is clearly a decision over which they had discretion. They could have kept many of the operational differences in place (at least for an extended period of time). But, again, the authors do not provide any insight on the organizational feasibility or costs of such a decision. To the extent that there are real operating synergies that have the potential for value creation, we can assume that significant coordination across the operations of these formally separate airlines would be necessary. If this is the case, then the cost of inconsistent operating procedures could conceivably be significant. Put differently, it is hard to imagine that it could be efficient for an organization in a single line of business to have disparate operating procedures in different parts of the organization that are engaged in practically identical activities. This is particularly true in an industry where standard operating procedures are so important.

The authors quote a former CEO of USAir who states that the mirror image strategy "turned out to be an irritant to everyone—PSA and Piedmont employees and their customers." Significant organizational change is always a source of irritation for participants, but this does not make it suboptimal, only inevitable. One way to reconcile this issue is to see if there are any other airlines that possess heterogeneous operating procedures to the degree that the authors believe USAir should have implemented.

The two issues I have raised point to the difficulty of this type of research. If the goal is to judge the quality of decisions made during the implementation process, we must judge these decision against alternative choices that could have been made. While it is clearly not possible to turn back the clock, it is important to recognize the trade-offs, and in some cases insights may be gained from the experiences of other firms that have taken an alternative approach. That said, I am sympathetic to the difficulty of capturing all these trade-offs, especially since the authors have already provided a fairly in-depth description of this particular merger.

Finally, the authors state that the USAir case provides support for Williamson's (1985) conjecture that internal equity issues can limit the boundaries of the firm. The idea is that maintaining differences in compensation across separate units will lead to dysfunctional behavior in the lower-paid unit. Hence, whatever benefits arise from the merger of two firms may be offset by such dysfunctional behavior. Given that Williamson's discussion on this issue is a bit imprecise, it may be the case that the USAir case applies. However, I do not believe it should if the Williamson conjecture has any bite.

Researchers and practitioners in human resource management have long recognized that pay equity is a critical element of any compensation system. Workers judge whether they are being paid fairly by comparing their pay to the pay of other workers engaged in a similar or related task, weighted by their level of contribution relative to this same other worker. There are two main sources of distortion here. First, workers may overestimate their level of contribution relative to others. Second, their basis of comparison will not just be similarity of task, but also, simply working for the same organization. The second distortion is most relevant for Williamson's conjecture. It is the mere fact that two workers are in the same organization that leads to comparison where it would not otherwise occur. In other words, there is a psychological difference between the internal and external labor markets. A current notable example of this problem has arisen as commercial banks have entered investment banking. Suddenly, commercial bankers feel compelled to compare their compensation to their "colleagues" in the investment banking unit who receive significantly higher compensation. Hence, to Williamson's point, related diversification leads to internal equity issues that would not otherwise arise.

In the USAir case, workers at Piedmont are going to compare themselves with workers at USAir that are doing nearly identical tasks. What rationale is there for USAir to pay them differently? Moreover, had the merger not occurred, it would have made complete sense for the Piedmont employees to point to USAir's higher wages in future collective bargaining sessions, especially since both airlines had the same unions. To be sure, the disgruntlement created by two workers doing the same tasks but being paid differently influenced USAir's decision to raise Piedmont wages. But this simply reflects disparities in wages between two airlines created in past negotiations with the same union. Now we have a single airline anticipating negotiations with the same union.

References

Haspeslagh, Philipe C., and David B. Jemison. 1991. *Managing acquisitions: Creating value through corporate renewal.* New York: Free Press.

Hayward, Mathew L., and Donald C. Hambrick. 1997. Explaining premiums paid for large acquisitions: Evidence of CEO hubris. *Administrative Science Quarterly* 42:103–27.

Williamson, Oliver E. 1985. *The economic institutions of capitalism.* New York: Free Press.

Paths to Creating Value in
Pharmaceutical Mergers

David J. Ravenscraft and William F. Long

6.1 Introduction

In the 1980s, the pharmaceutical industry underwent a period of tremendous growth and profitability. This growth was reflected in a 959 percent increase in a stock index of pharmaceutical firms from 1980 to 1992. During the same period, the S&P increased by 386 percent. Growth was driven by innovations resulting in part from the adoption of more rational, scientific approaches to drug discovery and by a market structure that allowed annual price increases in the 8 to 12 percent range. However, in

David J. Ravenscraft is the Julian Price Distinguished Professor of Finance at Kenan-Flagler Business School, University of North Carolina, Chapel Hill. William F. Long is president of Business Performance Research Associates, Inc., an applied microeconomics consulting firm in Bethesda, Maryland.

The authors thank the following individuals for sharing their time and knowledge: David Barry, CEO, Triangle Pharmaceuticals (former director of worldwide research and executive director, Burroughs Wellcome plc); Rick Beleson, senior analyst, Capital Research; Paul Brooke, managing director, Morgan Stanley; Cliff Disbrow, senior vice president of technical operations, GlaxoWellcome Inc.; Stuart Essig, managing director, Goldman Sachs; Clint Gartin, managing director, Morgan Stanley; Henry Grabowski, pharmaceutical economist, Duke University; Tom Haber, chief executive, Hadley Investment (former CFO, Glaxo Inc.); Rebecca Henderson, pharmaceutical economist, MIT; Douglas Hurt, CFO, GlaxoWellcome Inc.; Robert Ingram, CEO, GlaxoWellcome Inc.; Greg Ireland, portfolio manager, Capital Research; Suzanne Nora Johnson, partner, Goldman Sachs; Robert Jones, head of strategic planning, GlaxoWellcome plc; Rick Kent, director of worldwide research, GlaxoWellcome plc; George Morrow, group VP commercial operations, GlaxoWellcome Inc.; Mike Overlock, managing director, Goldman Sachs; Bob Postlethwait, president of neuroscience division, Eli Lilly; Michael Pucci, director sales and training, GlaxoWellcome Inc.; Charles Sanders, former CEO, Glaxo Inc.; Phil Tracy, former CEO, Wellcome Inc.; and John Vernon, pharmaceutical economist, Duke University. The authors also received valuable research assistance from Stéphane Chrétien and Carl Ackermann and helpful comments from Rob Gertner and George Baker. The views expressed here are those of the authors and do not necessarily reflect the views of any of the above named individuals.

true Schumpeterian fashion, booms sow the seed of their own destruction (Schumpeter 1950). Enhanced buyer power, increased competition from generic and "me too" drugs, the rise of biotechs as an alternative research approach, increased government pressure, rising research cost, and a rash of major patent expirations dramatically changed the growth and profit outlook of pharmaceutical companies. Beginning in the early 1990s, pharmaceutical firms' stock prices dropped and average price increases nearly vanished.

To maintain profitability, pharmaceutical firms had to negate these new influences by limiting buyer power, improving research and development (R&D) productivity, or cutting costs. Mergers played an important role in helping pharmaceutical firms meet all three of these challenges. Pharmaceutical firms vertically integrated by purchasing pharmacy benefit managers (PBMs) to help counteract the rising buyer power.[1] They sought to improve their pipeline and research capabilities through the acquisition of biotech firms. However, the most dramatic approach—and the focus of this paper—involved growing through large horizontal acquisitions.

The pharmaceutical industry, therefore, provides a rich and active market for studying how recent mergers create value. Over the last decade, more than $250 billion of assets were acquired in over four hundred deals involving a pharmaceutical or biotech firm. In terms of value, over half of these deals occurred during the years 1994 to 1996 (fig. 6.1). These mergers dramatically increased firm size. The value of the transactions was over $1 billion in approximately fifty pharmaceutical mergers and these deals account for roughly 70 percent of the merger value. Most of the very largest deals involved the combination of two large pharmaceutical firms. Ten of the top fifteen pharmaceutical deals are horizontal. (Three of the remaining five are vertical acquisitions and two are diversifying.) The announcement of the top sixty-five drug acquisitions created $18.8 billion of value for the combined bidder and target. However, if we look at only the horizontal deals, those deals alone created even more value—$19.5 billion.

The largest of these pharmaceutical deals, Glaxo's 1995 hostile acquisition of Burroughs Wellcome, illustrates these trends, challenges, and value

---

1. There were two main motivations for purchasing PBMs. First, pharmaceutical firms thought that owning a PBM could help ensure that their products were on the formulary list—a list of drugs that determined if insurance companies, HMOs, and hospitals would reimburse the patient for the drug. Where comparable drugs existed, PBMs were using formularies to gain price concessions from drug companies. In particular, Medco demonstrated to the drug companies that it had the power to move market share. There is some evidence that Merck's acquisition of Medco did increase the number of Merck drugs on Medco's formulary list and increased Merck's market share. After the third PBM merger, the Federal Trade Commission (FTC) imposed constraints on the three PBM purchasers—Merck, SmithKline Beecham, and Eli Lilly—that limited this ability to influence PBM formulary decisions. The second motivation was to acquire the vast information that PBMs collected on pharmaceutical usage and the skills in analyzing these data.

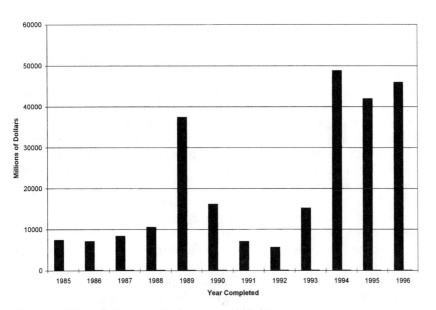

Fig. 6.1   Value of pharmaceutical mergers, 1985–96
Source: Security Data Corporation.

creation. Glaxo's sales increased from £618 million to £5,656 million between 1980 and 1994. This growth was led by the best selling prescription drug in history, Zantac (a peptic ulcer treatment that was launched in 1981). For much of this period, Zantac accounted for over 40 percent of Glaxo's sales. Wellcome's sales increased from £1,005 million to £2,662 million between 1986 (the first full year of public reporting) and 1994. Its leading product, Zovirax (a treatment for genital herpes and shingles first sold in 1982) also accounted for over 40 percent of Wellcome's sales and was the fourth best-selling drug in the industry for much of the 1990s. The U.S. patents on these two products expired in 1997. Thus, Glaxo and Wellcome faced the challenges of a changing industry environment and the decline of their major sources of growth. By combining two firms with similar problems, GlaxoWellcome created over $2 billion in stock market value upon the announcement of the merger.

How did GlaxoWellcome and other large horizontal pharmaceutical mergers create value? For research-intensive, global pharmaceutical firms the complete answer is complex. These acquisitions create value by reducing cost and enhancing revenue. Cost savings stem from economies of scale or scope, reduction of excess capacity, and elimination of inefficiencies. Revenue enhancement results from expanded global reach, broader product lines, expanded application of current and future technology, and sharing skill, information, and best practices. These mergers are also driven by the firms' desire to use a consistent flow of internal funding for

R&D in an industry where the discrete nature of blockbuster drugs makes many cash flow profiles volatile.

Because of the recent nature of these mergers, the cost savings are much more apparent at this time. Fortunately, these cost savings appear to be substantial. Despite these savings, creative approaches have been needed to keep bidders' shareholders from losing on the deal. Part of the problem is that the savings can be offset by the postintegration cost. For example, Glaxo estimates that it will cost $1.8 billion to cover the expenses of achieving the merger cost savings. This does not include the tremendous temporary disruption and loss of momentum from trying to combine two large organizations. Given that Glaxo paid a 40 percent premium (or $3.8 billion) for Wellcome, GlaxoWellcome must create $5.6 billion in 1995 discounted dollars plus the nonaccounting postmerger integration cost to earn a return for Glaxo shareholders.

In section 6.2 of this paper, we show the changes in the pharmaceutical industry and how they create incentives for mergers. Next, in section 6.3 we present evidence that value is created in pharmaceutical mergers, that targets and some bidders were underperforming the market before the merger, and that cost-cutting in large horizontal deals plays a critical role in value creation. In section 6.4, we demonstrate how an active market for corporate control in pharmaceuticals arose and the impact that corporate governance structure had on this market and the ability of bidders to capture value for their shareholders. Section 6.5 begins the focus on Glaxo-Wellcome with a brief history of the firms and a description of the events leading to the merger. Using GlaxoWellcome, we illustrate how and why horizontal mergers cut costs, the potential revenue gains from the merger, and the postmerger integration problems that must be overcome to capture this value. Section 6.6 discusses how these insights contribute to the academic debate surrounding mergers and pharmaceutical economics.

The paper's findings are based in part on extensive interviews with investment bankers, industry experts, and present and former pharmaceutical company executives. We interviewed five senior investment bankers responsible for pharmaceutical deals—Paul Brooke and Clinton Gartin of Morgan Stanley, and Stuart Essig, Suzanne Nora Johnson, and Michael Overlock of Goldman Sachs. We talked with five industry experts including two research analysts or portfolio managers—Rick Beleson and Greg Ireland of Capital Research—and three pharmaceutical economists—Henry Grabowski and John Vernon of Duke University and Rebecca Henderson of MIT. To gain the perspective of executives that left the firm after the merger, we interviewed two former Wellcome senior managers—David Barry, worldwide R&D director, and Phil Tracy, CEO Wellcome Inc.—and two former Glaxo senior managers—Tom Haber, CFO, and Charles Sanders, CEO Glaxo Inc. We spoke with one senior pharmaceutical executive outside of GlaxoWellcome, Bob Postlethwait, president of neuroscience division, Eli Lilly. Finally, we interviewed seven current executives of GlaxoWellcome, covering finance, research, commercial, sales, operations, and strategy. The executives of the U.S. operations were Cliff Disbrow, senior vice president for technical operations; Douglas Hurt, CFO; Robert Ingram, CEO; George Morrow, group vice president for commercial operations; and Michael Pucci, director of sales and training. The worldwide operations executives included Robert Jones, director of strategic planning, and Rick Kent, director of worldwide research. All of these executives continued to play an important role in the combined organization often in even more senior positions in the worldwide organization. Where possible, we attempted to verify consensus views with data supplied by the interviewees and archival data on industry characteristics, merger and acquisitions information, and stock market evidence.

6.2 The Changing Pharmaceutical Industry

The pharmaceutical industry displays several key characteristics that are critical to understanding its challenges. It is a highly risky business with long-term payoffs and lumpy outputs. On average, it takes fourteen to fifteen years to go from discovery of a drug to Federal Drug Administration (FDA) approval. The odds of a compound making it through this process are around 1 in 10,000, while the cost of getting it through is around $200 million. To cover this cost and risk, the drug companies depend on a few blockbuster drugs. Even for a large firm, it is not uncommon for one drug to account for almost half of its revenue. The result is often a very lumpy cash flow profile. Yet, the firms depend on internal funding of R&D because of well-known problems of asymmetric information (Myers and Majluf 1984) and moral hazard (Leland and Pyle 1977).[2]

Despite these challenges, pharmaceutical firms earned consistently high accounting profits and growth rates throughout the 1970s and 1980s. An important contributing factor was the way in which drugs were purchased. Unlike most products, the decisionmakers (doctors), the consumers (patients), and the payees (insurance companies) were all separate groups. This led to a relatively inelastic demand and annual price increases in the 8 to 12 percent range for much of the 1980s (see fig. 6.2 below).[3] Competition was also somewhat muted. Developing a generic drug was relatively expensive until after the 1984 Hatch Act. Pharmaceutical companies also appeared to develop fewer "me too" drugs in the 1970s. The primary research method was serendipity or random searches. This method led to

---

2. Hall (1992) summarizes the theoretical and empirical arguments for a positive relationship between internally generated cash flow and R&D expenditures.

3. These price increases were for the United States. Price increases vary greatly around the world. For example, over this same period pharmaceutical prices were declining in Japan.

less spillover across companies relative to the current rational, scientific-based drug research design (Henderson and Cockburn 1996).

The consequence of this inelastic demand and muted competition was impressive increases in drug company stock prices in the 1980s (see fig. 6.3 below). Between 1980 and 1992 pharmaceutical stocks rose 959 percent relative to a 386 percent increase in the S&P.[4] This long-run supranormal performance may also have led to some organizational slack and inefficiency.

Toward the late 1980s and early 1990s, the profit and growth environment began to change dramatically. On the demand side, strong new constraints on pharmaceutical prices arose. Bundled purchasing, managed care, hospital consolidation, and growing government intervention gave the buyer strong new powers to negotiate drug prices. The pharmaceutical companies also got hit with a group of three-letter acronyms—PBMs (pharmacy benefit managers), HMOs (health maintenance organizations), DURs (drug utilization reviews), and DRGs (diagnosis-related groups for Medicare). While the primary purpose of these organizations and reviews were different, they all served to dramatically strengthen buyer power. By the early 1990s, 82 percent of the pharmaceuticals in the United States were sold through PBMs, chain pharmacies, or hospitals. As a consequence, "the weighted average price discount to distributors grew from 4% in 1987 to 16% in 1992" (MacAvoy 1995, 8). The enhanced buyer power was also instrumental in aggravating two other demand side trends: generic drugs and competition between therapeutically similar patented drugs.

The rise of the generic drug industry dates back to the 1984 Hatch Act. This act greatly reduced the previously large cost of getting a generic drug approved (Grabowski and Vernon 1992). The full impact of the act was delayed by three factors. First, until the role of the buyer changed, doctors and pharmacists lacked strong incentives to encourage generic substitution. Second, it took time to overcome public distrust of generic drugs and this process was made worse by plant closings, bankruptcies, and FDA bribery charges involving generic firms in 1987. Third, strategies by drug companies forestalled generic substitution. These included improved formulation, distinct product appearance, production economies, and reformulation of dosages.[5] By 1992, cost-cutting incentives were increased and public trust in generics improved. Grabowski and Vernon (1996) show that between 1989 and 1992 generic market share had increased from 47 to 72 percent.

4. When calculating long-run price indexes it can be important to adjust for relative risks or β. However, for pharmaceutical firms the average β is very close to one.

5. See MacAvoy (1995) for a more detailed account of these demand side trends and the strategies used by pharmaceutical firms to forestall them.

Industry sources also suggest that there has been a rise in the number of "me too" drugs. This appears to be occurring despite the widespread belief that these drugs are often unprofitable. The cause of this rise is unclear. One possibility is that the rational, scientific research method has increased the ability of firms to learn from each other's announcements of successes and failures at each stage of the development process (Henderson and Cockburn 1996). Regardless of the cause, it is true that a substantial number of the drugs in development are targeting the same disease. The number of drugs in development in 1996 included more than 200 cancer medicines (48 for breast cancer), 132 drugs targeting aging-related illnesses (20 for arthritis and 22 for Alzheimer's), and 110 for AIDS and related diseases.[6] Perhaps even more important than trends in "me too" drugs is the ability of large buyers to leverage the competition between similar drugs through formularies. Formularies reduce transaction costs and increase buyer power by restricting the number of drugs that can be used to treat an illness. Pharmaceutical firms are forced into fierce competition to get their drug on a formulary. To make matters worse, McKinsey claims that they can design a formulary that can "meet 95% of the current drug needs . . . with only 247 drugs . . . 70% of these drugs are already generic, and this number will rise to almost 90% by 1998" (Pursche 1995, 20).

A final factor that negatively affected drug prices was politics. Because pharmaceutical products are priced well above marginal cost and because drug price increases throughout the 1980s had consistently exceeded the consumer price index, pharmaceutical companies became an easy target for Hillary and Bill Clinton's 1992 health care reforms. Although these reforms were substantially scaled back, they did put enormous political pressure on pharmaceutical firms to restrain price increases.

The consequence of these demand side trends is clearly illustrated in the Bureau of Labor Statistics (BLS) Drug Producer Price Index shown in figure 6.2. Sometime in 1991, the ability of pharmaceutical firms to consistently increase prices ended. While this BLS series has some known biases, they cannot explain the sudden drop in price increases in 1991. With the exception of one small blip, the inability to raise drug prices has continued into 1996.

Drug companies were also getting squeezed on the cost side. A pharmaceutical industry association estimates that the average 1995 constant dollar cost of internally discovering and developing drugs has risen from $125 in 1986 to $400 in 1995. Despite this cost increase (or maybe because of it), the amount that pharmaceutical companies invest in R&D rose

6. The statistics come from the pharmaceutical organization *PhRMA's Facts and Figures* 1996.

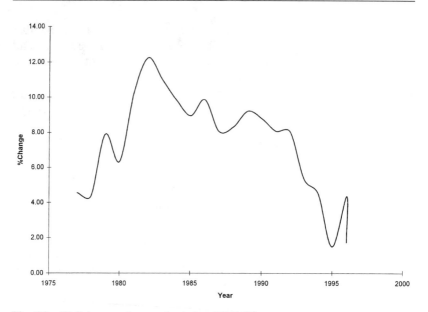

Fig. 6.2   BLS drug producer price index, 1976–96

continuously. Total pharmaceutical R&D has increased from $4.1 billion in 1985 to $8.4 billion in 1990 and to $15.8 billion in 1996. A similar increase is observed in R&D expressed as a percentage of sales. This number rose from 14.8 percent in 1984 to 15.9 percent in 1990 to 19.0 percent in 1996.[7] Henderson and Cockburn (1996, 43) also observe this dilemma, "Perhaps the most dramatic effect visible in the time-series aggregates is the continuing increase in research spending despite the fact that the mean cost per important patent rose dramatically from 1975 onwards."

Competition on the research side also arose in the form of small entrepreneurial pharmaceutical companies that are most commonly identified as "biotechs." The number of these companies in the United States increased from 333 in 1980 to 1,072 in 1990. The number of biotech products in clinical development almost doubled in the five-year period 1989 to 1993.

A final challenge facing pharmaceutical firms in the early 1990s was the forthcoming patent expiration of a large number of blockbuster drugs without clear indication of replacements. There were twenty-one "billion-dollar-a-year" products in 1993. Many of these were slated to go off patent by the year 2000. Yet not a single new drug was expected to reach this blockbuster status during that same time period. As a consequence, many

7. PhRMA (1996).

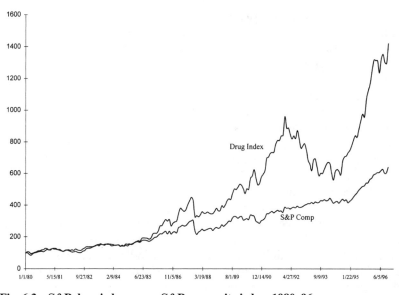

Fig. 6.3   S&P drug index versus S&P composite index, 1980–96
Source: Datastream International.

drug companies were flush with cash but short on the critical steady cash flow profile needed to continuously fund R&D.[8]

The critical nature of these challenges became apparent to the stock market at the end of 1991. As figure 6.3 demonstrates, collectively pharmaceutical companies experienced their first sharp long-term decline in over a decade. Drug firms began to underperform and buying drugs on Wall Street rather than in the research lab began to look attractive.[9]

These facts concerning the state of the pharmaceutical industry make it clear that pharmaceutical firms were at a critical turning point in the early 1990s. If they were going to sustain the growth rates that were driving their pre-1991 stock prices, they would have to do so through one or more of three basic approaches—counteract buyer power, develop unique drugs quicker, or cut costs.

The industry used mergers and acquisitions to address all three approaches. The three large vertical mergers, Merck-Medco, SmithKline Beecham–Diversified, and Eli Lilly–PCS, were attempts to address buyer

8. The information in this paragraph comes from the article "A Dry Period," *Forbes,* 24 April 1995, which also explains that this lack of research productivity arises more from the nature of scientific breakthroughs than from incompetence on the part of pharmaceutical firms.

9. Note that the drug stock index does begin to rise sharply again in late 1994, but only after the industry began to address some of these problems through mergers.

power by either co-opting that power or managing it through information. If they were successful, they would have increased the challenges faced by the rest of the industry who lacked access to PBMs and their information capabilities.[10]

Since the rise of biotechs, large pharmaceutical companies have accepted the value of acquisitions and alliances with these firms. The concept of a virtual corporation—what Eli Lilly calls "research without walls"—has been developing steam in this industry. The number of strategic alliances, which averaged around 150 per year during the years 1986 to 1989, rose to almost 400 per year in 1992–94 (PhRMA 1996). However, this trend raises questions about the optimal level of R&D inside large pharmaceutical firms.

The conditions faced by the pharmaceutical industry in the early 1990s are best described by the concept of "free cash flow" (Jensen 1986).[11] The culmination of demand constraints, cost increases, alternative research mechanisms, and declining pipelines strongly indicates that research productivity was declining. When firms failed to address these changes through cost cutting, their stock prices fell. Pharmaceutical firms flush with cash from past R&D successes could purchase products by taking over other companies cheaper and faster than they could through internal R&D. This action was even more important for firms whose blockbuster products were coming off patent and who did not have a sufficient pipeline to replace them. By using mergers to consolidate operations and cut out the excess industry capacity, the bidder could pay for the premium needed to acquire another firm's pipeline.

Recently, two articles have strongly demonstrated the potential advantages and impact of these cost-cutting mergers. McKinsey estimates that the changes in the pharmaceutical industry have led to sufficient excess capacity that a total of $60 to $90 billion in net present value could be cut from the U.S. pharmaceutical industry alone. "To put this number in perspective, the total value of fulfilling all disease-based unmet medical needs in the U.S. (through drug usage) is on the order of $120 billion

10. However, a 1995 study by the General Accounting Office (GAO) suggested the PBM acquisitions did not substantially help the pharmaceutical acquirers. The fact that two of the three PBM acquisitions were undone within five years after the merger suggests they did not produce the anticipated gains.

11. Jensen used the characteristics of the oil industry in the early 1980s to illustrate the concept of free cash flow. It is interesting to note that the pharmaceutical industry in the 1990s shares many of these same characteristics. Both industries have projects with substantial uncertainty, high upfront costs, and long payout periods. They both experienced a period of substantial price increases that led to some false expectations of this continuing. However, there are also important differences between these industries. In particular, it is very difficult for raiders to take over R&D firms using debt financing. The consolidation in the pharmaceutical industry had to be done by other large pharmaceutical firms.

NPV" (Pursche 1995, 19). After interviewing senior human resource managers at six U.K. pharmaceutical companies, Jones (1996, 30) concludes that "the views expressed by the six respondents indicate that leading pharmaceutical companies no longer see R&D as a core activity. This change represents an attempt to reduce R&D spending and improve efficiency in response to the many external pressures which face the industry." While both of these statements seem a little extreme, they illustrate how the changing pharmaceutical environment has created potential gains from consolidating through large horizontal mergers.

6.3 Characteristics of Value Creation

Measuring the value creation from pharmaceutical mergers is challenging for two reasons. First, the majority of mergers took place in the period 1994–96. For this paper, the postmerger time series is too brief for ex post measures such as changes in accounting profits or patent counts. Second, the pharmaceutical industry is very dynamic. The business press is filled with a constant stream of news about the industry and individual firms. Announcements concerning new drug discoveries, regulatory changes, legal matters, alliances, and individual drug cash flow projections are common. This makes it difficult to assign long-term changes to any one event without a large sample to reduce the noise. Given these constraints the best measure is the stock market reaction using fairly narrow windows.[12]

The average abnormal stock market reactions to the announcement of sixty-five pharmaceutical deals occurring between 1985 and 1996 are 13.31, −2.12, and 0.59 percent for the target, bidder, and combined firms, respectively. The target and bidder abnormal returns are statistically significant, but the combined returns are not. These acquisitions include all deals over $500 million for which the bidder and the target have stock market data.[13] A merger or acquisition was considered a pharmaceutical transaction if Security Data Corporation listed either the bidder or target as a pharmaceutical or biotech company. The market's reaction was calculated using standard event study methodology with a three-day event

12. Even the narrow window can be somewhat problematic. For example, Glaxo announced a decline in sales of its leading drug Zantac on the same day that it announced the Wellcome merger. Three days later, Glaxo announced the acquisition of Affymax, a leader in combinatorial chemistry, for $592 million. In the same month of the merger announcement, Glaxo received U.K. approval for an over-the-counter (OTC) version of Zantac, while the FDA rejected an OTC version of Wellcome's Zovirax. Both of these events significantly influenced the firms' stock prices.

13. The bidder or the target were non-U.S. companies in 45 percent of these deals. Because of the broad worldwide coverage of Datastream International, there were only fourteen deals in the over $500 million category for which we could not find data.

window centered around the first announcement of the winning bid.[14] The market model was estimated for 240 days to 40 days before the announcement of the transaction. Consistent with the findings from the general population of mergers occurring since 1980 (e.g., Bradley, Desai, and Kim 1988), the target shareholders gain and the bidder shareholders lose in the typical pharmaceutical deal.[15]

The combined firm abnormal return was calculated as the weighted average of the bidder and target abnormal returns with the weights being the market value of the firm forty days before the merger announcement. The 0.59 percent return value is the simple average of the combined firm value for all sixty-five firms. Thus, on average pharmaceutical mergers create a small amount of value for the combined shareholders. A more accurate way of computing total value created is to compute the dollar value created for each merger (target abnormal return times target market value plus bidder abnormal return times bidder market value). The sum of the dollar value created for all sixty-five mergers is $18.76 billion (U.S.).

Pharmaceutical acquisitions differ across a number of key characteristics. In table 6.1, the impact of these characteristics on the abnormal return to the target, bidder, and combined firm is explored. With respect to shareholder value creation, two characteristics stand out—large horizontal mergers and cross-border transactions. Large horizontal mergers are defined as the combination of two of the top thirty firms whose primary industry is pharmaceuticals. A listing of these top firms and mergers is given in figure 6.4. These mergers generate statistically significant (at the 10 percent level) abnormal return of 9.84, 4.97, and 7.60 percent for the target, bidder, and combined shareholders relative to other pharmaceutical deals. To put this in perspective, the sum of the combined shareholder dollar value created for the ten large horizontal drug mergers is $19.47 billion. This is more than the total value creation of the entire sample of sixty-five pharmaceutical acquisitions.

Deals that cross national boundaries also earn impressive returns for all shareholders. The target, bidder, and combined returns are 6.40, 4.25, and 3.53 percent relative to other drug acquisitions with all but the target re-

14. We also used an eleven-day window centered around the announcement day. The target firm returns were slightly higher and the bidder firm returns were slightly lower. A disadvantage of narrow windows around the first announcement date is that we do not capture leaks, rumors, or prior announcements with other bidders. Hoechst's acquisition of Marion Merrell Dow illustrates this point. Marion Merrell Dow was thought to be a target for over six months before a final deal with Hoechst was announced. There was little reaction in Dow's stock price when the deal was finally announced (see table 6.2). Thus, we have probably underestimated the return to targets and the total value created in the deal. A sensitivity test, which eliminated any deal that does not display a significant positive reaction to the target, does not affect the results.

15. These bidder losses occur despite the fact that we arbitrarily assigned bidder status to one of the two partners in the mergers of equals. As table 6.2 shows, the shareholders of these merger of equals "bidders" earned over 13 percent in above market returns.

Table 6.1   **Regressions of Abnormal Stock Market Returns on Deal Characteristics for Sixty-Five Top Pharmaceutical Transactions, 1985–96**

	Target Return	Bidder Return	Combined
Intercept (%)	17.05	−4.04	−1.13
	(4.75)	(−2.51)	(−0.78)
Horizontal (%)	9.84	4.97	7.60
	(1.79)	(2.01)	(3.47)
Partial acquisition (%)	−16.98	1.06	−1.74
	(−4.26)	(0.59)	(−1.10)
Cross border (%)	6.40	4.25	3.53
	(1.62)	(2.39)	(2.24)
Hostile (%)	18.97	−0.98	0.74
	(2.54)	(−0.29)	(0.25)
Vertical (%)	14.58	−2.96	−0.29
	(1.66)	(−0.75)	(−0.08)
Relative size (%)	−10.91	−3.39	−1.09
	(−1.69)	(−1.25)	(−0.45)
R^2	0.43	0.20	0.28

Note: The parentheses contain *t*-statistics. Partial acquisition equals one if the target was a subsidiary of a publicly traded company or the target was a divested unit of a publicly traded company. Cross border equals one if the bidder and target home country were not the same. Hostile equals one if the target was put into play through a hostile acquisition. Vertical equals one if the target was a PBM. Relative size is the target market value divided by the bidder market value.

turn statistically significant. This positive impact of cross-border acquisitions supports the general theoretical and empirical work on international acquisitions (Harris and Ravenscraft 1993). Cross-border deals like SmithKline Beecham and Pharmacia Upjohn expand global marketing by pushing one firm's products through the other firm's sales force.

Hostile takeovers and vertical integration deals pay significantly higher target premiums and partial acquisitions and smaller deals pay significantly lower premiums. However, these differences are not sufficient to statistically affect the bidder or combined return.

A closer look at the stock market's reaction to individual deals provides additional insight into the impact of deal characteristics. The individual returns for the top fifteen deals are given in table 6.2. Eleven of the fifteen deals created value for the combined shareholders. However, three of the losses were large—over $1.4 billion. Two of the three big losers were vertical, pharmacy benefit managers deals (Merck-Medco and Lilly-PCS).[16] The other deal that created large losses for shareholders was Kodak's di-

---

16. Analysts suggest that the remaining large vertical deal created value because of the way it was structured. The SmithKline Beecham–Diversified acquisition was not dilutive for SmithKline, in part because U.K. firms can immediately deduct the massive goodwill that

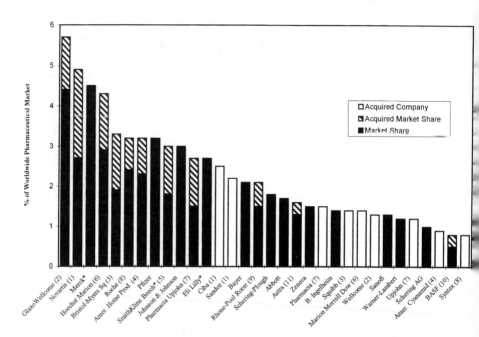

Fig. 6.4   Pharmaceutical market share of top companies (excluding Japanese firms), 1995

Source: Goldman Sachs and IMS.

Note: When company is not present in 1994, market shares at the acquisition date are used. The numbers in parentheses link the acquired and acquiring firms. Acquired firms 10 (Boots) and 11 (Fisons) are not shown.

*Company was engaged in a large vertical pharmacy benefit manager acquisition.

sastrous diversification attempt into pharmaceuticals through the purchase of Sterling Drugs.[17]

On the more positive side, six of the fifteen deals created over $1 billion in stock value during the three days surrounding the announcement. All of these were large horizontal acquisitions and five of the six occurred after 1993. The one early deal was Beecham's merger with SmithKline. This was a cross-border deal that also benefited from U.K. accounting rules. Two of the other large value-creating horizontal deals also benefited from the global reach that comes from a cross-border deal. As the regressions in table 6.1 reveal, however, large horizontal mergers generate substantial value even after controlling for cross-border advantages.

The industry pressures discussed in section 6.2 applied to all firms in

gets created in these deals. While this deduction does make earnings numbers look better, it would be surprising if this explained the market reaction. The goodwill deduction is an accounting change that does not carry with it a real side impact such as increased tax deductions.

17. Interestingly, the purchase of Gerber by Sandoz, which represented a diversification out of pharmaceuticals, was well received by the market, creating almost $1 billion in value.

Table 6.2 Market-Adjusted Returns to the Top Fifteen Pharmaceutical Mergers (1985–96) with Stock Market Data

Target Name	Target Nation[a]	Acquirer Name	Acquirer Nation[a]	Type[b]	Date Announced	Date Effective	Value of Transaction ($millions)	Percentage of Target Stock Return	Percentage of Acquirer Stock Return	Percentage of Weighted Stock Return	Total Stock Value Created ($millions)
Ciba-Geigy AG	SW	Sandoz AG	SW	H, ME	03/07/96	12/17/96	32,641	19.12	13.74	16.80	9,636
Wellcome PLC	UK	Glaxo Holdings PLC	UK	H	01/20/95	05/01/95	14,285	43.55	−8.18	3.93	1,520
Squibb Corp	US	Bristol-Myers Co.	US	H	07/27/89	10/04/89	12,094	27.46	−9.46	3.60	796
American Cyanamid Co.	US	American Home Products Corp.	US	H	08/02/94	12/21/94	9,561	48.40	−0.51	9.72	2,213
SmithKline Beckman Corp.	US	Beecham Group PLC	UK	H, CB	03/31/89	07/26/89	7,922	17.63	3.62	9.99	1,356
Marion Merrell Dow Inc.	US	Hoechst AG	GR	H, CB	02/28/95	07/18/95	7,121	0.38	−3.26	−2.08	−381
Pharmacia AB	SW	Upjohn Co.	US	H, CB, ME	08/21/95	11/02/95	6,989	14.22	17.36	16.27	1,620
Medco Containment Services Inc.	US	Merck & Co. Inc.	US	V	07/28/93	11/18/93	6,226	15.02	−4.99	−3.23	−1,511
Syntex Corp.	US	Roche Holding AG	SZ	H, CB	05/02/94	11/03/94	5,307	61.82	1.69	13.24	2,247

(continued)

Table 6.2 (continued)

Target Name	Target Nation[a]	Acquirer Name	Acquirer Nation[a]	Type[b]	Date Announced	Date Effective	Value of Transaction ($millions)	Percentage of Target Stock Return	Percentage of Acquirer Stock Return	Percentage of Weighted Stock Return	Total Stock Value Created ($millions)
Sterling Drug	US	Eastman Kodak Co. Inc.	US	D	01/25/88	02/29/88	5,100	7.41	−15.27	−11.93	−2,146
Wellcome PLC-OTC Products	UK	Warner-Lambert Co.-OTC Products	US	H, CB	07/28/93	06/30/94	4,397	6.69	2.39	3.53	467
PCS Health Systems (McKesson)	US	Eli Lilly & Co.	US	V	07/11/94	11/21/94	4,000	33.49	−16.05	−7.80	−1,494
Gerber Products Co.	US	Sandoz AG	SZ	D	05/23/94	12/19/94	3,686	47.52	−0.70	6.92	999
AH Robins Co. Inc.	US	American Home Products Corp.	US	H	12/23/87	12/15/89	3,194	21.45	−0.24	4.04	523
Diversified Pharmaceutical	US	SmithKline Beecham Corp.	US	V	05/03/94	05/27/94	2,300	13.50	4.62	6.26	622

Source: Security Data Corporation Mergers and Acquisitions Data Base and Datastream International

[a]SW = Sweden, UK = United Kingdom, US = United States, GR = Germany, SZ = Switzerland.

[b]H = horizontal, V = vertical, ME = merger of equals, CB = cross border, D = diversifying.

Table 6.3   **Industry-Adjusted Long-Run Premerger and Postmerger Performance of the
Bidder and Target in Large Horizontal Mergers**

	Cumulative Stock Return between 87 Weeks and 9 Weeks *before* the Merger	Cumulative Stock Return between 9 Weeks and 87 Weeks *after* the Merger
Targets		
American Cyanamid	−12.92	
Syntex	−47.64	
Wellcome	−27.52	
Marion Merrell Dow	−1.23	
Targets average	−22.33	
Bidders		
American Home Products	−20.40	
Roche	120.80	
Glaxo	−19.61	
Hoechst	4.42	
Bidders average	21.30	
Merged Firms		
American Home Products		13.01
Roche-Syntex		−19.21
GlaxoWellcome		−8.21
Hoechst Marion		20.31
Merged average		1.48

the industry. What factors led some firms to pursue or to be the target of large horizontal acquisitions? The stock market evidence in table 6.3 can provide a partial answer. This table gives the market performance of firms involved in a large horizontal merger for a period of one and one-half years before and after the merger. (In a few cases, we only had one year of postmerger data.) Target and bidder performance is measured relative to an index of pharmaceutical firms that did not engage in horizontal or vertical pharmaceutical mergers. Because we are interested in explaining why firms become bidders or targets, we want to eliminate any change in stock values associated with rumors of the merger. Thus, we eliminate the eight weeks immediately preceding the merger announcement. Similarly, we eliminate the eight postmerger weeks to focus on only postmerger events that are not associated with the deal announcement.

To construct this table, we began with the complete list of major pharmaceutical firms given in figure 6.4. This figure shows the market shares before and after mergers for the leading firms. We wanted a list of horizontal merger firms and a control group of firms that did not engage in pharmaceutical mergers. From that list, we eliminated firms with incomplete weekly stock data from 1990 to the middle of 1996. To focus on only recent, horizontal mergers with clear bidders and targets, we also eliminated firms engaged in vertical mergers, pharmaceutical mergers before 1990, or mergers of equals. This left us with a sample of four large pharmaceutical mergers (American Home Products' acquisition of American Cyanamid in 1994, Roche's acquisition of Syntex in 1994, Glaxo's acquisition of Wellcome in 1995, and Hoechst's acquisition of Marion Merrell Dow in 1995) and six control firms (Pfizer, Johnson and Johnson, Bayer, Abbott, Sanofi, and Schering). We created an equal-weighted index of the control firms and subtracted it from the target, bidder, or merged firm's return. Finally, we cumulated the adjusted return over the premerger and postmerger period.

The returns to the target firms are very consistent. All of the target firms were underperforming their peer group in the eighteen months before they became a target. On average, the targets lost 22 percent of their value during this period. Target firms were either failing to address the challenges of this changing industry or they had additional difficulties (such as the impending patent expiration of Wellcome's Zovirax). The evidence on the bidder returns is less clear. Two of the firms, Glaxo and American Home Products, displayed stock losses similar to the targets. One firm, Roche, dramatically outperformed its industry in the premerger period. The postmerger findings for the combined firms is equally mixed. This suggests that there is no systematic reevaluation of the merger announcement stock returns discussed above.

6.4   The Market for Corporate Control in the Pharmaceutical Industry

A wave of pharmaceutical mergers was feasible because this market is so unconcentrated. The dispersed nature of this industry is clear from figure 6.4. Before the recent wave began, the top ten firms controlled only 29 percent of the worldwide market. Even after substantial merger activity, the top ten firms control only 38 percent of the market. There are still a substantial number of firms that have not participated in the large horizontal consolidation. One industry expert indicated that there are probably forty companies for which consolidation still makes sense.

A significant amount of research in finance has shown a link between ownership and performance.[18] The difficulty is that the relationship is complicated. A large shareholder can provide important monitoring of corporate activity including the decision to acquire or be acquired (Fama and Jensen 1983). When the large shareholder is management or is aligned with management, entrenchment can harm performance and block changes in corporate control (Stulz 1988). Many firms in the pharmaceutical industry have a single shareholder or shareholder group with over 5 percent ownership. This concentrated ownership structure stems from three sources. First, many of the pharmaceutical companies began as family-owned businesses and the family or related endowment maintained a significant stake (e.g., G. D. Searle, Richardson-Vicks, Eli Lilly, Johnson

---

18. See Servaes and Zenner (1994) for a review of this literature.

and Johnson, Upjohn, Roche, Merck AG, Wellcome plc). Second, large global pharmaceutical companies often reside in countries where significant ownership is a common form of corporate governance (e.g., Astra, Novo Nordisk, Sandoz, Rhone-Poulenc, Schering, Synthelabo, and almost all of the Japanese pharmaceutical companies). Third, the pecking order hypothesis suggests that if internal funds are unavailable then the next best solution to the R&D-related information asymmetry and moral hazard problems is large block equity ownership (e.g., SmithKline Beecham, Syntex, and Zeneca).[19] Corporate theory suggests that this concentrated ownership structure should both facilitate and block merger activity. Both outcomes are evident in pharmaceuticals. A number of firms on the above lists have been acquired, while a similar number of small- to medium-size players have remained independent. It is also clear that some pharmaceutical firms are willing to use hostile acquisitions to overcome managerial entrenchment. The support of the Wellcome Trust for Glaxo's hostile takeover of Burroughs Wellcome illustrates the important role of these corporate governance issues.

From our discussions with industry experts, it is clear that an active industry merger market creates unique opportunities and challenges for bidders. These include increased strategic focus, a time trade-off between reduced uncertainty and scarcity, and the ability to adapt the acquisition method to escalating premiums.

Two pioneering mergers led firms to more actively focus on acquisitions as the potential solution to the challenges they faced. Merck's acquisition of Medco in 1993 encouraged other firms to look carefully at the vertical integration option. American Home Products' hostile takeover of American Cyanamid demonstrated that horizontal combinations could be used to dramatically cut costs. These deals escalated the intensity with which firms, consultants, and investment banking consider mergers, acquisitions, and takeovers. For example, it is not uncommon for major subsidiaries and their parents to independently consider alternative merger candidates. This increased scrutiny probably increases deal efficiency if it allows firms to become proactive rather than reactive. However, a fear is that this environment will encourage entrenched managers to seek acquisitions to avoid becoming a target. Surprisingly, we did not find evidence from our interviews of this acquire-or-be-acquired attitude.

This active merger market also creates a critical trade-off between reduced uncertainty and scarcity. Pioneering mergers face greater risk.[20] The potential success of the strategy is unknown. Therefore, investors are likely to discount the estimated synergies. Subsequent mergers can learn from

19. Information on ownership was taken from Worldscope and Compact Disclosure.
20. For example, even the CEO of Glaxo, Sir Richard Sykes, expressed skepticism about American Home Products' bid for American Cyanamid. According to the *Wall Street Journal,* "Sir Richard scoffed at claims that drug giants could easily boost profits by gobbling up weak rivals like American Cyanamid and slashing cost" (9 September 1994, p. B2).

the successes and failures of the pioneers. However, since there is often a limited number of good targets, competitive pressures may force firms to pay the full value of the synergies.

A mechanism used to avoid escalating premiums is a merger of equals. In these deals, the stocks of both firms are exchanged for the newly created stock of the merged company. No premium is paid. The merger gains are shared between the two firms. A merger of equals, however, faces what is known as "interloper risk," in which another firm is encouraged to bid for one of the two firms. Shareholders might prefer the certainty of receiving a target premium over the promised future synergies of the merger of equals. Thus, for a merger of equals to avoid interloper risk, it is critical that the future synergies be quickly incorporated into the stock value on the announcement of the merger. Because American Home Products had demonstrated the potential cost-cutting savings from horizontal mergers, horizontal merger efficiency claims were credible. Thus, subsequent announcements of mergers of equals resulted in immediate and dramatic increases in both parties' stock value (e.g., Pharmacia and Upjohn and Sandoz and Ciba-Geigy).

6.5   GlaxoWellcome Case

Glaxo and Wellcome have a long and distinguished history dating back over one hundred years. Glaxo's history can be traced back to the late 1800s and the Nathan family trade and dairy business in New Zealand. Their first manufactured product was a dried milk that was trademarked as Glaxo (which was derived from *lacto*). In the 1920s it expanded into vitamins by licensing a vitamin D extraction process, using it to reinforce baby food and produce its first pharmaceutical, a drop-dose version of vitamin D. During the Second World War, Glaxo scientists developed a new method for the mass production of penicillin that proved to be critical for Britain's war effort and led to a leading position in antibiotics. Prior to Wellcome, Glaxo's most important acquisition was of a U.K. firm, Allen & Hanburys, which brought them not only a leading manufacturer of infant foods and insulin, but more importantly a brilliant scientist, Dr. David Jack. For twenty-six years he directed Glaxo's R&D, developing a leading position in respiratory and gastrointestinal ailments. (Jack retired in 1987 and was replaced by Dr. Richard Sykes, Glaxo's current CEO.) Glaxo also displayed its marketing prowess by beating out Tagamet in the peptic ulcer market, even though its product Zantac was developed six years after Tagamet. "Me too" drugs are not supposed to be blockbusters. Glaxo's international roots expanded in the 1970s and 1980s, including a 1978 entry into the United States.

In 1880, Silas Burroughs and Henry Wellcome, two American pharmacists, formed Burroughs Wellcome & Co. in London. Their purpose was to supply Britain with U.S. compounded medicines. After Burroughs's death in 1895, Wellcome became the sole owner of the company. When Wellcome died in 1936, he willed the company to the Wellcome Trust to ensure that the company's profits went to medical research and education. Wellcome became a public company in 1986 when Wellcome Trust sold 25 percent of its ownership to the public. It sold another 35 percent in 1992. Henry Wellcome gave Wellcome a firm foundation in research, global outlook, and marketing. He established the first in-house pharmaceutical research facilities in 1894, starting a tradition of research that led to four Nobel Prizes for Wellcome scientists, including a 1988 prize for pioneering the rational drug approach. This academic-like research tradition helped give Wellcome the premier position in antivirals. In the early 1970s, Wellcome scientists did what many thought was impossible. They found a way to destroy a virus without harming its host cell. This led to Wellcome's two leading products, Zovirax and AZT. Henry Wellcome also established an early tradition in globalization by forming a U.S. subsidiary in 1906 and a floating laboratory on the Nile in the early 1900s that helped Wellcome become a leader in tropical diseases.

6.5.1 Premerger Challenges

Glaxo and Wellcome's phenomenal successes with Zantac and Zovirax turned out to be a double-edged sword. Their successes helped fuel the growth of large organizations. However, with half of their sales in the United States and U.S. patents set to expire in 1997, replacing that fuel was proving difficult. Glaxo and Wellcome were employing the classic defenses of these products including improved formulation, litigation to delay early entry, and moving to OTC status before expiration (although Zovirax was denied FDA approval for OTC). Despite these efforts, analysts estimated that both products would lose two-thirds or more of sales by the year 2000.

Replacing blockbusters is especially difficult given the changes in the pharmaceutical industry. Generic drug firms were ready to move as soon as Zantac and Zovirax patents expired. By the end of 1996, three firms had production facilities with tentative FDA approval ready to produce a generic Zantac. Valtrex, Wellcome's improved formulation of Zovirax, already faced competition from a similar SmithKline Beecham drug, Famvir. Multiple sources of competition for new unique successful drugs developed by Glaxo, like the migraine drug Imitrex, were just on the horizon (including one developed by Wellcome). While Wellcome retained its premier position in antivirals, competition in this area was increasing. The U.S. government continued to put pressure on Wellcome to keep AZT prices down and the French government has complained about the high price of Imitrex. Hospitals, HMOs, and PBMs have been successful in obtaining rebates on Wellcome and Glaxo products even before patent expiration and the new competition. As with all pharmaceutical companies, the cost of doing research continued to rise. Zantac and Zovirax were generating enough money to cover these costs and still build up cash reserves, but time was running out. If action was not taken, downsizing and layoffs would be necessary. (In fact, Glaxo was starting to shrink through attrition.) Furthermore, their declining stock price relative to other pharmaceutical firms (table 6.3) and cash reserves could make them an attractive takeover target.

While each firm faced similar challenges, how they reacted to them was somewhat different, perhaps because Glaxo, being three times the size of Wellcome, could pursue more and larger options. Glaxo pursued all three merger-related approaches. Concerns about growing buyer power, Merck's acquisition of Medco, and the informational requirements of new disease management programs led Glaxo to consider vertical integration through a joint venture with Johnson and Johnson and McKesson to run McKesson's pharmacy benefit manager division, PCS Health Systems. However, when McKesson saw SmithKline Beecham follow Merck by purchasing the PBM Diversified Pharmaceutical, McKesson decided to shop PCS around before joining in a joint venture. That strategy worked and Eli Lilly bid $4 billion for PCS. Johnson and Johnson and Glaxo's decisions not to join in the bidding suggest that they did not see the same value in PCS that Lilly saw. Glaxo decided to pursue more modest alliances with downstream firms.

Glaxo also was active in biotech joint ventures, licenses, and acquisitions. The most dramatic of these was Glaxo's 1995 acquisition of Affymax, the leader in combinatorial chemistry, for over $500 million. Using high throughput screening and robotics, combinatorial chemistry allows compounds to be evaluated in a fraction of the time used by more established techniques. In the race to be the first drug in a class to market and to increase the time distance with "me too" drugs, increased research productivity is critical. Still, the payback from this acquisition is long (possibly ten years) and uncertain. These types of acquisitions would not address the Zantac problem. Licensing could help, especially because it directly addresses the potential excess capacity problems Zantac would create. Since Glaxo's inception, when it licensed the process to create dried milk, it has had success in licensing. A recent example is Glaxo's license of the HIV drug, 3TC, from Biochem Pharma in 1991. This was Glaxo's first product in the antiviral area. However, competition for licenses is intense and it would be difficult to replace Zantac with licensed products.

Wellcome was considering many of the same options, but at smaller levels. However, they also were relying on their strong research tradition. They felt optimistic that their pipeline had the potential to replace Zovirax with Valtrex, an improved formulation. They predicted that combination therapies including AZT and 3TC would show great promise in fighting

AIDS. They even tried to license 3TC from Glaxo. While competitors had closed the gap, Wellcome still led in antivirals and thought they had the size and a number of promising new products (including 1592, Vertex Protease, FTC, and Wellferon) to maintain their leadership position. They were working on strengthening some other areas, like central nervous system (CNS), to gain economies of scope. But even these areas contained some promising products including a competitor to Glaxo's migraine drug Imitrex, called 311C. (The FTC felt that 311C showed enough promise as a unique competitor to Imitrex that it required 311C's divestiture.) Also, preliminary tests revealed that their antidepression product Wellbutrin showed promise in helping patients to stop smoking. Their declining stock price, however, suggested that the market disagreed with these optimistic projections. Some disappointments in prior Wellcome management claims, particularly in the cardiovascular area, had hurt Wellcome's credibility in the market. This put Wellcome in a difficult position. If they were correct in their forecasts, their undervalued stock price just made them a more attractive target. If they were wrong, a sharp downsizing would be needed.

6.5.2 Glaxo-Wellcome Merger

On 20 January 1995, Glaxo announced its boldest and most direct approach to dealing with the changing pharmaceutical industry and the Zantac problem—the acquisition of Wellcome. A shocked Wellcome management quickly rejected the offer and began seeking a white knight. In part because of a pledge by Wellcome Trust to sell their 40 percent to Glaxo, no white knight materialized. On 7 March 1995, Wellcome agreed to the merger.

Using just the announcement-day stock returns, an event study analysis of the merger reveals that Glaxo paid a 40.7 percent premium for Wellcome, increasing Wellcome shareholder value by $3.8 billion. On the day of the announcement, Glaxo shareholders earned an abnormal return of −5.5 percent for a loss in shareholder value of $1.9 billion. Thus, based on the day of the announcement (which was truly a surprise to the market and even some senior managers at Glaxo), the merger created $1.9 billion. This is probably a lower bound. On the same day of the merger, Glaxo announced a decline in Zantac sales of 4 percent. Thus, some of the loss in market value may be due to this new forecast. Prior announcements concerning declines in Zantac had reduced Glaxo's shares by as much as 2 percent. In addition, the market may have been concerned that Glaxo would get in a bidding war. Glaxo's shareholders did earn a positive abnormal return of 3.8 percent when Wellcome finally agreed to the original offer. Thus, it might be reasonable to assume that Glaxo shareholders were unaffected by the merger announcement. Under this assumption, the merger created $3.8 billion in net shareholder value.

There are two clear corporate governance issues in the Glaxo-Wellcome merger. First, the role of the blockholders in facilitating mergers is demonstrated by the Wellcome Trust. They made it possible for Wellcome to become a target and helped Glaxo avoid a bidding war.[21] Second, mergers sometimes require a change in top management. Sir Richard Sykes replaced Sir Paul Girolami as CEO just six months before the Wellcome acquisition. Girolami strongly favored organic growth over large acquisitions that would add debt and take funds away from R&D.

In an interview with *Management Today,* Glaxo's CEO Sir Richard Sykes explained why they merged with Wellcome. "Why merger? Two reasons, he says. First, the squeeze on health-care costs caused by recession. Drug companies with what is perceived as their arbitrary pricing of products, are easy targets for governments trying to cut costs. And second, Zantac. You cannot continue to grow organically if you have got a 2.4 billion pound product that is going on the decline, however clever you are. . . . Why Wellcome? Because says Sykes, it is the right size to be managed, the right shape to be easily integrated, and it had a weakness that made it an easier prey than others: it was 40%-owned by the Wellcome Trust, a charitable foundation which had a fiduciary duty to maximize its income" (*Management Today,* December 1995, p. 58).

Not everyone agreed with Sykes's motive or selection. William Steere, CEO of Pfizer, echoed a common skepticism. "I don't know what you get out of consolidation, frankly. Just being bigger is not particularly better" (*Business Week,* 13 January 1997, p. 110). Others thought that Glaxo had only traded a single "Z" problem (Zantac) for a "double Z" problem (Zantac and Zovirax). We now turn to how consolidating these two problems might improve GlaxoWellcome by $2 billion to $5 billion.

6.5.3 Sources of Value Creation—Cost Savings

As discussed above, the simplest answer is through an estimated $1 billion a year cost savings. GlaxoWellcome expected to achieve these annual savings by the end of 1998. The savings in 1995–97 appear to just about cover (on a discounted basis) the $1.8 billion integration cost, which primarily includes severance and early retirement pay and costs in closing sites. Using a discount rate of 13 percent, we can discount the post-1997 savings back to beginning of 1995 and compare them to our estimates of value creation and the premium paid for Wellcome.[22] These cost savings would need to be sustained through the year 2000 to cover the stock mar-

---

21. On the other hand, Wellcome management felt betrayed by the Wellcome Trust. Wellcome management had a written agreement with the Wellcome Trust that management would be informed and have a voice in any change in control. The Trust overruled this agreement because of their perceived fiduciary responsibility to effectively manage the Trust.

22. The 13 percent was the median discount value reported in the merger filings of a contemporaneous merger, Pharmacia Upjohn.

ket's lower bound estimate of value creation, and through 2006 to cover the premium paid for Wellcome and the stock market's upper bound estimate.

This exercise is somewhat academic for several reasons. First, three sets of projections must be accurate for the cost-savings estimate to be correct. The cost savings are calculated as the difference between the sum of Glaxo's and Wellcome's independent projections prior to the merger and the projections of the newly formed GlaxoWellcome. Second, these savings ignore other costs and benefits. They do not include the revenue-enhancing merger gains, nor do they include the nonaccounting post-merger integration costs. They also assume that the tax impacts of the cost savings are offset by the tax savings from the increased debt.[23] Finally, this exercise assumes that the cost cutting does not lower revenue. These are a lot of assumptions even for an economist. However, the estimates reveal how difficult it is to create value in mergers, especially for the bidder. To break even Glaxo must grow and then sustain a $1 billion annual cost savings over a substantial length of time.

How reasonable are GlaxoWellcome's assumed cost savings? Table 6.4 compares GlaxoWellcome's estimates of the projected cost savings and headcount reductions to seven other large horizontal mergers. All of these mergers project substantial cost savings of between 11 and 29 percent of the target's sales and 8 to 20 percent of the combined firm's workforce. Furthermore, most of these deals have achieved or are well on their way to achieving the estimated savings. For example, Roche-Syntex reached their estimated cut of five thousand jobs in the first eighteen months after the acquisition. Further rationalizations are also possible. On the basis of target sales, GlaxoWellcome's cost-saving estimates are higher than any of the other horizontal mergers. On the other hand, GlaxoWellcome's estimated headcount reduction relative to combined headcount is about average. Investment banking estimates and press reports put the estimate at as high as fifteen thousand. This would push headcount reduction to 23 percent of combined value, which would also be at the top of the list.[24] In any

23. If we were to assume that there were no tax benefits from the merger, then the cost savings would be reduced by around 30 percent (Glaxo's worldwide tax rate). With this adjustment, the cost saving would need to be sustained through the year 2002 to achieve the stock market's estimated lower bound merger synergies. The cost savings would need to be sustained forever to cover the premium paid for Wellcome. While even a crude estimate of the merger-related tax savings is difficult for a multinational R&D company like GlaxoWellcome, the potential tax savings are sufficiently large (the merger was financed with almost $9 billion in debt) that assuming the tax liabilities from the cost savings are covered by the tax saving from the merger seems more reasonable than no merger tax savings.

24. It is not surprising that GlaxoWellcome's estimated savings are higher than other companies'. They have closer geographic overlap than any of the other mergers. Each firm had 40 to 45 percent of their sales in the United States and 30 to 35 percent in Europe. Both had worldwide headquarters in the United Kingdom and U.S. headquarters in the same state. Both were also facing substantial declines in their leading products.

Table 6.4   Synergy Estimates and Headcount Reduction for Large Horizontal Pharmaceutical Mergers

	Merger Date	Estimated Annual Cost Saving at Maturity ($millions)	Combined Sales at Time of Merger ($millions)	Cost Saving as a Percentage of Smaller Co. Sales	Estimated Headcount Reduction	Combined Headcount at Time of Merger	Headcount Reduction as a Percentage of Total Headcount
Novartis[a]	1996	1,500	29,247	12	10,200	102,500	10
Pharmacia and Upjohn[a,b]	1995	800	6,949	15	4,100	34,500	13
Glaxo-Wellcome[c]	1995	1,000	11,960	29	7,500	64,400	12
Roche-Syntex[a]	1994	450	15,645	21	5,000	65,000	8
AHP-Cyanamid[d]	1994	700	12,500	17	7,630	77,950	10
Bristol-Myers Squibb[e]	1989	420	9,190	16	5,000	54,100	9
SmithKline Beecham[f]	1989	320	6,840	11	5,500	55,000	10
Marion Merrell Dow[e]	1989	170	2,350	16	1,970	9,844	20

Source: Data from Goldman Sachs, the Monitor Company, annual reports, and "Major Mergers in the Pharmaceutical Industry."

[a] Management estimates of cost synergies only.

[b] Originally $500 million in synergies was announced.

[c] GlaxoWellcome 1995 Annual Report.

[d] Company progress report on cost/headcount reduction, and Morgan Stanley extrapolation of these to maturity.

[e] Inferred from actual operating profit improvements and sales-adjusted headcount two to three years after merger.

[f] Actual number of headcount reduction offered by company.

event, table 6.4 shows that cost savings are an important part of large
horizontal pharmaceutical mergers and that the insights gained from
GlaxoWellcome should generalize.

To demonstrate how the cost cutting works, the typical cost structure
of a pharmaceutical firm—before and after a merger—is illustrated in
figure 6.5. The cost as a percentage of sales for the average U.S. and European firms in 1996 can be divided into administration (5 percent), marketing and sales (30 percent), R&D (15 percent), and cost of goods sold (30
percent) for an operating profit of 20 percent. Cost savings may come
from the acquired or acquiring company, but for illustrative purposes we
will assume that all of the savings come out of the target firm expenditures.
Experts estimate that much of the target's overhead can be eliminated in
the merger. R&D in the target company can be cut by several percentage
points, and R&D laboratories may be combined and marginal R&D projects can be cut. Substantial saving can come from combining sales forces
and eliminating redundancy. Excess capacity exists in the manufacturing
operations of most pharmaceutical companies. By consolidating production into fewer plants, those plants can be operated more efficiently and
other plants can be sold. A 5 percentage point reduction in the target's
commercial operation and a 10 percentage point reduction in manufacturing operation are obtainable. These reductions total 20 percent of the target's sales, which is the average reduction in table 6.4. This improves the

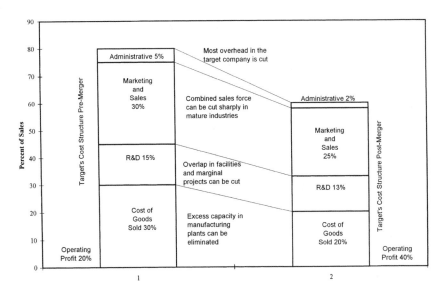

Fig. 6.5   Cost savings from horizontal pharmaceutical mergers
Source: Morgan Stanley presentation on average operating statistics for U.S. and European
pharmaceutical companies. Size of cuts comes from authors' discussions with industry experts.

target's operating profit to 40 percent with a total cost savings of $800 million on the average target's sales of $4 billion.

Initial evidence from the Glaxo-Wellcome merger demonstrates that these cost savings are feasible. Administrative cost savings are clear. Glaxo and Wellcome were both research-oriented firms with 100 percent of sales in pharmaceuticals and extensive geographic overlap in all of their primary markets. They had similar organizational structures revolving around geography and function. Thus, most of the major administrative positions were redundant. Once the decision was made as to which individual got the comparable position in the new organization, human nature generally drove the other individual to accept early retirement or a severance. Similarly, the staff associated with these administrative positions and functions could also be reduced.

The combined firm inherited more than sixty production sites. Wellcome had key manufacturing plants in Dartford (U.K.), Greenville (N.C.), and Kobe (Japan). Glaxo had three plants in the United Kingdom and key sites in Zebulon (N.C.), Verona (Italy), and Singapore. The other sites consisted of numerous secondary plants in many countries. This extensive system of secondary production sites was driven in part by local content requirements and by a belief that local production helps sales. There is substantial potential for savings by consolidating these plants. Many of the secondary production sites can be combined. However, this will take time because most of the countries that encourage local production also discourage plant closings and layoffs. Most of the large cost savings will come from selling the main plants. Wellcome's Greenville, North Carolina, plant was sold. This plant makes primary chemicals, packaged chemicals (tablets, creams, and ointments), and steriles. The primary chemicals were transferred to Singapore, the packaged chemicals to Glaxo's Zebulon, North Carolina, plant. The large state-of-the-art steriles facility at Greenville was built in anticipation of growth that had not yet materialized and therefore was not needed by GlaxoWellcome. The Singapore and Zebulon plants had sufficient excess capacity that Greenville's production could be added without major changes in facilities or staff. The Greenville plant employed nineteen hundred workers. By 1997, Greenville was the only major plant to be sold. However, a team was carefully evaluating worldwide production. Expectations were that this effort could easily equal the Greenville savings. If realized, manufacturing could account for a significant amount of the total cost savings.

An analysis of the savings on the commercial side is more complex. Until recently, the industrywide trend was to reduce the sales force. Better information allowed firms to be more selective in targeting which doctors could affect sales and corporate executives held the belief that the concentration of power into HMOs, PBMs, and large hospital chains had diminished the role of the doctor in determining prescriptions. New studies indicate that the doctor's role is still critical and firms have been reinstating sales forces. Glaxo's plans had been to reduce the sales force through attrition in anticipation of Zantac's decline. However, GlaxoWellcome is also trying to counteract the decline with new product introductions. Demands on the sales force are at a peak for new product introduction. All of these factors were changing around the merger, making premerger forecasts (which are the foundation of cost-savings estimates) obsolete.

Adding to this complication is the discrete nature of the sales force production function. Doctors tend to limit the sales discussion to a maximum of two to three drugs. Thus, a sales representative will generally handle a maximum of four to five drugs. Since most of Glaxo's products were sold to general practitioners, some of Glaxo's sales force could add Wellcome drugs to their portfolio, but others could not. For products that were sold to specialists, the economies were clearer. For example, Glaxo's sales force were calling on neurologists with one product, Imitrex. Wellcome had a co-promotion agreement with Dupont to sell Wellcome's Lamictal to neurologists. With only training costs, Glaxo's neurologist sales force could combine Lamictal and Imitrex, saving on the co-promotion agreement. The combination would also improve the sales force's ability to gain access to more doctors.

After a complex analysis that included accounting for the industry trends and the decline in Zantac and Zovirax, GlaxoWellcome's best estimate is that the merger will allow the U.S. sales force (including contract workers) to be reduced. These estimates suggest that the percentage of headcount reductions in the commercial area is similar in magnitude to the percentage of headcount reductions for the whole company.

GlaxoWellcome's mission statement begins with "GlaxoWellcome, a research-based company. . . ." Survival in the pharmaceutical industry depends on top-line growth through innovative products. Toward this end, Glaxo recently built a billion-dollar research complex in the United Kingdom at Stevenage, and acquired the leading firm in combinatorial chemistry, Affymax, for over $500 million. Developing new products and improving research productivity remain the firm's primary focus.

Nevertheless, GlaxoWellcome did use the merger to reduce research costs in two ways. First, they took a new look at each research project. Starting from a clean slate, they eliminated or put on hold marginal research projects. (They also identified some underfunded projects.) Second, they closed Wellcome's main U.K. research facility in Beckenham, which housed fifteen hundred scientists and staff. Some of the scientists and projects at Beckenham were transferred to Stevenage, but a significant number were cut. Stevenage was designed before the merger with enough capacity to combine two of Glaxo's older labs in Ware and Greenford. Therefore, it was a challenge to accommodate the added research from Beckenham. These two forms of cost savings are, of course, related. Given the difficulty in estimating the net present value of a research project in its early stages, projects are often decided on the basis of opportunity costs. Reducing the space increases the opportunity cost of any one project.

6.5.4 Sources of Cost Savings

What mechanism allows GlaxoWellcome to cut costs without jeopardizing net present value projects? Economists discuss two fundamental paths to true cost savings—economies of scale or scope and elimination of inefficiencies. In theory, these concepts are distinct. Economies of scale and scope refer to the shape of the cost curves for efficiently operated firms. Inefficiency is defined as a firm operating inside of its production possibility curve. In practice, these curves can be estimated with sufficiently detailed data. However, for the time period and cost factors that we are investigating, such detailed data do not exist.[25]

The source of cost savings can be inferred from our discussion of the ways costs were cut. Given that economies of scale are size-based cost advantages assuming firms are operating efficiently, these types of savings would need to meet three conditions. First, they would need to be savings that Glaxo and Wellcome could not have achieved on their own. Second, they would have to be savings that another efficiently operated firm that is smaller than premerger Glaxo is not achieving. Third, they would need to be savings that do not stem from excess capacity, that is, savings that result from the decline in Zantac or from the changing industry conditions discussed in section 6.2 (with the exceptions of conditions that would increase scale economies).

Some of the cost savings clearly meet these conditions. The cuts in administrative costs could not have occurred without the added size brought on by the merger. On the surface, it would appear that any merger can achieve these economies because you do not need two CEOs, accounting departments, legal departments, and so forth. However, the less related the two organizational structures, the less overlap there is to cut and the more likely bureaucracy and bonded rationality will offset any cuts. The similarity in focus, organizational structure, and location makes the administrative economies of scale feasible for GlaxoWellcome.

On the other hand, the main manufacturing cost savings do not stem

---

25. The only reports in the literature with sufficiently detailed pharmaceutical data to estimate production functions are Cockburn and Henderson (1995) and Henderson and Cockburn (1996). Their data contain confidential internal records of ten pharmaceutical firms between 1961 and 1988. Their production function relates one input research on new compounds to various outputs, most notably important patents. Thus, even if these data were available and updated to include the 1990s, it would cover only R&D cost savings.

from economies of scale but from a reduction in excess capacity, which is achieved by closing the plants with the greatest excess capacity and operating the remaining plants more efficiently.[26] An exception may be a regulatory advantage to size caused by local content requirements. Individually, even a highly efficient firm would have to operate a production facility in a country with these requirements if it wanted to sell there. Combining these firms would allow firms to close one of these facilities.

The R&D cost savings do not fit either the economies of scale or reduced excess capacity explanations. Like manufacturing, Glaxo closed one of Wellcome's large R&D facilities. But it was not because Glaxo's new Stevenage facility had excess capacity. Sharing expensive indivisible laboratory equipment is a classic economies of scale example. Some of this may be occurring at Stevenage. However, the indicated source of R&D savings stemmed from reducing their scientific workforce and canceling, postponing, or delaying projects. These cuts appear to be a recognition of the new economics in the pharmaceutical industry and a substitution of internal for external R&D. In economic terms, the allocations of resources in premerger R&D were inefficient.

A problem with this source of cost savings, it may be argued, is that it could have been achieved without the mergers.[27] While this is true, the interviews we undertook made it clear that this argument ignores the organizational behavior realities of business. A merger allows firms to "start with a clean slate" and "take a fresh look at the organization." In R&D and most other areas, GlaxoWellcome used the merger to stimulate the organization into considering change.[28] If done properly, this change can be very positive for an organization.[29] By combining their problems and creating a discrete event, the firms could justify the disruption costs of solving their problems through downsizing rather than following their premerger strategy of reduction through attrition.

An alternative approach to addressing the question of the source of cost cutting is to focus on the timing. Why did GlaxoWellcome merge in 1995 and why was there a concentration of pharmaceutical mergers in the 1994–96 period? The evidence using this approach falls strongly in favor of

26. In theory, this excess capacity could be reduced without the merger through coproduction agreements, for example, GlaxoWellcome could have sold some of their production capacity to another firm. These agreements are rare in the pharmaceutical industry (and in many others). Even contract manufacturing to independent organizations is not fully utilized because of concern about the longevity and reputation of these firms.

27. There is an indirect excess capacity explanation. If both firms had cut back on R&D independently, these cuts would not have been enough to close major facilities.

28. For example, worldwide technical director Joe Blaker asked managers from each manufacturing site to justify their existence (*Financial Times,* 9 April 1996, p. 10).

29. One interviewee even paraphrased Napoleon, stating that "to motivate your troops you need to shoot a few."

inefficiencies and excess capacity created by the changing pharmaceutical economics and the decline of the firms' major products. There is little evidence that the economies of scale and scope have changed with respect to administrative, manufacturing, or commercial costs.

There are some significant new developments in R&D that could substantially change the economies of scale and scope and greatly stimulate the productivity of R&D. Two significant (and related) developments are mapping the genes of organisms —from microbes to human beings—and combinatorial chemistry. The cost and potential spillovers of the complete genomic sequencing are enormous. These projects will dramatically increase the number of new drug targets. Combinatorial chemistry automates the search process, increasing the speed by which compounds can be tested when new targets are found. The issue is to what extent are these going to be the domain of large firms. Smaller firms will still play an important innovative role. Affymax, the leader in combinatorial chemistry, was a start-up in 1989. Small, focused, genetic research companies are increasing in number. In addition, joint ventures and government-sponsored research offer an alternative approach to large size in obtaining these economies. The human genomic sequencing project is being led by the National Institutes of Health (NIH). GlaxoWellcome has formed a joint venture with SmithKline Beecham for genomic sequencing of disease-causing microbes. Still, large organizations will be able to participate in a greater array of these ventures and they will be able to cover the fixed cost of development with a larger number of projects. For example, the benefits of Affymax technology apply equally well to Wellcome's research. Thus, the $539 million acquisition cost of Affymax can be spread over a larger research base.

6.5.5   Asset Restructuring

Glaxo and Wellcome were highly focused organizations. Thus, the opportunities for asset restructuring were limited. However, there were two areas where Glaxo thought the assets' usage was higher in another organization. Glaxo did not have an interest in marketing OTC products. They sold Wellcome's OTC business to Warner-Lambert, a company with more experience in the OTC business, for $1.05 billion. Warner-Lambert was a natural buyer, because both Glaxo and Wellcome had joint venture agreements to help switch prescription drugs to OTC status near the end of their patent life. This reallocation of assets created significant value for both parties. GlaxoWellcome's abnormal return from the announced acquisition was 6.7 percent and Warner-Lambert gained 2.4 percent for a total value creation of almost $500 million. GlaxoWellcome also sold off Wellcome's Singapore-based cosmetics business for approximately $140 million. Finally, GlaxoWellcome received an estimated $225 million for the FTC-ordered divestiture of Wellcome's migraine drug 311C to Zeneca.[30]

6.5.6   Revenue

GlaxoWellcome believes there is significant potential for revenue growth from the merger. Top-line growth can come from a broader product line, the incorporation of each organization's best practices, scientific and technical gains, expanded global reach, and building a new corporate culture. The broader product line can increase access to doctors and help counteract buyer power. Through a careful selection of best practices, GlaxoWellcome can take advantage of each other's strengths. By leveraging modern technology and each organization's research skills, the merger can enhance the productivity of R&D. Also, combining Glaxo and Wellcome research at Stevenage will increase the exchange of ideas between projects (i.e., economies of scope). As the abnormal returns regressions indicate, the gains from expanding cross-border deals are substantial. Although there is a substantial overlap in Glaxo and Wellcome's vast global organizations, the combined organizations nevertheless have a stronger global presence and reach allowing them to capture some of the advantages of cross-border deals. Different corporate cultures can destroy value. However, GlaxoWellcome emphasizes the desire to build a new and better culture by combining the academic freedom of the Wellcome organization with Glaxo's business focus.

GlaxoWellcome admits, however, that articulating to outside parties these intangible benefits relative to the more certain and quantifiable cost savings is challenging. As noted, the cost savings are potentially large enough to create value for both Glaxo and Wellcome shareholders. Revenue gains are more important the faster cost savings are dissipated and the larger the intangible postmerger integration cost.

6.5.7   Postmerger

Many mergers fail because of postmerger integration problems (Smith and Quella 1995). Research has identified several key issues to assessing postmerger success. These include the extent of organizational autonomy, the speed of integration, the ability to maintain top management and key

---

30. The final divestiture agreement took a long time to hammer out, partly because strategies for divesting these types of intangible assets are at the forefront of antitrust. The FTC is asking the firm to help it create a competitor. FTC experience suggests that when the divestiture is not a separate entity with its own assets, the divesting firm has the potential and incentive to inhibit its future competitor. In this case, the FTC appointed a trustee to oversee the progress of the drug while the parties negotiated for the right buyer and a fair price. This issued played a major role in the 1997 Ciba-Geigy and Sandoz merger, in which the FTC ordered the licensing of dozens of gene therapies (see *Business Week,* 20 January 1997).

employees, and the communication of merger goals and procedures (Haspeslagh and Jemison 1991). How these issues are addressed depends on the nature of the acquisition synergies, the relative size of the two firms, and the culture of the two organizations. To achieve the cost and revenue savings in the Glaxo-Wellcome merger, organizational autonomy for Wellcome was impossible. Given Glaxo's inexperience with acquisitions, the other integration issues were addressed with the help of the Boston Consulting Group.

GlaxoWellcome decided that integration had to be achieved quickly. Prior horizontal mergers had been criticized for dragging out the merger integration process (especially Bristol-Myers Squibb and SmithKline Beecham). Speed was critical because serious work delays occur as employees worry about their jobs and morale suffers during the process even for the survivors. The task of integration involved twenty principal task forces that were then subdivided into numerous committees and subcommittees. It took only nine months for these task forces and committees to complete the main integration plans and to lay out the strategic direction for each functional and geographic area in the new organization. A special magazine devoted to the integration process was developed to communicate critical issues (e.g., "When will I know if I have a job?") to the employees. While there were complaints about some decisions being made too fast and, with hindsight, the task forces could have better identified and focused on the critical paths, the integration in general, appears to have handled the speed and communication issue well.

Retaining top management and key employees was more of a challenge. As discussed, almost nothing can prevent the loss of managers who do not get the equivalent of their old position in the new company. In some cases, this process creates an opportunity to prune marginal managers. However, talented managers are often lost and sometimes key employees whom they have mentored go with them. The net impact of these changes is difficult to assess. Several interviewees suggested that GlaxoWellcome lost more talent than they expected. In part, this was due to the generous nature of the retirement and severance pay.[31]

Perhaps the most controversial postmerger issue does not appear in the standard list given above. Often the terms *merger* and *acquisition* are used interchangeably. In this case, the words carried great meaning. Senior management decided that the Glaxo-Wellcome deal should be called a "merger" for the purposes of postmerger integration. For research- and marketing-driven pharmaceutical organizations, knowledge resides in the scientists and sales force. Glaxo needed to keep these employees if the merger was to succeed. They were also serious about creating value by

---

31. Even former managers gave GlaxoWellcome high praise for the way they treated departing employees. The retirement and severance packages were felt to be generous.

developing a new culture and employing the best practices of each organization. They felt that these objectives could not be met if Glaxo was "acquiring" Wellcome. Accomplishing this goal has proved to be difficult. Given that the merger began as a hostile transaction, many Wellcome employees remained skeptical. This skepticism increased as Glaxo's managers began obtaining a large number of senior positions, even though some of this imbalance was expected. Glaxo was three times Wellcome's size and many Wellcome managers were older and more likely to take early retirement (especially in countries like the United States where Wellcome had been since 1906 and Glaxo only since 1978). The downside of this strategy was that it also put Glaxo employees at risk. "Under US law, severance terms had to be offered to all employees of the combined company there" (*Financial Times,* 9 April, 1996). As a consequence, they lost valuable employees on both sides. Gains from applying the best practices of both organizations also came up against some roadblocks. There were cases in which Wellcome's procedure or equipment was superior but, because of Glaxo's size, it was cheaper and more expedient to adopt Glaxo's version.

In sum, integration leads to inevitable disruption and significant temporal losses. There is a period where the organization is more focused on the integration than on productivity. In general, GlaxoWellcome handled the postmerger integration issues extremely well. Still, managers admit to significant temporal losses from the integration process. The best concrete example is in sales. GlaxoWellcome had to totally reconfigure and retrain their sales force. Employees did not know what their job was or if they had a job. Although GlaxoWellcome resolved these issues extremely quickly, they still had to pull the sales force from their territories and stopped shipping samples for two months. During this time, they lost momentum, market share, and some key employees. What makes mergers so challenging from the bidder's perspective is that the synergies must be large enough to cover the premium paid and these postmerger disruption costs.

6.6 Discussion and Conclusion

This paper demonstrates the changing nature of the pharmaceutical industry and how these changes have led to value-creating horizontal mergers. By focusing on the Glaxo-Wellcome merger, we can illustrate how value is created and the roadblocks to achieving value creation. This detailed industry and firm case study yields insights into a number of issues debated in the academic literature. We find evidence that rapidly changing industry conditions do generate overcapacity (Jensen 1993) and free cash flow (Jensen 1986) that can be reduced through mergers. However, we find pharmaceutical managers engaged in restructuring without the need for high debt, raiders, or dramatic changes in compensation. In pharmaceuticals, industry and stock market pressures were sufficient to induce bidders to change, although target manager compensation was insufficient in some cases to convince them to give up without hostile actions. We find evidence for economies of scale and scope, but we also find that the primary motive for increased size stems from the elimination of excess capacity and inefficiencies induced by the changing industry structure and firm product portfolio. This is consistent with work by Henderson and Cockburn (1996) and Dimasi, Grabowski, and Vernon (1995), who show that economies of scale and scope exist in pharmaceuticals, but that they are exhausted at the size of the largest firm prior to these horizontal combinations.

With respect to the debate concerning how mergers affect R&D (Hall 1990; and Hitt et al. 1996), we find that neither captures the relationship in pharmaceuticals. Hall argues that R&D is not affected by mergers. However, R&D is cut in large pharmaceutical mergers. Hitt et al. argue that R&D is cut in mergers because of increased debt, managerial distraction, and the imposition of financial controls. However, R&D remains the cornerstone of the merged pharmaceutical firms. Cutbacks are a result of changing pharmaceutical economics making marginal internal projects less attractive and some external alliance projects more promising.

Finally, we provide insights into why bidders often experience declines in stock market value upon the announcement of a merger. The challenge for bidders is not only to create value in the merger, but to create enough value to cover a competitive premium and substantial postmerger integration costs. Creative bidding solutions, like negotiating with blockholders and exchanging shares through a merger of equals, help avoid overpayment. An early focus on postmerger integration issues, like integration speed, retaining new employees, and building a new culture, are also critical to the bidder's success.

References

Bradley, M., A. Desai, and E. H. Kim. 1988. Synergistic gains from corporate acquisitions and their division between the stockholders of target and acquiring firms. *Journal of Financial Economics* 21:3–40.

Cockburn, I., and R. Henderson. 1995. Do agency costs explain variation in innovative performance? Working paper, MIT's Program on the Pharmaceutical Industry.

Dimasi, J., H. Grabowski, and J. Vernon. 1995. R&D costs, innovative output and firm size in the pharmaceutical industry. *International Journal of the Economics of Business* 2:201–19.

Fama, E., and M. Jensen. 1983. Separation of ownership and control. *Journal of Law and Economics* 26:301–25.

Grabowski, H., and J. Vernon. 1992. Brand loyalty, entry and price competition in pharmaceuticals after the 1984 Act. *Journal of Law and Economics* 36:331–50.

———. 1996. Longer patents for increased generic competition in the U.S. *PharmacoEconomics* 10:110–23.

Hall, B. 1990. The impact of corporate restructuring on industrial research and development. *Brookings Papers on Economic Activity,* special issue, 85–124.

———. 1992. Investment and research at the firm level: Does the source of financing matter? NBER Working Paper no. 4096. Cambridge, Mass.: National Bureau of Economic Research.

Harris, R., and D. Ravenscraft. 1993. Foreign takeovers. In *The new Palgrave dictionary of money and finance,* ed. J. Eatwell, M. Milgate, and P. Newman, 1–8. London: Norton.

Haspeslagh, P., and D. Jemison. 1991. *Managing acquisitions: Creating value through corporate renewal.* New York: Free Press.

Henderson, R., and I. Cockburn. 1996. Scale, scope and spillovers: The determinants of research productivity in drug discovery. *Rand Journal of Economics* 27:32–59.

Hitt, M., R. Hoskisson, R. Johnson, and D. Moesel. 1996. The market for corporate control and firm innovation. *Academy of Management Journal* 39:1084–1119.

Jensen, M. 1986. Agency costs of free cash flow, corporate finance and takeovers. *American Economic Review* 76:323–29.

———. 1993. The modern industrial revolution, exit and the failure of internal control systems. *Journal of Finance* 48:831–80.

Jones, O. 1996. Strategic HRM: The implications for pharmaceutical R&D. *Technovation* 16:21–32.

Leland, H., and D. Pyle. 1977. Information asymmetries, financial structure and financial intermediation. *Journal of Finance* 32:371–87.

MacAvoy, P. 1995. Lederle: Strategies for dominating prescription drugs in heart disease, cancer and child vaccines. Yale School of Management Strategy Case Study Series, September.

Myers, S., and N. Majluf. 1984. Corporate financing decisions when firms have information that investors do not have. *Journal of Financial Economics* 17:187–220.

Pharmaceutical Research and Manufacturers of America (PhRMA). 1996. *Facts and figures.*

Pursche, B. 1995. Creating value from horizontal integration. *In Vivo: The Business and Medicine Report* 13:18–22.

Schumpeter, J. 1950. *Capitalism, socialism and democracy.* 3d ed. New York: Harper.

Servaes, H., and M. Zenner. 1994. Ownership structure. *Finanzmarkt und Portfolio Management* 8:184–96.

Smith, K., and J. Quella. 1995. Seizing the moment to capture value in a strategic deal. *Mergers and Acquisitions* 29:25–30.

Stulz, R. 1988. Managerial control of voting rights, financing policies and the market for corporate control. *Journal of Financial Economics* 20:25–54.

U.S. General Accounting Office. 1995. Pharmacy benefit managers: Early results on ventures with drug manufacturers. Washington, D.C.: U.S. Government Printing Office, November.

Comment   Robert Gertner

A good clinical paper shifts our prior assumptions by providing a detailed interpretative account of an industry or an event that the reader finds sufficiently compelling to merit some generalization. It also suggests areas that deserve more careful, systematic analysis. David Ravenscraft and William Long's analysis of the Glaxo-Wellcome merger achieves these goals from my perspective. A nice feature of a clinical paper is that different readers can reach very different conclusions. I am afraid that my conclusions may be quite different from those of the authors.

The papers in this volume fall into two categories: bad acquisitions and good acquisitions. The goal of the bad acquisition papers is to understand why managers make bad acquisitions, while the goal of the good acquisition papers is to understand the sources of value in mergers. This is so despite the fact that it may be difficult to categorize a merger without the benefit of 20/20 hindsight, and sometimes even with it. In any event, this paper falls into the good acquisitions category and focuses on value creation in the merger of Glaxo and Wellcome. Certainly, the stock market thought the merger was good news.

There are four broad reasons why a horizontal merger may enhance stock market value: (1) cost savings; (2) revenue enhancement unrelated to market power; (3) acquisition of market power; and (4) the market's expecting the companies to do something worse. This paper focuses on cost savings and, to some extent, revenue enhancement, but I wish to explore the last two explanations as well.

As Ravenscraft and Long point out, the pharmaceutical companies were prime candidates to make acquisitions in the 1990s, with torrents of free cash flow and reduced investment opportunities in their core business. A number of companies did make bad or at least questionable acquisitions, such as the vertical mergers into PBMs by Merck and Eli Lilly.

In such an environment, a horizontal merger that has little or no negative profit implications could raise stock market values. Incorrect expectations of very bad decisions can be a source of shareholder gains, but it would be a mistake to conclude that such a merger creates value.

The authors do not give much weight to the possibility that the merger increases market power. They base this conclusion on relatively low concentration in the pharmaceutical industry that is not greatly increased by the Glaxo-Wellcome merger. I do not think we can write off the market power story so easily. The new "rational" approach to research and development in the pharmaceutical industry is characterized by companies' fo-

Robert Gertner is professor of economics and strategy at the Graduate School of Business of the University of Chicago and a research associate of the National Bureau of Economic Research.

cusing on particular diseases. A merger could lead to a significant reduction in R&D competition within a particular class. I have no knowledge whether this is the case in the Glaxo-Wellcome merger nor do I know anything about entry barriers into R&D niches, but the potential concerns seem real. Further exploration, perhaps just to eliminate any concern, is merited.

Revenue enhancement is another possible source of value. The idea is that the merger may lead to an increase in competitive rents through mechanisms like brand-name extension. The authors do not seem to believe that revenue enhancement was an important motivation for the merger and I agree.

Cost savings from a merger can be divided into three types. First, there can be cost savings from exploiting economies of scale and scope. This is pushing out the production possibility frontier. Second, a merger may improve efficiency, thereby moving from the interior of the production possibility set toward the frontier. Third, a merger can lead to cost savings through capacity reduction, or more broadly, a reduction in scale. This last cost saving may not be an efficiency improvement at all. Costs go down but revenues may decline by as much or more. It may be difficult to know whether a reduction in capacity is an efficiency-enhancing elimination of excess capacity or simply a reduction in scale.

One advantage of a clinical paper is that it improves our chances of distinguishing among these possibilities; Ravenscraft and Long try to do just that. Unfortunately, the pharmaceutical industry is sufficiently complex that this is quite difficult even with detailed knowledge of the merger plans. Much of the anticipated cost savings derived from consolidation of production, reductions in R&D, and reductions in sales forces. It is very difficult to know if this is a reduction in scale, elimination of excess capacity, or scale economies. This is especially difficult for R&D reductions and sales force consolidation. A smaller sales force may result in reduced sales in the not-so-immediate future and reductions in R&D may show up in output reductions in only the very distant future. Accounting data will not help. The authors suggest that senior management itself would not know how to categorize sales force reduction among the three categories. The authors believe that reduction is a small part of the cost savings, but I do not see sufficient evidence to reach this conclusion.

I find the most interesting issue in the paper is the discussion of whether the cost savings could be achieved without the merger. The authors argue that enhanced efficiency of R&D could in theory. I would add that much of the reductions in production capacity and sales force probably could as well, given the large size of the two companies. The authors' interviews suggest that the merger provided an opportunity to "take a fresh look at the organization" in a way that we are to infer would be impossible without the merger. I wish the authors had pushed the managers to explain why. I understand why it is necessary to "take a fresh look at the organization" with the merger, but do not understand why it is impossible to do so without a merger. A \$3.8 billion premium is a very high price to pay for a commitment by management to increase value through capacity reductions. A new cost-cutting CEO should be able to do this for a lot less. A cost-cutting CEO may be expensive, but not this expensive.

I can think of two sets of reasons why a merger may facilitate efficient capacity reductions. One is that the disruptions and costs associated with the reductions are lower as part of a merger implementation. Everyone can see the logic and necessity of consolidation with the merger. It may be easier to keep good employees and maintain morale and productivity. The second set of explanations are managerial agency problems. Maybe managers do not like their companies to shrink and it may be very unpleasant for management to reduce capacity because of a lack of growth opportunities. Perhaps the target's employees bear most of the burden and therefore it is less unpleasant for the acquirer's management. Of course, this is all idle speculation, which is exactly what a good clinical paper like this one should generate.

Contributors

Jason R. Barro
National Bureau of Economic
  Research
1050 Massachusetts Avenue
Cambridge, MA 02138

Severin Borenstein
Haas School of Business
University of California
Berkeley, CA 94720

Charles W. Calomiris
Graduate School of Business
Columbia University
3022 Broadway Street, Uris Hall
New York, NY 10027

David M. Cutler
Department of Economics
Harvard University
Cambridge, MA 02138

Robert Gertner
Graduate School of Business
University of Chicago
1101 East 58th Street
Chicago, IL 60637

Paul M. Healy
Graduate School of Business
  Administration
Harvard University
Boston, MA 02163

Christopher James
Department of Finance
University of Florida
P.O. Box 117168
Gainesville, FL 32611

Steven N. Kaplan
Graduate School of Business
University of Chicago
1101 East 58th Street
Chicago, IL 60637

Jason Karceski
Finance, Insurance, and Real Estate
  Department
P.O. Box 117168
University of Florida
Gainesville, FL 32611

Anil K Kashyap
Graduate School of Business
University of Chicago
1101 East 58th Street
Chicago, IL 60637

Marc Knez
Graduate School of Business
University of Chicago
1101 East 58th Street
Chicago, IL 60637

Stacey R. Kole
William E. Simon Graduate School
  of Business
University of Rochester
Rochester, NY 14627

Kenneth Lehn
J. M. Katz Graduate School of
  Business
University of Pittsburgh
278 B Mervis
Pittsburgh, PA 15260

Frank R. Lichtenberg
Graduate School of Business
Columbia University
3022 Broadway
726 Uris Hall
New York, NY 10027

William F. Long
Business Performance Research
  Associates, Inc.
5715 Rossmore Drive
Bethesda, MD 20814

Mark L. Mitchell
Graduate School of Business
  Administration
Harvard University
Soldiers Field Road
Boston, MA 02163

Robert H. Porter
Department of Economics
Northwestern University
2003 Sheridan Road
Evanston, IL 60208

Raghuram Rajan
Graduate School of Business
University of Chicago
1101 East 58th Street
Chicago, IL 60637

David J. Ravenscraft
Kenan-Flagler Business School
University of North Carolina
CB #3490
Chapel Hill, NC 27599

G. William Schwert
William E. Simon Graduate School
  of Business
University of Rochester
Rochester, NY 14627

René M. Stulz
Max M. Fisher College of Business
Ohio State University
806A Fisher Hall
2100 Neil Avenue
Columbus, OH 43210

Paolo Volpin
163 Coolidge Street, No. 5
Brookline, MA 02446

Karen H. Wruck
Department of Finance
Ohio State University
Fisher Hall 832
2100 Neil Avenue
Columbus, OH 43210

Luigi Zingales
Graduate School of Business
University of Chicago
1101 East 58th Street
Chicago, IL 60637

Name Index

Subject Index